COMPARATIVE POLITICS

Comparative Politics: Rationality, Culture, and Structure examines the major research traditions in comparative politics, assessing knowledge, advancing theory, and in the end seeking to direct research in the coming years. It begins by examining the three research schools that guide comparative politics: rational choice theory, culturalist analysis, and structuralist approaches. Margaret Levi, Marc Howard Ross, and Ira Katznelson offer briefs for each of the schools, presenting core principles, variations within each approach, and fresh combinations. A second set of authors then applies the research traditions to established fields of scholarship. Samuel H. Barnes examines work on mass politics, Doug McAdam, Sidney Tarrow, and Charles Tilly synthesize studies of social movements and revolutions, Peter A. Hall contrasts new research on the political economy of established democracies, and Joel S. Migdal offers a new approach to studies of the state. The concluding section contains essays by Mark I. Lichbach and Alan S. Zuckerman, returning the focus to the theme of advanced theory in comparative politics. Lichbach offers a critical evaluation that draws on the schools' theoretical sources and Zuckerman calls for a reformulation of the standards for explanation in comparative politics as a way to advance theory.

CAMBRIDGE STUDIES IN COMPARATIVE POLITICS

General Editor

PETER LANGE   Duke University

Associate Editors

ROBERT H. BATES   Harvard University
ELLEN COMISSO   University of California, San Diego
PETER HALL   Harvard University
JOEL MIGDAL   University of Washington
HELEN MILNER   Columbia University
RONALD ROGOWSKI   University of California, Los Angeles
SIDNEY TARROW   Cornell University

OTHER BOOKS IN THE SERIES

Catherine Boone, *Merchant Capital and the Roots of State Power in Sénégal,* 1930–1985

Michael Bratton and Nicolas van de Walle, *Democratic Experiments in Africa: Regime Transitions in Comparative Perspective*

Donatella della Porta, *Social Movements, Political Violence, and the State*

Roberto Franzosi, *The Puzzle of Strikes: Class and State Strategies in Postwar Italy*

Geoffrey Garrett, *Partisan Politics in the Global Economy*

Miriam Golden, *Heroic Defeats: The Politics of Job Loss*

Frances Hagopian, *Traditional Politics and Regime Change in Brazil*

J. Rogers Hollingsworth and Robert Boyer, *Contemporary Capitalism: The Embeddedness of Institutions*

Ellen Imergut, *Health Politics: Interests and Institutions in Western Europe*

Thomas Janoski and Alexander M. Hicks, eds., *The Comparative Political Economy of the Welfare State*

Robert O. Keohane and Helen B. Milner, eds., *Internationalization and Domestic Politics*

David Knoke, Franz Urban Pappi, Jeffrey Broadbent, and Yutaka Tsujinaka, eds., *Comparing Policy Networks*

Allan Kornberg and Harold D. Clarke, *Citizens and Community: Political Support in a Representative Democracy*

David D. Laitin, *Language Repertories and State Construction in Africa*

Doug McAdam, John McCarthy, and Mayer Zald, eds., *Comparative Perspectives on Social Movements*

Scott Mainwaring and Matthew Soberg Shugart, *Presidentialism and Democracy in Latin America*

Joel S. Migdal, Atul Kohli, and Vivienne Shue, eds., *State Power and Social Forces: Domination and Transformation in the Third World*

Continued on page following the Index

COMPARATIVE POLITICS

Rationality, Culture, and Structure

MARK IRVING LICHBACH

University of Colorado

ALAN S. ZUCKERMAN

Brown University

CAMBRIDGE
UNIVERSITY PRESS

PUBLISHED BY THE PRESS SYNDICATE OF THE UNIVERSITY OF CAMBRIDGE
The Pitt Building, Trumpington Street, Cambridge, United Kingdom

CAMBRIDGE UNIVERSITY PRESS
The Edinburgh Building, Cambridge CB2 2RU, UK
40 West 20th Street, New York, NY 10011-4211, USA
477 Williamstown Road, Port Melbourne, VIC 3207, Australia
Ruiz de Alarcón 13, 28014 Madrid, Spain
Dock House, The Waterfront, Cape Town 8001, South Africa

http://www.cambridge.org

First published 1997
Reprinted 1998, 1999, 2000, 2001, 2002

Printed in the United States of America

Typeset in Garamond

A catalog record for this book is available from the British Library

Library of Congress Cataloging in Publication data is available

ISBN 0 521 58369 1 hardback
ISBN 0 521 58668 2 paperback

For
Faye
and
Roberta

CONTENTS

Preface and Acknowledgments   ix

Contributors   xi

Part I: Introduction   1

Chapter 1: Research Traditions and Theory in Comparative Politics:
    An Introduction   3
    Mark I. Lichbach and Alan S. Zuckerman

Part II: Research Traditions in Comparative Politics   17

Chapter 2: A Model, a Method, and a Map: Rational Choice in
    Comparative and Historical Analysis   19
    Margaret Levi
Chapter 3: Culture and Identity in Comparative Political Analysis   42
    Marc Howard Ross
Chapter 4: Structure and Configuration in Comparative Politics   81
    Ira Katznelson

Part III: Theory Development in Comparative Politics   113

Chapter 5: Electoral Behavior and Comparative Politics   115
    Samuel H. Barnes
Chapter 6: Toward an Integrated Perspective on Social Movements
    and Revolution   142
    Doug McAdam, Sidney Tarrow, and Charles Tilly

Chapter 7: The Role of Interests, Institutions, and Ideas in the Comparative
        Political Economy of the Industrialized Nations   174
    Peter A. Hall
Chapter 8: Studying the State   208
    Joel S. Migdal

Part IV: Social Theory and Explanations in Comparative Politics   237

Chapter 9: Social Theory and Comparative Politics   239
    Mark I. Lichbach
Chapter 10: Reformulating Explanatory Standards and Advancing
        Theory in Comparative Politics   277
    Alan S. Zuckerman

Subject Index   311
Author Index   313

PREFACE AND
ACKNOWLEDGMENTS

Comparative politics, the field whose intellectual forebears include Karl Marx, Max Weber, Emile Durkheim, Gaetano Mosca, Roberto Michels, and Vilfredo Pareto, has lost its way. The promise offered by the founders of the modern study of comparative politics three decades ago, Harry Eckstein, David Apter, Robert Dahl, Karl Deutsch, Gabriel Almond, and Sidney Verba, has not been fulfilled. Too few studies are nomothetic, creatively combining theory and cases and developing general propositions. Too many studies are idiographic, offering no more than a wave to the systematic development and assessment of powerful explanatory arguments. Unlike students of American politics, comparativists do not draw upon methodological advances to power their scholarship. Unlike students of international politics, comparativists do not debate grand questions of theory. A field established by the founders of social thought and reinvented by some of the most important political scientists of the postwar era needs to be discovered yet again.

The coeditors discussed these ideas at the Meetings of the American Political Science Association in 1994. Puzzled by the slow growth of theories in comparative politics and dismayed by the lack of systematic attention to the field's research traditions, we first lamented the decline of this subdiscipline and then resolved to do something about it. Since we view research schools, especially rational choice theory, culturalist analyses, and structuralist approaches, to be at the center of the development of theory, we asked several of the field's senior scholars to join us in an effort to return attention in comparative politics to the analysis of the research communities and traditions that have historically shaped our field. Their agreement, made concrete in the essays found in this volume, and the encouragement of Alex Holzman, our editor at Cambridge University Press, has enabled us to turn our lament and resolve into a book that we hope orients future theory and research in comparative politics.

It is significant that the coeditors first developed a shared interest in theory and comparative politics several decades ago. Zuckerman was then a rookie assistant professor, offering a seminar on approaches to comparative politics at Brown University, and Lichbach a first-year graduate student. The course itself derived from one that Zuckerman took when he pursued his graduate studies with Harry Eckstein at Princeton. Here, we return to these concerns. We offer a set of essays that recover the grand task that Eckstein and the other founders of the contemporary study of comparative politics laid out more than thirty years ago. We found the connection between theory and comparative politics exciting then and we find the possible connections even more energizing now. Just as this enthusiasm was passed on to us, we now pass it on to a new generation of comparativists.

A collaborative project such as this volume is self-evidently the work of many hands. We want first to thank the contributors for being superb team players, defying the dire predictions that works with many authors would always be held up by one or more persons unable or unwilling to meet deadlines. We had no such problems. Indeed, the contributors displayed as much enthusiasm for the project and labored as hard as we did. Our praise for Alex Holzman knows no bounds. Always encouraging, always available, and always appropriately hard-headed, he made it possible for this project to succeed. Several colleagues, Jeffrey Anderson, Roger Cobb, Peter Lange, Marc Howard Ross, Ronald Rogowski, and Sidney Tarrow, provided encouragement and advice at critical points, and we want to thank them. First drafts of the essays were presented at a conference at Brown University's Watson Institute for International Studies, May 4-5, 1996. We are very pleased to acknowledge the financial and administrative assistance of Vartan Gregorian, Brown's president, Darrell West, the chair of its Department of Political Science, and our colleagues at the Watson Institute, especially Jean Lawlor. We also want to recognize the aid of several graduate students in Brown's Department of Political Science — Lucas Swaine, Laurence Kotler-Berkowitz, Claudia Elliot, and Dennis Michaud – who worked to make the conference the success that it was. We presented second drafts of the essays at the 1996 Meetings of the American Political Science Association, and are pleased to thank Karen Remmer and Ronald Rogowski for recognizing the importance of our project. Finally, we note that we list our names alphabetically as coeditors of the book and as coauthors of the first chapter, because had we not done so, some might suppose that our collaboration was not one of equals. To that end, Zuckerman is happy to pay the price of having a family name that begins with the last letter of the alphabet.

We dedicate the volume to our wives, Faye Lichbach and Roberta Zuckerman, whose love, strength, and wisdom provided the most important elements in this collaborative effort.

CONTRIBUTORS

Mark Irving Lichbach is Professor of Political Science and Chair of the department at the University of Colorado. A theorist interested in social choice and a comparativist interested in European politics, Lichbach explores the connections between collective action theories and political conflict, as well as the connections between collective choice theories and democratic institutions. He is the author of *The Rebel's Dilemma,* a study of protest and rebellion from a collective action perspective; *The Cooperator's Dilemma,* a conceptual and theoretical evaluation of the collective action research program; *Regime Change and the Coherence of European Governments,* a study of the development of democratic institutions; and two dozen articles that have appeared in scholarly journals in political science, economics, and sociology.

Alan S. Zuckerman is Professor of Political Science at Brown University and has served as Fulbright Visiting Professor of political science at Tel-Aviv University and the University of Pisa, as well as Visiting Fellow at the University of Essex. Zuckerman's work examines the relations among social and political structures, exploring the bases of social and political cohesion. He has appeared in journals, monographs, and books in Hebrew, Italian, German, and English, covering topics as diverse as the determinants of stability in political preferences; individual responses to the Holocaust; political cleavages in interwar and contemporary Europe; political contacting; and party activists in Israel and Italy. His books include *The Politics of Faction: Christian Democratic Rule in Italy,* a study of clientelist politics; *The Transformation of the Jews,* a comparative analysis of Jewish communities in Europe, the United States, and Israel over the past two centuries (coauthored with Calvin Goldscheider); and *Doing Political Science: an Introduction to Political Analysis.*

Margaret Levi is Professor of Political Science, Harry Bridges Chair, and Director of the Center for Labor Studies, University of Washington. Her books include *Consent, Dissent and Patriotism* (Cambridge, 1997), *The Limits of Rationality* (coedited with Karen Cook, Chicago, 1990), and *Of Rule and Revenue* (California, 1988). She is currently codirector (with Karen Cook and Russell Hardin) of the Russell Sage Foundation Project on The Construction and Maintenance of Trust. She has held fellowships from the Center for Advanced Study in the Behavioral Sciences, German Marshall Fund, Research School of Social Sciences of the Australian National University, Exeter College of Oxford University, and the Max Planck Institute in Koln. She serves on the editorial boards of Politics and Society and Rationality and Society. With James Alt, she is cochair of the 1997 Meetings of the American Political Science Association in Washington, D.C.

Marc Howard Ross is William Rand Kenan, Jr. Professor of Political Science at Bryn Mawr College. His primary interests are in the study of conflict and its management in general and ethnic conflict in particular. He has recently written *The Culture of Conflict: Interpretations and Interests in Comparative Perspective* and *The Management of Conflict: Interpretations and Interests in Comparative Perspective,* as well as numerous articles on these questions.

Ira Katznelson is Ruggles Professor of Political Science and History at Columbia University. His most recent books are *Marxism and the City* (Oxford University Press, 1992), *Paths of Emancipation: Jews, States, and Citizenship* (edited with Pierre Birnbaum; Princeton University Press, 1995), and *Liberalism's Crooked Circle: Letters to Adam Michnik* (Princeton University Press, 1996). He is completing a book on the origins and character of liberalism in the United States since the New Deal.

Samuel H. Barnes was appointed Director of the Center for German and European Studies at Georgetown in 1991. He had spent his entire previous academic career at the University of Michigan where he served as Chairman of the Department of Political Science for six years and Program Director in the Institute for Social Research from 1969 until 1991. He has held Fulbright awards to Paris, Florence, and Rome; taught in the Michigan program in Florence; spent a sabbatical in London; served as a Fellow of the Center for Advanced Study in the Behavioral Sciences and of the Hoover Institution, both in Palo Alto; and lectured widely in Europe and elsewhere. His research has focused largely on politics, parties, opinions, and behaviors in advanced industrial democracies. Current projects include a joint-authored book on democracy and the Spanish public, based on four national surveys in 1978, 1980, 1984, and 1990; and surveys of mass orientations toward democracy in eleven central and eastern European countries. His major works include *Party Democracy, Representation in Italy, Politics and Culture,* and with others, *Political Action.*

Doug McAdam is Professor of Sociology at the University of Arizona and the author of *Political Process and the Development of Black Insurgency* (University of Chicago Press, 1982) and *Freedom Summer* (Oxford, 1988). He also coedited a recent collection of papers on the general topic of this volume, *Comparative Perspectives on Social Movements,* (Cambridge, 1996).

Sidney Tarrow is Maxwell M. Upson Professor of Government at Cornell, where he also teaches in the field of sociology. He is the author of numerous works on Italian politics and society, including *Peasant Communism in Southern Italy* and *Democracy and Disorder,* but has increasingly specialized in the study of social movements and contentious politics. His latest work in this field is *Power in Movement: Social Movements, Collective Action, and Politics* (Cambridge, 1994).

Charles Tilly, after teaching at Delaware, Harvard, Toronto, Michigan, and the New School, now teaches social science at Columbia University. He works chiefly on social change and political processes with special reference to Western Europe and North America.

Peter A. Hall is Professor of Government and Senior Associate of the Center for European Studies at Harvard University. He is the author or editor of *Governing the Economy: The Politics of State Intervention in Britain and France* (1986), *European Labor in the 1980s* (1987), *The Political Power of Economic Ideas: Keynesianism across Nations* (1989), and *Developments in French Politics* (1990), as well as many articles on comparative political economy and public policy making in Europe

Joel S. Migdal is the Robert F. Philip Professor of International Studies at the University of Washington's Henry M. Jackson School of International Studies. His latest books are the Chinese edition of *Peasants, Politics, and Revolution: Pressures Towards Political and Social Change in the Third World* (1996); *Palestinians: The Making of a People* (coauthored with Baruch Kimmerling, Harvard University Press, 1994); *State Power and Social Forces: Domination and Transformation in the Third World* (coedited with Atul Kohli and Vivienne Shue, Cambridge University Press, 1994); and *Rules and Rights in the Middle East* (coedited with Ellis Goldberg and Resat Kasaba, University of Washington Press, 1994). His current research is on the role of law in state-society relations.

PART I

INTRODUCTION

RESEARCH TRADITIONS AND THEORY IN COMPARATIVE POLITICS: AN INTRODUCTION

Mark I. Lichbach
Alan S. Zuckerman

THE COMMON HERITAGE OF COMPARATIVE POLITICS

Comparativists inherit their dream of theorizing about politics from the founders of social theory. Their intellectual forebears represent the pantheon of Western thought. In the classic survey of the field's intellectual origins, Harry Eckstein (1963) highlights the past masters.

> Comparative politics ... has a particular right to claim Aristotle as an an-cestor because of the primacy that he assigned to politics among the sci-ences and because the problems he raised and the methods he used are sim-ilar to those still current in political studies (Eckstein 1963: 3).

Machiavelli and Montesquieu, Hobbes and Smith are the progenitors who lived during the Renaissance and the Enlightenment. The classic theorists of social sci-ence – Karl Marx, Max Weber, Emile Durkheim, Vilfredo Pareto, Gaetano Mosca, and Roberto Michels – established the field's research agenda, mode of analysis, and contrasting theoretical visions. Several seminal theorists of contem-porary political science – Harry Eckstein, David Apter, Robert Dahl, Seymour Lipset, Karl Deutsch, Gabriel Almond, and Sidney Verba – drew on this heritage to rebuild and reinvigorate the field of comparative politics. A shared, grand in-tellectual vision motivates comparativists.

Comparativists want to understand the critical events of the day, a position that ensures that dreams of theory address the political world as it exists, not for-

3

mal abstractions or utopias. Just as Marx and Weber responded to the fundamental transformations associated with the rise of capitalism, just as Marx developed a general strategy for a socialist revolution and Weber grappled with the theoretical and normative demands of the bureaucratic state, and just as Mosca, Pareto, and Michels strove to understand the possibilities and limits of democratic rule, students of comparative politics examine pressing questions in the context of their immediate political agenda. The contemporary study of comparative politics therefore blossomed in response to the political problems that followed World War II. New forms of conflict emerged: Communist threats; peasant rebellions and revolutions; social movements, urban riots, student upheavals, military coups, and national liberation struggles swept the world. Government decisions replaced markets as foci for economic development. New states followed the disintegration of colonial empires, and the worldwide movement toward democratic rule seemed to resume after the fascist tragedies. The challenges of the current era – domestic conflict, state-building, the political bases of economic growth, and democratization, to note but a few – stand at the center of today's research, indicating that the need to respond to contemporary issues guides the field.

Comparative politics therefore asserts an ambitious scope of inquiry. No political phenomenon is foreign to it; no level of analysis is irrelevant, and no time period beyond its reach. Civil war in Afghanistan; voting decisions in Britain; ethnic conflict in Quebec, Bosnia, and Burundi; policy interactions among the bureaucracies of the European Union in Brussels, government agencies in Rome, regional offices in Basilicata, and local powers in Potenza; the religious bases of political action in Iran, Israel, and the United States; the formation of democracies in Eastern Europe and the collapse of regimes in Africa; and global economic patterns are part of the array of contemporary issues that stand before the field. Questions about the origins of capitalism; the formation of European states; the rise of fascism and the collapse of interwar democracies; and the transition to independence after colonial rule are some of the themes of past eras that still command our attention.

Second, comparativists assert an ambitious intellectual vision in that they approach these substantive concerns with general questions in mind. Anyone who studies the politics of a particular country – whether Germany or Ghana, the United Arab Emirates or the United States of America – so as to address abstract issues, does comparative politics. Anyone who is interested in who comes to power, how, and why – the names, places, and dates of politics in any one place or other – in order to say something about the politics of succession or the determinants of vote choice, is a comparativist. In other words, students of comparative politics examine a case to reveal what it tells us about a larger set of political phenomena, or they relate the particulars of politics to more general theoretical ideas about politics.

Comparativists therefore insist that analysis requires explicit comparisons. Because events of global historical significance affect so many countries in so short a period of time, studies of single countries and abstract theorizing are woefully inadequate to capture epoch-shaping developments. More than three decades ago, when the founders of the contemporary field of comparative politics initiated the most recent effort to merge theory and data in the study of politics, they therefore established another of the field's guiding principles: The proper study of politics requires systematic comparisons.[1]

Finally, comparativists assert a grand intellectual vision in that their generalizations are situated in the context of the Big Questions of social thought: Who rules? How are interests represented? Who wins and who loses? How is authority challenged? Why are some nations "developed"? These questions have produced much contemporary theorizing about the connections among social order, the state, civil society, and social change, especially in democracies. Comparativists engage the basic issues that inform social and political thought.

In sum, comparative politics follows the lead of the grand masters in their approach to substantive issues, to the scope of inquiry, to the nature of theory-building, and to the enduring problems of social thought. As comparativists address politically significant matters, explore a range of political phenomena, propose general explanatory propositions based on systematic evidence from multiple cases, and address Big Questions, they move along a path first marked by the founders of social science.

THE COMPETING TRADITIONS IN COMPARATIVE POLITICS

In spite of this shared dream, long-standing disagreements separated the field's forebears and contrasting research schools characterize current efforts to build theories in comparative politics. When many of today's senior scholars were graduate students, their training included courses that compared psychological and culturalist approaches, institutional studies of political organizations, structural–functional and systems analyses, cybernetics and modes of information theory, pluralist, elitist, and Marxist analyses, modernization theory and its alternatives of dependency and world-systems theories, and rational choice theory, to name the most obvious. Most of these perspectives have disappeared and some have formed new combinations. Today, rational choice theories, culturalist approaches, and structural analyses stand as the principal competing theoretical schools in comparative politics. Rational choice theorists follow a path laid out by Hobbes, Smith, and Pareto; culturalists continue work begun by Montesquieu and developed by Weber and Mosca; and structuralists build on Marx's foundations and add to Weber's edifice. The themes and debates of contemporary comparative politics are therefore rooted in the enduring questions of social thought. They continue to lie at the center of work in all the social sciences.

[1]Classic works that appeared to herald the emergence of comparative politics as a subdiscipline of political science include Almond and Coleman (1960), Almond and Verba (1963), Beer and Ulam (1958), Dahl (1966; 1971), Eckstein and Apter (1963), Holt and Turner (1970), Huntington (1968), La Palombara and Weiner (1966), Lipset and Rokkan (1967), Moore (1966), Przeworski and Teune (1970); Pye and Verba (1965), Riker (1962), and Sartori (1970). At the same time, two journals, *Comparative Politics* and *Comparative Political Studies,* appeared, helping to institutionalize the subfield.

Rationalists begin with assumptions about actors who act deliberately to maximize their advantage. This research school uses the power of mathematical reasoning to elaborate explanations with impressive scope. Analysis begins at the level of the individual and culminates in questions about collective actions, choices, and institutions. Following the path first charted by Downs (1957), Olson (1968), and Riker (1962), rational choice theory has spread to address diverse problems: from electoral choice to revolutionary movements, from coalitions to political economy, and from institution formation to state-building. Here, the clarity of mathematical reasoning takes pride of place; powerful abstract logics facilitate a shared understanding among the members of the research school.

As comparativists engage in fieldwork in diverse societies, they grapple with the need to understand varied ways of life, systems of meaning, and values. As students who cut their teeth on the abstractions of modernization and dependency theory encounter the realities of particular villages, political parties, and legislatures, they seek to ground their observations in the politics that is being analyzed. Following the lead of social and cultural anthropologists, many comparativists adhere to Geertz's (1973) admonition to provide "thick descriptions." Culturalists therefore provide nuanced and detailed readings of particular cases, frequently drawn from fieldwork, as they seek to understand the phenomena being studied. This stance usually joins strong doubts about both the ability to generalize to abstract categories and the ability to provide explanations that apply to more than the case at hand.

Structuralists draw together long-standing interests in political and social institutions. Many emphasize the formal organizations of governments; some retain Marx's concern with class relations; some study political parties and interest groups; some combine these into analyses of how states and societies interact; and some emphasize the themes of political economy. Although these scholars display diverse patterns of reasoning, from mathematical models to verbal arguments, and many modes of organizing empirical evidence, they continue to follow Marx's and Weber's contention that theory and data guide social analysis.

As Alan Zuckerman's essay indicates, these research traditions take strong positions on the methodological issues that divide comparativists.[2] Rational

---

[2]There is also a long-standing debate in comparative politics about methodology. As comparativists propose explanations that cover sets of cases, perhaps based on causal accounts, they grapple with questions that relate to theory-building, concept formation, and case selection: How do concepts carry across cases? What is the value of treating concepts as variables that are measured by indicators? What is the proper use of case-specific information in theories that cover many cases? How does the choice of cases affect the general propositions offered? Are there requirements that define the number of cases that need to be included in an analysis? What is the relevance of single case studies to the development of theory? How can single case studies be used to speak to general sets of phenomena? Is it possible or desirable to include all relevant instances in the analysis? Is it possible to devise an adequate methodology that permits powerful generalizations based on the observation of a small number of cases? These questions raise problems of external validity, the ability to generalize beyond the case being observed.

Nearly thirty years ago, Sartori (1970) drew attention to fundamental questions of concept formation. At that same time, Lijphart (1971) and Przeworski and Teune (1970) initiated a controversy about

choice theorists seek to maximize the ability to provide universal laws that may be used in nomothetic explanations. They consider problems of reliability – the concern with the evidence required to support generalizations from the particular to sets of cases – as a challenge to research design. Cultural interpreters maximize the importance of reliability as they describe the constellations of particular cases and minimize the value of generalist research expectations. They interpret particular events, decisions, and patterns, eschewing any need to tie explanations to general principles. Structural analysts who follow Marx offer universal theories that include causal accounts. At the same time, they struggle to tie reliable descriptions into powerful generalizations; they grapple self-consciously with the requirements of case selection and how best to move from the particular analysis to the set of cases about which they seek to theorize. Comparativists' long-standing debates over method thus reappear in the three research traditions.

However, as Mark Lichbach's essay indicates, the dispute among the schools goes beyond the ideographic–nomothetic divide. The traditions differ with respect to ontology: Rationalists study how actors employ reason to satisfy their interests, culturalists study rules that constitute individual and group identities, and structuralists explore relations among actors in an institutional context. Reasons, rules, and relations are the various starting points of inquiry. The traditions also differ with respect to explanatory strategy: Rationalists perform comparative static experiments, culturalists produce interpretive understandings, and structuralists study the historical dynamics of real social types. Positivism, interpretivism, and realism are the possible philosophies of social science.

Moreover, as both Zuckerman and Lichbach indicate, no school displays a rigid and uniform orthodoxy. Rationalists debate the utility of relaxing the core assumption that defines individuals as maximizers of their self-interest. They differ as well over the proper form of explanation, some seeking covering laws and others proposing causal accounts, as they debate the necessity of transforming formal models into accounts of events. Continuing the debate initiated by Marx and Weber, structuralists differ over the ontological status of their concepts: Are social class, ethnicity, state, and other concepts that characterize this research school natural types? Are political processes best seen as determined and closed-ended or probabilistic and open-ended processes? Structuralists differ as well over

the proper methodology of comparative research, in which Eckstein (1975), Ragin (1987), Ragin and Becker (1992), and Skocpol and Somers (1980) have offered significant alternative positions (see Collier 1993 for a review of this literature). Most recently, Collier and Mahon (1993), Collier (1993), and Sartori (1994) illustrate further developments concerning the proper formation of concepts, and King, Keohane, and Verba (1994; 1995) initiated a productive debate over issues of research design in comparative politics. On the latter, see especially Bartels (1995), Brady (1995), Caporaso (1995), Collier (1995), Laitin (1995), Mohr (1996), Rogowski (1995), and Tarrow (1995). There is a natural affinity between studies of research design and comparative method that is frequently overlooked. King, Keohane, and Verba (1994; 1995) argue that there is only one scientific method. Hence, their strictures resemble those proposed by Cook and Campbell (1979).

the utility of nomothetic and causal explanations. Culturalists disagree over the theoretical importance of generalizations drawn from their fieldwork. May one derive or test general propositions from the analysis of a particular village? Do public opinion surveys provide an adequate picture of people's goals, values, and identities? They differ over the nature of explanation in comparative politics as well. Some culturalists reject any form of covering law or causal accounts, offering only interpretations of political life in particular places; others move toward the mainstream of comparative politics, incorporating values and systems of meaning into theories that adhere to the standard forms of explanation. In short, as Lichbach makes clear in his essay, ideal-type rationalists, culturalists, and structuralists need to be identified so that we may recognize how practicing comparativists employ a battery of ideal-type strategies in their concrete empirical work.

Comparative politics is dominated today by rationalist, culturalist, and structuralist approaches. What explains the imperialist expansion of these schools and the disappearance of earlier approaches? As Lichbach's and Zuckerman's essays in this volume demonstrate, these schools share an ontological and epistemological symmetry. They offer – indeed force – choices along the same dimensions. Furthermore, at a more fundamental level, the themes of the research schools rest at the heart of the human sciences. Reason, rules, and relations are unique to social theory. Focusing on these themes sets research in the social sciences apart from the physical sciences, providing a fundamental basis on which to theorize about political phenomena. Rationalist, culturalist, and structuralist theories are thus embedded in strong research communities, scholarly traditions, and analytical languages.

ADVANCING THEORY IN COMPARATIVE POLITICS: AN OVERVIEW OF THE ESSAYS IN THIS VOLUME

The extraordinary range and importance of the topics examined by comparativists, the powerful and competing research schools that characterize the field, and the scholarly pedigree of its work invite periodic assessments of the state of comparative politics. In the early 1960s, Harry Eckstein and David Apter (1963) edited a collection of essays that established the field's questions. In 1970, Robert Holt and John Turner gathered together a set of contributions that raised the level of theoretical sophistication. Both volumes guided research in comparative politics.[3]

---

[3]Some other early studies of the relationship between the research schools and theory in comparative politics include Bill and Hardgrave (1973), La Palombara (1974), Mayer (1972), Merkl (1970), and Merritt (1971). Recent works include Almond (1991), Cantori and Ziegler (1988), Chilcote (1994), Crotty (1991), Dogan and Kazancigil (1994), Dogan and Pelassy (1984), Mayer (1989), Rogowski (1993), Rustow and Erickson (1991), Weiner and Huntington (1987), Wiarda (1990), and Zuckerman (1991).

A field advances through explicit dialogue about the relative strengths and weaknesses, successes and failures of the research traditions of which it is composed. Theory is a collective but contentious enterprise. While scholarship is the work of single scholars, knowledge accumulates as competing groups of scholars accept and reject claims about the world. We have therefore organized this volume around the theme of competing research traditions in comparative politics. Because so much analysis in comparative politics is guided by the expectations, assumptions, methods, and principles of rational choice theory, culturalist analyses, and structuralist approaches, assessments of the state of theory and prospects for advancing theory need to focus on these research schools. As the authors of the essays in this volume examine the research traditions in comparative politics, they assess knowledge and advance theory, seeking to direct research in the coming years.

Because research in comparative politics centers around distinctive topics, we have also selected four themes around which to examine the interplay between theory and the three schools: the analysis of mass politics (especially regarding electoral behavior), social movements and revolutions, political economy, and state–society relations. Why did we choose these topics? Taken together, they encompass much of the research done in comparative politics. Each displays a history of sophisticated theoretical and empirical work that stretches over several decades. The comparative study of voting behavior begins in the interwar years. Because most people who engage in political activities do so only at the ballot box, this research examines the political behavior of the largest set of people; here the study of politics moves its focus away from politicians and bureaucrats, government agencies and political parties, and the abstractions of state and society. The systematic analysis of social movements and revolutions descends directly from Marx and Weber. It also links to studies of regime transformations and the bases of stable democracies. Beginning with Adam Smith's theories, the analysis of the political economies of advanced industrial societies has become the focus of the largest segment of research on the political institutions and public policies of established democracies. As comparativists study state–society relations, they follow a path first marked by Marx, Weber, Mosca, Michels, and Pareto. As they study the formation of states, they blend abstract theorization and detailed empirical studies.

A study of these particular topics has the additional virtue of moving the analysis beyond the field of comparative politics. Examining the successes of the research schools with regard to each of these topics also casts light on the utility of various analytic techniques: Electoral analyses typically use quantitative techniques to study survey results and work on state–society relations includes the results of qualitative studies, while research on both social movements and revolutions and political economy varies in the use of quantitative and qualitative modes of analysis. Finally, these research themes also cast light on the relations between theories developed in comparative politics and those that characterize related fields in political science and the other social sciences. The research

themes thus tell us about the utility of hypotheses devised to explain electoral behavior and social movements in the United States, the value of methods and arguments drawn from economists in the study of political economy, and the significance of anthropological approaches for the analysis of state–society relations.
In sum, as we analyze these four research topics, we shed light on central issues
of theory in comparative politics and the social sciences more generally.

We have divided the essays into three units. The first, containing the chapters written by Margaret Levi, Marc Howard Ross, and Ira Katznelson, offers
briefs for each of the research schools. The essays summarize each analytic tradition's core principles, noting variations within the approach and presenting recent work that points to new combinations. The next unit contains the chapters
written by Samuel H. Barnes on mass politics, Doug McAdam, Sidney Tarrow,
and Charles Tilly on social movements and revolution, Peter A. Hall on the political economy of established democracies, and Joel S. Migdal on state–society
relations in newly formed states. The concluding unit contains essays by Mark I.
Lichbach and Alan S. Zuckerman, returning the focus to the theme of advancing
theory in comparative politics.

THE ESSAYS

Margaret Levi contends that rational choice theory displays several critical
strengths. It demonstrates the potential gap between personal interest and the
public good, individual behavior and collective action. It offers testable theories,
providing the ability to make sense of a correlation or a set of events through a
plausible and compelling story that identifies causal mechanisms and universal
principles. Rationalists in comparative politics, she maintains, are committed to
explanation and to generalization. Levi also sets out differences within the research school. Members of this analytic tradition differ in the extent to which
they believe that the core principles can be tested directly. They vary as well in
the form of explanation: Some search for covering laws and others offer causal explanations. Levi maintains that the major task confronting comparative rationalists is to offer explanations that compel both logically and empirically. To that
end, she develops the method of analytic narratives, in which rational choice theory provides the principles that guide a narrative history of a political process.
This method offers a bridge between rationalists and the other research schools.
No matter the detail in an analytic narrative, maintains Levi, rationalists remain
distinctive. They are almost always willing to sacrifice nuance for generalizability, detail for logic.

Marc Howard Ross argues on behalf of culturalist analyses. He maintains
that two distinct, but not unrelated, features of culture are relevant to comparative politics. First, culture is a system of meaning which people use to manage
their daily worlds, large and small; second, culture is the basis of social and political identity which affects how people stand and how they act on a wide range
of matters. Culture is a framework for organizing the world, for locating the self

and others in it, for making sense of the actions and interpreting the motives of others, for grounding an analysis of interests, for linking collective identities to political action, and for motivating people and groups toward some actions and away from others. The effects of culture on collective action and political life are generally indirect, and to appreciate fully the role of culture in political life, it is necessary to inquire into how culture interacts with interests and institutions. Ross proposes that a postmodern, intersubjective understanding of politics is compatible with the belief that comparison is central to social science, no matter the complexity of social phenomena. Interpretations, Ross maintains, lie at the center of cultural analysis. The interpretations of particular political significance are built from the accounts of groups and individuals striving to make sense of their social and political worlds, and the term refers both to the shared intersubjective meanings of actors and also to the explicit efforts of social science observers to understand these meanings and to present them to others. Ross presents interpretations as a methodological tool in the comparative study of culture and politics for understanding processes like the construction of ethnic and national identities.

Ira Katznelson develops a macroanalytical mode of analysis. Katznelson presents a picture of society that is composed of important and significant social relationships, political processes, and economic interactions. Individuals are defined by these connections, as structures constrain their perceptions and choices. Katznelson believes that the most significant processes shaping human identities, interests, and interaction are such large-scale features of modernity as capitalist development, market rationality, state-building, secularization, political and scientific revolution, and the acceleration of instruments for the communication and diffusion of ideas. He offers an approach that examines the relationship of history and analytical social science; structural theory after Marxism; the special status of the state; and the question of behavioral and strategic microfoundations. He proposes a configurative approach, standing in opposition to the microanalytical and postpositivist currents that are increasingly important in political science. Finally, he offers a stirring call for a return to the world-historical vision of structuralists like Barrington Moore.

Samuel H. Barnes reviews the research traditions with regard to mass political behavior, concentrating first on turnout in national elections and then on partisan choice in established democracies. He maintains that research on the determinants of the decision to take part in an election display the strengths and weaknesses of each of the research schools. None has solved this problem, whether conceived as a question of aggregate variation across various countries and different points in time, or as the single act of casting a ballot for any one person. Barnes regards partisan choice as a more complex problem. Reviewing evidence that the mobilization of publics in established democracies has shifted from social to political to cognitive bases, he maintains that there is parallel support for the claim that rationalist perspectives have replaced structuralist arguments in this research area.

Doug McAdam, Sidney Tarrow, and Charles Tilly synthesize approaches to the analysis of social movements and revolution, denying either the need or the utility of deciding among them. Research in this area, they maintain, requires theories that join structural and rationalist factors – political opportunity and mobilization structures – with cultural factors – framing processes. Charting a research agenda, they call for comparisons across different types of contentious actions and movements and across different political settings that take into account particular national histories. Their chapter introduces a research agenda that includes the analysis of patterns that flow over time, taking seriously the metaphor of cycles and revolutions. Here, they lead comparative politics back to the theoretically informed study of a single country. Their effort joins with other process models, displaying a mode of explanation that accounts for political phenomena without offering a single general covering law or one general causal explanation.

Peter A. Hall examines theories of the political economy of advanced industrial societies that emphasize interests (drawing on rational choice theory), ideas and values (the work of culturalists), and institutions (structural approaches). In a systematic and comprehensive survey, Hall reflects on the accomplishments of each of the research schools, noting as well the lacunae present. The essay examines the potential for integrating themes, underlining exciting developments that lie at the intersections of the schools. Noting that much recent research has concentrated on explaining cross-national differences in economic policies and performance, Hall concludes by stressing the need to return to broad and fundamental themes: the relationship between the state, seen as the custodian of a general interest, and the market, seen as a mechanism for interchange among private interests, and the consequences of this interaction for the overall distribution of well-being in society.

Joel S. Migdal defends the centrality of the state against recent attacks on its analytic importance. The analysis of the state, he maintains, is unnecessarily cut off from other political phenomena. Locating the source of the problem in the overwhelming influence of Weber on the study of the state, Migdal maintains that the various perspectives – culturalist, rationalist, and structuralist alike – have tended to isolate it as a subject of study, peering into its innards and poring over its organization in order to understand how it succeeds in gaining obedience and conformity from its population. This sort of analytic isolation of the state, he claims, has led to a mystification of its capabilities and power. Finally, Migdal develops an argument on behalf of the "limited state." He seeks to accomplish this goal by blending the largely ignored culturalist perspective with the more dominant institutionalist approach, as well as shifting the analytic focus away from the state as a freestanding organization and toward a process-oriented view of the state-in-society.

Mark I. Lichbach addresses the central problem of this volume: the interpretation and understanding of the debate among the competing research traditions that characterize contemporary comparative politics. He offers a four-part thesis on improving the state of theory in comparative politics. First, if we approach theory by believing that our field consists only of a "messy center," our search for better theory will end almost immediately. Second, if, on the other hand, we embrace creative confrontations, which can include well-defined syntheses among the strongly defined research communities in our field – the rationalists, culturalists, and structuralists – reflexive understanding of theorists and their theories will flourish. Third, contemporary comparativists can get the most out of such a dialogue by appreciating the historical context of the development of social theory. Finally, contemporary comparativists can also gain from such a dialogue by recognizing that the approaches offer a critical commentary on the challenges of modernity which, in turn, help us appreciate the significance of rationalist, culturalist, and structuralist thought.

Alan S. Zuckerman also addresses the central problem of this volume. He does so by directing attention to the relationship between theory and the standards for explanations in comparative politics. He notes that the accepted forms of explanation – covering laws and causal accounts – display significant deficiencies, providing unreasonable standards for assessing explanations. Furthermore, Zuckerman maintains that nomological and causal explanations share an ontology that includes linear and frequently determined relationships among variables, clocklike patterns, parity in the size of cause and effect, and microprocesses as determinants of structures. Both utilize point predictions as the means for testing explanatory hypotheses. The successes of theories in comparative politics that share these conceptualizations of reality notwithstanding, argues Zuckerman, there is strong reason to view the political world as also composed of nonlinear relationships among variables, probabilistic outcomes and structures, aperiodic systems, unpredictable phenomena, chance factors, and open-ended possibilities. There is reason, therefore, to propose standards for explanation in comparative politics that accommodate these complex patterns. Zuckerman maintains that changing the standards for explanation in comparative politics allows fresh combinations of ideas to appear. Assumptions, modes and levels of analysis, and theoretical principles may be drawn from more than one research school. Process models that apply to particular cases join cross-national comparisons; complex statistical techniques join methods that assume linear relationships among variables; analyses join individual and structural variables. New theories emerge, maintains Zuckerman, and the ability to explain political phenomena advances.

THE WAY AHEAD

The rationalist, culturalist, and structuralist research traditions set the agenda in contemporary comparative politics, just as they do in the study of American politics, international politics, and social science even more generally.[4] Advancing theory in comparative politics therefore requires that we understand and assess these three research schools. Absent a focus on these approaches, symposia on the

[4]This point is documented in Lichbach's essay.

state of theory in comparative politics cannot succeed.[5] We hope that as comparativists – especially graduate students and young faculty – read *Comparative Politics: Rationality, Culture, and Structure,* they will place theoretical reflection again on their field's agenda.

We also have grander ambitions. While theoretical discussions of rules, reasons, and relations appear in the literature on social theory and the philosophy of social science, this is the first set of case studies of the rationalist–culturalist–structuralist debate to appear. Hence, we also hope that the essays in this volume guide research and theoretical reflections well beyond the boundaries of comparative politics. Our intellectual forebears in classic social theory and contemporary political science would have appreciated that *chutzpah*.

REFERENCES

Almond, Gabriel A. 1991. *Schools of Political Science.* Beverly Hills: Sage.

Almond, Gabriel A., and James S. Coleman, eds. 1960. *The Politics of Developing Areas.* Princeton: Princeton University Press.

Almond, Gabriel A., and Sidney Verba. 1963. *The Civic Culture: Political Attitudes and Democracy in Five Nations.* Princeton: Princeton University Press.

Bartels, Larry. 1995. "Symposium on Designing Social Inquiry." *The Political Methodologist,* 6:8-11.

Beer, Samuel H., and Adam B. Ulam, eds. 1958. *Patterns of Government: The Major Political Systems of Europe.* New York: Random House.

Bill, James A., and Robert L. Hardgrave. 1973. *Comparative Politics: The Quest for Theory.* Columbus, OH: Charles E. Merrill.

Brady, Henry E. 1995. "Symposium on *Designing Social Inquiry.*" *The Political Methodologist,* 6:11-14.

Cantori, Louis J., and Andrew H. Ziegler, Jr., eds. 1988. *Comparative Politics in the Post-Behavioral Age.* Boulder: Riener.

Caporaso, James. 1995. "Research Design Falsification, and the Qualitative–Quantitative Divide," *American Political Science Review* 89:457-60.

Chilcote, Ronald H. 1994. *Theories of Comparative Politics: The Search for a Paradigm Reconsidered,* 2nd ed. Boulder: Westview.

Collier, David. 1993. "The Comparative Method." In Ada W. Finifter, ed., *Political Science: The State of the Discipline II.* Washington, D.C.: American Political Science Association.

————. 1995. "Translating Quantitative Methods for Qualitative Researchers: The Case of Selection Bias." *American Political Science Review* 89:461-6.

Collier, David, and James Mahon. 1993. "Conceptual 'Stretching' Revisited: Adapting Categories in Comparative Analysis." *American Political Science Review* 87: 845-55.

Cook, Thomas D., and Donald T. Campbell. 1979. *Quasi-Experimentation: Design and Analysis Issues for Field Settings.* Boston: Houghton Mifflin.

---

[5]See for example the special issue of *World Politics* (October 1995).

Crotty, William, ed. 1991. *Looking to the Future – Volume 2: Comparative Politics, Policy, and International Relations.* Evanston: Northwestern University Press.

Dahl, Robert A., ed. 1966. *Political Oppositions in Western Democracies.* New Haven: Yale University Press.

———. 1971. *Polyarchy: Participation and Opposition.* New Haven: Yale University Press.

Dogan, Mattei, and Ali Kazancigil, eds. 1994. *Comparing Nations: Concepts, Strategies, Substance.* Oxford: Blackwell.

Dogan, Mattei, and Dominique Pelassy. 1984. *How to Compare Nations: Strategies in Comparative Politics.* Chatham, NJ: Chatham House.

Downs, Anthony. 1957. *An Economic Theory of Democracy.* New York: Harper & Row.

Eckstein, Harry. 1963. "A Perspective on Comparative Politics, Past and Present." In Harry Eckstein and David E. Apter, eds., *Comparative Politics: A Reader.* New York: The Free Press of Glencoe.

———. 1975. "Case Study and Theory in Political Science." In Fred Greenstein and Nelson Polsby, eds., *Handbook of Political Science VII.* Reading, MA: Addison-Wesley.

Eckstein, Harry, and David E. Apter, eds. 1963. *Comparative Politics: A Reader.* New York: The Free Press of Glencoe.

Geertz, Clifford. 1973. *The Interpretation of Cultures.* New York: Basic Books.

Holt, Robert T., and John E. Turner, eds. 1970. *The Methodology of Comparative Research.* New York: The Free Press.

Huntington, Samuel P. 1968. *Political Order in Changing Societies.* New Haven: Yale University Press.

King, Gary, Robert O. Keohane, and Sidney Verba. 1994. *Designing Social Inquiry: Scientific Inquiry in Qualitative Research.* Princeton: Princeton University Press.

———. 1995. "The Importance of Research Design in Political Science." *American Political Science Review* 89:475-81.

Laitin, David. 1995. "Disciplining Political Science." *American Political Science Review* 89:454-6.

La Palombara, Joseph. 1974. *Politics within Nations.* Englewood Cliffs, NJ: Prentice-Hall.

La Palombara, Joseph, and Myron Weiner, eds. 1966. *Political Parties and Political Development.* Princeton: Princeton University Press.

Lijphart, Arend. 1971. "Comparative Politics and Comparative Method." *American Political Science Review* 65:682-93.

Lipset, Seymour M., and Stein Rokkan, eds. 1967. *Party Systems and Voter Alignments: Cross-National Perspectives.* New York: The Free Press.

Mayer, Lawrence. 1972. *Comparative Political Inquiry: A Methodological Survey.* Homewood, IL: Dorsey.

———. 1989. *Comparative Political Inquiry: Promise Versus Performance.* Beverly Hills: Sage.

Merkl, Peter H. 1970. *Modern Comparative Politics.* New York: Holt, Rinehart, and Winston.

Merritt, Richard L. 1971. *Systematic Approaches to Comparative Politics.* Chicago: Rand McNally.

Mohr, Lawrence. 1996. *The Causes of Human Behavior: Implications for Theory and Method in the Social Sciences.* Ann Arbor: University of Michigan Press.

Moore, Barrington, Jr. 1966. *Social Origins of Dictatorship and Democracy: Lord and Peasant in the Making of the Modern World.* Boston: Beacon Press.

Olson, Mancur, Jr. 1968. *The Logic of Collective Action: Public Goods and the Theory of Groups.* New York: Schocken.

Przeworksi, Adam, and Henry Teune. 1970. *The Logic of Comparative Social Inquiry.* New York: Wiley-Interscience.

Pye, Lucien W., and Sidney Verba, eds. 1965. *Political Culture and Political Development.* Princeton: Princeton University Press.

Ragin, Charles. 1987. *The Comparative Method.* Berkeley: University of California Press.

Ragin, Charles C., and Howard S. Becker, eds. 1992. *What Is a Case? Exploring the Foundations of Social Inquiry.* Cambridge: Cambridge University Press.

Riker, William H. 1962. *The Theory of Political Coalitions.* New Haven: Yale University Press.

Rogowski, Ronald. 1993. "Comparative Politics." In Ada W. Finifter, ed., *Political Science: The State of the Discipline II.* Washington, D.C.: American Political Science Association.

———. 1995. "The Role of Theory and Anomaly in Social-Scientific Inference." *American Political Science Review* 89:467-70.

Rustow, Dankwart, and Kenneth Paul Erickson, eds. 1991. *Comparactive Political Dynamics: Research Perspective.* New York: HarperCollins.

Sartori, Giovanni. 1970. "Concept Misformation in Comparative Politics." *American Political Science Review* 64:1033-53.

———. 1994. "Compare Why and How: Comparing, Miscomparing, and the Comparative Method." In Mattei Dogan and Ali Kazancigil, eds., *Comparing Nations: Concepts, Strategies, Substance.* Oxford: Blackwell.

Skocpol, Theda, and Margaret Somers. 1980. "The Uses of Comparative History in Macrosocial Inquiry." *Comparative Studies in Society and History* 22:174-97.

Tarrow, Sidney. 1995. "Bridging the Qualitative-Quantitative Divide in Political Science." *American Political Science Review* 89:471-4.

Weiner, Myron, and Samuel P. Huntington, eds. 1987. *Understanding Political Development.* Boston: Little, Brown.

Wiarda, Howard J., ed. 1990. *New Directions in Comparative Politics.* 2nd ed. Boulder: Westview.

Zuckerman, Alan S. 1991. *Doing Political Science: An Introduction to Political Analysis.* Boulder: Westview.

PART II

RESEARCH TRADITIONS IN COMPARATIVE POLITICS

A MODEL, A METHOD, AND A MAP: RATIONAL CHOICE IN COMPARATIVE AND HISTORICAL ANALYSIS

Margaret Levi

Throughout history, rulers have reacted to political and economic constraints by establishing a wide array of institutional arrangements for both raising revenue and stimulating economic growth (Greif et al. 1994; Kiser 1994; Levi 1988; Milgrom et al. 1990; North 1981; North and Weingast 1989). Throughout the world, villagers have traditionally owned livestock privately and land in common. The Swiss of Torbel (Ostrom 1990: 61-5) are still successful in "governing the commons,"[1] but by the 1960s the pastoral Galole Orma people of northeastern Kenya no longer were (Ensminger 1992). Unions and social democratic parties (Golden 1990; Golden 1996; Przeworski 1985; Przeworski and Sprague 1986; Wallerstein 1989), religious parties (Kalyvas 1996; Gill forthcoming), and political coalitions (Kitschelt 1989; Rogowski 1989) have had varying capacities to organize and achieve political ends over time. Political officials have also differed in their abilities to effect reforms in developing societies (Ames 1987; Bates 1983; Bates and Krueger 1993; Geddes 1994; Oi 1989; Shirk 1993).

These are a small sampling of the historical and comparative macrophenomena rational choice theorists attempt to explain. The first example illustrates institutional establishment and change. The second is a case of a system of property rights long maintained and then, in some places, abandoned. The third exemplifies variations in the capacity of organizations and parties to achieve political

---

[1]This phrase is, of course, borrowed from the title of Elinor Ostrom's 1990 book.

ends. Although widely different in subject matter, time, and place, all of these works do what rational choice does best: reveal how intentional and rational actors generate collective outcomes and aggregate behavior. Although the choice of each actor may be intentional and individually rational, the results to all may be unintentional and socially irrational. If it has done nothing else, rational choice has done quite a lot by laying to rest, conclusively, the myths that individual interest equals collective action or that collective action necessarily produces a collective good.[2]

The strength of rational choice in comparative and historical analysis is also evident in its capacity to spawn testable theory with clear scope conditions,[3] its ability to make sense of a correlation or a set of events by providing a plausible and compelling story that identifies the causal mechanisms linking the independent and dependent variables,[4] and its universalism that reveals generalizable implications applicable to cases beyond those under immediate investigation. Rationalists in comparative politics are committed to explanation and to generalization. This does not mean that all rational choice scholars engage in exactly the same enterprise. Few would claim that the assumption of rationality is directly testable or even observable, but there are those (e.g., Diermeier 1995; Fiorina 1995) who believe it is impossible to directly observe – let alone test – the causal pathways their formal models reveal. They tend to be proponents of Hempel's covering law approach rather than of causal explanations.[5] Others, however, claim that it is incumbent upon rational choice to reveal and evaluate causal mechanisms. They tend to believe that causal explanations might be possible after all. What unifies rationalists is not their views on causation or testability but their commitment to some form of causal inference (the term preferred by King, Keohane, and Verba 1994), universalism, and empirical social science that will produce falsifiable hypotheses.

The major task confronting comparative rationalists is how to offer explanations that compel both logically and empirically. Arguably, the source of progress in empirical social science is the coupling of theory and data in a systematic fashion. The contemporary fascination with certain kinds of theory – be it of the more formal or the more interpretive variety – has combined with the backlash against behavioralism to produce a serious neglect of facts, evidence, and data. For those who believe the task of social scientists is to develop theory and then evaluate it against data that actually can mediate between competing hypotheses, both the mathematical modeler and the Foucaultian postmodernist are maddening. Too often economists are guilty of generating a hypothesis whose "valid-

---

[2] The first paradox is Olson's (1965) contribution and the second Arrow's (1951). More recently, Bates (1991) and Hardin (1995) make these points powerfully.

[3] For an explication of this argument, see Kiser and Hechter (1991) and Kiser (1997).

[4] Others have also made this point. See, e.g., Elster (1989 and 1993), Kalyvas (1996:15-17), Laitin (1995:6), Przeworksi and Sprague (1986:181), and Rogowski (1995:469-70).

[5] This appears to be the view advocated by Lichbach (this volume). Also, see Somers (1996) for an interesting discussion of this problem.

ity" they "demonstrate" with a single example that makes their point. Many postmodernists fail to appeal to any facts at all or, when they do, there is no way to falsify their claims.

Good empirical theory may not be enough, however, to convince all consumers of comparative research of the advantages of rational choice. Most rational choice scholars have experienced considerable hostility from area specialists and historians, who find rational choice accounts inadequately sensitive to the historical, political, and cultural context or who believe the findings could be discovered and stated just as well without the edifice of formal theory. Other critics doubt that rational choice has yet to produce significant empirical contributions, even in American politics (Green and Shapiro 1994).

There are also those who clearly recognize the value of certain rational choice contributions (e.g., Hall this volume; McAdam, Tarrow, and Tilly this volume) but who either believe in the superiority of another approach or argue for a synthetic methodology. This chapter adopts a stance closer to those advocating some convergence. A line in the sand remains, nonetheless. Rationalists are almost always willing to sacrifice nuance for generalizability, detail for logic, a forfeiture most other comparativists would decline.[6]

THE MODEL OF RATIONAL CHOICE: NEITHER NEOCLASSICAL ECONOMICS NOR PUBLIC CHOICE

INFLUENCES

Many scholars have made significant contributions to advances in rational choice as an empirical social science. Anthony Downs's *An Economic Theory of Democracy* (1957) made spatial modeling a key component of analyses of voting and electoral processes. In the hands of William Riker (e.g., 1962, 1987) and those directly influenced by him, spatial modeling became an invaluable tool in the investigation of the origins and maintenance of such political institutions as federalism. In *The Logic of Collective Action* (1965) Mancur Olson emphasizes strategic interaction; each individual makes her decision based on the probable decision of others. His popularization of the free rider problem to account for variation in collective action and the production of collective goods reduces to a fiction models based on the automatic translation of interests into organization. Simultaneously, it stimulates systematic investigation of the conditions under which individuals will join together to influence government or each other and the conditions under which it is even possible for government and other organizations to deliver what constituents demand. The emphasis in

---

[6]Since Popkin's book on peasants (1979), there have been numerous works in comparative politics that used rational choice to simplify. Some of the most recent are: Gambetta 1993; Firmin-Sellers 1996; Ramseyer and Rosenbluth 1993; Tsebelis 1995; and Verdier 1994.

Douglass North's *Structure and Change in Economic History* (1981) is on the combination of strategic interaction and institutions that prohibit certain options and facilitate others. His advocacy of transaction cost theory, his advances in economic institutionalism, and his recognition of the role of relative bargaining power stimulate systematic investigation of the variation in both state action and outcomes throughout history. With *Institutions, Institutional Change and Economic Performance* (1990), North emphasizes path dependence and informal institutions, thus raising issues of historical determinacy and cultural influences on action.

The underlying model that produces these pathbreaking works derives from the neoclassical economic model in which the outcome of analytical interest is the consequence of the aggregation of the decisions of many rational individuals maximizing their egoistic interests. Rational choice theory is not, however, neoclassical economics (Bates 1988). Its attention to institutions and norms, to the richness of context, to questions of conflict and power, and, on occasion, to non-egoistic motivations differentiate it sharply from the straightforward application of economics to politics that characterized the early public choice school. Moreover, its aims are empirical and explanatory rather than normative and exhortatory. Whereas James Buchanan and Gordon Tullock (1965) use their models to attack the role of the state in the economy, the practitioners of rational choice seek to explore and understand what role the state, politics, groups, and organizations have actually played in economic and political development.

When individuals operate within the framework of the free market, the result is both personally and socially efficient – or so the neoclassical claim goes. In contrast, the institutions of politics do not necessarily lead to Pareto-optimal outcomes; the combined decisions of rational individuals often generate nonrational collective choices. This was, of course, the earlier and important finding of Kenneth Arrow (1951), whose paradox was both an explicit normative critique of majority rule democracy and an implicit demand for institutional innovation. Olson and North share with Arrow a concern with the reality of paradox and inefficiency, but their goal is more empirical: to understand when such results occur and why they do not always. For Olson, the reason that optimal or more proximately optimal outcomes are sometimes achieved rests in the provision of selective incentives. For North, the reason that we can explain structure and change rests in institutions and norms that constrain or facilitate choices, on the one hand, and that increase or decrease the transaction costs, on the other. Both North and Olson give politics an important role in economic analysis; actors with distributional agendas can influence the choices rational individuals make by altering the relative prices of the options in their choice set. For example, union officials can make it more rational for potential members to join and pay dues by controlling access to employment (Olson 1965), or rulers can create secure property rights that influence where investors place their funds (North 1981).

THE MODEL OF RATIONAL CHOICE

Empirical rational choice models now take for granted the contributions of Arrow, Downs, Riker, Olson, and North. Their emphasis is on rational and strategic individuals who make choices within constraints to obtain their desired ends, whose decisions rest on their assessment of the probable actions of others, and whose personal outcomes depend on what others do. The approach is methodologically individualist, yet its focus is not on individual choice but on the aggregation of individual choices. Rational choice is, as Lichbach (this volume) notes, a model that offers the microfoundations of macroprocesses and events. It does this by means of an equilibrium analysis in which actors respond to each others' decisions until each is at a position from which no improvement is possible. Sometimes, of course, there is no such position, and the result is either cycling or chaos. However, general equilibrium analysis permits the investigator to model and explain this outcome as well as more static outcomes. Keys to the model, then, are the assumption of rationality, the forms of constraint, the nature of the strategic interaction, and the search for an equilibrium solution.

Several applications of rational choice analysis will help in the explication of the essential elements of the model. These illustrations and most of the others referred to in this chapter tend to reflect the influence of Olson and North more than that of Arrow, Downs, Riker, or Buchanan and Tullock. Although there is considerable comparative work done by rationalists using spatial models and other such tools, the emphasis here is on research that raises issues of collective action and institutional arrangements.

The first application draws from Elinor Ostrom's *Governing the Commons* (1990) in which she compares several small communities reliant on inland fisheries. Some have been more successful than others in protecting their common pool resources, but all have escaped the imposition of a solution by centralized government. The second draws from my research on revenue production and taxation (Levi 1988) and on war and conscription (Levi 1997), which accounts for variation in government success in introducing compulsory contributions. The first example is a problem of cooperation among those who draw their livelihood from the common pool resource. The second is a problem of cooperation between government actors and citizens.

Both analyses assume that actors are making rational decisions in situations of uncertainty. They are assessing the expected costs and benefits and acting consistently with their preferences. They vary in their discount rates (how much they care about the future) and in their capacities to assess the risks they face. Thus, the appropriators of resources may or may not care about the long-term sustainability of the fishery, and they may or may not have good knowledge about how many fish there are and what natural disasters might befall them. They are uncertain about the effects of actions they and others take; they cannot even be absolutely certain about when others from within or outside their community will overfish. To Ostrom (1990: 34), this means that "the only reasonable assumption about the calculation process employed is that appropriators engage in a considerable amount of trial-and-error learning." In the military service case, many of the men likely to be conscripted probably had very high discount rates; they were extremely young, willing to take high risks, and probably believed in their invulnerability. Nonetheless, they lacked hard information on how long or how bloody the war would be or what traumas it might cause them over time. They were, however, facing a set of decisions that, most likely, were extraordinary rather than the recurring problems faced by the appropriators of fish or other natural resources. Thus, they could not use trial and error to develop their best course of action; rather they had to seek guidance from the past, their peers, their governments, or whatever other source they felt could offer good guidance.

The assumption of rationality is the subject of much of the criticism of rational choice. Even among the practitioners, there are the serious issues of what it means to be rational and of how much it matters whether individuals are actually rational or not.[7] However, the rationality assumption most useful for comparative research is a fairly thin variant in which individuals act consistently in relation to their preferences. The trick is in defining the preferences in general, ex ante to a particular application. In many instances, this is not difficult, requiring only a fairly straightforward observation of what is of principal concern to the class of actors under consideration. For example, if they are people buying and selling, maximizing wealth seems a reasonable assumption. If they are peasants in risky environments, maximizing security has some appeal. In the case of government actors, the presumption is that they want to stay in power. The utility functions of citizens are trickier to clarify given the range of interests citizens might have; there is nothing comparable to the economics dictum of getting the most for the least for one's money in the marketplace. Thus, any maximand will lead to hypotheses that can account for a smaller part of the variation in citizen behavior than in politician or economic consumer behavior.

Rational choice is not bound by the utility or wealth-maximizing assumptions that characterize economics. Rational choice does not even require the assumption that individuals are self-interested. However, the addition of non-egoistic considerations or motivational norms — such as the community standards Ostrom stresses or the fairness principles I stress — does increase the complexity and difficulty of the analysis. The advantage of assuming utility-maximization is that it is both parsimonious and extremely general, but it can also produce tautology: Whatever people do becomes a "revealed preference." The advantage of

---

[7] On the meanings of rationality, Elster's work (e.g., 1979, 1983a, 1983b, 1989, 1993) provides some of the most important considerations. On the importance of the validity of the rationality assumption, see Plott (1990) reporting on experiments in which the market aggregates the decisions of seemingly nonrational individuals into exactly the outcomes one would predict from a rational choice assumption. There is, of course, also the "as if" argument made famous by Milton Friedman.

the more specific wealth-maximizing assumption is that it produces observable implications but with a narrow conception of human motivation. The advantage of an assumption in which actors consider net payoffs that include both material and ethical factors is that it may better approximate reality albeit at the sacrifice of a neater and more parsimonious model. Nonetheless, as the maximand more closely approximates reality, the more reality it should capture.

The real action in the model does not, however, come from the internal considerations of the actor but from the constraints on her behavior. Thus, Ostrom (1990: 38), following Popper (1967), "... accepts Popper's methodological advice to emphasize the way we describe the situations in which individuals find themselves so that we can use observable variables to reject our theories, rather than internal, in-the-mind, subjective variables, which are far more difficult to measure."

Constraints have two major sources. The first, derived straightforwardly from neoclassical economics, is scarcity; individuals maximize within the confines of their available resources. An individual without money cannot make the investments that would make her richer, and an individual who lacks the vote cannot directly influence who is in government, no matter how much it might be in her interest to elect a certain party.

The other important constraints are institutional and organizational. Institutions are sets of rules (and sanctions) that structure social interactions and whose existence and applicability are commonly known within the relevant community.[8] Institutions, so defined, structure the individual choices of strategic actors so as to produce equilibrium outcomes, that is outcomes that no one has an incentive to alter. In game theory, they are the rules of the game that structure the interactions among players. In legislatures they are the rules that structure the order of votes, the method of aggregation of votes, and the like. An operational definition developed by Greif (forthcoming: 7) is the "technologically determined constraints on behavior which are self-enforcing."[9] All institutions are embodiments of rules, all have a legalistic aspect, and all possess enforcement mechanisms. They are considered political institutions when the state enforces the rules, social institutions when enforcement is through mechanisms such as approval and shunning, and economic institutions when enforcement is by means of profit and loss.[10]

---

[8]Of course, institutions can also facilitate action. However, the emphasis in this section is on their role in constraining choice.

[9]Organizations are "groups of individuals bound by some common purpose to achieve objectives" (North 1990: 5) or, what is essentially the same thing, "collective actors who might be subject to institutional constraint" (Knight 1992). Institutions and organization are closely intertwined, and often the same term is used to describe a particular example of both, e.g., firm, Congress, family. The legal institution of the firm is not exactly the same as the actual shareholders, managers, and employees who people the firm. Nor are the informal societal rules that guide family behavior in complete identity with the choices made by the actual family. The institution regulates behavior but cannot totally determine it. The organization, that is the individuals whose fates are tightly interwoven by an overarching common purpose, may not always be regulated.

[10]Michael Lipsky helped me to perceive this distinction.

Organizations – and expectations – are "institutional components," which are not determined technologically (Greif forthcoming: 7). Whether or not institutions and organizations are as distinct as North and Knight both argue,[11] organizations not only introduce a new player into the interaction, they can also affect what information and payoffs are available to the relevant actors. For example, in the study of CPRs (common pool resources), the firm and state are organizations that operate with and within the institutional framework of the property rights system. In my recent research within the institutions of democratic decision making, governments, political parties, and interest groups interact with each other in order to design military service policies.

Strategic action is the third pillar of the rational choice model. In the powerful price theory of neoclassical economics, the consumer lets the market transform the choices of others into a price and range of products that form the basis of her choice. The actor does not have to consider what others are going to do before making her choice. In most political and social situations, however, an evaluation of the behavior of other relevant actors comes prior to the choice. The decision whether to free ride, overfish, or pasture too many cows depends, at least in part, on an assessment of what others are likely to do. The vote of a legislator, the compliance of a citizen with government, the willingness to engage in collective action or even rebellion are all acts that depend on beliefs about the likely actions of others. A young man is likely to volunteer for military service if he believes he is going to be one of very few soldiers on the front lines, and an assessment that too many others will free ride may transform an opponent of conscription to a supporter. The outcome for all depends on the choice of each. In order to make a choice in a context of strategic interaction, each decision maker has to have expectations about the other players. For most purposes, the decision maker simply assumes common knowledge of rationality, that is, the decision maker assumes that other decision makers are also instrumentally rational and will thus make the same inferences from the same information.[12]

Theoretical work on strategic action, particularly in its game theoretic forms, has contributed to unraveling several puzzles in comparative politics. For example, Michael Taylor (1987 [1976]) and, later, Robert Axelrod (1984), make a strong case for the importance of the tit-for-tat strategy in iterated prisoner dilemma situations that meet certain clearly specified, and observable, criteria; by this means they extend the circumstances under which it is instrumentally rational to cooperate. Taylor labels this conditional cooperation and uses the concept to help explain both the origin of the state (1987 [1976], 1982) and the location of revolutionary action (1988; see also Lichbach 1995). Russell Hardin stresses the advantages of successful coordination in solving a variety of collective action problems (1982, 1990) as well as unsuccessful coordination in forestalling

---

[11]They claim that institutions are the rules of the game and organizations the players and their strategies.

[12]For a more complete explication of this assumption, see Hargreaves Heap and Varoufakis (1995: 23-8).

violent conflicts (1995). Although both Taylor and Hardin are primarily theorists, their findings have proved extremely useful for those engaged in original empirical research. Ostrom, for example, has to consider the hypotheses generated by this work in accounting for the variation in choices made by the actors she studies. I developed the concept of quasivoluntary compliance (1988) and, more recently, contingent consent (1997) to capture the fact that many citizens act reciprocally, complying if many others are and withdrawing compliance when there are expectations or evidence that they are among the few complying.

The final component of the model is its assumption of equilibrium. To reiterate: This is not an assumption that all behavior is static, or even that all interactions among rational individuals produce an equilibrium. Indeed, Arrow's paradox and other important findings in rational choice rest on the opposite finding. Nor are all equilibria efficient. The research on collective action problems is an explicit recognition of the conditions under which the logic of rational action is likely to produce suboptimal equilibria and of the kinds of arrangements that make it more likely for rational individuals to produce more optimal equilibria. Ostrom points to the herders of Torbel, Switzerland and the *zanjera* irrigation systems of the Philippines as examples of long-enduring CPRs, but there are also groups – she points to cases in Sri Lanka, Turkey, and California – who have trouble finding and sustaining solutions to their CPR problems. In my work, volunteering proved an inefficient equilibrium, at least from the point of view of the military during a large-scale war, but altering that equilibrium took substantial political effort by legislators and other government officials who shared the military's view. Greif (forthcoming) offers numerous examples of institutional arrangements that, although promoting commerce, were not necessarily the most efficient means for doing so.

THE TRADITIONAL METHOD OF RATIONAL CHOICE

Rational choice theory in comparative and historical analysis is a model that has only recently begun to be explicit and self-conscious about its method, that is, what distinguishes it from neoclassical economics, what formalization can and cannot do, and how to bring in narrative material appropriately and systematically. One thing is clear: The power of rational choice lies in its parsimony and testability. Thus, although it is essential that analysts more competently address "the real world," this should not be done at too great a sacrifice of analytical rigor. This is the difficult path many are now trying to walk.

COMPARATIVE STATICS

The presumption of equilibria permits the analyst to consider what would disrupt a particular equilibrium. Recall that in an equilibrium, no one has an incentive to change her choice. However, it is obvious that choices change regularly and constantly, whether they be in the realm of consumer, political, or social decision making. To understand these changes requires a set of hypotheses concerning what exogenous shocks or alterations in the independent variables will have what effects on the actions of the individuals under study. Ostrom (1990) relies on comparative statics when she is able to identify the factors, such as population pressures or state intervention, that undermine a traditional set of arrangements for protecting common pool resources. In a very different context, Levi (1988) shows that, given the assumption that a ruler maximizes revenue to the state, the ruler will change the form of taxes and tax collection with changes in the transaction costs of collecting and enforcing certain kinds of taxes, the relative bargaining power of those likely to be taxed, and the expenditure requirements of the ruler. Moreover, particular outcomes should be predictable, i.e., there will be no income tax until the costs of assessing and collecting income are sufficiently low to make it pay for the ruler.

PATH DEPENDENCE

To capture the critical moments and actions of the particular case also requires an understanding of the constraints that derive from past actions. The sequence in which events occur is causally important, and events in the distant past can initiate particular chains of causation that have effects in the present.

Path dependence does not simply mean that "history matters." This is both true and trivial. Path dependence has to mean, if it is to mean anything, that once a country or region has started down a track, the costs of reversal are very high. There will be other choice points, but the entrenchments of certain institutional arrangements obstruct an easy reversal of the initial choice. Perhaps the better metaphor is a tree, rather than a path.[13] From the same trunk, there are many different branches and smaller branches. Although it is possible to turn around or to clamber from one to the other – and essential if the chosen branch dies – the branch on which a climber begins is the one she tends to follow.

The notion of path dependence originated to explain the persistence of socially suboptimal technologies, such as the QWERTY typewriter. This happens, according to Paul David, under three necessary conditions: "strong technical interrelatedness, scale economies, and irreversibilities due to learning and habituation (1985: 336)." W. Brian Arthur (1989) adds a fourth condition: increasing returns within a decentralized and laissez-faire market. The application of path dependence to social arrangements, such as horizontal or vertical linkages, requires specification of the political, economic, and social factors that are most analogous to David's and Arthur's conditions. The model of path dependence suggests that not only major technological changes but also major regime changes would alter other interconnected features of the society.

[13]This is what William Sewell, Jr. argued to me.

There have actually been few successful attempts at applying the concept of path dependence in comparative politics. Putnam (1993), following North (1990), turned path dependence into an overly deterministic concept in which events of the fourteenth century produced – it seems, inexorably – the "virtuous cycle" of civic engagement in Northern Italy and its "vicious cycle" of distrust in Southern Italy.[14] More compelling are path dependent explanations of party formation in Europe provided by Kitschelt (1989, 1994) and Kalyvas (1996), who do not use the concept explicitly.

One possible avenue is provided by Avner Greif (1996) in his research on the Commercial Revolution. Greif identifies various forms of expectations that coordinate action and, in some instances, give rise to organizations that then influence future economic development. The expectations arise out of the complex of economic, social, political and cultural, as well as technological, features of a society. The existence of a coordination point in itself makes change difficult since it requires considerable effort to locate and then move enough others to a different coordination point (see, e.g., Hardin 1995). When organization develops, the path is even more firmly established, for organization tends to bring with it vested interests who will choose to maintain a path even when it is not optimal.

ANALYTIC NARRATIVES

As comparative and historical rational choice develops, it has increasingly become a form of institutional analysis. Institutions clearly enter the model as constraints, but they also play critical roles in reducing the individual's information costs and in providing focal points for action. The demands of applying game theory to empirical research have only enhanced the institutional features of the model. There are two important problems posed by game theory that institutions help resolve. First, there is the unreasonably high calculative capacity assumed of the decision makers. Second, there is the folk theorem, the finding that in a majority of conceivable multiperson interactions, the outcome is indeterminate. At first, the recognition of these problems produced skepticism about the relevance of game theory to empirical analysis (see, e.g., Hechter 1990, 1992), but it simultaneously produced useful evaluations of "the games real actors play" (Scharpf 1997).

Herbert Simon won the Nobel prize for recognizing the demands rationality places on the calculative capacity of the decision maker. Strategic action increases the requirements, for individuals must figure out what others are likely to do in order to devise their own best strategy. The assumption of common knowledge among actors about each other assumes as given a considerable amount of information and fails to reckon the costs of acquiring such information. However, for many of the actors and in many of the situations of

---

[14]For critiques of Putnam's usage see Levi (1996) and Sabetti (1996).

interest to comparativists, institutions do much of the work of calculation and information provision. They have this effect because they convey expectations both about sanctions and about the behavior of others. This information then enables each actor to make an informed strategy choice.[15] For example, the institution of the income tax informs potential taxpayers of the nature and probability of punishments for personal evasion, but it also lets them know that most others cannot or are unlikely to free ride. The information has a deterrence role and, at the same time, encourages reciprocity as a motivation for payment (Levi 1988).

At the heart of current empirical rational choice is the folk theorem. In the more technical language of economics, the folk theorem asserts that there are often multiple equilibria in games in which numerous individuals engage in repeated play. Once again, however, institutions save the day by providing focal points[16] and other means for coordinating action. Some of the most interesting explorations of the way institutions produce relatively stable equilibria are in economic history, most notably in papers by North and Weingast (1989; also see their paper with Milgrom 1990) and Greif (1989; 1993; 1994a; 1994b; 1996; with Milgrom and Weingast, 1994). This research investigates the creation of self-enforcing institutions, often nonstate institutions, that make possible credible commitments between actors and thus expand exchange and reduce conflict.

Moving toward an even more complicated consideration of situations, institutions, and focal points makes it harder to use traditional rational choice methods, however. Comparative statics is still at the heart of research design, but to generate satisfying hypotheses and to test them requires a far more detailed knowledge of the case than was previously expected of rational choice scholars. This assessment led to the development of what a set of collaborators (Robert Bates, Avner Greif, Margaret Levi, Jean-Laurent Rosenthal, and Barry Weingast) have come to label analytic narrative (in process).[17] This approach eliminates many of the dichotomies by which both proponents and critics distinguished rational choice from other enterprises. At the same time, it makes certain tensions within rational choice the source of creativity.

An analytic narrative presumes that the outcome or event to be explained derives from the aggregation of individual choices. The analytic narrative rests on the behavioral postulates of rational choice: Individuals are the decision makers, they are rational in the sense that they act consistently on their preferences and their choices are meant to serve their ends, they are strategic in that the choice of

---

[15]This definition is consistent with the claim of North (1990) and others that institutions are rules that regulate recurrent interactions and, thus, reduce the uncertainty that arises from otherwise unpredictable behavior.

[16]The idea of focal points derives from Schelling (1978), of course.

[17]This is not, however, the only such effort. Also see Fritz Scharpf (1997). Sociologists have also given considerable attention to the issue of narratives and how to make them more analytical. See, for example, Abell (1987) and Kiser (1997).

each is affected by the likely choices of others, and the variation in choice is a function of the constraints on the actors. An analytic narrative requires the researcher to clearly identify the key actors, their strategic considerations, and the relevant technological, social, political, or economic constraints, and this specification depends on a detailed knowledge of the case.

Once the case has been mastered sufficiently to identify the key actors, their strategies, and their constraints, then it is possible to begin the process of developing explanations and testing hypotheses. Thus, the next step is to derive a specific model that indicates the links between independent and dependent variables and leads to an account of the causal mechanisms. The model can take the form of an expected utility equation, as in Mancur Olson's work, or it can derive from the logic of game theory, as in David Laitin's recent work (1992, 1995). The game theoretic approach has several advantages, for it allows one to specify not only the comparative statics and path dependence, equally available from general equilibrium theory, but also the behavior off the equilibrium path.

WHAT'S OFF THE EQUILIBRIUM PATH, OR THE PROBLEM OF COUNTERFACTUALS[18]

In a famous essay on "Objective Possibility and Adequate Causation in Historical Explanation," Max Weber argued for the explicit and systematic use of counterfactuals as aspects of the empirical world that are contrary to fact but not to logical or "objective" possibility (1949 [1905]). Counterfactuals are indispensable in most comparative and historical work, since the possible causal factors are so numerous and interrelated and since the number of similar cases is seldom sufficient. However, Weber's efforts to formulate some general principles for evaluating the plausibility of "objective possibility" lack adequate theoretical grounds for justifying and circumscribing his counterfactual assumptions (Elster 1978: 180).

Until recently (Fearon 1991, 1996; Tetlock and Belkin 1996), there has been little effort to systematically evaluate the role counterfactuals do play and can play in social scientific analyses. Nor, until recently, has there been much success in giving counterfactual assumptions theoretical justification. However, game theory does provide a means to do just that. It outlines the range of sequential choices available to the actors. To understand why one of the paths becomes the equilibrium path, it is necessary to understand why the actors did not follow other possible paths (see, especially, Weingast 1996, Bueno de Mesquita 1996). Thus, the model generates testable hypotheses about: (1) what the beliefs of the actors had to be and what they could not have been; and (2) what the critical junctures were in the decision-making process.

---

[18]This discussion largely derives from Kiser and Levi (1996), who consider the role counterfactuals play in the analysis of revolution.

WHAT MATTERS IN THE PAST AND WHAT DOES NOT

While it is certainly the case that good theory often elaborates contingencies or points to the path where a different action or event may have changed the outcome, it is also the case that theory should delimit the possibilities. There is a tension in the work of most structuralists who, on the one hand, tend to make their theory extremely deterministic and, on the other hand, insist on conjunctural analysis that opens up too wide a range of possibilities. Here analytic narrative offers an important alternative approach. It facilitates both causal inference and the revelation of critical junctures or choice points. At its most successful, it can offer an account of why one path and not another is followed and then maintained. However, formal models only make sense of a revolutionary sequence of events when they can illuminate and interrogate the actual details of the case.

PROBLEM AND CASE SELECTION

Geddes (1997) offers a strong set of claims about what rational choice, and indeed any good empirical analysis, might accomplish and what it cannot. She argues against those who set their caps too high, who try to account for all revolutions or all developments; they invariably, in her view, build sand castles subject to the relentless shifts in paradigms. Rather, she argues for more modest, albeit still ambitious, projects. In her own case (1994), this involved identifying the links between electoral institutions and the kinds and timing of reform. If, as Elster (1989: 7) and Taylor (1988) claim, the best explanations are "fine-grained," this is a further impetus for defining questions in a way that enables one to spell out the direct relationship between one variable and another.

In general, Geddes has been proved right. The work that best succeeds in meeting social scientific criteria of evidence and falsifiability, the work that can be used as a solid building block rather than a sand castle, is work that precisely models a set of causal mechanisms and clearly delimits their domain of operation. Scholars can still ask big questions, but only certain kinds of big questions. For example, Rosenthal (1992) tells us a considerable amount about the relationship between the state, property rights, and economic development by means of a detailed investigation of sewage and drainage in postrevolutionary France. Bates and Lien (1985), Levi (1988), and Kiser (1994) contribute to the theory of the state and arguments about political change through studies of seemingly arcane government tax collection policies.

The kinds of problems chosen combine with the commitment to analytic narratives to produce two very different bases for case selection. The first is substantive; there is a time- and place-specific puzzle that one wishes to investigate. Thus, Barry Weingast (in his contribution to Bates, Greif, et al. in progress) is perplexed by the accounts he has read of the precipitants to the United States Civil War, and Robert Bates (1997) is eager to understand why coffee producers organize as they do. In these instances, the puzzle is embedded in a particular case, which is obviously what is to be studied. For those concerned with unraveling a theory-driven puzzle, such as what accounts for the variation in distributional coalitions (Olson 1981), free riding (Hechter 1987), state forms (Levi 1988), or economic growth (Greif 1994b), the basis of case selection is quite different. It requires investigating a range of cases that might reveal the mechanisms at work. Thus, I considered the rise and decline of tax farming in ancient Rome, the introduction of the income tax in 1799 in England, and the problems of tax evasion and avoidance in 1980s Australia as a means of getting at different features of the theory of predatory rule.

A MAP FOR THE FUTURE OF EMPIRICAL RATIONAL CHOICE: INADEQUATELY EXPLORED TERRAIN

Rational choice cannot explain everything, nor does it unravel all puzzles equally well, but it can illuminate and advance the explanation of a wide range of phenomena in a large variety of countries and time periods. There are, however, other interesting problems, seemingly more susceptible to microanalysis but apparently harder to fathom with the tools of rational choice. The most striking are why so many people vote and why we witness so many instances of large-scale collective actions in the form of protests and revolutions.

Comparative and historical researchers who wish to combine a nuanced understanding of the complexity of a particular (often unique) situation or set of events with a general theoretical understanding demand more of rational choice than it has so far delivered. First, neoclassical economics and its increasing mathematization and formalization is powerful and parsimonious, but it tends to rely on stylized facts rather than on the observations and details that enrich both the narrative and our confidence that we have explained an actual occurrence. Second, even when a rational choice analysis offers a logical story consistent with the facts, this hardly constitutes a validation of the explanation. Third, the presumption that changes in behavior reflect changes in relative prices, that is the emphasis on tangible incentives, fails to capture some of the most interesting behavior, such as large-scale collective actions or cooperation within firms or with government. Fourth, there is the question of the extent to which the findings of rational choice can be used to inform not only our understanding but also our capacity to improve the world in which we live.

The first problem is clearly the most tractable. Analytic narrative is a label that applies to a growing number of comparative rationalists, and it has long fit some of the best work in economic history. The others are more difficult.

FALSIFICATION

Analytic narrative does not in itself eliminate all competing accounts. It provides a means to tell a "compelling tale" (Przeworski and Sprague 1986: 181), but there might be other, equally compelling tales. At the least, what makes a tale compelling is that the causal mechanisms it identifies are plausible. The credibility of these mechanisms is enhanced significantly by demonstrating their generalizability to other cases. In the best of all possible worlds, this means applying the explanatory model to other, out of sample, cases. There is the occasional scholar who takes this maxim seriously enough to apply it. Few, however, know enough about cases other than their own to adequately analyze other cases. More often, the explanation is thrown into the marketplace of ideas where, if it is compelling enough, others attempt to use it, either to give it additional support or to disconfirm it.

Another means of subjecting the findings to the norms of falsification is through demonstration that another methodology altogether produces the same results. Survey and experimental evidence, as well as mathematical proofs of formal theorems, add weight to the findings of case studies. If the mechanisms identified in the case studies are valid, they should hold up elsewhere. Triangulation is one of the buzzwords of the day, but although many scholars will appeal to support provided by other forms of research, few actually investigate their problems with a variety of methods.[19]

Findings from elsewhere are not only an additional source of falsification; they may also be important in revealing mechanisms worth exploring in the field. Some of the recent work on trust reflects such an effort.[20]

RECONSIDERING THE BEHAVIORAL ASSUMPTION

The third problem, the narrow behavioral assumption of most rational choice analysis, is more difficult to overcome. North certainly acknowledges this problem, especially in his more recent work (1990; with Denzau 1994) and has consequently begun to explore the role of culture, norms, mental models, and other ideational and cognitive factors in decision making. John Ferejohn (1991) offers an alternative approach; he advocates supplementing the analysis generated by rational choice with an analysis generated by an interpretive approach as a means to offer a more complete explanation.

My own recent work (1991; 1997) reflects an effort to model actors as both rational and ethical beings. Although rational choice models do not necessarily assume that individuals are selfish, many rationalists have in fact made precisely that assumption or have failed to adequately consider the role that ethical concerns, such as fairness, play in decision making. Rational choice has been very successful in accounting for why so many people fail to vote, contribute, or par-

[19]Elinor Ostrom stands out in this regard, but there are beginning to be others. For example, Shane Fricks is writing a Ph.D. dissertation that combines experiments, case studies, and game theory; Toshio Yamagishi increasingly combines surveys and experiments.

[20]A Russell Sage Foundation project on "The Construction and Maintenance of Trust," coordinated by Karen Cook, Russell Hardin, and Margaret Levi, is holding workshops and beginning to produce papers and books that demonstrate this tendency.

ticipate in various forms of collective action. It is less successful in explaining why they engage in such behaviors when they do. To put this another way, the model predicts more free riders than there often are. It is not enough, however, to add ethical ends to the preference function; this produces tautology, not explanation, and certainly not testable hypotheses. Rather, the aim must be to specify the conditions under which more instrumental motivations are triggered, more ethical considerations dominate, and when, as I suspect is true in many cases, individuals are willing to act ethically even if it means bearing some tangible costs.

The models that flow from an assumption of rational but ethical actors will be less parsimonious than those that flow from the simpler assumption of narrow self-interest. In many instances, the more parsimonious model may be all that is necessary. However, where there are large-scale collective actions and ideologically driven decisions to change institutions, then a more complex model may be both necessary and right.

Such an approach may have a moral as well as empirical advantage: If, as some have argued and as some experiments seem to bear out (Frank 1987), the emphasis on instrumental rationality influences how people act, then a model that also stresses the norm of ethical rationality may be superior. There is, however, always the danger of morality becoming the grounds for disregarding the interests or denigrating the moral positions of others, a danger that a focus on self-interest often avoids (Hardin 1995).

FROM EMPIRICAL TO NORMATIVE

The breakdown of communism and the recurring problems of poverty, unemployment, and ethnic conflict, even in the so-called developed world, produce a demand for theory that guides as well as informs, arguments that meet our normative as well as empirical requirements. The rational choice approach, properly understood and undertaken, offers empirically grounded theoretical work that can account for our current arrangements and suggest possible alternatives. This is because rational choice, properly understood and properly undertaken, rests on an increasingly realistic psychology of individual action and interaction, an institutional framework that accounts for what constrains and facilitates human behavior, and a powerful model of the aggregation of individual choices.

Social science is an empirical science whose central aim should be explanation. Explanations are but scholastic exercises unless they can be translated into understanding that aids in improving political, economic, and social life generally. To translate first-rate and basic social science into practical guidelines is not such an easy undertaking, and perhaps the best we, as social scientists, can do is clarify where our scholarly research might inform political decision making.

Some rational choice work is immediately appropriable. For example, Olson's *Logic of Collective Action* clearly resonated with community organizing and union building efforts. Indeed, when I read the book as an undergraduate, I thought Olson was an advisor to Saul Alinsky, the famed community organizer and author of *Reveille for Radicals*. Another example of theoretically informed arguments with clear policy implications is Elinor Ostrom's *Governing the Commons*.

The current interest in the new rational choice institutionalism is equally useful but not so quickly appropriable. Douglass North tells stories of disappointing those who ask him for advice about institutional designs meant to speed up growth and democracy in Eastern Europe and elsewhere; he argues that it takes a long time to build strong informal institutions, the necessary prerequisite for political and economic development. Recent work on federalism is prescriptive, as are the growing bodies of literature on trust and compliance.

There is yet another group of scholars who are fundamentally concerned about how to produce institutions that achieve fair, equitable, and just outcomes and who use explanations derived from rationalist empirical research as data in their arguments. Jack Knight (1992) and Brian Barry (1995) count among these although they do not themselves do the empirical work. Others, e.g., Frohlich and Oppenheimer (1992) and Rothstein (1992; forthcoming) do.[21]

CONCLUSION

Empirical rational choice in comparative analysis is in its relative infancy. It is still in the process of making the transition from analytics to analytic narrative. Even so, it has become one of the leading paradigms in the field and produced some major and influential work on a range of subjects, places, and periods. Although the divide between rationalists and many of those in this volume may be shrinking as rationalists become more concerned with context and nonrationalists recognize collective action problems, voting cycles, and other insights from rational choice, the divide remains nonetheless. Structuralists and rationalists are in the same conversation, but they persist in very different views of the origins and effects of institutions and preferences. Many rationalists are taking on board the concerns of culturalists with providing a more complete account of preferences and strategies, but they continue to disagree on the uses of those accounts. What divides rationalists from culturalists and structuralists is not method in the sense of mathematics versus statistics, fieldwork, observation, and archival research; there are many rationalists who rely on precisely these tools. What divides them is method in the sense of how to construct theory, organize research findings, and address the issues of falsifiability and plausibility.

Rational choice will continue to have its serious detractors in comparative politics. It simplifies the world and human psychology more than suits the tastes of many comparativists, especially those committed to area studies or interpretivist explanations. Its positivist ethic may be unpalatable to postmodernists and

[21]Rothstein is not a rational choice scholar per se, although he uses some rational choice theory in his work.

others. The very commitment of rationalists to scientific progress by means of fact-finding, testability, and partial universalism will remain repugnant to some critics and an impossible goal to others. Rationalists must continue to refine and clarify their models so as to increase their explanatory power, and they must find more satisfying means for arbitrating among competing accounts. These are the tasks incumbent on all comparative social scientists committed to explanation. Continued competition among paradigms may improve our ability to accomplish such tasks. The argument of this chapter has been more modest, however: The confrontation between deductively derived models and empirical research has already contributed to better rational choice models and explanations and holds the promise of even better theory.

REFERENCES

Abell, Peter. 1987. *The Syntax of Social Life: The Theory and Method of Comparative Narrative.* Oxford: Oxford University Press.

Ames, Barry. 1987. *Political Survival: Politicians and Public Policy in Latin America.* Berkeley: University of California Press.

Arrow, Kenneth. 1951. *Social Choice and Individual Values.* New Haven: Yale University Press.

Arthur, Brian. 1989. "Competing Technologies, Increasing Returns, and Lock-in By Historical Events." *The Economic Journal* 99 (March):116-31.

Axelrod, Robert. 1984. *The Evolution of Cooperation.* New York: Basic Books.

Barry, Brian. 1995. *Justice as Impartiality.* Oxford: Oxford University Press.

Bates, Robert H. 1983. *Essays on the Political Economy of Rural Africa.* Berkeley: University of California Press.

———. 1988. "Contra Contractarianism." *Politics & Society* 16 (1).

———. 1991. *Beyond the Miracle of the Market.* New York: Cambridge University Press.

———. 1997. *Open Economy Politics: The Political Economy of the World Coffee Trade.* Princeton: Princeton University Press.

Bates, Robert H., Avner Greif, Margaret Levi, Jean-Laurent Rosenthal, and Barry Weingast. In process. *Analytic Narratives.*

Bates, Robert H., and Anne O. Krueger. 1993. *Political and Economic Interactions in Economic Policy Reform.* Cambridge, MA: Basil Blackwell.

Bates, Robert, and Da-Hsiang Donald Lien. 1985. "A Note on Taxation, Development and Representative Government." *Politics & Society* 14 (1):53-70.

Buchanan, James M., and Gordon Tullock. 1965. *The Calculus of Consent: Logical Foundations of Constitutional Democracy.* Ann Arbor: University of Michigan Press.

Bueno de Mesquita, Bruce. 1996. "Counterfactuals and International Affairs: Some Insights from Game Theory." In Philip E. Tetlock and Aaron Belkin, eds., *Counterfactual Thought Experiments in World Politics.* Princeton: Princeton University Press.

David, Paul. 1985. "Clio and the Economics of QWERTY." *American Economic Review* 75 (2):332-7.

Denzau, Arthur T., and Douglass C. North. 1994. "Shared Mental Models: Ideologies and Institutions." *Kyklos* 47 (1):3-31.

Diermeier, Daniel. 1995. "The Role of Theory." *Critical Review* 9 (1-2, Winter-Spring):59-70.

Downs, Anthony. 1957. *An Economic Theory of Democracy.* New York: Harper.

Elster, Jon. 1978. *Logic and Society.* New York: John Wiley & Sons.

————. 1983a. *Explaining Technical Change: A Case Study in the Philosophy of Social Science.* New York: Cambridge University Press.

————. 1983b. *Sour Grapes: Studies in the Subversion of Rationality.* New York: Cambridge University Press.

————. 1989. *Nuts and Bolts for the Social Sciences.* New York: Cambridge University Press.

————. 1993. *Political Psychology.* New York: Cambridge University Press.

Emsinger, Jean. 1992. *Making a Market: The Institutional Transformation of an African Society.* New York: Cambridge University Press.

Fearon, James D. 1991. "Counterfactuals and Hypothesis Testing in Political Science." *World Politics* 43 (2):169-95.

————. 1996. "Causes and Counterfactuals in Social Science." In Philip E. Tetlock and Aaron Belkin, eds., *Counterfactual Thought Experiments in World Politics.* Princeton: Princeton University Press.

Ferejohn, John. 1991. "Rationality and Interpretation: Parliamentary Elections in Early Stuart England." In Kristen Renwick Monroe, ed., *The Economic Approach to Politics.* New York: HarperCollins.

Fiorina, Morris P. 1995. "Rational Choice, Empirical Contributions, and the Scientific Enterprise." *Critical Review* 9 (1-2, Winter-Spring):85-94.

Firmin-Sellers, Kathryn. 1996. *The Transformation of Property Rights in the Gold Coast.* New York: Cambridge University Press.

Frank, Robert H. 1987. "If Homo Economicus Could Choose His Own Utility Function, Would He Want One with a Conscience?" *American Economic Review* (September):593-604.

Frohlich, Norman, and Joe A. Oppenheimer. 1992. *Choosing Justice.* Berkeley: University of California Press.

Gambetta, Diego. 1993. *The Sicilian Mafia: The Business of Private Protection.* Cambridge: Harvard University Press.

Geddes, Barbara. 1994. *The Politicians' Dilemma.* Berkeley: University of California Press.

————. 1997. *Paradigms and Sand Castles in Comparative Politics of Developing Areas.* Ann Arbor: University of Michigan Press. A paper version of this was published in William Crotty, ed., *Political Science: Looking Forward to the Future.* Boston: Northwestern University Press, 1991.

Gill, Anthony. Forthcoming. *Rendering unto Caesar: The Political Economy of Church–State Relations in Latin America.* Chicago: University of Chicago Press.

Golden, Miriam. 1990. *A Rational Choice Analysis of Union Militancy with Application to the Cases of British Coal and Fiat.* Ithaca: Cornell University Press.

————. 1996. *Heroic Defeats.* New York: Cambridge University Press.

Green, Donald, and Ian Shapiro. 1994. *The Pathologies of Rational Choice.* New Haven: Yale University Press.

Greif, Avner. 1989. "Reputation and Coalitions in Medieval Trade: Evidence on the Maghribi Traders." *Journal of Economic History* XLIX (4 December):857-82.

———. 1993. "Contract Enforceability and Economic Institutions in Early Trade: Evidence on the Maghribi Traders' Coalition." *American Economic Review* 83 (3):June.

———. 1994a. "Cultural Beliefs and the Organization of Society: A Historical and Theoretical Reflection on Collectivist and Individualist Societies." *Journal of Political Economy* 102 (5 October):912-50.

———. 1994b. "On the Political Foundations of the Late Medieval Commercial Revolution: Genoa During the Twelfth and Thirteenth Centuries." *Journal of Economic History* 54 (4 June):271-87.

———. 1996. "On the Study of Organizations and Evolving Organizational Forms through History: Reflections from the Late Medieval Firm." *Industrial and Corporate Change* 5 (2).

———. In press. "Micro Theory and Recent Developments in the Study of Economic Institutions through Economic History." In David M. Kreps and Kenneth F. Wallis, eds., *Advances in Economic Theory.* New York: Cambridge University Press.

Greif, Avner, Paul Milgrom, and Barbara R. Weingast. 1994. "Coordination, Commitment and Enforcement: The Case of the Merchant Guild." *Journal of Political Economy* 102 (4):745-76.

Hardin, Russell. 1982. *Collective Action.* Baltimore: Johns Hopkins University Press.

———. 1990. "The Social Evolution of Cooperation." In Karen S. Cook and Margaret Levi, eds., *The Limits to Rationality.* Chicago: University of Chicago Press.

———. 1995. *One for All.* Princeton: Princeton University Press.

Hargreaves Heap, Shaun P., and Yanis Varoufakis. 1995. *Game Theory: A Critical Introduction.* London: Routledge.

Hechter, Michael. 1987. *Principles of Group Solidarity.* Berkeley: University of California Press.

———. 1990. "On the Inadequacy of Game Theory for the Solution of Real-World Collective Action Problems." In Karen S. Cook and Margaret Levi, eds., *The Limits of Rationality.* Chicago: University of Chicago Press.

———. 1992. "The Insufficiency of Game Theory for the Resolution of Real-World Collective Action Problems." *Rationality & Society* 4 (January):33-40.

Kalyvas, Stathis N. 1996. *The Rise of Christian Democracy in Europe.* Ithaca: Cornell University Press.

King, Gary, R. Keohane, and S. Verba. 1994. *Scientific Inference in Qualitative Research.* Princeton: Princeton University Press.

Kiser, Edgar. 1994. "Markets and Hierarchies in Early Modern Tax Systems: A Principal–Agent Analysis." *Politics & Society* 22 (3):285-316.

———. 1996. "The Revival of Narrative in Historical Sociology: What Rational Choice Theory Can Contribute." *Politics & Society* 24 (3):249-71.

Kiser, Edgar, and Michael Hechter. 1991. "The Role of General Theory in Comparative-Historical Sociology." *American Journal of Sociology* 97:1-30.

Kiser, Edgar, and Margaret Levi. 1996. "Using Counterfactuals in Historical Analysis: Theories of Revolution." In Philip E. Tetlock and Aaron Belkin, eds., *Counterfactual Thought Experiments in World Politics.* Princeton: Princeton University Press.

Kitschelt, Herbert. 1989. *The Logics of Party Formation: Ecological Politics in Belgium and West Germany.* Ithaca: Cornell University Press.

————. 1994. *The Transformation of European Social Democracy.* New York: Cambridge University Press.

Knight, Jack. 1992. *Institutions and Social Conflict.* New York: Cambridge University Press.

Laitin, David. 1992. *Language Repertoires and State Construction in Africa.* New York: Cambridge University Press.

————. 1995. "National Revivals and Violence." *Archives europeennes de sociologie* 36:3-43.

Levi, Margaret. 1988. *Of Rule and Revenue.* Berkeley: University of California Press.

————. 1991. "Are There Limits to Rationality?" *Public Choice* 32:130-41.

————. 1996. "Social and Unsocial Capital: A Review Essay of Robert Putnam's *Making Democracy Work.*" *Politics & Society* 24 (1):45-55.

————. 1997. *Consent, Dissent and Patriotism.* New York: Cambridge University Press.

Lichbach, Mark. 1995. *The Rebel's Dilemma.* Ann Arbor: University of Michigan Press.

————. 1997. *The Cooperator's Dilemma.* Ann Arbor: University of Michigan Press.

Milgrom, Paul R., D. C. North, and B. R. Weingast. 1990. "The Role of Institutions in the Revival of Trade: The Medieval Law Merchant, Private Judges, and the Champagne Fairs." *Economics and Politics* 2 (1):1-23.

North, Douglass C. 1981. *Structure and Change in Economic History.* New York: Norton.

————. 1990. *Institutions, Institutional Change, and Economic Performance.* New York: Cambridge University Press.

North, Douglass C., and Barry R. Weingast. 1989. "Constitutions and Commitment: The Evolution of Institutions Governing Public Choice in Seventeenth-Century England." *Journal of Economic History* 49 (4):803-32.

Oi, Jean. 1989. *State and Peasant in Contemporary China: The Political Economy of Village Government.* Berkeley: University of California Press.

Olson, Mancur. 1965. *The Logic of Collective Action.* Cambridge: Harvard University Press.

————. 1981. *The Rise and Decline of Nations.* New Haven: Yale University Press.

Ostrom, Elinor. 1990. *Governing the Commons: The Evolution of Institutions for Collective Action.* New York: Cambridge University Press.

Plott, Charles R. 1990. "Rational Choice in Experimental Markets." In Karen S. Cook and Margaret Levi, eds., *The Limits to Rationality.* Chicago:University of Chicago Press.

Popkin, Samuel. 1979. *The Rational Peasant.* Berkeley: University of California Press.

Popper, Karl R. 1967. "Rationality and the Status of the Rationality Principle." In E. M. Classen, ed., *Le Fondements Philosophiques des Systems Economiques Textes de Jacques Rueff et Essais Redges en son Honeur.* Paris: Payot.

Przeworski, Adam. 1985. *Capitalism and Social Democracy.* New York: Cambridge University Press.

Przeworski, Adam, and John Sprague. 1986. *Paper Stones: A History of Electoral Socialism.* New York: Cambridge University Press.

Putnam, Robert. 1993. *Making Democracy Work: Civic Traditions in Modern Italy.* Princeton: Princeton University Press.

Ramseyer, J. Mark, and Frances Rosenbluth. 1993. *Japan's Political Marketplace.* Cambridge: Harvard University Press.

Riker, William. 1982. *Liberalism Against Populism.* Prospect Heights, IL: Waveland Press.

———. 1986. *The Art of Political Manipulation.* New Haven: Yale University Press.

Rogowski, Ronald. 1989. *Commerce and Coalitions: How Trade Affects Domestic Political Alignments.* Princeton: Princeton University Press.

———. 1995. "The Role of Theory and Anomaly in Social-Scientific Inference." *American Political Science Review* 89:467-70.

Rosenthal, Jean-Laurent. 1992. *The Fruits of Revolution.* New York: Cambridge University Press.

Rothstein, Bo. 1992. "Social Justice and State Capacity." *Politics & Society* 20 (1):101-12.

———. Forthcoming. *Just Institutions Matter.* Cambridge: Cambridge University Press.

Sabetti, Filippo. 1996. "Path Dependency and Civic Culture: Some Lessons from Italy about Interpreting Social Experiments." *Politics & Society* 24 (1):19-44.

Scharpf, Fritz. 1997. *Games Real Actors Could Play.* New York: Westview Press.

Schelling, Thomas C. 1978. *Micromotives and Macrobehavior.* New York: W. Norton.

Shirk, S. L. 1993. *The Political Logic of Economic Reform in China.* Berkeley: University of California Press.

Somers, Margaret R. 1996. "'We're No Angels': Realism, Rational Choice, and Relationality in Social Science." Ann Arbor: Department of Sociology, University of Michigan.

Taylor, Michael. 1982. *Community, Anarchy and Liberty.* Cambridge: Cambridge University Press.

———. 1987 [1976]. *The Possibility of Cooperation.* Cambridge: Cambridge University Press.

———. 1988. "The Rationality of Revolution." In *The Rationality of Revolution,* ed. Taylor, Michael. New York: Cambridge University Press.

Tetlock, Philip E., and Aaron Belkin, eds. 1996. *Counterfactual Thought Experiments in World Politics.* Princeton: Princeton University Press.

Tsebelis, George. 1995. "Decision Making in Political Systems: Veto Players in Presidentialism, Parliamentarism, Multicameralism, and Multipartyism." *British Journal of Political Science* 25:289-326.

Verdier, Daniel. 1994. *Democracy and International Trade: Britain, France, and the United States, 1860–1990.* Princeton: Princeton University Press.

Wallerstein, Michael. 1989. "Union Organization in Advanced Industrial Democracies." *American Political Science Review* 83:481-501.

Weber, Max. 1949 (1905). "Objective Possibility and Adequate Causation in Historical Explanation." In Max Weber, ed., *The Methodology of the Social Sciences.* New York: Free Press.

Weingast, Barry R. 1996. "Off-the-Path Behavior: A Game-Theoretic Approach to Counterfactuals and Its Implications for Political and Historical Analysis." In Philip E. Tetlock and Aaron Belkin, eds., *Counterfactual Thought Experiments in World Politics.* Princeton: Princeton University Press.

3

CULTURE AND IDENTITY IN COMPARATIVE POLITICAL ANALYSIS*

Marc Howard Ross

INTRODUCTION

In this essay I argue that two distinct, but not unrelated, features of culture are relevant to comparative politics. First, culture is a system of meaning that people use to manage their daily worlds, large and small; second, culture is the basis of social and political identity that affects how people line up and how they act on a wide range of matters. Culture is a framework for organizing the world, for locating the self and others in it, for making sense of the actions and interpreting motives of others, for grounding an analysis of interests, for linking collective identities to political action, and for motivating people and groups toward some actions and away from others. At the same time, two caveats are in order: One is that to be useful culture cannot be defined so broadly as to include all behaviors, beliefs, institutions – in short, any domain of life – although it is appropriate to consider the cultural dimensions of specific domains; two, the effects of culture on collective action and political life are generally indirect, and to fully appreciate the role of culture in political life, it is necessary to inquire how the impact of culture interacts with interests and institutions.

It should not be surprising that cultural analyses in comparative politics take many forms, for unlike rational choice theory, cultural approaches are less clear about exactly what domains of politics to examine, and there is even less of a con-

*I wish to thank the organizers and participants in the Symposium on Theory in Comparative Politics for their comments on my presentation. In addition, Donald Campbell, Katherine Conner, Barbara Frankel, Carol Hager, Phil Kilbride, Mark Lichbach, and Alan Zuckerman offered detailed comments on earlier versions of this article.

sensus concerning the methods and tools to employ.[1] Lichbach (this volume) distinguishes between subjective and intersubjective views of culture; the subjective emphasizes how individuals internalize individual values and attitudes that become the object of study, while the intersubjective focuses on the shared meanings and identities that constitute the symbolic, expressive, and interpretive part of social life. I argue here for the merits of a postmodern intersubjective understanding of culture (with attention to subjective elements). This strong view of culture is completely compatible with the belief that comparison is central to the social science enterprise (while not denying its complexities), although this is not the position some radical interpretivists hold. In making this argument here, an important task is to situate important or exemplary works in the field in terms of crucial questions that cultural approaches to politics address. However, this essay is not a review article, and there are many additional studies that would be included if reviewing the field were my goal.

This essay offers an opportunity to emphasize (even advocate) what an intersubjective cultural approach can contribute to comparative politics. In contrast to rational choice approaches, which are well entrenched in the discipline, and institutional approaches, which have dominated the field in one form or another since its inception, cultural contributions to political analysis are relatively rare and far less developed. Few graduate students take culture very seriously, and if one peruses the annual list of dissertations in comparative politics over several years, it is difficult to place cultural analyses in the trinity of comparative politics, as the editors of this volume have done.

It is not hard to identify the reasons why studies that give culture a central role are rare in comparative politics. Most basically, culture is not a concept with which most political scientists are comfortable. For many, culture complicates issues of evidence, transforming hopes of rigorous analysis into "just so" accounts that fail to meet widely held notions of scientific explanation. Culture violates canons of methodological individualism while raising serious unit of analysis problems for which there are no easy answers. Culture to many, neo-Marxists and non-Marxists alike, seems like an epiphenomenon offering a discourse for political mobilization and demand-making while masking more serious differences dividing groups and individuals. Finally, employing the concept of culture puts political scientists into a series of controversies over which proponents of cultural analysis in anthropology themselves are deeply divided.[2] Each of these objections is more or less addressed in this essay, and while I do not argue that they are unimportant, I do not view them as sufficiently damaging to warrant throwing the baby out with the bath water.

[1] It is possible to identify differences within culturalist approaches to politics in terms of methods, levels of analysis, substantive questions, and willingness to compare and generalize across cases. In this essay, other than distinguishing between what I call weak and strong cultural understandings, I emphasize what I view as the useful core of the approach much more than differences within it.

[2] Among the issues that divide anthropologists are relativism, the importance of searching for generalizations, the possibility of comparison, and the role of psychological mechanisms in cultural explanations.

Cultural analysis of politics takes seriously the postmodern critique of behavioral political analyses and seeks to offer contextually rich intersubjective accounts of politics that emphasize how political actors understand social and political action (Merelman 1991). In cultural analyses, for example, interests are contextually and intersubjectively defined, and the strategies used to pursue them are understood to be context-dependent. Central to cultural analysis is the concept of interpretation. The interpretations of particular political significance are built from the accounts – stories if one prefers – of groups and individuals striving to make sense of their social and political worlds, and I use the term to refer both to the shared intersubjective meanings of actors[3] and to the explicit efforts of social science observers to understand these meanings and to present them to others (Taylor, 1985). Shared interpretations of actors – worldviews – are important in any cultural analysis as they offer an important methodological tool, along with an examination of rituals and symbols, for examining both systems of meaning and the structure and intensity of political identity.

This essay has four parts. The first discusses five contributions that the concept of culture defined as a system of meaning and identity makes to comparative political analysis: culture frames the context in which politics occurs; culture links individual and collective identities; culture defines the boundaries between groups and organizes actions within and between them; culture provides a framework for interpreting the actions and motives of others; and culture provides resources for political organization and motivation. The second part examines five central themes (some might say approaches) in cultural analyses of politics: culture and personality studies; the civic culture tradition; culture and political process (an approach that originated in anthropology); political ritual; and culture and political violence. Third, I identify five critiques of cultural studies of politics: unit of analysis issues; the problem of within-culture variation; the difficulty of distinguishing culture from social or political organization; the static nature of culture and explaining political change; and the need to identify underlying mechanisms that suggest "how culture works." The fourth section examines the role of interpretation in cultural analysis as an effort to link the contextually rich political details found in particular political settings (be they small communities or countries) to general domains of political life such as authority, community, and conflict. I discuss the concept of psychocultural interpretations and their methodological relevance in the comparative study of culture and politics for understanding processes such as ethnic and national identity construction. I conclude that culture is too often ignored as a domain of political life and that cultural analyses can enrich the way we conceptualize areas such as political economy, social movements, and political institutions in a number of useful ways, often complementing the insights derived from interest and institutional approaches.

---

[3]Taylor uses the term "common reference world" (1985:38) to refer to what members of a culture share.

CULTURE AND CULTURAL ANALYSES OF POLITICS

CULTURE

Culture, a central concept in anthropology, has been defined in a wide variety of ways that variously emphasize culture as social organization, core values, specific beliefs, social action, or a way of life (Kroeber and Kluckholm 1952). Most contemporary analyses, however, begin, as I do here, with Geertz's definition of culture as "an historically transmitted pattern of meaning embodied in symbols, a system of inherited conceptions expressed in symbolic forms by means of which men communicate, perpetuate, and develop their knowledge about and attitudes towards life" (1973b: 89)[4] This view emphasizes culture as public, shared meanings; behaviors, institutions, and social structure are understood not as culture itself but as culturally constituted phenomena (Spiro 1984). Culture from this perspective is a worldview that explains why and how individuals and groups behave as they do, and includes both cognitive and affective beliefs about social reality and assumptions about when, where, and how people in one's culture and those in other cultures are likely to act in particular ways (see also Berger 1995).[5] For purposes of political analysis, I want to emphasize that shared understandings occur among people who also have a common (and almost invariably named) identity which signals distinctions between the group and outsiders. Culture, in short, marks "a distinctive way of life" characterized in the subjective we-feelings of cultural group members (and outsiders) and is expressed through specific behaviors (customs and rituals) – both sacred and profane – which mark the daily, yearly, and life cycle rhythms of its members and reveal how people view past, present, and future events and understand choices they face (Berger 1995). Cultural metaphors have both cognitive meaning, which describes group experience, and high affective salience, which emphasizes the unique intragroup bonds – almost like a secret code – that set one group's experience apart from that of others.

It should be pointed out that in a shared meaning and identity system the fact that different individuals and groups understand each other does not imply agreement that widely held meanings are necessarily acceptable to all. Rather, meaning and identity, control over symbols and rituals, and the ability to impose one interpretation rather than another on a situation are frequently bitterly contested (Scott 1985). In this same vein, Laitin (1988) contends that culture highlights points of concern to be debated (1988: 589) and not just areas of agreement. Sharing a culture does not mean that people are necessarily in agreement on specifics, only that they possess a similar understanding of how the world works.

---

[4]D'Andrade (1984: 88) points out that the radical shift from the view of culture as behavior that could be understood within a stimulus-response framework to culture as systems of meaning is found in a number of fields. For a more complete discussion of culture as meanings and symbols see the excellent discussions in Schweder and LeVine (1984).

[5]I use worldview to include affective elements, whereas often the concept of social schema only emphasizes cognitive elements. Anthony Wallace's concept of mazeway is a parallel to worldview (1970).

Placing the concept of culture at the center of analysis affects the questions asked about political life (Brysk 1995; Merelman 1991: 45). For example, an interest in distinctive worldviews and identity leads to questions about how differences in worldviews might explain such phenomena as the emergence of certain leaders and reactions to them, the organization of political decision making, social movement mobilization, or perception of external threats. At the same time, an interest in culture and cultural difference discourages inquiry into the role of rational self-interest in political choice making, for such questions presume that interest maximization is more or less invariant across cultures and does not need a theory of cultural variation to explain what is viewed as constant (Wildavsky 1987).

My goal is to suggest how cultural analysis enhances our understanding of politics, not to comprehensively review the field, which defined broadly, could include every study that includes a cultural variable in a regression equation on the one hand to the most hermeneutically informed textual analysis on the other. Here I emphasize work that gives a central role to the concept of culture as a system of meaning and identity, and in the next few pages I suggest core questions in comparative political analysis that profit from attention to the concept of culture. Underlying my presentation is the belief that most political scientists have not thought a great deal about culture; that many consider it an epiphenomenon to be explained away rather than to be incorporated into theories and explanations; and that many who do invoke culture define it so thinly that they do not develop analyses of cultural dynamics that are terribly insightful.[6]

Culture Frames the Context in Which Politics Occurs

Culture orders political priorities (Laitin 1986: 11), meaning it defines the symbolic and material objects people consider valuable and worth fighting over, the contexts in which such disputes occur, the rules (both formal and informal) by which politics takes place and who participates in it. In doing so, culture defines interests and how they are to be pursued. For example, anthropologist Napoleon Chagnon (1967) invokes the cultural importance of the value of fierceness (*waiteri* complex) to explain the prevalence of high warfare among Yanomamo communities; political scientist Edward Banfield (1958) explains the absence of political participation and civic society in southern Italy in terms of a cultural pattern he calls amoral familism; and political scientists Gabriel Almond and Sidney Verba (1963) explain differences in political attitudes and patterns of participation among the United States, Great Britain, Germany, Italy, and Mexico in terms of differences between participant, subject, and parochial political cultures. To understand the cultural framing of politics, consider how culture influences beliefs about, and the organization of, community, authority, and conflict (Ross 1988).

---

[6]Laitin (1986; 1988) describes "the two faces of culture," referring to culture as a system of meaning on the one hand and culture as a resource for instrumental action on the other. While I find the distinction useful and his analysis very consistent with my own, this twofold distinction is too brief for my purposes here.

Cultural understandings are at the core of the definition of political communities since people in a community share, in Geertz's (1973b) words, "schematic images of the social order," common meanings which Taylor says are the basis of community (1985: 39). Communities are distinct, but also nested, entities. People are invariably part of more than one community and develop multiple loyalties whose interrelationship can take a variety of forms. Authority in any political community is culturally constituted and consists of regularized procedures that members of a community consider more or less legitimate – meaning that they have been arrived at by a procedure they consider fair, although the issue may continue to be highly contested – for distributing tangible and symbolic goods. The establishment of legitimate authority is a historical process for a community (Arendt 1958) and a psychological one for individuals, linking people through a sense of common fate captured in the historical accounts people in a community share. The establishment and maintenance of political authority is often explained in cognitive and cost–benefit terms and threats of coercion but also involves ritual activity, including religious action, which connects people's everyday experience and anxiety to those of the collectivity (Edelman 1964; Kertzer 1988; Shils and Young 1953; Turner 1957, 1968). Conflict occurs in virtually all communities, and all cultures have norms about what is reasonable to fight about and how conflicts are to be managed. Cultures shape conflict, defining what is appropriate social action, how the motives of others should be understood, and what is worth fighting about (Ross 1993a). Thus, at the same time, culture constitutes the social order and is a tool for domination, and conflict over the nature and make-up of the political community and authority within it are regular features of political life.

Culture Links Individual and Collective Identities

Culture offers an account of political behavior that makes particular actions more or less likely and connects the fate of individuals and the group. The crucial connection at work is that of identification, which renders certain actions reasonable and removes alternatives that on other grounds might be equally plausible. Individual and collective action, this view suggests, are motivated, in part, by the sense of common fate people in a culture share and involve two distinct elements: the strong reinforcement between individual and collective identity that renders culturally sanctioned behavior rewarding and the sense that outsiders will treat oneself and other members of one's group in similar ways.

Identification dynamics involve the construction of internal images of the external world out of the developmental and historical experiences group members share. Many objects of identification are associated with primary sensations such as smell, taste, and sound that acquire intense affective meaning and only later acquire a cognitive component. People sharing cultural attachments have common experiences that facilitate the developmental task of incorporating group identity into one's own sense of self. Anderson (1991) writes of imagined communities, which can link the person and collective identities.

The process of within-group identity formation overemphasizes what it is that group members actually share. It gives greater emotional weight to the common elements, reinforcing them with an ideology of linked fate. It overvalues the uniformity within groups, emphasizing both affectively and cognitively the common elements individuals share, and exaggerating differences with outsiders (Turner 1988). Deviations from the norm are selectively ignored or negatively reinforced as incompatible with group solidarity and its myth of shared historical experiences.

It should be stressed that culture is only one basis for linking individual to social identity. It can be a particularly powerful one, however, in situations of threat and uncertainty because cultural attachments are connected to very primary feelings about identity. While much of our language, in western thought generally and psychoanalysis in particular, emphasizes an inherent conflict between the group and the individual, an emphasis on identity draws attention to ways in which social attachments are an integral way of strengthening individual identity (Turner 1988).

Culture Defines Group Boundaries and Organizes Actions Within and Between Them

As culture defines identity groups, it also specifies expectations concerning patterns of association within and between groups. Consider such basic questions as who lives with whom, who spends time together, to whom one is most attached emotionally, who controls scarce resources, how property is transferred between generations, and how work is organized. The world's cultures provide very different answers to each of these questions, but most important the evidence shows that how any group answers any of these questions has significance for how people act and expect others to behave (Levinson and Malone, 1981; Naroll 1970).

Cultural definitions of social groups – whether they are defined by kinship, age, gender, or common interests – entail clear expectations about how people are to act, even when these definitions are continually contested (Greif 1994; Scott 1985). How such social categories and groups are defined and the rules that regulate their behavior vary cross-culturally. Cultural norms regarding intergroup relations (here we can consider relations between groups in the same culture such as age or ritual groups, or groups from different cultures) can be highly elaborate. Cultures differ in how and when they restrict (and how they enforce such restrictions on) relations, but few are silent on these questions.

People don't often think about the social origin of groups with which they identify, for most groups are seen as natural, often biological in character, when in fact they are cultural and political constructions whose "reasonableness" needs to be regularly reasserted and taught to succeeding generations (Anderson 1991). Weber, for example, shows how the nineteenth-century French state, through the institutionalization of a national education system, investment in transportation, and universal male military service, created a sense of national identity out of a myriad of regional loyalties (1976).[7] All cultures, of course, provide specific, but not always explicit, socialization regarding in-group and out-group distinctions. Cultural learning involves messages about groups' motives, their behavior, and how one is to act toward members of each category.

Cross-culturally, the rigidity of social distinctions is highly variable, and variation in the permeability of boundaries means that functioning categories are both contextual and changing over time. This is clearly seen in the literature on "situational ethnicity," which shows how distinctions among groups can depend upon what other groups are in a social environment and what the particular political stakes are in a conflict. In East Africa, for example, speakers of *Kiluhya*, whose homeland is in western Kenya, gradually developed a political and social identity as Luhya people through contact with other ethnic communities in Nairobi, Mombasa, Kampala, and other urban centers since 1900. Earlier, however, their identity was primarily as Marigoli, Busia, or Samia, more localized Baluhya subgroups.

Culture Provides a Framework for Interpreting the Actions and Motives of Others

Actions, like words, are highly ambiguous, and making sense of them requires a shared cultural framework to assure that the message that is sent is similar, if not identical with, that which is received. Few behaviors are so universal that they require little or no interpretation. The work on the cross-cultural (and even cross-species) interpretability of specific facial gestures (Ekman, Friesen, and Ellsworth 1972; Masters and Sullivan 1989), while fascinating, is also testimony to how few domains of human action are coherent outside of a shared cultural framework. Because most political and social action is complex, a capacity to decode only facial and other obvious physical gestures doesn't get one very far in understanding political life. It also provides little assistance in placing action in a broader context – one that includes motives, which offer an account of what someone has done but, in addition, says why they acted as they did.

Motives are central to cultural analysis because they offer a mechanism to link individual action to a broader social setting (D'Andrade and Strauss 1992). This contrasts with Geertz's focus on "inspecting events" and making sense of actors' interpretations of them but his rejection of the idea that we should examine mental structures (1973a: 10-12). D'Andrade's (1992) cultural analysis of motives develops the notion of a schema (not unlike what I am calling worldviews), "a conceptual structure which makes possible the identification of objects and events" (1992: 28). Schemas, he argues, are culturally acquired and produce "motivational strivings." He emphasizes the importance of understanding the context-dependent nature of schemas as interpretive devices and the need to spell out

[7]Certainly the comparative analysis of state-building has long recognized the role of cultural practices and political control over them, as well as the role of political leaders who become cultural icons, linking previously disparate groups in a single state and in the process defining newer, broader identities.

how they are acquired. Both D'Andrade and Strauss argue that we need to see cultures as "both the public actions, objects and symbols that make shared learning possible ... and the private psychological states of knowledge and feeling without which these public things are meaningless and could not be recreated" (Strauss 1992: 6).[8]

In many ways motives in cultural analysis are much like interests in rational choice theory. In statements such as "They were motivated by fear of their ancestors and so they sacrificed half of their livestock" or "The blips had an interest in weakening the military capability of their enemy," both motives and interests offer a "reasonable" account of why individuals or groups behave in a certain way. Yet there are also significant differences in the use of motives and interests as explanatory mechanisms that are central to the difference between cultural and rational choice explanations. Most basically, while interests are assumed to be more or less transparent (some would say given) and universal, motives are knowable only through empirical analysis of particular cultural contexts.[9] As a result, while turning to interests suggests that more or less any human group would behave the same way in a certain situation, an emphasis on motives focuses on explaining variation in behavior across groups. Wildavsky (1987) argues that rational choice theorists make a serious error in taking interests as given. In fact, he says, an empirically based cultural analysis reveals systematic variation in interests across cultures.

In an analysis of intracultural behavior, the difference between motives and interests is not always consequential, for in fact when interests are shared they can operate like motives, offering a readily available account of why people behave as they do. However, when we consider cross-cultural encounters, the difference between interests and motives can be more significant. Consider the statement above that a group of people motivated by fear of their ancestors and therefore sacrificed half their domestic animals. To people in another culture in which such fears are unknown, they are not plausible motives for action, and such behavior is not comprehensible. Trying to transform such an explanation into an interest statement ("They had an interest in not making the ancestors angry") still begs the question of why the group understands the world in terms of "fear of the ancestors." Only an analysis that seeks to explain why this motive is important in one culture but not another is adequate here.

Interest accounts of political action are imperialistic, dominating other explanations and insisting in what is often a tautological fashion that whatever action occurs can be understood in terms of individual (or group) interest maxi-

---

[8]This sort of rich understanding of culture is not one that it is possible to develop exclusively from survey data. Although such data can make a significant contribution to what I have called subjective cultural analysis, the data by themselves are insufficient for building an intersubjective cultural account.

[9]There have been efforts to identify a fixed number of human motives such as Murray's (1938) and McClelland's (1961) work on three particular motives – achievement, affiliation, and power. It is important to recognize that in both of these cases – especially McClelland's – the relative importance of any single motive varied both cross-culturally and across individuals.

mization. The power of interest explanations lies in their hypothesized connections between thought and action; their weakness, however, is that they begin with actor's action and then identify interests that are consistent with the pursuit of such action. All too infrequently is there an effort made to see if actors themselves make the same connections. More interesting from a cultural perspective is the almost complete absence of concern with the nature of specific interests in interest theories.[10] To the extent that groups and individuals are seen as having invariant interests, such as the maximization of wealth or political power, this question is somewhat uninteresting. However, to the degree to which important interests vary from culture to culture, the matter of what constitutes crucial political interests for groups or individuals is worthy of serious empirical study. Cultural explanations, as a result, do not deny the relevance of interests but see them as contextually defined and one motive among many. Even though it views interests as cultural constructions rather than objectively identifiable universals, cultural theory can complement rational choice and other interest theories. Its different emphasis does not necessarily lead to competing propositions that put the two theories in conflict with each other; rather, cultural theory's concern with the construction of interests addresses an issue about which interest theories have little to say.

In cross-cultural encounters people most often make sense of other groups' behavior, i.e., attribute motives to them, by drawing on their own cultural worldview. However, it is worth pointing out that cultural worldviews provide two contrasting strategies for encounters with outsiders. One is to apply the rules of one's own culture because they are, after all, what is best known (and often all that is known), believing that outsiders will respond as insiders do. The second is to search for different rules, assuming that outsiders share few motives with people in one's own culture, hence will respond in "heathen" ways and are likely to take advantage of any weakness shown to them – for they will not follow what are viewed as "civilized norms." The first strategy is that of generalization, whereas the second is one of differentiation.[11]

Few people ever subject shared cultural frameworks to self-conscious analysis, since most people deeply internalize cultural assumptions and hence rarely articulate them consciously or view them as problematic. Yet even in times of stress

[10]However, see Levi (this volume) and her recognition of early rational choice theory's lack of interest in this question and current attention to it, including an interest in the role of culture as a source of interests (e.g., Greif 1994).

[11]An important question is the extent to which any culture characteristically exhibits generalizing or differentiating behaviors in encounters with outsiders, at least in certain domains. In a cross-cultural study of internal and external conflict and violence, I found that in some cultures the levels of internal and external conflict are quite similar (generalizers) while in others they are highly differentiated. The differences between the two groups of societies are quite clear: Differentiating societies are characterized by many ties that link diverse groups in the society and that clearly mark them off from outsiders, while generalizing societies are those without strong mechanisms of internal integration. Probably a key reason why insiders and outsiders are treated somewhat the same is because whether one is an insider or outsider vis-à-vis a group is defined contextually and not in absolute terms (Ross 1993a: Chapter 7).

there is a widespread (if not universal) ethnocentric tendency to suggest that "there is something wrong" with a person who fails to offer or misreads an obvious cultural signal and to take such behavior as evidence that something is "wrong" with that person or of the inferiority of the other group. For the most part, culturally shared worldviews are protected, and people will go to great lengths to resist changes that challenge their core elements.

Culture Provides Resources for Political Organization and Mobilization

Culture offers significant resources that leaders and groups use as instruments of organization and mobilization (Brysk 1995; Edelman 1964; Kertzer 1988; Laitin 1986). For example, Tilly has developed the concept of repertoires of collective action referring to "a limited set of routines that are learned, shared, and acted out through a relatively deliberate process of choices. Repertoires are learned cultural creations" (1995: 26; also see Tilly 1986; Traugott 1995; McAdam, Tarrow, and Tilly this volume). Anthropologist Abner Cohen (1969; 1974; 1981) spells out more generally the political uses of culture, emphasizing the importance of cultural organizations (formal or informal groups organized around specific cultural practices such as a religious or age group) as a political tool in situations where "normal politics" is not possible for one reason or another; in fact, the theory is much more widely relevant. In Cohen's analysis of Hausa traders in Ibadan (Nigeria) and Creoles in Freetown (Sierra Leone), the two were small minorities, so that using electoral strategies to pursue their economic and political goals would have likely resulted in massive defeats. Instead, the two groups organized around cultural issues – a religious revival focused on the Tijaniyyi brotherhood in the case of the Hausa, and Freemasonry for the Creoles. In each case these cultural responses to changing political situations provided intense within-group interaction and social exchange that prevented the loss of control over long-distance trade in the case of the Hausa and protected the Creoles's domination of the state's administrative elite.

Frequently groups use cultural organizations (not always consciously, as Cohen points out) to achieve goals that cannot be pursued directly. Cohen identifies six political problems addressed by cultural organizations that bolster group solidarity and effective mobilization (Cohen 1969: 201-10). (1) Such organizations help define a group's distinctiveness, meaning its membership and sphere of operation within the context of the contemporaneous political setting, through myths of origin and claims to superiority; descent and endogamy; moral exclusiveness; endo-culture; spatial proximity; and homogenization (201-4). (2) Cultural organizations meet the political need for intense internal communications among the group's constituent parts (205). (3) Cultural organizations offer mechanisms for decision making involving some formulation of general problems confronting the group and taking decisions about them (206). (4) They provide authority for implementing decisions and for speaking, where appropriate, on behalf of the group (207). (5)

Cultural organizations can provide a political ideology often rooted in the language of kinship and ritual, which gives legitimacy to power and converts it into authority (208-10). (6) Finally, cultural organizations meet the need for discipline, through ceremonials and rituals that connect the ideology to current problems of the community (210-11).[12]

In discussing religion, the prototypical cultural basis for political organization, Cohen points out that:

> Religion provides an ideal 'blueprint' for the development of an informal political organization. It mobilizes many of the most powerful emotions which are associated with the basic problems of human existence and gives legitimacy and stability to political arrangements by representing these as parts of the system of the universe. It makes it possible to mobilize the power of symbols and the power inherent in the ritual relationship between various ritual positions within the organization of the cult. It makes it possible to use the arrangements for financing and administering places of worship and associated places for welfare, education, and social activities of various sorts, to use these in developing the organization and administration of political functions. Religion also provides frequent and regular meetings in congregations, where in the course of ritual activities, a great deal of informal interaction takes place, information is communicated, and general problems are formulated and discussed. The system of myths and symbols which religion provides is capable of being continuously interpreted and reinterpreted in order to accommodate it to changing economic, political and other social circumstances. (210)

Although Cohen's analysis is about the coping strategies of small cultural minorities, it is clearly relevant to understanding how leaders of large ethnic groups (often, but not always, majorities) have come to, and held onto, political power. African politics since the 1960s provides many examples of mobilization around cultural symbols and fears, and so do European settings such as Northern Ireland, France with a strong antiimmigrant, antiforeigner party, and Germany with its numerous outbreaks of antiforeigner violence. It is, however, in Eastern Europe and the former Soviet Union where we perhaps have the most to learn about the political manipulation of cultural symbols and rituals and their sometimes disastrous consequences. Here we must ask why the appeals to Serbian, Armenian, or Hungarian identity are all so powerful. However, as Campbell (1983) has suggested, any such answer that relies on mechanisms of individual benefit only makes sense if we can also account for the strength of individual attachments to groups such as those defined in cultural terms.

---

[12]Cohen's analysis is quite compatible with the one resource mobilization theorists offer in their discussion of social movements, especially in their willingness to consider cultural as well as material resources (McAdam, Tarrow, and Tilly this volume).

CULTURAL ANALYSES OF POLITICS

Although one could make a cogent argument that cultural analyses are among the oldest works of political analysis, here I discuss a selected number of more recent studies that illustrate key concepts and methods associated with a cultural approach in comparative politics. My focus here is on approaches that give a central role to the concept of culture, not ones in which one or two cultural variables appear but are neither theoretically significant nor well developed. I discuss five different (but not necessarily mutually exclusive) approaches that are important because of their widespread influence within comparative politics and/or because of their potential to provide important insights. Under each I discuss a few important studies that illustrate the approach, without suggesting they are the only, or best, examples of it.

Culture, Personality, and Politics

The merging of the theoretical perspectives of psychoanalysis and cultural anthropology in the 1940s and early 1950s provided a framework linking macro- and micro-level phenomena to explain cross-cultural differences in behavior. A popularized branch of this work, national character studies, combined Ruth Benedict's (1934) view that cultures were highly patterned with psychoanalysis' stress on the importance of infant and child socialization to offer profiles (some would say caricatures) of large countries, such as Japan, Russia, and the United States, to explain, among other things, their political institutions and political styles (Benedict 1946; Gorer and Rickman 1946; Mead 1942). Emphasizing (often with weak data) the link between socialization (defined in terms of a country's modal patterns), personality (often not directly measured), and political behavior, these studies offered sweeping generalizations about American individualism, Japanese militarism, and Russian totalitarian rule. Within a few years, a wide range of critiques emerged emphasizing problems in these works, including assumptions of within-country homogeneity, lack of evidence linking key elements in the theory, and its inability either to account for political change or to speak to the zigs and zags in political life in the countries under study. Clearly, transferring culture and personality theory and methods from small-scale preindustrial societies to the largest modern, industrial nations was not successful on either theoretical or methodological grounds.[13]

However, two political scientists, Lucien Pye (1962) and Edward Banfield (1958), found sufficient merit in the approach that they borrowed from it in two widely read, influential studies, while trying to address some of the most tren-

---

[13]Much of the critique of national character research was also relevant to studies in small-scale societies typically studied by anthropologists. For example, Wallace (1970:152-54) argued that while culture and personality theories would predict that a large proportion of the people in a small society would exhibit a similar personality profile, when he administered standardized tests to a community of Tuscarora Indians only 37% fit the modal pattern. Also see Inkeles and Levinson (1968) and LeVine (1973).

chant critiques of national character research. Pye, in an ambitious study of Burma in the 1950s, sought to explain the country's search for national identity. Keenly aware of the criticism that the personalities of political elites might be significantly different from those of the mass public and the need to study personality directly, Pye produced data on the crucial psychological variables through in-depth psychoanalytic interviews with Burmese elites. Emphasizing identity issues in an Eriksonian framework, Pye developed the link between the problems of individual identity among the elites he interviewed and Burmese nation-building. Development, he concluded, was not just about economic policies and institution-building but was intimately linked to the worldviews and psychological capacities of a country's elites.

Banfield developed a far less psychoanalytic framework to examine the absence of collective social or political action among peasants in a town in southern Italy where on self-interest grounds an outsider might expect to find it. His answer was that amoral familism, the rule that one can only trust and cooperate with the members of one's immediate family, is taught from an early age and supported in a variety of domains of daily life. Wider cooperation fails to gain a toehold because no one can imagine that cooperation will be reciprocated or sustained. Consequently, the culture of amoral familism is a powerful configuration (as Ruth Benedict might have used the term) and difficult to overcome despite the likely benefits from doing so.

The Civic Culture Tradition

Without a doubt, when most political scientists think about cultural analysis of politics, Almond and Verba's *The Civic Culture* (1963) quickly comes to mind. Utilizing data collected from large national samples in five countries – the United States, Britain, Germany, Italy, and Mexico – the authors sought to explain different levels of support for, and participation in, democratic political practices. Almond and Verba identify three distinctive political cultures – the participant, subject, and parochial – which differ in the attitudes citizens express toward the political system, trust in political authorities, beliefs concerning the efficacy of individual and collective political actions, and levels of political involvement. Thus, individual subjective attitudes and behaviors are the basis for assigning individuals to patterns, and the distribution of a country's individuals determines where the country is categorized in Almond and Verba's scheme. As a result, Almond and Verba's indicators of political culture cohere far more loosely than the constituent parts of culture do for Benedict, Geertz, and most anthropologists (Merelman 1991: 52; see also Almond 1980).[14]

Although the civic culture data are more or less consistent with the authors' theory, there are large questions that remain from a study using individual level

---

[14]An additional criticism of the civic culture tradition is the impoverished, generally implicit, unilineal view of the world's political cultures on a single continuum with the United States at the high end, rather than a multidimensional, more complex image of cultural difference.

survey data to discuss national political patterns, such as how to explain the some-times large numbers of people who do not fit a country's dominant pattern, the role of political institutions, the weak conception of culture that emerges from their in-dividualistic approach, and the relationship between political and other domains of culture (Verba 1980). The relatively low correlations among attitudes, the very small number of respondents who fit ideal-typical patterns, and the subjective, but not intersubjective nature of survey data mean that survey evidence alone is insuf-ficient to describe the existence and significance of cultural meaning systems. In contrast, Merelman's (1991) comparative study of political culture in the United States, Canada, and Britain is based on a richer view of culture as a system of mean-ing and includes intersubjective cultural data derived from television programs, corporate publications, textbooks, and magazine ads along with survey data.[15]

Nonetheless, survey research in literally dozens of countries has produced hundreds of studies in the civic culture tradition, including another large-scale study in which Verba and his colleagues examined political participation in seven countries (Verba, Nie, and Kim 1978). Perhaps, however, Inglehart (1977; 1988) is the political scientist who has most faithfully carried out work in the civic cul-ture tradition, emphasizing culture in interpreting cross-national survey data using the yearly Euro-Barometer surveys. For example, he has explained in cul-tural terms the strong political and life-style differences between individuals who emphasize what he calls materialist and postmaterialist values, i.e., emphasis on order and the economy versus participation and free speech. Arguing that politi-cal scientists often develop explanations that give short shrift to cultural factors, Inglehart links the strength of a syndrome of attitudes he calls civic culture – per-sonal life satisfaction, political satisfaction, interpersonal trust, and support for the existing social order – to democratic stability and economic development (1988).

Finally, although it does not rely on survey data as exclusively as Almond and Verba or Inglehart, Putnam's work on the political differences in the civic cultures in northern and southern Italy is also squarely in this tradition (1993). To the survey evidence he presents, Putnam also adds data on governmental per-formance, aggregate economic and political participation data, and interviews with political elites. Using these different data, Putnam argues that democracy and democratic innovations are most effective where there is a strong tradition of civic participation. When he examines alternative explanations for the relative success of Italian regionalization in 1976, he argues that those regions in which civic participation has flourished for perhaps the past 800 years are most likely to be those in which effective regional governments developed, whereas in re-gions without such cultural traditions (such as the one Banfield studied), the governments are less effective.[16]

[15] In another interesting example using a cultural indicator of collective political orientations, Regan (1994) relates sales of war toys and popularity of war movies to U. S. militarization.

[16] There has been extensive discussion of Putnam's (1993) work and its relevance beyond Italy, which is not my focus here. For two critical views of his theory pertinent to my discussion of culture, see Laitin (1995b) and Tarrow (1996).

Culture and Political Process: The Extended Case

Although political anthropology has existed as a field for decades, only a few political scientists have found its theoretical insights or methods of great interest (Barkun 1968; Bates 1983; Easton 1959; Friedrich with Horwitz 1968; Laitin 1986; Masters 1964). Much of this is probably due to the field's emphasis on documenting variations in political structure in human communities. Among these works one finds Fortes and Evans-Pritchard (1940), who provide detailed descriptions of eight African states and stateless societies in which kinship forms the basis of political organization and who argue strongly that politics does not require a state with a monopoly over the means of legitimate force, as Weberians have argued. Others illustrate the complex ways in which different societies deal with leadership succession, political decision making, and conflict management (Goody 1966; Kuper and Richards 1971; Pospisil 1971). Cross-cultural studies in this tradition examine patterns among political variables and relations between them and social, economic, and ecological factors (Murdock 1949; Ross 1986, 1988). From the point of view of cultural approaches to comparative politics, most structural studies in political anthropology, while documenting differences among societies, do not pay much explicit attention to culture per se.

In contrast to structural studies, works that put political process at their core have greater theoretical and methodological relevance for comparative politics. Initially developed by Max Gluckman and his followers in field research in southern Africa (and later known as the Manchester School), these studies focused on explaining how and why particular political outcomes occur, providing rich details about political conflict in which culture's role is at center stage (Gluckman 1942; Mitchell 1956; Epstein 1958; Turner 1957; 1968; Cohen 1969; 1974). These studies, which particularly influenced Africanists, offered a deeply contextualized account of particular events or problems to develop broad middle-range theory that is especially useful in comparative political analysis.[17] For example, in one study, Victor Turner (1957) analyzed how the Ndembu of Zambia cope with the strong conflicting structural demands between their norms of political succession and postmarital residence. He argued that strong cross-cutting ties in their society provide the basis for the extensive use of ritual, which emphasizes what members share and integrates a group that often finds itself bitterly divided on other grounds. Abner Cohen, whose work was discussed in detail above, argues that culture provides a strategic, although not necessarily conscious, basis for political mobilization of groups whose positions cannot be defended through more conventional political means. An examination of ethnic mobilization in the last decade in Eastern Europe (and elsewhere) shows the power of his analysis, which few political scientists have examined, and offers a theoretical context for explaining the behavior of political leaders whose ability to survive in multicultural contexts is uncertain.

---

[17]Gluckman, for example, wrote about the importance of studying what he called "trouble cases" in his work on African law, but it is clear that he saw this as a much more general methodological strategy as well.

The extended cases of interest here are those that use culture to explain why and how a political conflict takes the course it does. For example, Scott (1985) analyzes the responses to irrigation and the institutionalization of double cropping in Sedaka, a village in Malaysia, in terms of how the richer and poorer rice farmers understand the demands of traditional norms and obligations in light of new opportunities and challenges. His study includes several detailed cases, one concerning the village gate and another involving a politically motivated village improvement scheme, that are especially effective at showing how the competing interests are manifest within a culturally homogeneous village. Scott demonstrates that it is only because the villagers' shared understandings are so great that small actions that an outsider might easily miss can contribute to the continuing battle over access to resources.

Political Ritual and Identity

Before Murray Edelman published *The Symbolic Uses of Politics* (1964), few political scientists gave much serious thought to issues of political symbolism and ritual. Since then, comparativists ignore it at their peril. Edelman's core argument was simple but important. Politics, he said, is a passing parade of symbols to which we react on two levels: the cognitive, which involves the information any symbol communicates; and the affective, which consists of powerful feelings political symbols can invoke. The ability of leaders to provide symbolic reassurance to the masses allows organized groups to take the lion's share of material benefits for themselves. Edelman and the many people he influenced more indirectly have made the study of political symbolism and ritual central to analyses of political institutions and dynamics. For our point of view here, this work is crucial because it shows how cultural frameworks render political symbols and rituals significant in a wide range of settings and to a wide number of political dynamics (Brysk 1995).

Whereas earlier analyses, for example, emphasized elections as citizen choice making, a more cultural analysis would also pay attention to how political parties and candidates, in their quest for power, use culturally shared metaphors and culturally rooted fears in their appeals to citizens. Policy positions or candidate choices, we now understand, are not just about the issue preferences of individuals; we also must ask how such orientations are or are not consonant with shared cultural understandings and identities. The invocation of symbols and use of rituals do not just indicate points of consensus; they are also efforts to overcome contradictions in situations of disjunction (Kurtz 1991: 149).

This richer understanding of politics' cultural roots has produced an interest in how political rituals create (rather than just reflect) meanings and shape actions (Gusfield 1966). There is attention to high-visibility political rituals such as the torchlight marches in East Germany in the waning days of the old regime in 1989, and how participation in these events provided the courage for citizen participation under a regime that earlier made such action

unthinkable. More generally, political transitions, such as the changes in Eastern Europe or in South Africa between 1990 and 1994, can only be explained
effectively when we make sense of the interaction between substantive change
and ritual action.

An even stronger position is that political rituals are particularly critical to
constructing political reality for most people (Edelman 1988; Kertzer 1988: 77-
101) and that the power to control ritual is important.

> Indeed, ritual is an important means of influencing people's ideas about po-
> litical events, political policies, political systems, and political leaders.
> Through ritual, people develop their ideas about what are appropriate po-
> litical institutions, what are appropriate qualities in political leaders, and
> how well the world around them measures up against these standards.
> (Kertzer 1988: 79)

In short, rituals are important instruments of control and from a Gramscian
point of view are central mechanisms for obtaining and maintaining power. Detailed analyses of meaning-construction rituals would examine social movements
as well as the mass media, which increasingly for citizens of mass democracies
provide not only access to core knowledge but also the framework for making
sense of it (Dayan and Katz 1992).

Political rituals offer meaning in ambiguous, uncertain situations and are
crucial to the dynamics of identity construction and maintenance, particularly in
periods of change. In bringing certain people together, culturally rooted rituals
simultaneously exclude others. Powerful political rituals are those that utilize
culturally rooted metaphors and meanings to offer a vision of reality; often this
involves pitting one group against another by raising fears and threats to the
point that people are all too ready to undertake strong action in the name of the
group.

Culture and Political Conflict

In many analyses culture plays a central role in explaining the level and form
of political conflict and violence. Culture in these analyses provides a system of
meaning to make sense of the actions and motives of opponents and a mechanism
for building and maintaining identity. Within-group worldviews are reinforced
as groups increase in-group solidarity and out-group hostility increases. Not all
cultural mobilization in conflict situations leads to violence, however, and one
important comparative question concerns when this turn to violence occurs and
when it does not.

For example, Laitin (1995a) offers a controlled comparison emphasizing culturally constituted differences in social organization to explain the high use of
political violence in the Basque protest in Spain and its relative absence in nearby Catalonia. He identifies as a significant difference between these subcultures
the relative importance of autonomous male groups with strong norms of honor
in the small towns in the Basque region and their relative absence in Catalonia.

When these small, local male groups engage in protest that produces some limited and mainly symbolic successes, violence becomes self-sustaining.[18] As a result, the differences in the use of violence between the regions are not a function of objective differences or relative deprivation within them but of the cultural organization of each community, which affects the likelihood that the ethnic revivals in each community will turn to violence.

Ross (1993a) provides a more general cross-cultural analysis to explain differences in levels and targets of conflict and violence. He finds that psychocultural variables – low warmth and affection in child rearing, harsh socialization, and male gender identity conflict – were excellent predictors of a society's overall level of violence, while social structural factors, such as the strength of crosscutting ties or the presence of exclusive male groups, determined whether targets were within the same society, in another society, or both. He goes on to argue that cultural worldviews determine how groups see outsiders and the motives attributed to them. In addition, the culture of conflict is a crucial determinant not just of a group's level of conflict but also of how conflict is managed when it occurs (Ross 1993b).

Raymond Cohen (1990; 1991) demonstrates how culture provides a framework through which political leaders understand the actions and words of others in his examination of how cultural assumptions complicate the task of diplomatic negotiations. First through an analysis of Egyptian–Israeli negotiations over time (1990), and then through an examination of how cultural miscommunication has affected U.S. negotiations with Mexico, Egypt, China, India, and Japan, Cohen (1991) suggests that differences in time frames and in the importance of context, language, and individualistic versus collectivist ethos all are important in either inhibiting or facilitating negotiated efforts to deal with international issues. Focusing only on "substance," he contends, leads to serious missed opportunities and failures where successes might have emerged.

Finally, culture is central in the ethnic and identity disputes that have seemingly proliferated in recent years. In intransigent conflicts between groups with very different systems of meaning and distinct identities, cultural factors easily become the focal point of many conflicts when they are central to the parties' definition of the dispute (Ross 1997). In such situations, each group readily sees itself as a threatened minority whose very existence is precarious (Horowitz 1985). Frequently, in conflicts such as the one in Northern Ireland, differences are framed so that central elements of one culture are seen as powerful threats to the other; in these cases one can only imagine a resolution that addresses these culturally rooted fears head-on (Mulvihill, Ross, and Schermer 1995).

---

[18]In many ways his argument is similar to fraternal interest group theory in anthropology, which says that in the absence of centralized authority, coresident related males are likely to defend what they see as their core interests through organized violence (Paige and Paige 1981; Ross 1993a).

CRITIQUE OF CULTURAL ANALYSES OF POLITICS

Cultural studies of politics have been subject to a number of important criticisms about which proponents cannot remain silent. Perhaps the most significant problems arise over methodological issues such as the vagueness of culture as a unit of analysis or the issue of within- versus between-cultural variation. Others are concerned with the vagueness of the concept of culture and the difficulty in distinguishing culture from related concepts such as social organization, political behavior, and values. Some are worried that, since culture suggests relatively fixed, unchanging patterns of behavior, it is not terribly useful in accounting for changes in behavior and beliefs, a key feature of most contemporary political systems. Finally, there is concern that cultural analyses are not sufficiently explicit concerning the mechanisms linking culture and political action. Each of these criticisms is worth some brief comments. However, it should be clear that my view is that none of these problems is fatal and that in the cultural approach to comparative politics, like those rooted in interests or institutions, the best way to address the conceptual and methodological problems is through a multi-method search for convergence rather than abandonment of the theory.

Unit of Analysis Issues

Defining the unit of analysis precisely – be it voters, states, wars, or international organizations – is one of the first lessons of most methods seminars in political science. "What is a culture?" some political scientists ask, meaning "How do I know one when I see one?" since culture is not a unit of social or political organization with readily identifiable boundaries. Furthermore, the imprecision of common language use makes it very unclear what are a culture's key properties. As a result we hear references to western culture, French culture, Breton culture, rural Breton culture, etc. Where does the parsing stop? Conceptually the best answer is that the appropriate level of analysis depends on what one wants to explain. However, this is not always an easy-to-use methodological guide in empirical research.

Huntington offers a similar answer when he describes a range of what he calls cultural entities starting with villages and moving to regions, ethnic groups, nationalities, religious groups, and civilizations. Each has distinct cultural features that distinguish it from similar units in other cultural entities. The key for him is that the civilization is "the highest grouping of people and the broadest level of cultural identity people have short of that which distinguishes humans from other species" (1993: 24). Following Horowitz (1985), he says that the level of cultural identity that is the most salient at any moment depends upon where someone is and what they are doing with whom.

The unit of analysis problem is about what constitutes the core of a culture and also how to identify its edges (Barth 1969). Where does one culture stop and another begin? Since cultures, unlike states or political parties, are not formal units of organization, treating them as independent units of political analysis can be troubling indeed. While this may seem like a devastating critique to some, it is just as true that neither states nor voters are as independent as our political and methodological theories lead us to believe. For purposes of most analyses we emphasize the independence of all these units. What is probably more useful is to be more sophisticated about interaction effects and the influence of one unit upon another.[19]

Probably the best answer to these methodological problems is to begin with the recognition that cultural identity is layered and situationally defined.[20] People hold multiple identities, some identities partially overlap, and the group boundaries can shift across issues. Despite the methodological problems this can present, we cannot ignore culture if we think it is important, and we should make decisions about units of analysis based on what we are trying to explain rather than on abstract criteria intended to identify a set of cultural units akin to a list of all UN member states.[21] In addition, there are a number of other procedures we can use to define cultural units in particular pieces of research. For example, we can use operational criteria such as asking people how they identify themselves and others and use social consensus about particular cultural groups and their boundaries. The point is that the task for research is to identify relevant groupings in whatever situation is under study. The fact that people can have multiple identities or that identities can change over time does not invalidate such analysis, it just makes the research more complicated. Good longitudinal data on socially defined cultural identities might be of real importance, for example, in understanding the breakdown of Yugoslavia and its recent civil war.

Political culture research in the Almond and Verba tradition ought to solve the problem by defining culture as the aggregate of individual orientations. Almond and Powell, for example, define political culture as "the pattern of individual attitudes and orientations towards politics among members of a political system" (1966: 23). Reducing culture to the sum of individual attitudes is hardly

---

[19]Galton's Problem refers to the fact that in cross-cultural (and cross-national) samples, assumptions about the independence of units are often inappropriate and that substantive correlations among culture traits can reflect diffusion and borrowing rather than functional association. The most useful response is not to ignore this problem but to build diffusion hypotheses into models to test the relative power of each pattern (Ross and Homer 1976).

[20]Another answer comes from Thompson, Ellis, and Wildavsky (1990), who argue that culture is seen in distinct ways of life, which they define in terms of Mary Douglas's grid-group analysis. Group refers to the extent to which an individual is incorporated into bounded units, whereas grid refers to the degree to which a person's behaviors are circumscribed by externally imposed restrictions. Different individuals or states can, in their view, exhibit different degrees of each of the five combinations they identify over time. However, viable social units, they argue, are not characterized by the presence of only one culturally defined way of life. While I find much of their analysis of the interaction between values and social structure quite useful, it is less evident to me that making the way of life the unit of analysis provides a guideline easy for researchers to use, since they say multiple orientations can exist in the same culture or subculture and that individuals may have different orientations across time and situations.

[21]This does not mean that such a list of societies that represent the world's cultures, such as one of the samples developed in cross-cultural research, is not useful in many research situations.

adequate, however, ignoring both the context in which particular attitudes are held and the shared understandings that organize clusters of intersubjective orientations (Merelman 1991). Culture, as a result, is no longer a system of meanings and identity; rather, it is simply a frequency distribution on a set of single attitude items – a kind of machine with totally interchangeable parts. While studying individuals is one way that we can understand culture, as both Taylor (1985: 37) and Geertz (1973a) argue, culture is not the property of single individuals, for it is rooted in social practice and shared understandings, and survey data alone cannot build a rich understanding of political culture. This explains why survey data alone are inherently limited as a tool for studying political culture; they must be used in conjunction with other data to provide a coherent portrait of any single culture or comparisons between cultures.

Within-Culture Variation Can Be Substantial

It often seems easy to say what members of formal groups have in common. But what exactly do people of a given culture share? My answer is shared meanings and a common identity. Operationally, this can be ambiguous, however, for we know that people who themselves identify with a culture (or any organized group) may also differ in terms of values, lifestyles, political dispositions, religious belief and practice, and ideas about common interests. In addition, Strauss cautions that while there may be some variation in schemas (what I have been calling worldviews) across individuals in the same culture, even those with very similar schemas may not internalize exactly the same things, and that the ambiguity of metaphor produces variation in responses (Strauss 1992: 10-11). However, this is not necessarily any more a problem in dealing with culture than with other units (or even intra-individual variation in behavior or attitudes over time). LeVine argues that emphasizing culture as common understandings of the symbols and representations they communicate does not mean there is necessarily a problem with within-cultural variation in thought, feeling, and behavior (1984: 68).

A second answer is that often what is more crucial politically than agreement on content is that people share a common identity, although this still leaves open the question of different degrees of identification and differences in the actions people are willing to undertake in the name of that identity. Shared identities mean that people see themselves as similar to some people and different from others and are open to potential mobilization on the basis of these differences. What an emphasis on identity stresses, once again, is that the relevant critical aspects of cultural similarity and difference are defined in specific political contexts. It is also the case that often what people believe they share may be at odds with reality because perceptions of cultural homogeneity overemphasize what is actually shared, minimizing within-group while stressing between-group differences. In this dynamic, in-group conformity pressures will lead people both to selectively perceive greater within-group homogeneity on critical characteristics than actually exists and to generate greater actual homogeneity and group conformity in situations where perceived threats to the culture are great.

Distinguishing Culture from Other Concepts

Some uses of the concept of culture, such as much of the early work on national character, defined culture so broadly as to include society, personality, values, and institutions. In fact, nothing was excluded.[22] The very broad use of the concept of culture is also seen among social scientists emphasizing culture as a source of the social integration of a society. This perspective, probably clearest in functional theory in British social anthropology, would use culture to refer both to distinct elements of social organization and to the "fit" between different parts of a cultural system and the integration of the whole. The problem here is not the concept of culture but the way it is used. As noted above, the current anthropological focus is on culture as meaning systems distinct from social structure and behavior. D'Andrade makes this particularly clear in his description of culture "as consisting of learned systems of meaning, communicated by means of natural language and other symbol systems, having representational, directive, and affective function, and capable of creating cultural entities and particular senses of reality. Through these systems of meaning, groups of people adapt to their environment and structure interpersonal activities" (1984: 116). I find Spiro's (1984) clear distinction between culture as a system of meaning, and what he calls "culturally constituted elements," referring to social structure, behaviors, beliefs, rituals, etc., particularly helpful here.

Spiro's (1984) distinction between culture and culturally constituted elements allows us to distinguish between cultural meanings and identity on the one hand and structure, behaviors, and individual beliefs on the other. Structure, from this perspective, is reflective of (and to some extent derived from) culture, but it is independently measurable, and an important empirical question concerns the conditions under which the correspondence between culture and various culturally constituted elements is high and when it is not. We also can examine hypotheses about change and examine how culture, structure, and other phenomena do and do not shift in patterned ways. Last, the distinction makes it feasible to compare societies in which the correspondence between culture and social structure are high and those in which they are low to test hypotheses about the impact of consistency on such things as citizen satisfaction with government, political involvement, and political stability.

Culture and Change

Cultures are commonly viewed as slow-changing entities. How, then, can the concept of culture help comparativists deal with issues of political change, especially relatively rapid developments such as the end of military rule in many Latin American states during the 1980s or the breakup of the Soviet empire?

---

[22]Pye says that national character analyses tended to treat "personality and culture as opposite sides of the same coin. Culture for them was the generalized personality of a people, in the sense that the modal personality of a people was their culture, and thus culture and personality were essentially identical factors shaping behavior" (1991: 494).

Three points are worth making. First, cultural analyses are no better than any other partial theories, such as interest or institutional ones, available in comparative politics. There are some phenomena for which each is most powerful, and some aspects of change are not best explained in cultural terms. Second, and interestingly, while it is not clear that cultural theories would have explained the fall of the Soviet empire very well (many other comparative political theories share this feature), a political cultural analysis is probably a good deal better at accounting for the ebb and flow of politics in the region since 1989 than many of its rivals (Fleron 1996). Particularly in unstructured, chang-ing settings, cultural interpretations and assumptions about the motivation of others can be especially important in accounting for political processes in which there are few or no institutionalized procedures to guide action. Third, few contemporary views see culture as a static, unchanging phenomenon marked by fixed beliefs and unalterable practices (Eckstein 1988). Rather, emphasis on the interactive, constructed nature of culture suggests a capacity to modify beliefs and behaviors, and for important shifts in the salience of particular cultural understandings and their connections to other cultural elements (Goode and Schneider 1994; Merelman 1991).

Culture can play a significant role in political change despite the fact that culture itself does not change rapidly, if, and when political demands are articulated through culturally meaningful accounts, which sharpen goal articulation and mobilize supporters. Defining culturally legitimate possible alternatives both builds support and can challenge a regime. Brysk argues that this is particularly powerful when it involves reframing elements of identity in a way that mobilizes supporters, produces agenda change, and challenges the legitimacy and authority of existing policies and institutions (1995: 580-2).

The Mechanisms Underlying Cultural Explanations

Asking "how culture works" raises two different questions: (1) How does the organization of any particular culture produce the specific effects attributed to it? and (2) why are appeals to cultural identity so powerful that people are willing to take high risks in their name? The first is about the organization of culture and the second about its mobilizing power.

Theories that give culture a central explanatory role must specify how the effects attributed to culture come about. It is not good enough to simply say, "They did it because they're Germans." While this statement implies that non-Germans (such as the Japanese or French) would have behaved differently, adding a clause to this effect doesn't really enhance the explanation a great deal. Only when one starts to say why Germans are likely to behave in a certain way that is different from how Americans behave (in what is presumed to be an equivalent situation) do we begin to have an adequate explanation that pays attention to the content of culture and also says something about how it is learned and reinforced

(Andrade, 1992; Strauss, 1992D).[23] Indeed this was a central concern of early political culture research, although few were very impressed with the adequacy of explanations it provided. Learning and reinforcement involve institutional contexts in which a person (child or adult) practices, and then masters, key behaviors, infusing them with emotional significance.[24]

Social experiences within institutions such as schools, religious organizations, kin groups, and later in work and leisure settings all provide cultural messages about values and expectations that are selectively reinforced. It certainly is the case that the messages from different domains are not always fully consistent. Sometimes there is a difference in emphasis; at other times there is an outright contradiction, e.g., peer groups and families don't necessarily give adolescents the same messages. However, what are most important from a cultural perspective are the beliefs, customs, rituals, behaviors, expectations, and motives that are internalized by individuals and widely shared among people in a culture even though they may also, at the same time, be highly contested. For example, Scott's (1985) study of a small rice-growing village in Malaysia shows how people can share meanings while at the same time compete over how specific elements are to be weighted and in what situations specific cultural elements are most relevant. Culture is about what is held in common and regularly reinforced; there is a reward for "getting it right" and a cost – which most people are willing to pay at times – for not doing so. Finally, it should be noted that cultural learning is not necessarily very conscious, occurring when individuals in institutional roles pass on culturally sanctioned beliefs and behaviors to others. Through these experiences culture prepares people to make sense of – to interpret–the world and act "effectively" in it.

The power of culture – the ability to mobilize action in its name – requires explanation, for it is not always the case that people can or will exhibit solidarity around cultural identity just because a leader (or anyone else) asserts that there is an external threat. Cultural mobilization builds on fears and perceived threats that are consistent with internalized worldviews and regularly reinforced through high in-group interaction and emotional solidarity. Such worldviews are expressed in daily experiences as well as significant ceremonial and ritual events that effectively restate and renew support for a group's core values and the need for solidarity in the face of external foes (Kertzer 1988). In potentially threatening situations, the ability of a group to organize collective ac-

---

[23]The point here is similar to Przeworski and Teune's (1970), that comparative political analysts should strive to replace proper names with variable names. While some interpretivists only want to consider the uniqueness of each culture and context, others are comfortable making comparisons while recognizing the potential problems inherent in any comparison and the generalizations derived from it.

[24]Beatrice Whiting (1980) discusses the importance cross-culturally of the placement of individuals in particular contexts, e.g., girls take care of younger siblings more than boys and boys are more likely to take care of animals in all the cultures for which she has data. Her data also show that cultures vary in the settings they "make available" to individuals, and she distinguishes between behaviors seen as "mundane" and those domains that are "projective" and infused with great emotional significance.

tion, which can range from unified voting to political demonstrations and violent action, is tied to the plausibility of a specific worldview – although the
view itself does not produce direct effects. Rather, these must be mediated
through institutions (Laitin 1986; 1995a). The resonance between the definition of a situation and group-based action is often not explicit, as Abner
Cohen's (1969) analysis points out. Nonetheless it is effective when group
members act in unified ways in the face of perceived threats. Closer examination of the dynamics of psychocultural interpretation in the next section suggests additional specific mechanisms at work.

THE CENTRALITY OF INTERPRETATION IN
CULTURAL ANALYSES OF POLITICS

At the core of contemporary intersubjective approaches to culture and politics is
the concept of interpretation. Culture in the Geertzian, postmodern view is a system of meaning and identity that accounts for why and how people in any particular setting act as they do, in contrast to the idea of culture as a set of norms
or behaviors that directly shape action. This culture-as-meaning-and-identity
perspective gives a central role to interpretation, the making of meaning from the
ambiguous and fragmented elements of daily life (Darnton 1985; Taylor 1985).
While there is widespread agreement that a subjective, meaning-centered conception of culture is richer than more mechanistic or material views, there is also
fundamental disagreement concerning the goals of cultural explanations of politics. More humanistically oriented political (and other social) scientists emphasize the role of particular contextual and historical forces that shape meaning for
actors. Their concern is with the uniqueness of each context as actors understand
it, and they have little interest in accounting for patterns of similarity and difference across settings. This emphasis on the uniqueness of each cultural context
and its particular meaning for actors readily leads to the conclusion that any
search for generalization is pointless, for the only generalizations that might be
offered are uninteresting. At the same time, this radical interpretivist view denies the value of any comparison at all and is not the one I develop here (Edgerton 1992: 23-45).[25]

---

[25]In anthropology where this debate has been particularly heated, two issues – evaluation of different cultures (cultural relativism) and comparison of cultures – are often fused. The relativism debate concerns the appropriateness of evaluating cultures other than one's own, while the comparison question turns
on the issue of whether it is possible to compare cultures and develop meaningful generalizations. Edgerton describes the anti-comparison position as "asserting far more than the self-evident point that people
in different societies live in somewhat different worlds of meaning. They are claiming that each of these
worlds is truly unique – incommensurable and largely incomprehensible – and that the people who in-
habit them have different cognitive abilities ... [and] various postmodern relativists and interpretivists
postulate fundamental differences from one culture to the next in cognitive processes involving logic,
causal inferences, and information processing" (Edgerton 1992:28).

In contrast, more social scientifically oriented investigators, while accepting the intersubjective and subjective character of culture, seek to identify the mechanisms that link culture and action, and to identify regularities in cultural behavior across settings. One approach found in psychological anthropology draws on both psychoanalytic and cognitive theories to explain how culture affects behavior (e.g., D'Andrade 1992; Spiro 1987). It emphasizes, for example, how individuals absorb, process, and modify cultural knowledge (information, affect, images) to develop images of the world, and how these images affect collective and individual action.

Here I discuss the conceptual and methodological importance of interpretations, arguing that they are key tools for understanding culture and politics. The rich accounts found in the images of the world's people point to key concerns, assumptions about how social and political relations are organized, and views about the possibilities for political action. These images of the world are obtainable, in part, through public and private accounts. However, simply presenting the transcripts of individuals' stories is insufficient for a number of reasons, including the important one that texts do not speak for themselves and without an intermediary they often make no sense to an outsider (Scott 1985: 138-41). Rather, the comparativist needs to frame accounts in both a cultural and comparative context and highlight the crucial elements (Kohli et al. 1995: 44-5).[26] Laitin (1988) says that connecting culture and action requires detailed local, ethnographic knowledge and experience. Without a rich contextual understanding, it is too difficult to derive much significance from the detailed, highly contextualized interpretations of the world that hardly ever speak for themselves.[27]

The interpretations of interest here are accounts of the world that people within a culture widely share (or at least easily understand).[28] Elsewhere I use the term psychocultural interpretations to describe how shared interpretations are acquired through individual-level psychological (and social-psychological) mechanisms that are widespread in a culture (Ross 1993a; 1995).[29] Psychocultural interpretations are the basis on which people in a culture understand the world and link specific worldviews to political action, offering rich data for comparative political analyses.

[26]Here the subjectivity of different social scientists and varying theoretical interests will certainly produce variation in the accounts that are rendered. Often this will reflect differences in emphasis. This is not necessarily a sign of the method's failure but of its complexity; as with other methods, efforts to obtain inter-subjective reliability among observers are important.

[27]This is the same claim that many students of the U. S. Congress have made over the years.

[28]Taylor proposes an interesting test of the utility of an interpretation when he writes, "We make sense of action when there is a coherence between the actions of the agent and the meaning of his situation for him" (1985: 24).

[29]The term psychocultural brings together the psychological processes central to the construction of these interpretations and cultural dynamics, emphasizing that these orientations are not just personal but, rather, are nurtured and socially reinforced, linking individuals in a collective process, amplifying what is shared, and emphasizing differences among groups (Mack, 1983).

Psychocultural interpretations offer plausible accounts of the world, emphasizing the motives of different actors and reinforcing those features that distinguish one's own group from others. When supported by one's social world, these plausible accounts offer psychic and social protection from the ambiguities and uncertainties of existence, reinforcing social and political bonds within groups. The power of psychocultural interpretations lies in their shared social character, not those idiosyncratic features that distinguish one person's account from another's. As Taylor writes, "They are not subjective meanings, the property of one or some individuals, but rather inter-subjective meanings which are constitutive of the social matrix in which individuals find themselves and act" (1985: 36).

At the core of psychocultural interpretations are internalized, shared orientations rooted in the earliest social relationships that help people in a culture make sense of the inherently ambiguous, highly charged events that characterize their lives (Ross 1995). Psychocultural interpretations draw attention not just to what people do to each other but also to what one group of people think or feel that another group of people are doing, trying to do, or wanting to do. In a context of suspicion and uncertainty, not only actions but also presumptions about the intentions and meanings behind the actions (or inactions) play an important role. This is crucial, for in few political situations do external events provide clear explanations for what is occurring; to develop these, individuals turn to internal frameworks which then shape subsequent behavior.

While participants in any dispute can often tell someone "just what the conflict is about," this precision is often illusory, and political scientists often see this as evidence of flawed decision making and/or faulty information processing. However, it is more useful to view these "errors" as important data about the social dynamics. In many situations, different parties don't always agree about what a conflict is about, when it started, or who is involved, for they operate from (but are not aware of) alternative frames of references that shape their actions. Many disputes, whether they are between families in a community or nations in the world, involve parties with a long history, which, of course, includes long lists of accumulated grievances that can be trotted out and appended to newer ones as political conditions shift (Scott 1985). In many situations, complex conflicts are about a range of issues that are not of equal interest to all parties. For example, Hager (1995) offers a particularly clear case in her examination of conflict in West Berlin over energy policy, which she examines in terms of both the public policy considerations and the democratization issues concerning the legitimation of citizen roles in decision making on technologically complex matters. Decision makers saw the issues as technical ones needing conflict management, while citizen groups emphasized the legitimation of citizen participation in decision making.

The same factors that push actors to make sense of a situation also lead to cognitive and perceptual distortion, because the desire for certainty is often greater than the capacity for accuracy. Not only are disputants likely to make systematic errors in the "facts" underlying interpretations, but the homogeneous nature of most social settings and cultural amplifiers reinforces these self-serving mistakes. What is most crucial, however, about interpretations of politics is the compelling, coherent account they offer to the parties in linking discrete events to general understandings. Central to such interpretations is the attribution of motives to parties. Once identified, the existence of such motives seemingly makes it easy to "predict" another's future actions, and through one's own behavior to turn such predictions into self-fulfilling prophesies. In this sense, it is appropriate to suggest that rather than thinking about particular objective events that cause conflicts to escalate, we ought to be thinking about the *interpretations* of such events that are associated with escalation and those that are not.[30]

Psychocultural interpretations are found in the stories parties recount about past experiences, present difficulties, and future aspirations. These accounts are valuable for revealing how participants think about and characterize their political worlds. In fact, as we listen to them it is important to consider the extent to which stories from different groups or factions differ without necessarily directly contradicting each other, as each selects key events in its effort to gain supporters and to make sense of its actual experience (Scott 1985).[31]

This can be seen vividly in stories about long-standing ethnic conflicts that contain the culturally rooted aspirations, challenges, and deepest fears of communities. Volkan (1988) uses the term "chosen trauma" to refer to a specific experience that comes to symbolize a group's deepest threats and fears through feelings of helplessness and victimization (1991: 13). Volkan and his collaborators provide many examples of such events including the Turkish slaughter of Armenians, the Nazi holocaust, the experience of slavery and segregation for African Americans, and the Serbian defeat at Kosovo by the Turks in 1389.[32] If a group feels too humiliated, angry or helpless to mourn the losses suffered in the trauma, Volkan suggests that it then incorporates the emotional meaning of the traumatic event into its identity and passes on the emotional and symbolic meaning from generation to generation.[33] In escalating intergroup conflicts, the key metaphors, such as the chosen trauma, serve both as a rallying point and as a way to make sense of events that evoke deep fears and threats to existence (Horowitz

---

[30]While there is no room to develop the point here, it is important to understand that in contemporary society, the media become politically significant as creators and interpreters of events (Dayan and Katz 1992: 83).

[31]For example in Northern Ireland, Protestant Unionists find great meaning in the story of William of Orange and the Battle of the Boyne in 1689, while Catholic accounts really say little about King Billy or the battle. In contrast, Catholic Nationalists emphasize the meaning of the 1916 Easter Uprising, which for Protestants is far less significant than their sacred pact committing themselves to resist Irish self-rule four years earlier. Even when an event enters into the stories of both sides, such as the Hunger Strikes of Nationalist prisoners in 1980–81, the metaphors and meanings associated with them can be so different that it is hard to realize one is hearing about the same events in two different ways.

[32]See the special issue of *Mind and Human Interaction* (1992) devoted to the question of ethnic and nationalistic traumas, and Volkan (1996) for a discussion of the meaning of Kosovo for Serbs.

[33]The flip side is the *chosen glory* in which a group perceives triumph over the enemy; this is seen clearly in the Northern Irish Protestant celebration of the Battle of the Boyne in 1689 every July 12 (Cecil 1993).

1985; Kelman 1978; 1987). Only when the deep-seated threats these stories represent are addressed, he suggests, is a community able to begin to formulate a more peaceful future with its enemies.

Psychocultural interpretations reflect but also strengthen the boundary between in-groups and out-groups. The process of telling and listening to – validating[34] if you will – stories of past traumas and glories strengthens the link between individual and group identity and emphasizes how threats to the group are also threats to individual group members. In long-term intransigent conflict, strong threats to identity are an essential part of the conflict dynamic, and any efforts to defuse such a situation must take seriously the stories that participants recount, and the perceived threats to identity. The point, after all, is not whether participants' accounts are true or false from some objective point of view but that they are meaningful to the parties involved.

Interpretations play a central role in the construction of ethnic and national identities (Anderson 1991; Brubaker 1996; Gellner 1983; Hobsbawm and Ranger 1983; Smith 1986; Tambiah 1986). The examination of interpretations over time is a tool for understanding the contested nature of history and for discerning how one account comes to be accepted as "what really happened" while other plausible stories of the past are rejected. Interpretations of the past are found in how people talk and write about it but are also found in the public rituals and myths built around key events in the national (or ethnic) past. The rituals and myths are significant because of the meanings and metaphors surrounding a group's history that they communicate and reinforce, and because of the political mobilizing potential they have in the hands of political entrepreneurs.

Interpretations As a Methodological Tool

At the core of cultural analyses of politics are people's accounts of their daily worlds. Comparative researchers of all persuasions easily recognize many of the forms in which such accounts appear, such as formal written materials, historical documents, public discourse, government records, law cases, systematic observations, and survey data. In addition, the rich accounts often needed in cultural analysis can only be obtained through ethnographic field research (Laitin 1988; Ross and Ross 1974); in-depth interviews and life histories; structured interviews; extended case analysis of trouble cases; popular culture (Merelman 1991); and public and semipublic myths and rituals. Certainly the process analysis Migdal, Tarrow, and Zuckerman all advocate in their chapters (this volume) is central to cultural analysis with its emphasis on interpretations.

The central goal of the culture as a meaning and identity perspective is to understand from the point of view of actors in a particular context why certain

---

[34]What is validated is the meaning of a story to participants on each side. This does not necessarily mean the acceptance of such accounts as accurate. The notion of empathy is useful here. It suggests an acceptance of the account as meaningful to the recounter without necessarily implying agreement on the part of the listener.

actions are undertaken and others are not. What this entails is developing a plausible account – and in the process examining rival accounts of action and showing why they are not as good. There can be a huge gap, however, between the elements in the stories actors offer and how a comparativist understands political action, just as there is a great difference between the content of a patient's dreams and the psychoanalyst's interpretation of how the elements fit together and the dreams' overall significance. Bridging the two requires calling on cultural understandings and building interpretations that both make sense to cultural insiders and can be appreciated by outsiders.[35]

With a few rare exceptions, the most successful work linking culture and politics will not rely on only one source of data or a single tool for data analysis. Our most interesting theories are complex and highly contingent and cannot be simply accepted or rejected on the basis of one crucial piece of evidence, as is the case in some natural sciences. Instead, we need to obtain areas of convergence between independent data collected using a wide range of methods in order to have confidence in a set of findings, as Campbell and Fiske (1959) advocated. Exclusive reliance on one type of data to study the interplay of culture and politics, as is found in some survey researchers such as Inglehart (1988), inevitably produces a thin, almost content-free sense of culture and points to few dynamics of how culture produces the political effects it does. Instead, a more useful approach is one such as Scott's (1985) or Laitin's (1986; 1995a) in which a range of evidence is marshaled to explain a phenomenon that is not self-evident: the presence of everyday, but not overt, resistance among third-world peasants; the absence of bitter conflict between Christians and Moslems in western Nigeria; or why in Spain, the Basque revival has been violent while under very similar circumstances, the Catalonian one was not. Another successful instance of bringing together a range of data is Merelman's (1991) comparison of liberal democratic cultures in the United States, Britain, and Canada, which analyzes television programs, corporate publications, textbooks, and magazine ads along with survey data.

CONCLUSION

Culture is a worldview offering a shared account of action and its meaning and providing people with social and political identities; it is manifested in a way of life transmitted (with changes and modifications) over time, and embodied in a community's institutions, values, and behavioral regularities. Politics, I have argued, occurs in a cultural context that links individual and collective identities,

---

[35]Carol Hager (personal communication) suggests that critical theory provides a set of guidelines for the empirical study of interpretations in political research with its attention to communication processes and concerns with the problems of mediating between a researcher's own interpretations and those of the people being studied.

defines the boundaries between groups and organized actions within and between them, provides a framework for interpreting the actions and motives of others, and provides resources for political organization and mobilization. Cultural accounts of politics emphasize how, through shared intersubjective meanings, actors understand and act in their daily worlds. Beginning with context-dependent accounts – worldviews – cultural analysis constructs plausible interpretations of political life that both seem reasonable to local actors and make sense to outsiders.[36]

I have argued for a "strong" view of culture and against the notion that it can be more simply approached in terms of specific values that people in a community hold. In fact, the significance of the presence or absence of consensus on any single item is often unclear without an analysis of the context. Culture as a system of meaning is not at all incompatible with strong disagreement on particular attitudes (Laitin 1988), and it is often those points of disagreement that are of real political significance and shed light on "tough" problems facing a society. For example, the bitter divisions in some European countries over questions such as the treatment of immigrants or further European political or economic integration are powerful points of tension involving complicated, alternative cultural constructions of what it means to be French or German or British. As a result, a cultural analysis might utilize survey data to document the nature of divisions in a country on these questions, but it would go a good deal further, trying to make sense of why and how they are important to people, the connections between these issues and political and personal identity, and the significance of bitterly contested political meanings and actions within a common cultural framework.

In principle, cultural analysis can enhance our understanding of politics in a number of domains. McAdam, Tarrow, and Tilly (this volume) describe important cultural contributions in the field of contentious politics and offer a model of how structural, interest, and cultural perspectives can complement each other in explaining significant political phenomena. Seeing social movements as both carriers and makers of meaning, they suggest, enriches older, more developed structural and resource mobilization perspectives. Cultural analyses emphasize framing of action and increase our understanding of the definition of political opportunities and the repertoires of action that are found in different settings. A focus on narrative structuring and symbolic politics expands our capacity to explain collective action in terms of changing preferences, changing identities, and changing responses to resources (Brysk 1995: 567)

---

[36]The issue of how local actors react to an interpretation has several components. One is the extent to which they or the social scientist have provided it. If it is the latter, to what extent do they see it as plausible? Another issue is how local actors react to a social scientist's interpretation. For example, Nancy Scheper-Hughes (1982: v-xi), writing about the severe personal and social dysfunctionality associated with the very high rates of schizophrenia in rural Ireland, reports how upset villagers were with her book describing this pattern. Interestingly, they didn't say she was wrong; rather, they chastised her for making public what were regarded locally as private matters.

Attention to culture would certainly address one of the most widely cited weaknesses of rational choice theory, its inattention to context-specific interests and cross-cultural differences in how interests are conceptualized and articulated. More broadly, political economy might be an area that would benefit from more explicit attention to cultural questions, as Hall (this volume) suggests. For example, political economists have long documented differences in equality of resource distribution across countries, noting places like Scandinavia and Sri Lanka where inequalities are relatively low. While there is a certain amount of lip service paid to "cultural differences" in these cases, a more profound analysis would inquire into cultural conceptions of social justice, linked fate, and perhaps the relationship between the individual and the collectivity. Similarly, there are probably strong cultural factors involved in explaining cross-national differences in the locus of decision making and control over the economy. Where economic theory would emphasize efficiency, it may be that culture is much more salient in determining not only how a country resolves such an issue but also how it implements economic and political programs.

Political institutions are another obvious candidate for more culturally oriented research, although such studies are certainly not totally absent. Many students of American legislatures, for example, have found culture particularly helpful in explaining their internal operation (Matthews 1962; Muir 1982). The "folkways" of the U. S. Senate that Matthews identifies to explain its functioning in the 1950s are both specific norms affecting any individual senator's behavior and also a system that cannot simply be understood in terms of its individual elements or the degree to which any senator thinks a particular norm is appropriate. Similarly, as Crozier (1964) demonstrated so effectively, culture can shape the behavior of both public and private bureaucracies, and a cultural model sharply contrasts with explanations derived from a more universal, rational-actor, bureaucratic routinization model.

Finally, conflict is cultural behavior, since culture shapes what people fight about, how they fight, with whom they fight, and how the conflict ends (Avruch 1991; Ross 1993b). Both group goals and group actions are linked to cultural notions of appropriate behavior in the development and pursuit of goals. As a result, culturally shared rules can guide behavior even in the absence of strong institutions to enforce them. Conflict involves both the pursuit of culturally defined competing interests and the parties' divergent interpretations and threats to identity. These interpretations offer alternative metaphors about what is at stake in a conflict and the intensity of the dispute. Only when we examine the cultural meanings from the point of view of the participants can we make sense of why any conflict took the particular course it did.

REFERENCES

Almond, Gabriel A. 1980. "The Intellectual History of the Civic Culture Concept." In Gabriel A. Almond and Sidney Verba, eds., *The Civil Culture Revisited.* Boston: Little Brown.

Almond, Gabriel A., and Sidney Verba. 1963. *The Civic Culture: Political Attitudes and Democracy in Five Nations.* Princeton: Princeton University Press.

Almond, Gabriel A., and G. Bingham Powell. 1966 *Comparative Politics: A Developmental Approach.* Boston: Little Brown.

Anderson, Benedict. 1991. *Imagined Communities: Reflections on the Origin and Spread of Nationalism.* London and New York: Verso.

Arendt, Hannah. 1958. "What Is Authority?" In Karl Friedrich, ed., *Nomos I: Authority.* Cambridge: Harvard University Press.

Avruch, Kevin. 1991. "Introduction: Culture and Conflict Resolution." In Kevin Avruch, Peter W. Black, and Joseph A. Scimecca, eds., *Conflict Resolution: Cross-Cultured Perspectives.* New York: Greenwood Press.

Banfield, Edward C. 1958. *The Moral Basis of a Backward Society.* New York: Free Press.

Barkun, Michael. 1968. *Law Without Sanctions: Order in Primitive Societies and the World Community.* New Haven: Yale University Press.

Barth Fredrik, ed. 1969. *Ethnic Groups and Boundaries.* Boston: Little Brown.

Bates, Robert H. 1983. "The Centralization of African Societies," In Robert H. Bates, *Essays on the Political Economy of Rural Africa.* New York: Cambridge University Press.

Benedict, Ruth. 1934. *Patterns of Culture.* Boston: Houghton Mifflin.

———. 1946. *The Chrysanthemum and the Sword.* Boston: Houghton Mifflin.

Berger, Bennett M. 1995 *An Essay on Culture: Symbolic Structure and Social Structure.* Berkeley and Los Angeles: University of California Press.

Brubaker, Rogers. 1996. *Nationalism Reframed: Nationhood and the National Question in the New Europe.* Cambridge: Cambridge University Press.

Brysk, Alison. 1995. "'Hearts and Minds': Bringing Symbolic Politics Back In." *Polity* 27:559-85.

Campbell, Donald T. 1983. "Two Distinct Routes Beyond Kin Selection to Ultrasociality: Implications for the Humanities and Social Sciences." In D. L. Bridgeman, ed., *The Nature of Prosocial Development: Theories and Strategies.* New York: Academic Press.

Campbell, D. T., and D. W. Fiske. 1959. "Convergent and Discriminant Validation through the Multitrait-Mulitmethod Matrix." *Psychological Bulletin.* 56:81-105.

Cecil, Roseanne. (1993). "The Marching Season in Northern Ireland: An Expression of Politico-Religious Identity." In Sharon Macdonald, ed., *Inside European Identities: Ethnography in Western Europe.* Ann Arbor: Berg Publishers.

Chagnon, Napoleon. 1967. "Yanomamo Social Organization and Warfare." In Morton Fried, Marvin Harris, and Robert Murphy, eds., *War: The Anthropology of Armed Conflict and Aggression.* Garden City, NY: Natural History Press.

Cohen, Abner. 1969. *Custom and Politics in Urban Africa.* Berkeley and Los Angeles: University of California Press.

———. 1974. *Two-Dimensional Man: An Essay on the Anthropology of Power and Symbolism in Complex Society.* Berkeley and Los Angeles: University of California Press.

———.1981. *The Politics of Elite Culture.* Berkeley and Los Angeles: University of California Press.

Cohen, Raymond. 1990. *Culture and Conflict in Egyptian-Israeli Relations.* Bloomington: Indiana University Press.

———. 1991. *Negotiating Across Cultures: Communication Obstacles in International Diplomacy.* Washington, D.C.: USIP Press.

Crozier, Michael. 1964. *The Bureaucratic Phenomenon.* Chicago: University of Chicago Press.

D'Andrade, Roy G. 1984. "Cultural Meaning Systems." In Richard A. Schweder and Robert A. LeVine, eds., *Culture Theory: Essays on Mind, Self, and Emotion.* Cambridge: Cambridge University Press.

———. (1992). "Schemas and Motivation." In Roy G. D'Andrade and Claudia Strauss, eds., *Human Motives and Cultural Models.* Cambridge: Cambridge University Press.

D'Andrade, Roy G., and Claudia Strauss. 1992. *Human Motives and Cultural Models.* Cambridge: Cambridge University Press.

Darnton, Robert. 1985. *The Great Cat Massacre and Other Episodes in French Cultural History.* New York: Basic Books.

Dayan, Daniel, and Elihu Katz. 1992. *Media Events: The Live Broadcasting of History.* Cambridge and London: Harvard University Press.

Easton, David. 1959. "Political Anthropology." In Bernard J. Siegel, ed.. *Biennial Review of Anthropology.* Stanford: Stanford University Press.

Eckstein, Harry F. 1988. "A Culturalist Theory of Political Change." *American Political Science Review* 82:789-804.

Edelman, Murray J. 1964. *The Symbolic Uses of Politics.* Urbana: University of Illinois Press.

———. 1988. *Constructing the Political Spectacle.* Chicago and London: University of Chicago Press.

Edgerton, Robert B. 1992. *Sick Societies: Challenging the Myth of Primitive Harmony.* New York: Free Press.

Ekman, Paul, Wallace V. Friesen, and Phoebe Ellsworth. 1972. *Emotion in the Human Face.* Elmsford, NY: Pergamon Press.

Epstein, A. L. 1958. *Politics in an African Urban Community.* Manchester: Manchester University Press.

Fleron, Fredric L. Jr. 1996. "Post-Soviet Political Culture in Russia: An Assessment of Recent Empirical Investigations." *Europe-Asia Studies* 48.

Fortes, M., and E. E. Evans-Pritchard. 1940. *African Political Systems.* Oxford: Oxford University Press.

Friedrich, Carl J., with Morton Horwitz. 1968. "The Relation of Political Theory to Anthropology." *American Political Science Review* 52:536-45.

Geertz, Clifford. 1973a. "Thick Description: Toward an Interpretive Theory of Culture." In Clifford Geertz, *The Interpretation of Cultures.* New York: Basic Books, Harper Torchbooks.

———. 1973b. "Religion as a Cultural System." In Clifford Geertz, *The Interpretation of Cultures.* New York: Basic Books, Harper Torchbooks.

Gellner, Ernest. 1983. *Nations and Nationalism.* Ithaca: Cornell University Press.

Gluckman, Max. 1942. *Analysis of a Social Situation in Modern Zululand.* Manchester: Manchester University Press.

Goode, Judith, and Joanne A. Schneider. 1994. *Reshaping Ethnic and Racial Relations in Philadelphia: Immigrants in a Divided City.* Philadelphia: Temple University Press.

Goody, Jack. 1966. *Succession to High Office.* Cambridge: Cambridge University Press.

Gorer, Geoffrey, and John Rickman. 1946. *The People of Great Russia.* London: Cresset Press.

Greif, Avner. 1994. "Cultural Beliefs and the Organization of Society: A Historical and Theoretical Reflection on Collectivist and Individualist Societies." *Journal of Political Economy* 102:912-50.

Gusfield, Joseph R. 1966. *Symbolic Crusade: Status Politics and the American Temperance Movement.* Urbana and London: University of Illinois Press.

Hager, Carol J. 1995. *Technological Democracy: Bureaucracy and Citizenry in the German Energy Debate.* Ann Arbor: University of Michigan Press.

Hobsbawm, Eric, and Terrence Ranger. 1983. *The Invention of Tradition.* Cambridge: Cambridge University Press.

Horowitz, Donald L. 1985. *Ethnic Groups in Conflict.* Berkeley and Los Angeles: University of California Press.

Huntington, Samuel P. 1993. "The Clash of Civilizations." *Foreign Affairs* 22-49.

Inglehart, Ronald. 1977. *The Silent Revolution in Europe: Changing Values and Political Styles Among Western Publics.* Princeton: Princeton University Press.

———. 1988. "The Renaissance of Political Culture." *American Political Science Review* 82: 1203-30.

Inkeles, Alex, and David J. Levinson. 1968. "National Character; The Study of Modal Personality and Sociocultural Systems." In G. Lindzey, ed., *Handbook of Social Psychology,* Vol II. Cambridge: Addison Wesley.

Kelman, Herbert C. 1978. "Israelis and Palestinians: Psychological Prerequisites for Mutual Acceptance." *International Security* 3:162-86.

———. 1987. "The Political Psychology of the Israeli-Palestinian Conflict: How Can We Overcome the Barriers to a Negotiated Solution?" *Political Psychology* 8:347-63.

Kertzer, David I. 1988. *Ritual, Politics and Power.* New Haven and London: Yale University Press.

Kohli, Atul et al. 1995. "The Role of Theory in Comparative Politics: A Symposium." *World Politics* 48: 1-49.

Kroeber, A. L., and Clyde Kluckholm. 1952. *Culture: A Critical Review of Concepts and Definitions.* Papers of the Peabody Museum of American Archeology and Ethnology, 47, No. 1.

Kuper Adam, and Audrey Richards, eds. 1971. *Councils in Action.* Cambridge: Cambridge University Press.

Kurtz, Donald V. 1991. "Strategies of Legitimation and the Aztec State." In Frank McGlynn and Arthur Tuden, eds., *Anthropological Approaches to Political Behavior.* Pittsburgh: University of Pittsburgh Press.

Laitin, David D. 1986. *Hegemony and Culture: Politics and Religious Change among the Yoruba.* Chicago: University of Chicago Press.

———. 1988. "Political Culture and Political Preferences." *American Political Science Review* 82:589-93.

————. 1995a. "National Revivals and Violence." *Archives Europeennes de Sociologie.* 36:3-43.

————. 1995b. "The Civic Culture at 30." *American Political Science Review* 89:168-73.

LeVine, Robert A. 1973. *Culture, Behavior and Personality.* Chicago: Aldine.

————. 1984. "Properties of Culture: An Ethnographic View." In Richard A. Schweder and Robert A. LeVine, eds., *Culture Theory: Essays on Mind, Self, and Emotion.* Cambridge: Cambridge University Press.

Levinson, David, and Martin J. Malone. 1981. *Toward Explaining Human Culture: A Critical Review of the Findings of Worldwide Cross-Cultural Research.* New Haven: HRAF Press.

Mack, John. 1983. "Nationalism and the Self." *Psychohistory Review* 2:47-69.

Masters, Roger D. 1964. "World Politics as a Primitive Political System." *World Politics* 16:595-619.

Masters Roger D., and Denis G. Sullivan. 1989. "Nonverbal Displays and Political Leadership in France and the United States." *Political Behavior* 11:121-53.

Matthews, Donald R. 1962. *US Senators and Their World.* New York: Norton.

McClelland, David C. 1961. *The Achieving Society.* Princeton: Van Nostrand.

Mead, Margaret. 1942. *And Keep Your Powder Dry.* New York: Morrow.

Merelman, Richard M. 1991. *Partial Visions: Culture and Politics in Britain, Canada, and the United States.* Madison: University of Wisconsin Press.

Mitchell, J. C. 1956. *The Kalela Dance: Aspects of Social Relationships among Urban Africans in Northern Rhodesia.* Rhodes-Livingstone Institute Papers No. 27. Manchester: Manchester University Press.

Muir, William K. Jr. 1982. *Legislature: California's School for Politics.* Chicago: University of Chicago Press.

Mulvihill, Robert F., Marc Howard Ross, and Victor L. Schermer. 1995. "Psychocultural Interpretations of Ethnic Conflict in Northern Ireland: Family and Group Systems Contributions." In Mark F. Ettin, Jay W. Fidler, and Bertrom D. Cohen, eds., *Group Process and Political Dynamics.* Madison, CT: International Universities Press.

Murdock, George Peter. 1949. *Social Structure.* New York: The Free Press.

Murray, Henry C. 1938. *Explorations In Personality.* New York: Oxford University Press.

Naroll, Raoul. 1970. "What Have We Learned from Cross-Cultural Surveys?" *American Anthropologist.* 72:1227-88.

Paige, Karen Eriksen, and Jeffrey M. Paige. 1981. *The Politics of Reproductive Ritual.* Berkeley and Los Angeles: University of California Press.

Pospisil, Leonard. 1971. *The Anthropology of Law: A Comparative Theory.* New York: Harper & Row.

Przeworski, Adam, and Henry Teune. 1970. *The Logic of Comparative Social Research.* New York: John Wiley.

Putnam, Robert D. 1993. *Making Democracy Work: Civic Traditions in Modern Italy.* Princeton: Princeton University Press.

Pye, Lucien D. 1962. *Politics, Personality and Nation Building: Burma's Search for Identity.* New Haven: Yale University Press.

————. 1991. "Political Culture Revisited." *Political Psychology* 12:487-508.

Regan, Patrick M. 1994. "War Toys, War Movies and the Militarization of the United States, 1900–85." *Journal of Peace Research.* 31:45-58.

Ross, Jennie-Keith, and Marc Howard Ross. (1974). "Participant Observation in Political Research." *Political Methodology.* 1:63-88.

Ross, Marc Howard. 1986. "Female Political Participation: A Cross-Cultural Explanation.: *American Anthropologist* 88:843-58.

―――. 1988. "Studying Politics Cross-Culturally: Key Concepts and Issues." *Behavior Science Research* 22:105-29.

―――. 1993a. *The Culture of Conflict: Interpretations and Interests in Comparative Perspective.* New Haven and London: Yale University Press.

―――. 1993b. *The Management of Conflict: Interpretations and Interests in Comparative Perspective.* New Haven and London: Yale University Press.

―――. 1995. "Psychocultural Interpretation Theory and Peacemaking in Ethnic Conflicts." *Political Psychology.* 16:523-44.

―――. 1997. "Cultural Contributions to the Study of Political Psychology and Ethnic Conflict." *Political Psychology* 18:299-326.

Ross, Marc Howard, and Homer, Elizabeth L. 1976. "Galton's Problem in Cross-National Research." *World Politics* 24:1-28.

Scheper-Hughes, Nancy. 1982. *Saints, Scholars and Schizophrenics: Mental Illness in Rural Ireland.* Berkeley and Los Angeles: University of California Press.

Schweder, Richard A., and Robert A. LeVine, eds. 1984. *Culture Theory: Essays on Mind, Self, and Emotion.* Cambridge: Cambridge University Press.

Scott, James C. 1985. *Weapons of the Weak: Everyday Forms of Peasant Resistance.* New Haven: Yale University Press

Shils, Edward, and Michael Young. 1953. "The Meaning of the Coronation." *Sociological Quarterly* 1:63-81.

Smith, Anthony D. 1986. *The Ethnic Origin of Nations.* Oxford: Basil Blackwell.

Spiro, Melford E. 1984. "Some Reflections on Cultural Determinism and Relativism with Special Reference to Emotion and Reason." In Richard A. Schweder and Robert A. LeVine, eds.. *Culture Theory: Essays on Mind, Self, and Emotion.* Cambridge: Cambridge University Press.

―――. 1987. "Culture and Human Nature." In *Culture and Human Nature: Theoretical Papers of Melford E. Spiro.* Chicago: University of Chicago Press.

Strauss, Claudia. 1992. "Models and Motives." In Roy G. D'Andrade and Claudia Strauss, eds. *Human Motives and Cultural Models.* Cambridge: Cambridge University Press.

Tambiah, Stanley Jeyaraja. 1986. *Sri Lanka: Ethnic Fratricide and the Dismantling of Democracy.* London: I. B. Tauris.

Tarrow, Sidney. 1996. "Making Social Science Work Across Space and Time: A Critical Reflection on Robert Putnam's *Making Democracy Work.*" *American Political Science Review* 90:389-97.

Taylor, Charles. 1985. "Interpretation and the Sciences of Man." In *Philosophy and the Human Sciences, 2.* Cambridge: Cambridge University Press.

Thompson, Michael, Richard Ellis, and Aaron Wildavsky. 1990. *Culture Theory.* Boulder: Westview Press.

Tilly, Charles. 1986. *The Contentious French: Four Centuries of Popular Struggle.* Cambridge: Harvard University Press.

―――. 1995. "Contentious Repertoires in Great Britain, 1758–1834." In M. Traugott, ed. *Repertories and Cycles of Collective Action.* Durham and London: Duke University Press.

Traugott, Mark, ed. 1995. *Repertories and Cycles of Collective Action*. Durham and London: Duke University Press.

Turner, John C. 1988. *Rediscovering the Social Group: A Self-Categorization Theory*. Oxford: Basil Blackwell.

Turner, Victor. 1957. *Schism and Continuity in an African Society*. Manchester: Manchester University Press.

———. 1968. "Mukanda: The Politics of a Non-Political Ritual." In Marc J. Swartz, ed., *Local-level politics*. Chicago: Aldine.

Verba, Sidney. 1980. "On Revisiting the Civic Culture: A Personal Postscript." In Gabriel A. Almond and Sidney Verba, eds., *The Civil Culture Revisited*. Boston: Little, Brown.

Verba, Sidney, Norman Nie, and Jue-on Kim. 1978. *Participation and Political Equality: A Seven-Nation Comparison*. Cambridge: Cambridge University Press.

Volkan, Vamik D. 1988. *The Need to Have Enemies and Allies: From Clinical Practice to International Relationships*. New York: Jason Aronson.

———. 1991. "On Chosen Trauma." *Mind and Human Interaction* 3:13.

———. 1996. "Bosnia-Herzegovina: Ancient Fuel of a Modern Inferno." *Mind and Human Interaction* 7:110-27.

Wallace, Anthony F. C. 1970. *Culture and Personality*. Second Ed. New York: Random House.

Weber, Eugen. 1976. *Peasants into Frenchmen: The Modernization of Rural France, 1870–1914*. Stanford: Stanford University Press

Whiting, Beatrice Blythe. 1980. "Culture and Social Behavior: A Model for the Development of Social Behavior." *Ethos* 8:95-116.

Wildavsky, Aaron. 1987. "Choosing Preference by Constructing Institutions: A Cultural Theory of Preference Formation." *American Political Science Review* 81:3-21.

4

STRUCTURE AND CONFIGURATION IN COMPARATIVE POLITICS

Ira Katznelson

By 1968, the year *Comparative Politics* was founded, the subfield had begun to change beyond recognition. The new journal marked, and sought to promote, this transition by promising to advance comparative politics as a constitutive part of behavioral political science. Taking note of the "reorientation of the discipline" since the Second World War, the editors explained they were motivated to transcend the older "country-by-country approach whose conclusions are discrete rather than cumulative." Announcing "skepticism about the value of institutional and legal analysis," they bemoaned the insufficient application of "the scientific method" and the neglect of such analytical tools as structural functionalism and political systems analysis and of such concepts as consensus, role, and socialization (Brown, Herz, and Rogow 1968: 1).

In 1986, *Studies in American Political Development,* a journal devoted to "the revival of scholarship on American institutions and the related turn by political scientists to history," arrived on the scene. The inaugural issue's preface explained that history is "the natural proving ground for the claim that institutions have an independent and formative influence on politics" and that history also "provides the dimension necessary for understanding institutions as they operate under varying conditions" (Orren and Skowronek 1986, vii). With the exception of this last phrase, there was no explicit mention of what was, in effect, the journal's central goal: to promote constructions of the American case via the pathway of historical institutionalism as a unit in the study of comparative politics. Long segregated as if epistemologically distinctive, American political studies, the editors clearly hoped, now would become part of a broader comparative enterprise. Though there had been important exceptions such as the deployment of the United States as one of the five cases in Almond and Verba's analytic study of political culture and chapters by Huntington on America's Tudor polity and by Hollingsworth on American political development in the last volume of the Comparative Politics series, by and large the American case had been excised from the universe of comparative political studies (Almond and Verba 1963; Huntington 1968; Hollingsworth 1978). After all, most students of American politics at least tacitly accepted as givens Hartz's portrait of liberal nondevelopment and "the relative statelessness of the United States" (Hartz 1955; Nettl 1968: 561).

But the editors of *Studies* did not seek to affiliate with the variable-centered comparative politics of the earlier journal. As their own work made clear (especially Skowronek's *Building a New American State,* which had demonstrated a close affinity with the state-centered project of the Social Science Research Committee on States and Social Structures) and as the title of the new publication itself signified (deliberately echoing, one assumes, the name "Studies in Political Development" of the nine-volume series sponsored from the early 1960s to the mid-1970s by the earlier SSRC Committee on Comparative Politics), the editors were particularly drawn to a more structural, historical, and macroanalytical style of comparative politics capable of discerning and explaining regime characteristics and jumbo changes, the kind of historical macroanalysis Charles Tilly was then calling "big structures, large processes, huge comparisons" (Tilly 1984). Equally clear was the editors' desire to reestablish political, especially state, structures and institutions at the center of research.

This influential attempt to cross subdisciplinary boundaries had rather more in mind than the behavioral revolution in comparative politics, especially when it was clothed in antiinstitutionalist garb. If the editors of *Comparative Politics* saluted "the ready availability of a stock of analytic categories developed primarily by sociologists" (Brown, Herz, and Rogow 1968: 1), the editors of *Studies,* looked mainly to a different sociological lineage. During the 1960s and 1970s, a remarkable group of audacious comparative-historical investigations, mainly written by political sociologists who grounded their work in the structural, historical, and organizational materialism of Karl Marx and Max Weber, constituted a research program and convened a bounded epistemic conversation that utterly had transformed the potential scope, ambition, and content of comparative politics. Turning the study of postfeudal modernity away from the realms of description and metaphysics, the treatments of immense historical change by scholars including Perry Anderson, Reinhard Bendix, Shmuel Eisenstadt, Samuel Huntington, Barrington Moore, Stein Rokkan, Theda Skocpol, Charles Tilly, Louise Tilly, and Immanuel Wallerstein, for all their considerable differences of theoretical genealogy and emphasis,[1] shared in the effort to elaborate on those lo-

---

[1]Their work was influenced by and overlapped in a nontrivial way with the more behavioral and process-oriented projects of *Comparative Politics* and the publications of the SSRC Committee on Comparative Politics; but their conceptual orientation, analytical foci, and ways of working nonetheless were distinctive.

cations where large-scale processes (including differentiation, state-building, war, capitalism, industrialization, urbanization, and cross-border flows of ideas, people, capital, and goods) and institutions (understood both as congeries of rules for cooperation, commitment, and conflict resolution and as formal organizations) actually meet (Anderson 1974a, 1974b; Bendix 1964, 1978; Moore 1966; Rokkan 1970; Skocpol 1979; Tilly, Tilly and Tilly 1975; Wallerstein 1974). Though hardly unitary in theoretical terms, the main contributors to this effort did promote a broadly common mode of structural and macroanalytical inquiry combining ontological and methodological commitments geared to account for the origins and character of postfeudal modernity and to the specification of macrofoundations for human action and social change.

The power of this body of work derived from its rejection of the main alternatives in the more than century-old debate between methodological collectivists, whose favorite term is society, and methodological individualists, whose preferred locution is action. The macroanalytical turn of the 1960s and 1970s spurned both frames as inadequate to the problem of ontology. They refused "society" in the sense associated with (overly simple) readings of Durkheim: as a distinct, unitary, comprehensive, integrated, lawful patterning of social relationships and cultural understandings contained inside defined spatial borders that overweeningly limit individual cognition and behavior. They insisted, by contrast, that social life and action in particular places is shaped by processes, relationships, and forms of interaction whose scale is both greater (as in global trade or the cross-border circulation of ideas) and lesser (as in patterns of kinship or regional cultures) than any single societal container can hold. In turn, they resisted the decomposition of social relations and processes into a congeries of undersocialized individuals whose cognition and choice motors their behavior without a consideration of how structured and relational situations constrain and enable human action.[2]

Instead, the macroanalytical scholars developed a probabilistic approach to structure, wagering that the most significant processes shaping human identities, interests, and interaction are such large-scale features of modernity as capitalist development, market rationality, state-building, secularization, political and scientific revolution, and the acceleration of instruments for the communication and diffusion of ideas (Daston 1988; Hacking 1990). "Society" in this orientation is replaced by the structured concatenation of processes. These, while not determinant of behavior in any strict sense, establish in specific times and places a calculus of cognitive and behavioral probabilities by creating situational orders within which individuals think, interact, and choose. Persons, in this view, are embedded agents operating within relational structural fields that distinguish the possible from the impossible and the likely from the less likely.

---

[2]Put differently, they refused the choice between sociological and economic theory Brian Barry so incisively posed in *Sociologists, Economists, and Democracy* (1970).

The ambitions, achievements, and advantages of structurally directed macro-analysis based in these conceptual orientations clearly inspired the new Americanist initiative. But not without a degree of irony concerning timing or a touch of cred-ulousness regarding epistemology and method. After all, not many years later when Princeton's Center for International Studies gathered a group of leading compara-tivists to consider "The Role of Theory in Comparative Politics" (Kohli et al. 1995),[3] the capacity of this kind of macroanalysis to define the commanding heights at the center of the enterprise had come into question. The symposium's main problem was defined, as Peter Evans put it, by whether the "center that has constituted the tra-ditional core of the study of comparative politics is in danger of being overrun" (Kohli et al. 1995: 2) by two assertive initiatives, each apparently unfriendly to the field's structural, historical, and institutional legacy: the strong methodological in-dividualism of rational choice theory imported from microeconomics and game the-ory; and the postmodern turn to signification that called the field's organizational and social structural materialism into question and, even more radically, debunked causal accounts as pseudoscience. At just the moment some Americanists sought to associate their scholarship with comparative historical and institutional analysis, the theoretical energy in comparative politics was being seized, or at least claimed, by just those scholarly trajectories that had already achieved a good deal of effect with-in American studies, both in the social sciences and the humanities. Though the large majority of publications in comparative politics continues to be located be-tween the poles of choice theory deductivism and antiscience interpretivism, the en-ergy, imagination, and leadership deployed by the macroanalytical orientation in the 1960s and 1970s have dissipated to a considerable degree. Even the most novel and interesting recent works in this genre – such as Silberman's epic comparison of the rise of rational bureaucratic states in the nineteenth century, de Swaan's innovative consideration of the rise of modern welfare states (both of which incorporate the United States in their comparative ken), Downing's return to Moore's themes of the origins of democracy and dictatorship via a consideration of alternative medieval configurations and military modernization in early modern Europe, Ertman's rich but parsimonious account of variations to state-building in medieval and early mod-ern Europe, and Luebbert's coalitional analysis of the origins of liberal, social demo-cratic, and fascist regimes in interwar twentieth-century Europe – have attracted far less attention and have proved to date a good deal less influential than the books of the earlier generation (de Swaan 1988; Downing 1992; Ertman, 1997; Luebbert 1991; Silberman 1993). Yet just these texts, considered together with key works written under the rubric of American political development (Bensel 1990; Skocpol 1992; Skowronek 1993), actually promise step-wise advances to macroanalysis and an integration of this tradition with more finely focused scholarship by historical in-stitutionalists. Their relative advantage lies in their combination of the kind of con-figurative macroanalysis pioneered by Moore with the deployment of institutions as middle-level mediations between large-scale processes and the microdynamics of agency and action (Tarrow 1987).

---

[3]The meetings took place during 1993–94.

Put differently, though I identify with the new historical institutionalism which mainly has focused on comparative interest representation, public policy, and political economy and has been the most visible successor to the grand macroanalytical scholarship of the 1960s and 1970s, I want to push back against what I think has been its not an entirely welcome substantive and conceptual retrenchment. Compared to the work of their predecessors, institutionalist scholars in comparative politics have shortened their time horizons, contracted their regime questions, and narrowed the range of considered outcomes. Such a constriction, of course, is not necessarily a bad thing. The comparative historical analysis of how transactions between states and citizens and between states and economies are contingently shaped within specific assemblages of institutional legacies and arrangements (Hall 1986; Immergut 1992; Pierson 1994; Samuels 1994; and Steinmo 1993) has successfully turned policy studies away from the mundane and aseptic temptations of the overly technocratic and ahistorical policy sciences and has effectively linked empirical work to basic normative questions in the liberal tradition, above all those concerned with interest representation (Berger 1981; Schmitter and Lehmbruch 1979). The focus in these studies has turned to the manner in which the contours of institutions shape the formation and aggregation of individual and group interests as an alternative both to less mediated versions of marxist class analysis that hinge on expectations of an ineluctable shift from classes in themselves to classes for themselves and to simple behavioral stories about how action makes preferences evident and how private preferences add up to a public edifice. Unlike the postpositivist impulse of postmodernism, historical institutionalism has refused to reduce reality to signification; and unlike rational choice, it has disallowed the reduction of agency to effectively utilitarian individuals in worlds where both the content and means of rationality vary by organizational, cultural, and historical configurations.

However, whereas both rational choice and postmodernism pose insurgent alternatives to mainstream practices in comparative politics, smaller-scale historical institutionalism has proved stronger a skeptical response to their respective atomistic and anything-goes orientations and has functioned more effectively as a motivating and persuasive, though underspecified, set of claims that institutions and history matter than as a sharply etched project of the kind the earlier and more adventurous macroanalytical scholarship appeared to propel (Immergut 1996; Koelble 1995; Robertson 1993; Steinmo, Thelen, and Longstreth 1992). In some measure, this is the healthy result of taking another look at the implicit assumptions embedded inside marxist, and marxisant, historical materialism. It also is the consequence of shifting attention from extraordinary moments of regime creation and transformation to the routinized contours of normal politics in different democratic capitalist regimes. But this relocation runs the risk of detaching the two kinds of enterprises and of recusing historical-institutional work from its more assertive ambitions to create not only a historically grounded social science but a social science history capable of working with, and exploiting, the tensions inherent in their joining.

The relative empirical and theoretical restraint of recent comparative historical institutionalism has been characterized by a cautious construction of comparable cases, a continuing reliance on John Stuart Mill's method of agreement and method difference (Hammel 1980; Mill 1852; Skocpol and Somers 1980),[4] a reduction in historical sweep, and a certain disconnection with the grand macroanalytical tradition. The result has been something of a loss to the élan and potential of comparative politics, especially at the core of the enterprise. The Princeton symposium, after all, reaffirmed that what Evans called "work that draws on general theories wherever it can but also cares deeply about particular historical outcomes" and what Katzenstein described as the "thick" version of the new institutionalism "concerned with both states *and* social structures" which "looks at social sectors, political coalitions, political institutions, and ideological constraints," remains at the very heart of the most compelling efforts in the field. In her spirited defense of this "middle way," Skocpol regretted that as compared to rational choice theorists and postmodernists, "those of us who do comparativehistorical social science often do not explain adequately ... the methods we use for investigation and for the presentation of results." In particular, she had in mind the connection between analytical choices and the construction of narratives as well as the manufacture of cases to make them susceptible to systematic comparison, whether empirical or counterfactual (Kohli et al. 1995: 4, 12, 44). In part, she thus claimed, the crisis of macroanalysis is a crisis of poor exposition.

Would this were so. This defensive posture is reminiscent of politicians who blame their lack of public standing on failures of communication. The slippage of historical macroanalysis from its critical hegemonic positioning in the 1970s is, rather, more the result of a certain lack of theoretical and methodological selfconsciousness and clarity especially at a time when marxism, which in fact had done much of the intellectual work for macroanalysis, has been called into question by global events and by challenges to its essentialism, functionalism, and teleology. Marxism's integrated material, historical, and macroanalytical account of epochal change in western history; its analysis of the logic and dynamics of class structures and modern capitalism; and its attempts at holistic social theory capable of inventing causal stories about specific capitalist societies understood in their entirety and not just as economies in fact, had provided (either as a goad or in some cases as a foil) the main themes, tools, and motors for the earlier macroanalysis, much of which had taken the form of extending or revising classical marxism's hierarchical delineation of structures, processes, identities, and interests. Divorced from these resources and the analytical work they had performed, and in the absence of comparable, content-rich, structural theory, the less well-specified orientation of historical institutionalism has come to bear more theoretical weight than it can be expected to hold. As a consequence, today's his-

---

[4]Skocpol and Somers' rich essay fails to remember that Mill not only proposed methods of agreement and difference but also of residues and concomitant variation, to which I return below. His work also contains an illuminating discussion of a plurality of causes to similar outcomes.

torical-institutional scholarship confronts choice theory and postmodernism as dual threats rather than as sets of useful tools and criticisms it might confidently engage, appropriate, and incorporate.

The result has been an unfortunate, and unnecessary, abdication. This essay takes up a number of key problems that must be addressed if structural macro-analysis is to reclaim its place at the core of comparative politics; not as what Evans describes as "an eclectic messy center" (Kohli et al. 1995: 4) but as a methodologically self-conscious research program.

The most important problem is that of cases and of comparison itself (Ragin and Becker 1992). "As I see it," Skocpol avers, "comparative politics people ... should *compare* – a startling idea! – and not simply study places in the world that are not America" (Kohli et al. 1995: 38). But compare what, and how, in light of the difficulties, even inappropriateness, of experimental and quasi-experimental designs given the small number of often deeply incom-mensurable cases with which we work? Comparativists have presented four principal answers to this question: what might be called the global or large-process, case-comparative, variable-comparative, and relational answers. The first, as in Wallerstein's work on the world system, Charles Tilly's and Hendrik Spruyt's competing accounts of European state-building, or Michael Mann's multivolume study of social power (Tilly 1990; Mann 1986, 1993; Spruyt 1994), endeavors to transcend the problem of cases by focusing on the larger relations and processes of which they are a part. The second seeks by a variety of more or less self-conscious efforts to justify the selection of cases and ma-neuver to overcome the problem of too many variables and too small an N by mustering soft versions of experimental and multivariate approaches, making particular cases place markers for variables (the United States for democracy or Nazi Germany for totalitarianism, for example) (Lipjhart 1971; Collier 1991). The third, by contrast, decomposes cases into variables that are analyzed and compared via a strong application of multivariate techniques (Barnes et al. 1979; Bartolini and Mair 1990; Dalton, Flanagan, and Beck 1984; Lipset, 1960, 1983; Lipset and Rokkan 1967). The fourth incorporates the gains of es-pecially the first two inside what might be called a relational and configurative form of analysis. I proffer the advantages of such an approach, drawing pri-marily on the model of Tocqueville's *Democracy in America,* Weber's *The Method-ology of the Social Sciences,* and a fresh look at Mill's *System of Logic* (Mill, 1852; Tocqueville 1966; Weber 1979). Configurative macroanalysis, I argue, can profit from the challenges of rational choice and postmodernism without sac-rificing its distinctiveness; it can effectively deploy without overburdening the tools of historical institutionalism; and it can reclaim the normative dimension that both weberian and marxist theory placed, albeit differently, at the center of comparative political studies.

The core of the essay thus takes up issues central to this fourth approach. These include: the relationship of history and analytical social science; struc-tural theory after marxism; the special status of the state; and the question of behavioral and strategic microfoundations. The value of a configurative comparative politics can best be assayed, at least implicitly, against the counteroption considered, in effect, by the *World Politics* symposium: the colonization of comparative politics by the microanalytical and postpositivist currents increasingly important to mainstream studies of the United States, a prescription echoing the one tendered by the editors of *Comparative Politics* in 1968 who had sought to advance their subfield by making it a variant of American political studies.

THE MACROANALYTICAL HEYDAY AND ITS AFTERMATH: REMARKS ON MOORE AND SKOCPOL

The subject matter of the historical macroanalysis of the 1960s and 1970s was vast. It is not too much of an oversimplification, however, to observe that this body of work was animated by a main theme, a dominant problem, and a primary elaboration. The theme was the systematic and comparative charting of diverse trajectories from a premodern to the modern Eurocentric world fashioned between the sixteenth and nineteenth centuries and the implications of these routes for the formation of social classes and political regimes. The problem was the intertwining of state and class. The elaboration, as noted, was of marxist theory, in particular its consideration of class as history's motor and its focus on the problem of the transition from feudalism to capitalism.

The breakthrough book that transformed the objectives and aspirations of comparative historical macroanalysis undoubtedly was Barrington Moore's *Social Origins*. Though he began his comparative analysis of routes to modernity in Britain, France, the United States, China, Japan, and India with deceptively bland language – "In the effort to understand the history of a specific country a comparative perspective can lead to asking very useful and sometimes new questions. There are further advantages. Comparisons can serve as a rough negative check on accepted historical explanations. And a comparative approach may lead to new generalizations" – he set to sea fishing for a very large substantive and methodological catch (Moore 1966: xiii). His effort to chart three distinctive routes to the modern world (via bourgeois revolution, abortive revolution, and communist revolution) did far more than hold in tension "the detailed investigation of specific cases" and the attempt to construct generalizations resembling "a large-scale map of an extended terrain." It linked extraordinary moments to the subsequent contours of normal politics. It demonstrated how class analysis could unlock secrets of political regimes. It treated Asian and European cases drawn from the "developing" and "developed" worlds as comparable units of analysis. Though peopled by many kinds of agents, the book was motored primarily by structural relationships whose powerful logics shaped and constrained the identities, aspirations, and actions of the actors. It made normative questions about the role of the social sciences in quests for truth and for a less oppressive world constitutive of its analytical questions. Moore's main goal, after all, was that of identifying the unusual braiding of circumstances capable of producing relatively free and decent versions of modernity (Moore 1965: xiv).[5]

The notion of "configuration" was located at the core of this effort. Moore aimed at "specifying configurations favorable and unfavorable to the establishment of modern western democracy" (Moore 1966: xiv). He did not slice and dice his cases into variables which themselves would be compared as if they were not enclosed and entwined inside cases of dense and distinctive complexity.[6] He considered each case with sufficient detail to stand alone as an analytically constructed, historically recognizable case study. Though deployed to a comparative purpose, each also was written as a coherent (and deliberately provocative) single-country investigation. Nor did Moore treat "revolution" and "class struggle" as processes independent of time and place. Rather, he constructed and deployed a limited repertoire of developmental configurations (Lasswell 1935)[7] as the means to avoid becoming hostage either to historical detail or to rather too simple stories about historical trajectories even with respect to complex questions of historical change on a very large scale. He achieved this goal by constructing his cases to show how each was dominated by a particular configuration of class, revolution, and political regime, yet how each also contained subordinate combinations and arrangements that became primary elsewhere. The product of a great and erudite mind working on a broad but bounded canvas, Social Origins advanced scientific inquiry by way of an aesthetic triumph.

It would not be easy to overstate the significance of this book. First, it demonstrated that the impulses of classical sociology and traditional moral and political theory to tame and make sense of large-scale social and historical change had not been destroyed by the overbearingly specialized and fragmented qualities of "normal" social science. Second, in no small tension with the volumes being produced by the Committee on Comparative Politics which focused "on conceptualizing political systems, identifying their universal functions, and describing the processes of political modernization and development" by parsing what it called "the developmental syndrome" into concepts (equality, capacity, differentiation) and crises (identity, legitimacy, participation, penetration, distribution), Moore's configurative orientation exhibited both more hubris and less

[5]The language of "truth" and "configuration" is Moore's.

[6]Thus avoiding the false science noted by Zolberg in his astringent remarks directed at the work of Lipset on working class formation ("Radicalism or Reformism"): "Albeit suggestive, Lipset's approach – shared by Rokkan as well – is marred by an attempt to apply multivariate techniques to macroanalytic materials and by the imprecise and questionable character of the variables themselves. The result is a historically ridiculous universe, in which pre–World War I Britain, Germany, France, and Russia are equated as having 'rigid' and largely 'feudal' patterns of social class, as against 'nonrigid' patterns in the United States, the Low Countries, and Switzerland; and in which Britain, where one cannot speak of a mass electorate before 1882, is equated with the United States as having achieved political citizenship 'early' while the Low Countries and Russia are equated as having done so 'late'" (Zolberg 1986: 450).

[7]Too rarely is credit given to Harold Lasswell for the notion of "developmental constructs" within a configurative social science.

(Pye 1971: vi-vii). More because his historical social science was leaner, wagering on fewer central variables; but less because he insisted on a tighter fit between concepts and situations. Third, the clearly marxist character of *Social Origins* was at odds not only with the main thrust of work by authors of the SSRC "Studies in Political Development" who had sought a conceptual/behavioral foundation for macroanalysis and who had underplayed the state as an institution in order to escape the arid formalism of early twentieth-century political science (which had taken a particularly desiccated character in the comparative study of "foreign governments"), but also with two other important currents: the realist and organizational weberian orientation such émigré scholars as Reinhard Bendix had brought to the task of analyzing early modern European state formation, and the market exchange models of power and participation increasingly dominant inside political sociology and political science at the time. The effect was to empower colleagues and students to emulate and promote the kind of enterprise Moore had pursued, to provide an alternative to mainstream approaches, and to convene a variety of efforts to build up and out from the edifice of *Social Origins.*

Though *Social Origins's* identification of multiple trajectories rather than a single pathway was not marxist in any orthodox sense, it remained embedded in a mode of production historical materialism. It broke neither with marxism's focus on class struggle as the basic datum of political life nor with its causal emphasis on economic rather than cultural, political, or ideational causes (Skocpol 1973). But like other key marxist works written in this structural and comparative macroanalytical vein – especially the volumes of Anderson and Wallerstein – Moore sought to connect a materialist class analysis to alternative types of states and regime outcomes. The considerable works of 1960s and 1970s historical macroanalysis thus sought to extend from marxism to what manifestly was, together with capitalism, the second great macroprocess of modernity, the creation and development of the sovereign state and the post-Westphalian system of sovereign states. Like another important current grounded in German realism, especially Hintze and Weber, represented most notably by Bendix's *Nation-Building and Citizenship,* the more dominant marxian work also came to grapple with the dualism Bendix identified (the "system is broken up by the twin revolutions of the West – the political and the industrial") and with the conjoining of problems of class and state he pursued ("In the emerging nation-states of Western Europe the critical political problem was whether and to what extent social protest would be accommodated through the extension of citizenship to the lower classes." (Bendix 1964: 67)).

But it was Theda Skocpol, first in a powerful critique of Moore written when she was his graduate student and then in her dissertation on comparative revolutions, who most successfully created a strong *structural* macroanalysis with one foot in marxian class inquiry and another in weberian state analysis. Her work displayed the virtues of structural macroanalysis in full efflorescence, yet its tilt away from agency also projected toward a subsequent narrowing, bifurcation, and dispersion of the comparative macroanalytical impulse. It was not so much *States and Social Revolutions* that produced this set of developments but the manner in which some of its core ideas and tendencies were followed up, not least by Skocpol herself. By contrast, as we shall see, the "polity-centered" perspective of her recent *Protecting Soldiers and Mothers,* a contribution to the effort inaugurated by *Studies in American Political Development,* helps point us toward a recrudescence of the macroanalytical impulse in a more configurative mode.[8]

The gist of Skocpol's spirited critique of Moore was the insistence that an autarchic marxism, however rich and elaborated, can take us only so far. She argued that Moore's emphasis on the structures and processes of class domination and relations left underspecified the political mechanisms any social class requires but which are not reducible to class interests and control. "Every property system, indeed every market," she wrote in a Polanyian vein, "requires political backing. The significant question to ask is not whether such support is present or absent, but rather *who controls the political mechanisms and how they are organized.*" (Italics in original.) Marxist political sociology, she insisted, too quickly conflates class interests and class capacities and treats as a closed rather than an open question whether state organizations and political leaders might not act against the interests of a given dominant class or mode of production. In short, without leaving class analysis behind, Skocpol sought to introduce the possibility of an independent state both in support of and in tension with class relations. Further, she sought to extend our span of attention beyond the boundaries of the nation–state itself. Unlike Moore, she insisted that modernization entails structural changes both to economic institutions and to integrative political ones, including bureaucracies and parties; and that "both occur under the impetus of foreign as well as domestic pressures." Unlike Bendix (and Huntington), she insisted that the potential autonomy of the political does not provide warrants for neglecting "the interrelationship or state institutions and class structures" or "class constraints on political elites' freedom of action." Yet unlike Wallerstein, who introduced the international dimension via the notion of a world system, she resisted the reduction of state forms and strength to the role they perform within the modern world capitalist class structure and division of labor (Skocpol 1973: 16, 30, 31).

In *States and Social Revolutions,* Skocpol sought to surpass her mentor in two main ways. Like Moore, her work stressed "a structural perspective, with special attention devoted to international contexts and to developments at home and abroad that affect the breakdown of state organizations of old regimes and the buildup of new, revolutionary state organizations." And like Moore, she stuck with the nation–state as her unit of analysis and treated historical agents as motivated rather unproblematically by their structural locations, thus eliding the issue of microfoundations as an independent problem. By contrast to Moore,

---

[8]Note that in his essay for this volume, Mark Lichbach deploys *States and Social Revolutions* as exemplary of structuralist analysis. For reasons I indicate below, I think Skocpol's recent work, particularly *Protecting Soldiers and Mothers,* better indicates the direction in which structural and configurative scholarship is, and should be, moving.

however, she argued that marxist class analysis is insufficient to account for out-comes and variations. Her strategy was additive. Turning for intellectual suste-nance to the tradition of German realism and to contemporary scholarship on early modern European state-building and state theory (Nettl 1968; Tilly 1975), she developed a template for analysis that yoked marxist and weberian strands of theory together, insisting that marxists "face more directly the questions of what states are in their own right" by taking "the state seriously as a macro-structure." The state, she argued,

> Properly conceived is no mere arena in which socioeconomic struggles are fought out. It is, rather, a set of administrative, policing, and military orga-nizations headed, and more or less well coordinated by, an executive author-ity. Any state first and fundamentally extracts resources from society and de-ploys these to create and support coercive and administrative organizations.

Unlike Moore, she insisted on the value added by this approach to states as macrostructures treated independently of their place in "abstractly conceived modes of production" or as "political aspects of concrete class relations and strug-gles" (Skocpol 1979: 28, 29).[9]

If a shift to the state in tandem with class analysis represented the first key revision to Moore's orientation, the second concerned a nuanced but significant alteration to the mix between "scientific" comparison and the place of distinctive historical instances. In a methodological paper she wrote with Margaret Somers just after the publication of *States and Social Revolutions,* Skocpol explained that three distinct logics of analysis and exposition were being deployed in compara-tive history: the "parallel demonstration of theory" aiming to reveal how a gen-eral theory holds for diverse instances; the "contrast of contexts" directed at showing how the particularity of cases affects and modifies more general social processes; and "'macro-causal analysis" which "uses comparative history primarily for the purpose of making causal inferences about macro-level structures and processes." She persuasively identified both her own book and Moore's with the third tendency, arguing that while they share a suspicion of theories that gener-alize at too great a remove from specific cases (implicitly recognizing that rela-tions among variables cannot be consistent from case to case), they also seek to use historical comparisons as the means to test more general propositions and causal hypotheses about large-scale change. The method deployed to grapple with the tensions inherent in the relationship between such propositions and spe-cific historical instances is that of a continuous oscillation "between alternative explanatory hypotheses and comparisons of relevant aspects of the histories of two or more cases" (Skocpol and Somers 1980: 175, 181, 182).

Though both efforts were located in this zone of macroanalysis, Skocpol ar-gued that they differed in their relative emphasis on the scientific and the his-

---

[9]At the core of this shift was her representation of the state as "Janus-faced, with an intrinsically dual-anchorage in class-divided socioeconomic structures and an international system of states" (Skocpol 1979: 32).

torical. Moore, she observed, was rather more interested in the "historical analysis of causal sequences specific to individual countries" than in reproducing in a qualitative mode the approach of multivariate analysis aimed at testing causal hypotheses about large-scale phenomena. By placing her work and Moore's in the same broad category, Skocpol avoided over-stressing their differences, but I believe, as she did, that these were important (though I draw different conclusions about their relative merits). Whereas Moore sought primarily to construct specific cases in their complexity as configurational historical constructs, Skocpol put more emphasis on distinguishing variables and their effects within specific cases. Deploying Mill's method of difference, she claimed it is possible to overcome the problem of lots of potential variables and a small number of comparable cases and thus achieve scientific status for macroanalysis. I believe this to be an instance of wishful thinking which, if pushed hard, inevitably produces distortions to the integrity of cases without achieving the vaunted goal of systematic social science.

To be sure, Skocpol's widening of the scope of historical macroanalysis to include modern states and state-building as potentially autonomous and constitutive domains of modernity conjointly with capitalism and class marked an important step beyond Moore's more autarchic if revisionist marxism, but her strong tilt in the direction of variable-testing promised a good deal more than macroanalysis can deliver persuasively. In seeking to move beyond configurative analysis of the type promoted by Moore, Skocpol soon sought in work focused on the comparative study of welfare states to affirm that state and state-related variables more powerfully account for interesting outcomes, including the success or failure of various policy initiatives by social groups and classes, than what she claimed are competing economy- or society-centered possibilities (Skocpol and Finegold 1982; Skocpol and Ikenberry 1983; Orloff and Skocpol 1984). When such stylized causal accounts actually are deployed, however, they do violence to the integrity of the cases by forcing an artificial choice between key factors, when what matters is the terms of the relationships governing their transactions. After all, no state-centered account can make sense of the presence or absence of social democratic outcomes unless it locates them in interaction with the dispositions and collective actions of groups and social classes just as, in turn, society-centered explanations cannot possibly be compelling if they avoid grappling with the specificity of the modern state. Unlike Moore, who approached his cases in their configurational complexity, Skocpol, especially after *States and Social Revolutions* but before her *Protecting Soldiers and Mothers,* labored to justify mannered alternatives between clusters of variables.

Her structural macroanalysis, like Moore's, advanced historical research well beyond the typical causal indistinctness of too many historical narratives, but her pursuit of a causal hierarchy elided the problem of microfoundations. Moore's marxism had solved this problem by theoretically specifying the important historical agents and by making their dispositions and preferences immanent to their positionality. Skocpol had rejected his privileging of class relations, but her disapprobation was accompanied by an even more radical downplaying of the independent causal status of agents and agency. In stressing how structural relations place agency well beyond intentionality, she pushed limitations on voluntary action so far as to recommend that scholars should "emphasize objective relationships and conflicts among variously situated groups and nations, *rather than* the interests, outlooks, or ideologies of particular actors" (Skocpol 1979: 291; italics added). The resultant portrait of revolutions without revolutionaries not only left her macroanalysis without microfoundations virtually as a matter of principle, but it implied that there were no plausible alternative outcomes to those history had dealt, thus suggesting that history unfolds without human discretion and decision (Sewell 1985; Laitin and Warner 1992). When the main actors are structures and institutions rather than group or individual anthropological subjects, meaning, action, contingency, and negotiation, not to speak of the surprises of history, unfortunately recede (Trevor Roper 1980).

The best of the recent historical-institutional policy studies on health, taxation, labor relations, and other substantive arenas[10] has been premised on the three main moves Skocpol made when she revised Moore's legacy: the transcendence of a marxian materialism by a more cross-sectional and static organizational materialism; a very strong tilt in the direction of structure as an alternative to a focus on agency; and a shift from configurative comparative strategies to case comparative research strategies.[11] These shifts became the attributive grammar of the new scholarship, giving it coherence and power but also constraining its reach and range. For a more expansive configurative comparative politics to thrive again, albeit differently than for Moore, these three predicates must be reexamined. Any such review must begin with a consideration of the degree of theoretical conceit with regard to history appropriate to historically oriented social science.

REVIVING MACROANALYSIS: HISTORY AND THEORY, STRUCTURE AND CONFIGURATION

To simplify: For behaviorists, history is variable-specific and variable driven. It is imagined as sets of time-series. The materials on which they work are long-term data sets of opinion, war, voting, and the like (Page and Shapiro 1992). For rational choice theorists, history provides material with which to illustrate the capacity of deductive theory and it provides targets of explanation based on a small number of axiomatic assumptions about human motivation, the possession of in-

---

[10]Much of this scholarship has been written by Skocpol's students, coauthors, and close colleagues.

[11]Inside Perry Anderson's *Lineages,* we can see at work a contrast between an exclusively structuralist macroanalysis and a configurative, process-orientated macroanalysis. His treatment of Eastern Europe is entirely structuralist in contrast to the more configurational treatment of Western Europe (Anderson 1974a).

formation, and the patterning of interactions under conditions of scarcity. It also becomes an object of explanation shaped by the play of actors seeking to efficiently secure preferences and by the endogenous creation of institutions as byproducts of this action under conditions of strategic interdependence.[12] For postmodernists, history, though lacking an architecture or a telos, presents multiple sites of repression and resistance best understood in terms of the constant flux of identity formation and reformation (Mitchell 1988).

Historical macroanalysts have no a priori grounds on which to rule out any of these moves as ways of illuminating human structures and agency, but they are suspicious of the degree of simplification required by each. History is more than context, raw material, or a site for the play of the microdynamics of power. As the protean record of the human experience, history's thick inexhaustibility defies the taming instincts of historians but especially those of social scientists. It should not surprise that for most historians gaining a kind of demonic control of sources and constructing narrative interpretations (even if the causal stories are murky) are the considerable achievements for which they strive. Social science in its various modes, by contrast, willfully distorts for the purpose of ascertaining patterns, meaning, and truth in history by deploying often timeless analytical tools and by asking theory- and concept-driven questions (Cohn 1980). Though their styles of knowledge creation vary enormously to include various strategies of experimental design, postulation, hypothetical modeling, probabilistic analysis, and historical derivation (Crombie 1994), social scientists share in common a tendency to shift between the mediation of history by strong theory and the mediation of strong history by concepts (Bonnell 1980).

Now it is possible to argue, as, say, the late sociologist Philip Abrams and the anthropologist John Comaroff have, that there ought to be no "relationship" between history and social science "since there should be no division to begin with"; that all social science is historical and all history to be explicable must be analyzed utilizing tools of social science; that, as Eric Hobsbawm has averred, "the social sciences are trivial unless they come to terms with ... the way men get their living and their material environment ... [and] their ideas, since their relations with one another are expressed and formulated in language which implies concepts as soon as they open their mouths." Comparative historical macroanalysts perforce have no choice but to agree with these various calls for the mutual constitution of history and social science because they know, as Hobsbawm has insisted, that a small number of principles are essential to this craft: History has chronology and thus must be concerned with what actually happened; the history of society consists of "specific units of people living together and definable in sociological terms"; and the researcher "must have a hierarchy of assumptions

---

[12]Thus, for example, Levi asserts as a hypothesis rather than as a conclusion based on the deployment of evidence that predatory motivations with regard to the extraction of revenue are characteristic of history's rulers, the chief executives of state institutions, in spite of enormous variation in time and place (Levi 1988: 3-4).

about what counts." The making of histories on these terms thus represents a "collaboration between general models of social structure and change and the specific set of phenomena which actually occurred" (Abrams 1982; Comaroff 1982: 144; Hobsbawm 1974: 4-5, 9-10).

Perhaps, in principle, there is, or should be, no distinction between history and social science because each is essential to the constitution of the other, but in practice this is far too simple and seductive an elision. For every effort to assert the absence of a distinction, there is another that can strongly argue for their incompatibility.[13] After all, there is a considerable divide distinguishing, say, histories of war from histories of specific wars. I think a third position is more compelling. Though separate, history and social science cannot be constituted meaningfully without each other; hence what matters is the *terms* of their inescapably tension-ridden connections. These cannot be fixed by rule. Necessarily they shift in aim and method depending on scales of time,[14] the character of cases, the content of concepts, and, above all, the level of explanatory ambition (Knapp 1990).

The configurative position does not lack assertive objectives, but these are tempered by the modesty history and its variety demand. At stake is a particular kind of narrativity: less than the metanarrativity of presuppositional narratives about such grand concepts as progress and enlightenment or such commanding but general processes as the creation of mass society and class struggle, but more than the emplotment of the many stories history offers up. Rather, a configurative macroanalysis aims at an analytical narrativity that deploys spatial and temporal concepts "to reconstruct and plot over time and space the ontological narratives and relationships of historical actors, the public and cultural narratives that inform their lives, and the crucial intersection of these narratives with other relevant social forces" (Somers 1992: 604-5). It is by the selection of tools for the construction of cases as analytical narratives that even single-country case studies become accessible to comparison. This consideration requires that case research be informed by an explicitly posed analytical agenda that can be applied to interrogate quite distinctive instances with the goal not of flattening but of illuminating differences. But it also stipulates a deeply inductive approach to inquiry as the

[13]When this kind of effort by some historians goes to excess, a battle for objectivity can ensue. Though we have become used to social scientists claiming the mantle of objectivity against the more slack mode of interpretation by historians, it is worth remembering these shoes can fit on other feet. Thus, in his inaugural lecture as Regius Professor of History at Cambridge University, Geoffrey Elton observed and exhorted, "But we, as historians, do not write history for the use of the moment; we are guardians and distributors of the truths of history and should at least try to make sure that when current partisans plunder history for their own purposes they have a non-partisan and real history to stand over them." To make clear who these partisans were, he promptly inveighed against the very practice of social science (Elton 1984).

[14]On history and time, Koselleck has "tried to show historiographically that temporalization was at the beginning of modern history which today is being studied from a historical angle with regard to general change ... theoretically that we depend on the distinction between different time levels in order to be able to work within social history ... [and that] historical time itself can be made empirically transparent" (Koselleck 1982: 126).

tools deployed to examine cases stick close to the ground while seeking to explain big events and cognate developments without being concerned as a main focus with the production of cross-case generalizations. The heuristics of comparison, from this perspective, are vital to the practice of a configurative social science rightly skeptical about too many regularities of motivation and action.

The greatest instance of such an effort remains the pioneer structural-con-figurative text, Tocqueville's *Democracy in America*. This remarkable analytical narrative treats the United States both as a complex configuration of elements and as an elaboration of the archetype of equality as the dominant model for the future more generally. America is treated simultaneously as a highly distinctive, even exceptional constellation of elements, yet also as a harbinger of things to come. Though the United States is Tocqueville's only case, it always is constructed against empirical (especially French) and conceptual counterfactuals. Further, the United States is situated in place and time not as a hermetically sealed "case" but as a relationally inscribed instance in three senses: First, its own history and special qualities of institutions, values, and demography are composed in relationship to the experiences of other countries and to global flows of information, ideology, and people. Second, its development is situated in relation to larger trends and processes that affect the modern, western world more generally, especially those of social and political equalization. Third, America, as the first egalitarian regime for white males, is presented as the most important cause shaping the prospects, choices, and trajectories of other countries by way of the effects of a visible demonstration.

Though *Democracy in America* contains a strong causal story about liberal and egalitarian political culture and the construction of particular kinds of agents and their associational ties under determinate structural conditions, it also underscores variation and complexity, especially with respect to questions of race and the confrontation of civilizations. The text carefully distinguishes levels of causation – those specific and limited to the American milieu; those shared broadly by the larger thrust toward social equality and the movement of masses into politics; and those of political culture deeply imbricated with the patterning of institutions like the law, religion, the press, and secular voluntary associations. Throughout, individual and group dispositions and collective actions are shaped by and reshape large-scale structural and ideological arrangements and trends. Human nature is not fixed either as benevolent or as interest-seeking; rather, human behavior is conditioned on the structural and institutional shaping of values and mores which, in turn, remake contextual conditions for action. Structures and actors make democracy and democracy remakes structures and actors. Motivated by broadly liberal values and fears in a revolutionary world, Tocqueville combined classification and typological thinking with the dense historical, sociological, and political depiction of a single, complicated, dense case. He understood that out of context the factors deployed in his analysis would lose their relational quality; yet he insisted that a configurative study of the United States contained deeply comparative lessons. As Raymond Aron has noted, Tocqueville "wanted to make history intelligible, but he did not want to do away with it," and he rejected vast and transhistorical syntheses which claimed either to tame or predict history's vagaries (Aron 1968: 232).

There is a close affinity between Tocqueville's mix of modesty and assertion and Max Weber's guidelines for historical configuration in the essay he published on objectivity in the social sciences on the occasion of the appearance of the new *Archiv fur Sozialwissenschaft und Sozialpolitik,* which he edited. Social science, he argued, should aim to construct situations so that individuals can ascertain the possible, either in the past or the present; that is, what they or other actors can, as opposed to what they must, do. This orientation, like Stretton's later restatement of it, considers ethical imperatives not as independent motivators or explanations but as only operative inside determinate situations analytically ordered by social and political analysts who reveal "constellations of norms, institutions, etc." (Weber 1979: 64) by focusing on the conceptually organized interconnections of elements in conjunction with narratives of events. Understanding that our values condition our interest in particular problems and in specific analytical narratives, Weber argued the case for a configurative macroanalysis. Such a social science, he wrote,

> seeks to transcend the purely *formal* treatment of the legal or conventional norms regulating social life. The type of social science in which we are interested is an *empirical science* of concrete *reality (Wirklichkeitswissenschaft).* Our aim is the understanding of the characteristic uniqueness of the reality in which we move. We wish to understand on the other hand the relationships and the cultural significance of individual events in their contemporary manifestation and on the other the causes of their being historically *so* and not *otherwise....* It too concerns itself with the question of the *individual* consequence which the working of these "laws" in an unique *configuration* produces, since it is these individual configurations which are *significant* for us. Every individual constellation which it "explains" or predicts is causally explicable only as the consequence of another equally individual constellation which has preceded it. As far back as we may go into the grey mist of the far-off past, the reality to which the laws apply always remains equally *individual,* equally *undeducible* from laws (Weber 1979: 72; italics in original).

The approaches of Tocqueville and Weber to which I am partial cannot be contained within the methods of agreement and difference proposed by John Stuart Mill, for under the conditions of comparing large and complex instances these cannot satisfy conditions of proof or discovery. Indeed, we would do well to recall that Mill himself introduced two "elements of complexity" into his attempt to turn qualitative analysis into an experimental method. The first of these was what he called the "Method of Residues" which understands that any specific situation in which factors interconnect in a constellation can only be apprehended by understanding its often tacit and sometimes hidden presumptions and antecedents. This method, he insisted, though inevitably uncertain as to the surety of its claims, "is the most fertile in unexpected results; often informing us of sequences in which neither the cause nor the effect were [sic] sufficiently conspicuous to attract themselves to the attention of observers" (Mill 1852: 230). Louis Hartz's contentious claim about the hidden but powerful status of liberalism in the American experience took just this form (Hartz 1955).

Even more significant was Mill's final move: an insistence on the significance of concomitant variation in specific historical constellations "because it by no means follows when two phenomena accompany each other in their variations, that the one is cause and the other effect" (Mill 1852: 233). Both may have a common antecedent cause and both may be mutually constitutive. Such situations, he points out, make it impossible to apply the method of difference; what matters is not the causal relation of variables in such circumstances but the configuration of the constellation of elements. Indeed, by way of a profound irony, it was the development of just those statistical tools in the nineteenth century that aimed to elucidate causal relations with certainty which, by introducing the notion of probability into social analysis, had the effect of shattering certainty and of making a configurative historical social science appealing, even compelling, especially in the face of our circumstances as analysts who are inside the very world for which we seek objective, though not neutral perspectives.

Read together, Tocqueville, Weber, and Mill point to a distinctive way of constructing cases for comparative analysis, focusing less on the causal importance of this or that variable contrasted with others but more on how variables are joined together in specific historical instances. They do so by wagering on key factors, deployed as ideal-types, in interaction with others, but not on ideal-types too distant from situations on the ground. Running the risk of selection bias (Lustick 1996), this orientation to comparison prefers ideal-types that are realist and concrete rather than nominalist and abstract, preferring theory to guide investigations, say, about Catholicism and Protestantism rather than religion or about class relations within capitalism rather than structures of inequality.

Unlike the approach to comparison that identifies a given case with a given type, in this approach cases are understood to be combinations of elements rather than manifestations of one or another theoretically derived instance in a typology. In Moore's work, for example, each country contains a hierarchical combination of ideal-types, and the definition and complexity of each case are shaped by the quality of their combinations.

The analytical narratives he composed were geared to establish the interconnections and play of these elements over time. None was freestanding. Each was the product of the trajectory of a nonrandom set of ties linking past, present, and future; each exists inside a larger pattern of trends and processes of which it is a part.

Utilizing a configurative compass with structural bearings to guide comparison points to and locates the significance of other modes of comparison. It situates cases inside the common elements stressed by the global or large-process point of departure. Its cases become names for analytically established categories that can be compared one to the other within a given epoch or at structurally equivalent times. It can even borrow, albeit skeptically, from variable-centered research by carefully reembedding the results of multivariate analysis in order to test propositions in thick context.

The role of theory in such circumstances, Hugh Stretton has observed, "may thus be seen as an organization of possibilities." The kind of theory he advocates for historical case studies like *Protecting,* where strict verification is precluded by the nature of the material and by a refusal to parse it too finely into isolated variables, is the kind that "leaves open the question whether people are doing what people would invariably do in these uniquely complicated circumstances, or are doing one of the comparatively few things which people (usually free) choose to do in such circumstances" (Stretton 1969: 326-7, 215). The product of such theorizing is a social science of guarded generalizations in situations where there can be no true universal hypotheses and where the number of discrete factors and actors is too small for statistical statements to secure any purchase.

But theory, after the hegemony of marxism in macroanalytical scholarship, of what kind? Quite simply, we possess no full-blown equivalent either to classical marxism or to post-Gramscian twentieth-century neo-marxism; nor, in light of the limitations of any such inclusive, autarchic, and holistic theory should we seek to find a replica. But we also pay a steep price for its absence; how is it possible to minimize the costs? By availing ourselves, I think, of what might be called the strategies of oscillation and of raising the level of abstraction which I identify, respectively, with Albert Hirschman and Ralf Dahrendorf.

In his Marc Bloch lecture of 1982, Hirschman addressed competing interpretations focused on the economic and noneconomic dynamics of market societies. He contrasted four theses: the *doux commerce* argument focusing on the beneficent gentle and civilizing features of markets as tamers of passions; the self-destruction proposition stressing how market-capitalist societies necessarily undermine the moral foundations of society; the feudal shackles thesis claiming that remnants from the past undermine positive market features by making market penetration of society too incomplete; and a feudal blessings thesis stressing, as Louis Hartz did for the United States, the hazards attendant on having been deprived of a feudal past. These alternatives, Hirschman shows, have developed as intellectual constructs in near-total isolation from each other. He sought to bring them together, transcend the question of which one is right, and demonstrate that when this is done we can see they compose a coherent ideological tableau. "However incompatible the various theories may be," he argued, "each might still have its 'hour of truth' and/or its 'country of truth' as it applies in a given country or group of countries during some stretch of time." He claimed, further, that accounts of particular times and places are most powerful when they combine these elements and hold them in tension. Thus, Hirschman observed by way of an illustration, not only is it possible for the *doux commerce* and self-destruction theses to hold at the same moment, but by a strategy of configuration we can see that modern capitalist society simultaneously is self-reinforcing and self-undermining as its moral basis is consumed and filled up at the same time. In his rendering, the focus of analysis shifts from tests of the relative truth value of competing propositions to the analysis of how apparent alternatives delineate mutual relations. "An excess of depletion over replenishment and a consequent crisis of the system is then of course possible, but the special circumstances making for it would have to be noted, just as it might be possible to specify conditions under which the system would gain in cohesion and legitimacy." He concluded, "is it not in the interest of social science to embrace complexity, be it at some sacrifice of its claim to predictive power?" (Hirschman 1982: 1481, 1483) Within such an oscillatory approach, marxism would have a continuing role to play as the generator of hypotheses and as the basis for claims to privilege of the analysis of social class and the logic of political economy, but only as one among other sources of claims about the elements to which we must attend in analytically constructing particular cases.

Though different, Dahrendorf's attempt to rescue the kernel of marxist dynamics and the capacity of its focus on structure from the sins of teleology and reductionism and from the narrowing traps of political economy likewise suggests how macroanalysis might continue to profit from its marxist (and marxisant) heritage. His *Class and Class Conflict in Industrial Society* (1959) sought to rescue marxian doctrine from the particularities of the historical moment in which it was founded. He did so both by lifting the level of abstraction, substituting a more general language of social structure and conflict groups for capitalism and social classes, and preserving marxism's analytical focus on social change and on the formation of groups in conflict. He superseded class conflict by subsuming it within a more inclusive category of authority conflict which unfolds within the hierarchical structures of society, including those of industry and the state. In designating the motor of social change as that of the presence of a structured and unequal distribution of authority, Dahrendorf insisted that the seats of such authority, hence of conflict, are multiple. They do not exclude property relations and class, of course, but these are given no a priori place of privilege. Their relative importance hinges on a historically distinctive arrangement and positioning of elements. In stressing this position, and in aiming to construct what Robert Merton had called theories of the middle range linking general theory capable of interrogating situations with concrete observations and specific cases (Merton 1949), Dahrendorf also embraced the normative quest, pursued by Moore, to discover a decent democratic modernity based on the recognition, rather than the suppression, of conflict.

What Hirschman and Dahrendorf, separately and together, demonstrate is that it is possible to pursue a relational and structural research program of considerable range and ambition even after marxism loses the hegemonic status it enjoyed in the work of Moore, Wallerstein, Anderson, and other pioneering figures in the macroanalytical revolution in comparative politics; and, moreover, that it is feasible to do so without making the shifts to cross-sectional comparison, to structure at the expense of agency, and to case comparative in lieu of configurative research strategies that Skocpol counseled after her critique of Moore.

It is important to underscore, alongside Hirschman and Dahrendorf, that the revival of a configurative comparative politics does not imply or require commitment to a particular theory, marxist or otherwise, but to an orientation to theory characterized by a cluster of ontological and methodological commitments; most prominently the claim that action and identity must firmly be placed inside structural macrofoundations that are not constantly in flux. Relations among collectivities and individuals are characterized by strong and quite persistent relations. Of course, structures themselves are the products of human agency, but in a wider scholarly division of labor it makes sense for configurative comparativists to focus mainly on the obverse—that is, on how structures constitute and cause identities and actions by tilting and organizing probabilities. The linkage between structure and agency in this perspective is primarily institutional, in the sense of institutions both as composing rules and as formal organizations that are loci for human interaction under conditions of differential power and authority.

INSTITUTIONS AS LIGATURES

In 1925, Harry Elmer Barnes convened an important symposium on "The History and Prospects of the Social Sciences" (which included papers devoted to history and biology). Walter James Shephard's essay on political science took note of the movement away from the state as a central object of analysis: "Metaphysical, deductive, and analytical studies of the state have not entirely disappeared, but they have been definitely pushed into the background." Instead, there had been a turn to investigations that "have provided a vast mass of facts regarding the structure and function of every political institution." Not quite a decade later, Frederick Watkins, then a graduate student of Carl Friedrich but later Professor of Political Science at Yale, published a brilliant historical and analytical consideration of "The State as a Concept of Political Science" in which he strongly urged a turn away from the state in particular to associations in general, and away from a determinate institutional analysis to a focus on behavioral power. As a senior scholar, Watkins contributed the entry on "The State" to the 1968 *International Encyclopedia of the Social Sciences.* He declared victory. The idea that political science begins and ends with the state or should treat the state as a distinctive kind of political association, he wrote, "no longer corresponds to the theory and practice of contemporary political scientists" (Shephard 1925: 425; Watkins 1934; 1968: 155).

The very same year, J. P. Nettl, starting from much the same observation ("The concept of state is not much in vogue in the social sciences right now"), drew a radically different conclusion, the imperative of "integrating the concept of state into the current primacy of social science concerns and analytical methods." Like other scholars who soon sought to "bring the state back in" on the grounds that the state's monopoly claims to sovereignty over people and territory, its uniquely inclusive and coercive ensemble of institutions, and its nation-defining normative qualities distinguish it from all other modern organizational forms (Evans, Rueschemeyer, and Skocpol 1985),[15] Nettl refused the reduction of the state to just one association or institution among many. The state, he told (and inspired many of) us, "summates a set of functions and structures in order to generalize their applicability," represents an irreducible "unit in the field of international relations," "represents an autonomous collectivity … as a distinct *sector* or arena of society," and is also what he called "a sociocultural phenomenon." Each of these elements, he insisted, is configured distinctively in specific locations and times (Nettl 1968: 559, 562, 564, 565).

The most important works in macroanalysis in the period just before and after the publication of Nettl's landmark essay either reflected or built on this turn to the state, treating it either as a companion macrostructure to modern capitalism or as an alternative focus competing with the social determinism of marxist class analysis (at just the moment marxism itself was discovering the relative autonomy of the state). But like all such counter-to-trend intellectual revolutions, the turn to the state and to state-centered explanations quickly became the obvious thing to have done. Who really would wish to deny the significance of the triumph of the sovereign state in early modern Europe as the most important political form against such competitors as the Hanseatic League or Italian city-states, or dispute the significance of this political form for the international arena after Westphalia, or gainsay its diffusion so that today virtually every person on the face of the earth is enclosed within a sovereign state that is a member of the international community of states (and equipped with all its cultural paraphernalia)? Quite soon, however, the state-focused research community found itself tightly constrained by a very bulky conceptual elaboration of Nettl, which tended to reduce his rich and complex array of dimensions to simple distinctions between weak versus strong, and federal versus unitary, states; to sneak normative preferences in by the back door (these typically were social democratic, preferring strong states to counter the capacities of capital) without sufficiently examining their assumptions or grappling with the deep illiberality of states as condensations of coercion; and to focus on the explanatory power of statist analysis as opposed to those of other scholarly traditions.

As a counter to these tendencies, the new historical institutionalism has come to a welcome rescue. Narrower than the older macroanalysis, this body of scholarship shifted away from the macrostuctures of the state, the economy, and civil society to focus on institutions understood both as rules of transaction between these sites and as the actual array of formal organizations inside each macrostructure and astride their interactions. Institutions emerged as ligatures fastening sites, relationships, and large-scale processes to each other. What came

---

[15]The volume was sponsored not only by the SSRC Committee on States and Social Structures but by the Joint Committees on Latin American Studies and West European Studies.

to distinguish historical institutionalism was an insistence that these bonds, though constructed of similar tools across instances, are configured distinctively in particular locations. It is these configurations, perforce, which must become our units of analysis. Further, the new institutionalism demanded that agents always be understood as embedded in institutional milieus; that causal relations of elements and variables always are patterned by context and circumstance; and that historical developments are contingently shaped by choices taken by actors about the content of the institutional links connecting state, economy, and society at key moments of historical indeterminacy (Immergut 1996).

The power and promise of this kind of institutional analysis lies not only in its ability to shift attention from macrostructures to transactions across macrostructural boundaries (after all, that is what the new institutionalism's main subjects of public policy, political economy, and interest representation are all about), but in the manner it connects institutional design to the formation and existence of political agents who possess particular clusters of preferences, interests, and identities. Unlike rational choice, which takes preferences as the point of departure, or behavioralism, which treats action as the site of revealed preferences, historical institutionalism has been vitally concerned with how particular configurations of preferences, interests, and identities come to be politically salient at particular times as products, not just causes; but as causes as well as products.[16] The institutionalist epistemology thus is relational, crossing the divide between structure and agency without seeking to eliminate the heuristic distinction between them.

An outstanding, but vastly underattended, contribution to institutionalist thinking along these lines is the 1986 series of lectures on "how institutions think" by the anthropologist Mary Douglas (Douglas 1986). These focus on how institutional milieus, both normative and organizational, shape human cognition and the dispositions of historical subjects to form solidary groups and to cooperate. Since, as methodological individualists rightly argue, only individual persons can think and act, at issue are the conditions under which thinking and feeling come to be sufficiently cognate to compose collective units of action. This, Douglas argues, is the contribution of institutions. They, in turn, are shaped and reshaped by individuals and groups whose thought and sentiments themselves have been fashioned in institutional contexts. The weak form of an institution is a convention that does not quite seem natural; institutions take strong forms when they appear as if part of the inevitable natural order of things. Early nineteenth-century markets, Polanyi reminds us, took the first form (Polanyi 1944); but late twentieth-century markets have achieved the second. Much the same might be said about state formation. From weak to strong, institutions confer identities by assigning properties to categories, by polarizing, excluding, and grading, and by

---

[16]In this orientation, it is closer to the approach to rationality drawn from cognitive science focusing on actors seeking to reduce uncertainty under conditions of incomplete or distorted information, associated above all with the bounded rationality perspective of Herbert Simon (Simon 1986).

distinguishing the visible and the obvious from the less visible and the murky. Institutions name and classify. They shape the very categories of plausible and possible thought. But institutions themselves are not natural; they are caused (Wildavsky 1987).

Douglas's text pushed key historical-institutionalist assumptions harder than many who work in this vein find comfortable (especially problematical is her affinity for Durkheim's functionalism and the abstract, at times contentless, quality of her presentation), but its value lies in its crystallization of the kind of work an institutional focus can perform for macroanalysis, not least by refusing an overly aseptic and rationalistic individualism as the only basis specifying microfoundations.

Just this, in part, is what makes Skocpol's *Protecting Soldiers and Mothers* (1992), a revisionist study of welfare state history in the United States, a significant advance on her earlier work. Most comparativists have failed to attend to this book, treating it as belonging to another subfield. This neglect is regrettable. More than any recent text explicitly belonging to comparative politics, *Protecting* revivifies large-scale macroanalysis on terms Skocpol herself once sought to obscure or ignore. The book's configurative approach contrasts with the fool's gold of the earlier multivariate tilt Skocpol first had introduced by way of a critique of Moore's work; and it diverges from her earlier excessive structuralism by tightly linking the organizational forms and identities of key political actors. Unlike the artificial dichotomy between explanations oriented either to the state or to society, what Skocpol now calls her "polity-centered" approach is explicitly and genuinely relational in quality. Moreover, the new book is profoundly interested in political identities, dispositions, and action. *Protecting* is a volume dedicated to understanding the manner in which political institutions and policies shape two-way exchanges between the state and civil society. In making these moves, the text joins the style of the grand macroanalysis of the 1960s and 1970s (with a tilt toward the configurative style of Moore that Skocpol once sought to revise) with the nuance and detail of fine-grained recent historical-institutionalist work in political economy and public policy.

Like the more general project of scholarship in American political development, Skocpol sought to set aside versions of American exceptionalism so strong that they invite consideration of the American case as simply *sui generis*. She did so by making three key moves. Via the route of periodization, she insisted the United States was not the welfare state laggard it often is portrayed as being. Well before the New Deal, it had deployed an extensive system of Civil War pensions (which soon transmuted into a dense and expensive system of transfers) and programs at the federal and state levels aimed at the well-being of children and their mothers. Via the route of an institutionalist analysis both of key characteristics of the federal American state and of the networks of groups and organizations in civil society seeking to influence policy outcomes, she argued there is an elective affinity between policy success and the fit between the form of interest organization and the form of the state. Marshaling this kind of argument, she continued her very first project aimed at transcending a too-simple class analysis, but now she performed the task without eliding issues of agency and identity or fabricating an affected competition between state- and society-focused variables (substantively, she sought to show why in the early decades of the twentieth century, cross-class coalitions led by professional women proved more effective in securing policy goals than those put together by organized labor). Finally, and most important, via the route of a theory of interaction and transactions, she constructed a dynamic configurative approach to the relationship between public policy, state capacity, and the political goals and capabilities of social groups. There were two central elements to this effort: first, the "fit" and terms of exchange between politicized social identities and group political orientations and capacities, on the one side, and governmental institutions, systems of partisan and interest representation, and the rules (in this case, liberal) of the game, on the other; second, the feedback effects of policies on politics (both on the organization of the state itself and on the identities and proclivities of social groups) (Skocpol 1992: 41-62).[17] This relational and configurative form of analysis made negotiations between the state and civil society the centerpiece of its analysis of specific areas of public policy. Not surprisingly, some historians are made nervous by the systematic qualities of this type of analysis, while some social scientists think its deeply historical qualities are purchased at the sacrifice of analytical elegance and rigor. Actually, these anxieties are the hallmarks of success for a configurative macroanalysis at the junction of history and social science.[18]

What is particularly heartening for the future of a configurative and institutional macroanalysis is that Skocpol's turn to microfoundations in tandem with this type of institutional analysis is hardly unique. Thus, for example, de Swaan (1988) has demonstrated how growth in the scale of both civil society and the state from the sixteenth to the nineteenth centuries radically altered the terms of their interaction, and how this alteration created new kinds of collective action that produced modern welfare states. Silberman (1983), drawing on notions of bounded rationality under conditions of imperfect information, has shown how leaders faced with different institutional conditions of uncertainty about succession and regime change acted to change institutions to make their circumstances

---

[17]This approach, though novel for Skocpol's corpus, displays a strong continuity with her rejection of simple socially determinist lines of explanation. As before, she continues to reject explanations that begin with socioeconomic situations and that treat the generation of demands by social groups as derived from those circumstances entirely prior to their deployment within a political milieu. For a discussion, see the section on "The Shared Limits of Existing Theories," pp.38-40.

[18]Yet somewhere between *States and Social Revolutions* and *Protecting Soldiers and Mothers,* Skocpol seems to have lost some of her taste for hortatory theoretical invocation. Perhaps because of its Americanist audience and ambitions, *Protecting*'s larger implications are masked as its theoretical and methodological discussions are presented, appropriately enough, only to the extent required to allow its author to quickly turn to the task it focuses on over some 600 printed pages: the calling into question of much received wisdom about the history of the American welfare state. The result is a surprising reticence about theorizing just those issues *Protecting* makes central to its account, including puzzles of comparison and the challenge of microfoundations.

less equivocal. Padgett and Ansell have established how the factional networks in renaissance Florence produced parties and identities: "rules induce roles, which induce interests, which induce strategic exchanges, which lock in patterns of collective action that depend on the rules" (Padgett and Ansell 1993). These various moves inside macroanalysis were uncommon before the new institutionalist impulse took flight.

And yet, though the tools for striking advances are now available, there are no grounds for complacency. Ironically, at a time when most of the best historical-institutionalist scholarship inside the subfield of comparative politics has limited its scope while deepening its power, studies in American political development happily have refused this choice. Though primarily limited to the single case of the United States, it is not just Skocpol's study of social policy but other considerable texts like Bensel's story of the emergence of a one-party state after the Civil War and Skowronek's analytical treatment of the presidency (Bensel 1990; Skowronek 1993) that have recovered much of the audacity of the project of macroanalysis characteristic of the sweep in the scholarship of Moore and Skocpol on revolutions while also inserting the connecting tissue of institutions linking structure and agency within determinate and contingent historical configurations. Like the great texts of old, these works suggest playful periodizations (Skowronek rejuggles presidential administrations, the oldest organizing feature of studies of American politics, into categories shaped by what he calls political time) and propose fresh bases for comparison (thus Bensel argues that post–Civil War nineteenth-century America had more in common with the one-party twentieth-century developing states of Mexico and India than with the European instances usually treated as foils for American history). Having stood just to the side of the elaboration of European macroanalysis when it rushed headlong into structure at the expense of agency and toward state-centered analyses at the expense of relational and configurative accounts, these American studies may well be our richest current source of nourishment for the growth of comparative macroanalysis. Such configurative American political studies, inscribed by the new institutionalism but undogmatic about their ties to behavioralism, rational choice, and the turn to signification, may well do far more than originally intended by the editors of *Studies in American Political Development* a decade ago. Located at the periphery of both American and comparative politics, this genre of work has begun to recover the dimensions of invention and surprise that attracted many of us to political science and to comparative politics two and three decades ago.

REFERENCES

Abrams, Philip 1982. *Historical Sociology.* Ithaca: Cornell University Press.
Almond, Gabriel A., and Sidney Verba. 1963. *The Civic Culture: Political Attitudes and Democracy in Five Nations.* Princeton: Princeton University Press.
Anderson, Perry. 1974a. *Lineages of the Absolutist State.* London: New Left Books.

————. 1974b. *Passages from Antiquity to Feudalism.* London: New Left Books.

Aron, Raymond. 1968. *Main Currents in Sociological Thought.* London: Penguin Books.

Barnes, Samuel Henry, Max Kaase, and Klause R. Allerbeck. 1979. *Political Action: Mass Participation in Five Western Democracies.* Beverly Hills: Sage Publications.

Barry, Brian M. 1970. *Sociologists, Economists and Democracy.* London: Collier-Macmillan.

Bartolini, Stefano, and Peter Mair. 1990. *Identity, Competition, and Electoral Availability: The Stabilisation of European Electorates 1885–1985.* Cambridge: Cambridge University Press.

Bendix, Reinhard. 1964. *Nation-Building and Citizenship: Studies of Our Changing Social Order.* New York: John Wiley.

————. 1978. *Kings or People: Power and the Mandate to Rule.* Berkeley: University of California Press.

Bensel, Richard Franklin. 1990. *Yankee Leviathan: The Origins of Central State Authority in America, 1859–1877.* Cambridge: Cambridge University Press.

Berger, Suzanne D., ed. 1981. *Organizing Interests in Western Europe: Pluralism, Corporatism, and the Transformation of Politics.* Cambridge: Cambridge University Press.

Bonnell, Victoria. 1980. "The Uses of Theory, Concepts, and Comparisons in Historical Sociology." *Comparative Studies in Society and History,* 22:156-73.

Brown, Bernard E., John H. Herz, and Arnold A. Rogow. 1968. "A Statement by the Editors." *Comparative Politics* 1:1-2.

Cohn, Bernard S. 1980. "History and Anthropology: The State of Play." In *Comparative Studies in Society and History,* 22:198-221.

Collier, David. 1991. "The Comparative Method: Two Decades of Change." In Dankwart Rustow and Kenneth Paul Erickson, eds., *Comparative Political Dynamics: Global Research Perspectives.* New York: HarperCollins.

Comaroff, John. 1982. "Dialectical Systems, History, and Anthropology: Units of Study and Questions of Theory." *The Journal of Southern African Studies* 8:143-72.

Crombie, A. C. 1994. *Styles of Scientific Thinking in the European Tradition.* 3 volumes. London: Duckworth.

Dahrendorf, Ralf. 1959. *Class and Class Conflict in Industrial Society.* Stanford: Stanford University Press.

Dalton, Russell J., Scott Flanagan, and Paul Allen Beck, eds. 1984. *Electoral Change in Advanced Industrial Democracies: Realignment or Dealignment?* Princeton: Princeton University Press.

Daston, Lorraine. 1988. *Classical Probability in the Enlightenment.* Princeton: Princeton University Press.

de Swaan, Abram. 1988. *In Care of the State: Health Care, Education and Welfare in Europe and the USA in the Modern Era.* New York: Oxford University Press.

Douglas, Mary. 1986. *How Institutions Think.* Syracuse: Syracuse University Press.

Downing, Brian M. 1992. *The Military Revolution and Political Change: Origins of Democracy and Autocracy in Early Modern Europe.* Princeton: Princeton University Press.

Elton, G. R. 1984. *The History of England.* Cambridge: Cambridge University Press.

Ertman, Thomas. 1997. *Birth of the Leviathan: Building States and Regimes in Medieval and Early Modern Europe.* Cambridge: Cambridge University Press.

Evans, Peter B., Dietrich Rueschemeyer, and Theda Skocpol, eds. 1985. *Bringing the State Back In.* Cambridge: Cambridge University Press.

Hacking, Ian. 1990. *The Taming of Chance.* Cambridge: Cambridge University Press.

Hall, Peter A. 1986. *Governing the Economy: The Politics of State Intervention in Britain and France.* Cambridge: Polity Press.

Hammel, E. A. 1980. "The Comparative Method in Anthropological Perspective." *Comparative Studies in Society and History* 22:145-55.

Hartz, Louis. 1955. *The Liberal Tradition in America.* New York: Harcourt, Brace, and World.

Hirschman, Albert O. 1982. "Rival Interpretations of Market Society: Civilizing, Destructive, or Feeble?" *The Journal of Economic Literature* 20:1463-84.

Hobsbawm, E. J. 1974. "From Social History to the History of Society." In M. W. Flinn and T. C. Smout, eds., *Essays in Social History.* London: Oxford University Press.

Hollingsworth, Rogers J. 1978. "The United States." In Raymond Grew, ed. *Crises of Political Development in Europe and the United States.* Princeton: Princeton University Press.

Huntington, Samuel P. 1968. *Political Order in Changing Societies.* New Haven: Yale University Press.

Immergut, Ellen M. 1992. *Health Politics: Interests and Institutions in Western Europe.* Cambridge: Cambridge University Press.

———. 1996. "The Normative Roots of the New Institutionalism: Historical Institutionalism and Comparative Policy Studies." In Arthur Benz and Wolfgang Seibel, eds., *Beitrage zur Theorieentwicklung in der Politik- und Verwaltungswissenschaft.* Baden-Baden: Nomos Verlag.

Knapp, Peter. 1990. "The Revival of Macrosociology: Methodological Issues of Discontinuity in Comparative-Historical Theory." *Sociological Forum* 5:545-67.

Koelble, Thomas A. 1995. "The New Institutionalism in Political Science." *Comparative Politics* 27:231-43.

Kohli, Atul, Peter Evans, Peter J. Katzenstein, Adam Przeworski, Susanne Hoeber Rudolph, James C. Scott, and Theda Skocpol. 1995. "The Role of Theory in Comparative Politics: A Symposium." *World Politics* 48:1-49.

Koselleck, Reinhart. 1982. "Concepts of Historical Time and Social History." In David Carr, ed., *La philosophie de histoire et la pratique historienne d'aujourd'hui.* Ottawa: University of Ottawa Press.

Laitin, David, and Carolyn M. Warner. 1992. "Structure and Irony in Social Revolutions." *Political Theory* 20:147-52.

Lasswell, Harold. 1935. *World Politics and Personal Insecurity.* New York: McGraw-Hill.

Levi, Margaret. 1988. *Of Rule and Revenue.* Berkeley: University of California Press.

Lijphart, Arend. 1971. "Comparative Politics and the Comparative Method." *American Political Science Review* 65:682-93.

Lipset, Seymour Martin. 1960. *Political Man.* New York: Doubleday.

———. 1983. "Radicalism or Reformism: The Sources of Working Class Politics." *American Political Science Review* 77:1-18.

Lipset, Seymour Martin, and Stein Rokkan, eds. 1967. *Party Systems and Voter Alignments.* New York: Free Press.

Luebbert, Gregory M. 1991. *Liberalism, Fascism, or Social Democracy: Social Classes and the Political Origins of Regimes in Interwar Europe.* New York: Oxford University Press.

Lustick, Ian S. 1996. "History, Historiography, and Political Science: Multiple Historical Records and the Problem of Selection Bias." *American Political Science Review* 90:605-18.

Mann, Michael. 1986, 1993. *The Sources of Social Power: Volume I: A History of Power from the Beginning to A. D. 1760* and *Volume II: The Rise of Classes and Nation-States, 1760–1914.* Cambridge: Cambridge University Press.

Merton, Robert K. 1949. *Social Theory and Social Structure.* Glencoe: Free Press.

Mill, John Stuart. 1852. *A System of Logic: Ratiocinative and Inductive.* New York: Harper and Company.

Mitchell, Timothy. 1988. *Colonizing Egypt.* Cambridge: Cambridge University Press.

Moore, Jr., Barrington. 1966. *Social Origins of Dictatorship and Democracy: Lord and Peasant in the Making of the Modern World.* Boston: Beacon Press.

Nettl, J. P. 1968. "The State As a Conceptual Variable." *World Politics* 20:559-92.

Orloff, Ann Shola, and Theda Skocpol. 1984. "Why Not Equal Protection? Explaining the Origins of Public Social Welfare in Britain, 1900–1914, and the United States, 1880's to 1920's." *American Sociological Review* 49:726-50.

Orren, Karen, and Stephen Skowronek. 1986. "Editors' Preface." *Studies in American Political Development* 1:vii-viii.

Padgett, John F., and Christopher K. Ansell. 1993. "Robust Action and the Rise of the Medici." *American Journal of Sociology* 98:1259-319.

Page, Benjamin I., and Robert Y. Shapiro. 1992. *The Rational Public: Fifty Years of Trends in Americans' Policy Preferences.* Chicago: University of Chicago Press.

Pierson, Paul. 1994. *Dismantling the Welfare State? Reagan, Thatcher, and the Politics of Retrenchment.* Cambridge: Cambridge University Press.

Polanyi, Karl. 1944. *The Great Transformation: The Political and Economic Origins of Our Time.* New York: Rinehart and Company.

Pye, Lucian. 1971. "Foreword." In Leonard Binder et al. *Crises and Sequences in Political Development.* Princeton: Princeton University Press.

Ragin, Charles C., and Howard S. Becker, eds. 1992. *What Is a Case? Exploring the Foundations of Social Inquiry.* Cambridge: Cambridge University Press.

Robertson, David Brian. 1993. "The Return to History and the New Institutionalism in American Political Science." *Social Science History* 17:1-36.

Rokkan, Stein. 1970. *Citizens, Elections, Parties: Approaches to the Comparative Study of the Process of Development.* Oslo: Universitetsforlaget.

Samuels, Richard J. 1994. *Rich Nation, Strong Army: National Security and the Technological Transformation of Japan.* Ithaca: Cornell University Press.

Schmitter, Philippe C., and Gerhard Lehmbruch, eds. 1979. *Trends Toward Corporatist Intermediation.* Beverly Hills: Sage Publications.

Sewell, Jr., William. 1985. "Ideologies and Social Revolutions: Reflections on the French Case." *Journal of Modern History* 57:57-85.

Shephard, Walter James. 1925. "Political Science." In Harry Elmer Barnes, *The History and Prospects of the Social Sciences.* New York: Alfred A. Knopf.

Silberman, Bernard S. 1993. *Cages of Reason: The Rise of the Rational State in France, Japan, the United States, and Great Britain.* Chicago: University of Chicago Press.

Simon, Herbert A. 1986. "Theories of Bounded Rationality." In C. B. McGuire and
    Roy Radner, eds., *Decision and Organization: A Volume in Honor of Jacob Mar-
    shak*. Minneapolis: University of Minnesota Press.
Skocpol, Theda. 1973. "A Critical Review of Barrington Moore's *Social Origins of Dic-
    tatorship and Democracy.*" *Politics and Society* 4:1-34.
———. 1979. *States and Social Revolutions: A Comparative Analysis of France, Russia,
    and China*. Cambridge: Cambridge University Press .
———. 1992. *Protecting Soldiers and Mothers: The Political Origins of Social Policy in the
    United States*. Cambridge: The Belknap Press of Harvard University Press.
Skocpol, Theda, and Kenneth Finegold. 1982, "Economic Intervention and the Early
    New Deal." *Political Science Quarterly* 97:255-78.
Skocpol, Theda, and John Ikenberry. 1983. "The Political Formation of the Ameri-
    can Welfare State in Historical and Comparative Perspective." *Comparative
    Social Research* 6:87-148.
Skocpol, Theda, and Margaret Somers. 1980. "The Uses of Comparative History in
    Macrosocial Inquiry." *Comparative Studies in Society and History* 22:174-97.
Skowronek, Stephen. 1993. *The Politics Presidents Make: Leadership from John Adams
    to George Bush*. Cambridge: The Belknap Press of Harvard University
    Press.
Somers, Margaret R. 1992. "Narrativity, Narrative Identity, and Social Action:
    Rethinking English Working Class Formation." *Social Science History*
    16:591-630.
Spruyt, Hendrik. 1994. *The Sovereign State and Its Competitors*. Princeton: Princeton
    University Press.
Steinmo, Sven. 1993. *Taxation and Democracy: Swedish, British, and American Ap-
    proaches to Financing the Modern State*. New Haven: Yale University Press.
Steinmo, Sven, Kathleen Thelen, and Frank Longstreth, eds. 1992. *Structuring Poli-
    tics: Historical Institutionalism in Comparative Perspective*. Cambridge: Cam-
    bridge University Press.
Stretton, Hugh. 1969. *The Political Sciences: General Principles of Selection in Social Sci-
    ence and History*. London: Routledge & Kegan Paul.
Tarrow, Sidney. 1987. "Big Structures and Contentious Events: Two of Charles Tilly's
    Recent Writings." *Sociological Forum* 2:191-204.
Tilly, Charles, ed. 1975. *The Formation of National States in Western Europe*. Princeton:
    Princeton University Press.
———. 1984. *Big Structures, Large Processes, Huge Comparisons*. New York: Russell
    Sage Foundation.
———. 1990. *Coercion, Capital, and European States, AD 990–1990*. Oxford: Basil
    Blackwell.
Tilly, Charles, Louise A. Tilly, and Richard Tilly. 1975. *The Rebellious Century,
    1830–1930*. Cambridge: Harvard University Press.
Tocqueville, Alexis de. 1966. *Democracy in America*. Ed. J. P. Mayer. New York: Harp-
    er & Row.
Trevor Roper, H. R. 1980. "History and Imagination." *Valedictory Lecture as Regius
    Professor of History*. Oxford: Oxford University Press.
Wallerstein, Immanuel. 1974. *The Modern World System: Capitalist Agriculture and the
    Origins of the European World-Economy in the Sixteenth Century*. New York: Aca-
    demic Press.

Watkins, Frederick Mundell. 1934. *The State As a Concept of Political Science.* New York: Harper and Brothers.

———. 1968. "State." In David Sills, ed., *International Encyclopedia of the Social Sciences,* volume 15. New York: Macmillan.

Weber, Max. 1979. *The Methodology of the Social Sciences.* New York: Free Press.

Wildavsky, Aaron. 1987. "Choosing Preferences by Constituting Institutions: A Cultural Theory of Preference Formation." *American Political Science Review* 81:3-21.

Zolberg, Aristide R. 1986. "How Many Exceptionalisms?" In Ira Katznelson and Aristide R. Zolberg, eds., *Working-Class Formation: Nineteenth-Century Patterns in Western Europe and the United States.* Princeton: Princeton University Press.

PART III

THEORY DEVELOPMENT IN COMPARATIVE POLITICS

5

ELECTORAL BEHAVIOR AND COMPARATIVE POLITICS

Samuel H. Barnes

INTRODUCTION

The comparative study of mass publics has made impressive advances over the past generation. There are two principal reasons for this progress: One is the development and widespread applicability of large-scale representative sample surveys that provide data about individual attitudes and behavior; the other is the existence of a substantial body of normal science in this research arena carried out in the advanced industrial democracies of North America, Europe, and a few other areas. The former makes possible the use of sampling theory, statistical analyses, mathematical modeling, and hence rigorous quantitative standards. The latter has stimulated substantial theoretical, methodological, and software developments that provide a rich background of empirical knowledge and research experience, so that increasingly sophisticated inquiries are possible.

There are, of course, many ways to study mass publics, and several, including the analysis of social movements, are represented in this volume. Still others include the use of electoral, demographic, economic, and related aggregate data; events data; content analysis; extended open-ended interviews; and participant observation and other anthropological approaches. Several methods, however, and especially the more concentrated and intensive ones, do not deal adequately with the mapping or sampling problem, so we often know a lot about certain sets of people but do not know to what universe the generalizations really apply.[1]

This chapter will concentrate on studies utilizing national representative sample surveys. In addition to confronting the sampling and generalization problems directly, these studies have the advantage of being, in principle, universally applicable, limited only by the varying quality of survey organizations and the

---

[1]It should be recognized that survey methods can be applied to any clearly defined universe, hence surveys have widespread use other than the study of national or large-scale samples.

difficulties of constructing questionnaires that are equally suitable to various populations. This problem of equivalence is mitigated by research designs in which the substantive meaning and the context of topics being investigated do not differ excessively, though complete agreement is unlikely as to where and when such goals are achieved. Studies of such topics as values, attitudes, political participation, electoral behavior, and others in widely disparate parts of the world suggest that problems of equivalence are questions of degree, and that the future is bright for research designs of potentially wide applicability.

A major strength of representative surveys is that they permit researchers to design inquiries, to formulate questions and batteries of questions that provide useful indicators of individual attitudes and behaviors, and to use these indicators to explore relationships in which the researcher is interested. Researchers are not limited to the data provided by fortune, the needs of government, or international trade. Although opinions will continue to differ as to the utility of doing so in particular cases, in principle there are few topics that cannot be investigated in this manner. Some issues are difficult to reduce to the simplicity required in large-scale surveys. Yet respondents can respond yes or no to questions posed or can be placed in mutually exclusive categories along some dimension, providing nominal levels of measurement; respondents can also usually be placed in some "more or less" categories on variables, providing ordinal indicators. With even these levels of measurement, statistical analysis and model building are greatly facilitated. These are of great benefit to all of the approaches that concern us in the present volume. There is no intellectual or scientific substitute for the empirical testing of theoretical propositions. In many research areas, sample surveys are a major source of data for this testing. The present chapter will concentrate on theoretically relevant studies of mass publics, using survey research. Of special interest are those few studies that deal systematically with more than one country. There are excellent studies of elections and electoral behavior in many individual countries. An extensive series was edited by Howard Penniman and others over a period of years (the *At the Polls* series) and published by the American Enterprise Institute and later by Duke University Press. Hundreds of studies of individual countries have been made available through national data archives and large collections such as those at the archives of the Interuniversity Consortium for Political and Social Research.

Many of these country studies have been utilized in cross-national inquiries in the *Beliefs of Government* series on European publics. Eurobarometer biannual surveys also provide an important source of data on electoral behavior. The project on the "Comparative Study of Electoral Systems" merits attention (Rosenstone 1996). Directed by an international group of scholars, in 1996 it had commitments from more than 50 countries to execute a common research design. This study holds great promise for the development of a database for truly crossnational electoral research. It should contribute greatly to the resolution of many of the concerns raised in this chapter.

Although methodological issues abound, there is little disagreement about the main points of methods such as sampling, questionnaire construction, interviewing techniques, and even data analysis. There are, of course, many unsolved problems and areas that cry out for treatment. But improvements are likely to emerge in the process of carrying out research and not from general discussion.

This chapter will focus not only on *what* the public believes and does but, where possible, *why* it does so. Most attention will be devoted to the advanced industrial democracies, because that is where most systematic research has been carried out and hence where theoretical issues relating to this approach to studying mass publics have received the most attention.

In this chapter I will first introduce my understanding of the relationships among the three approaches on which this volume focuses. I will then use them to review two substantive areas of research on electoral behavior. The first is voting turnout, which demonstrates clearly the strengths and weaknesses of the rational actor approach, as well as the role of institutions and culture. The second area is partisan choice, a more complicated topic. This analysis begins with the argument that the mobilization of publics in advanced democracies has shifted from social, to political, and then to cognitive patterns. Analysis of several discrete research traditions or areas suggests a similar progression from the dominance of sociological and cultural approaches to an increasing reliance on rational actor approaches in the study of electoral choice.

APPROACHES TO THE STUDY OF ELECTORAL BEHAVIOR

As subsequent analysis will demonstrate, the study of electoral behavior has progressed in an ad hoc manner, largely unconcerned with the grander theoretical issues of political science as a discipline or with the great isms of the twentieth century. Because of the applied and practical nature of much of the research on electoral behavior, it has been generally – though not completely – spared the ideological disputes common to most political science fields. Early work utilized aggregate electoral returns, and these are still important data sources for much research on the topic. The survey tradition on which this chapter focuses is newer, and work is generally seen as beginning in the 1930s with the development of sampling techniques and survey organizations. The importance for democratic theory of the study of electoral behavior is paralleled by its value to campaign directors who are interested mostly in the horse race aspects of campaigns. Much electoral polling has little scholarly value. From its beginning in the 1930s, however, scholars have utilized survey research to investigate electoral behavior in depth and with rigor.

Without being overly concerned with theory, electoral research nevertheless reflects the pattern of theoretical innovation in political science as a whole. It flourished simultaneously with the behavioral revolution in the social sciences. The emphasis on measurement, statistics, models, and hypothesis testing of the movement fits neatly with the needs of students of voting; the methodological individualism and quantification of surveys made electoral research a cutting edge of the behavioral movement. The disciplinary origin of much of this innovation, even for political science, was sociology and psychology, and social-psychology in particular. It focused on the individual and on individuals interacting in groups.

Little attention was paid to culture, which was treated by some as a residual category, a "black box" into which could be poured most of the variance left unexplained by individual-level measures of variables. The avoidance was encouraged by the national, single-country nature of most electoral research. Such designs minimized cultural differences. Many subjects of a collective nature, such as identity, norms, and shared meaning, were ignored. These topics are of course relevant to the study of political participation in cross-national perspective, but the narrower topic of national electoral behavior did not seem to suffer from their omission. Anthropologists and others studying less complex societies could deal with culture; scholars dealing with complex industrial democracies largely abandoned the topic. Yet the development of comparative politics was greatly influenced by anthropological research, as that field was the sole source of information about much of the world. So the study of culture prospered more in comparative politics than in behavioral science.

There are many ways to study culture and culturalists do not agree among themselves as to methods.[2] At one extreme are those who emphasize interpretation, "thick description," and sensitive understanding of what culture means to the people being studied. Many of these scholars find large-scale surveys, with their necessary simplifications and crude attempts at measurement, unacceptable as sources of data. Students of mass behavior, including electoral behavior, in turn find much in the interpretive approach unappealing. When analysts move from little societies to large and complex ones, the deep and intimate knowledge possible of a village gives way to less empirically grounded observations about larger entities. Surveys have a major advantage over ethnographic approaches in dealing with complex societies. They also have a disadvantage, one that is less serious in complex societies.

A principal advantage of the study of culture through surveys is that it largely solves the sampling problem: To what universe do our generalizations apply? The sampling problem remains whether acknowledged or not. Cultural patterns differ from group to group, from social stratum to social stratum, from region to region. In dealing with complex societies, insights into cultural patterns become less interpersonally transmissible and less convincing. Cultural explanations are viewed as mere interpretations or impressions, subjective and lacking in empirical grounding. The sampling problem can largely be resolved through survey research. Although inadequate attention has been devoted to the development of valid indicators of cultural variables for use in surveys, surveys do solve the sampling problem.

[2]The issues in this section are discussed at greater length in Barnes (1994).

A disadvantage of studying culture through surveys is that this method does not deal well with the I/we problem: Culture is what *we* believe, not what *I* believe. It is the shared assumptions of a group interacting in particular times and places. The group is not merely a statistical category from a survey. The tendency has been to equate aggregated individual opinion with cultural assumptions. In advanced industrial societies with vast resources and much freedom of choice, the two may be very much the same. As will be discussed below, people in such societies essentially choose or create much of their culture. Hence the study of individual attitudes and behavior is a close approximation of the study of cultural assumptions.

But for much of the world, culture – conceived of as shared assumptions about what is correct and proper in most situations – is not something individuals may accept or reject. Rather, it is something they must live with and work around. They need not believe in it, in the sense that they have internalized it and follow its norms even when no one is looking; but they are subjected to sanctions of varying degrees if they go against it. It is largely in modern democracies that individuals have a wide range of choices, and even in those societies alternatives are hardly unlimited. It is important, consequently, not to think of culture as something that is always voluntary in its impact on behavior. Culture can constrain behavior much as institutions can. It rewards some behaviors and sanctions others. Like institutions, it conditions behavior, it conditions choice.

One general criticism of the culturalist approach, whether of the survey or ethnographic tradition, is that it does not deal adequately with change (but see Baker, Dalton, and Hildebrandt 1981). It is common to view culture as something basic and unchanging and, hence, to find the lack of continuity in most components of culture an argument against cultural explanations. But culture is learned. It must be reproduced across generations. Not everything that is taught is learned. Especially in changing societies, much of what elders want to transmit is simply irrelevant for the younger generation and hence is abandoned. As long as elite recruitment remains stable, those committed to change can be filtered out. But in times of transition, new skills, new sources of power, make it impossible to maintain cultural continuity.

The major source of cultural change is generational replacement. People's orientations toward cultural norms change little beyond a certain age. But as the older generation retires and dies off, the young possessing different views about many things (but never about everything!) replace them. Hence populations change but individuals don't. Change in transitional periods is accelerated by the greater adaptability of the young to new situations and the inability of the old to adapt. Over time, it becomes apparent that many older cultural components remain, for culture is the default option in guiding choice.

A culturalist perspective is useful in understanding institutions in comparative perspective. Culture has a huge impact on institutions: They are not only sets of rules and behaviors; they exist within particular cultures and they are very much influenced by the cultures of which they are a part. They also develop their own internal organizational cultures (see Ott 1989 and Schein 1985). Comparativists know that how an institution functions is very much affected by the environment around it, and that merely transferring organizations into a new setting does not guarantee that they will function as they did in the old. It is not as widely acknowledged that institutions also develop their own internal set of shared assumptions, their organizational cultures, and that these affect how the institution performs. Within a particular society, or within societies with rather similar political cultures, a change in institutions may have roughly the same effect, as is observed when electoral institutions are altered. But where the political cultures differ greatly, there is no reason to expect that institutions will generate the same set of behaviors when transplanted. Therefore comparativists find it difficult and perhaps impossible to view institutions as something independent from culture.

As in many other areas of political science we are presented with a classic problem of causal analysis, a chicken and egg situation. A recurring question since *The Civic Culture* of Almond and Verba (1963) has been whether it is cultural norms that lead to the proper functioning of democratic institutions or whether their proper functioning is itself the origin of the norms of democracy. This issue demonstrates the relationship of institutional analysis to other approaches. Institutions obviously make a difference. But the difference must stem as much from the culture of the larger society as well as the culture of the institution – the shared assumptions of those involved in it – as from the table of organization, administrative laws, patterns of routine behavior that they prescribe, and managerial oversight. Otherwise, similar institutions would not function so differently in different cultures.

At this point the place of utility maximization in comparative politics and in the study of electoral behavior can be clarified. Publics pursue their goals within the institutional and cultural constraints of particular societies. Rewards and sanctions are an integral component of institutions and are key in the structuring of rational behavior. Goals are also pursued within the constraints of shared assumptions as to what is desirable, permissible, right, wrong – in short, the cultural norms of a society. How confining these are varies greatly around the world, and contemporary advanced democracies offer great choice in the cultural as they do in the political identities available. Culture plays an important role in understanding why people believe and act as they do, and as long as comparativists are interested in this understanding, culture should remain a core interest.

In a classic statement, Milton Friedman argued that a predictive science should focus on what people *do* or should do to pursue their goals, and not their reasons for choosing these goals (1953). Much of the elegance of rational choice analysis derives from this and related formulations that avoid dealing with "tastes," with preference formation, with cognitive and psychological processes. However, within political science, rational choice approaches have assumed that a variety of types of goals can legitimately be analyzed from this perspective. While formally not representing a reconceptualization of rational action, the practical consequences of this widening of the notion of utility maximization are to make it possible to include virtually any goal in a utility maximization approach, including the goal of adhering to cultural norms. This has the potential of incorporating cultural analysis into the study of public choice. As much of recent advances in this study have focused on institutions, positive theory can make the claim to have absorbed the other two approaches. This claim will be evaluated in the years ahead.

ELECTORAL TURNOUT

In *The Logic of Collective Action,* Mancur Olson (1965) explored a basic point of contention in the application of the rational actor model to the study of mass publics: Why does anyone engage in collective action? This is especially relevant in the decision to vote (see Barzel and Silberberg 1973). No one can expect to cast the determining ballot, so the rational individual should not bother. Yet turnout in most democracies is quite high.

Turnout has been a thorny issue for positive theorists – Grofman, following Fiorina, labels turnout, "the paradox that ate rational choice theory" – and there have been many attempts to explain it within the paradigm (Grofman 1993). These have taken the form of demonstrating that voting is in fact a rational thing to do from the utility perspective or because it can achieve some personal, though not necessarily material, need. Much creativity has been expended on this task of reconciliation.

There are several utilitarian explanations. Uhlaner (1989) suggests that the role of groups in elections and the consumption benefits they bring make turning out to vote quite rational. In a similar vein, though without data, Morton (1991) developed a strategic calculus of voting models that incorporates groups. Others argue that too much is made of the paradox, that it is a low-cost activity with low benefits (Aldrich 1993). In an especially original contribution, Brunk (1980) claims that people vote because they are misled by false information about the utility gained from voting. Citing experimental data, he argues that as more people understand the irrationality of voting, turnout will decline. Size is considered an important variable in estimating the probability that one individual's political action will be decisive for the outcome. Lohmann, following Ledyard, argues that "the probability that one individual's political action will be decisive for the outcome is strictly positive in a finite-sized society" (Lohmann 1993: 320). The converse is that "turnout is close to zero if the electorate is large and imperfectly or incompletely informed" (Palfrey and Rosenthal, cited in Lohmann 1993: 320).

Among others, Riker and Ordeshook (1968) offered the sense of civic duty as an explanation. Moon, building on this theme, added a variety of individual level determinants of turnout (1992). Other analysts have emphasized that fulfilling one's sense of civic duty makes one feel good. Overbye adds the desire to invest in a good reputation as an explanation (1995). Such arguments seem to open the door to the inclusion of any psychological variable or cultural norm needed to improve the amount of variance explained. The paradox of voting causes rational choice theorists considerable discomfort, as credible resolutions of the paradox seem to require abandoning the simple version of the utility model in favor of one that incorporates variables widely viewed as affective and cultural in their origins.

This is not a problem peculiar to comparative politics. On the other hand, the question of why turnout varies among democracies is important for comparativists. While rational choice does not have a simple answer to why people vote, it does, in combination with institutional data relating to the ease of voting, explain much of the variance in turnout (see Grofman 1996 on why people vote and variations in turnout). There is strong evidence that, confronted with similar institutions and political situations, people respond in a similar fashion. There seems to be universal agreement that institutions play the principal role in turnout variations across democracies. Several major studies document their impact. Voting laws and the related issue of ease or difficulty of registration are shown to be especially relevant (see Aldrich 1993; Jackman 1987; Jackman and Miller 1995; Powell 1986; Teixeira 1987, 1992; Wolfinger and Rosenstone 1980). Some of these deal only with the United States; others include all or most advanced industrial democracies.

The explanatory power of institutional arrangements is impressive. With regressions of voter turnout on five institutional characteristics for 19 industrial democracies for the 1971–80 period, Jackman explains 74.8% of the variance. With the addition of dummy variables for the United States and Switzerland, which are the major outliers in analyses of voting turnout, 96% is explained (1987: 412). Replicating the latter analysis with 1960–1970 data, he obtained a remarkably similar 97% explained (416). These results and others led Jackman and Miller (1995) to argue for the superiority of rational choice explanations over cultural and historical ones.[3] These are impressive results, and it would seem difficult to improve on them. However, no cultural (or historical) variables were included in the analysis.[4] These advanced industrial democracies share many, indeed most, norms concerning electoral institutions, so that institutional mechanisms can hardly be considered to be independent of the norms of political culture. Moreover, there has been a decline in turnout in Europe over the past decade, a decline evident in almost all countries, yet no institutional changes seem responsible (Borg 1995). Crepaz argues that the levels of polarization and postmaterialism – political rather than institutional variables – are responsible for high levels of turnout (1990).

It could be deemed arbitrary to attribute motivations to a single class of variables. Admittedly, from the viewpoint of elegant theory, explaining the variance in turnout with the success of Jackman suggests that institutional variables are

---

[3]The data employed are aggregate, not survey, data.

[4]For an analysis employing cultural variables (values and religion), see Borg (1995). Lane and Ersson state that "special knowledge" is necessary to understand why the United States, Switzerland, Japan, and Ireland are deviant cases (1990).

sufficient. But attributing causation is not always straightforward. For example, turnout has been high in many of the elections in the new postcommunist democracies in Central and Eastern Europe. Is this due to the perceptions of rational actors of the critical importance of supporting democracy? This could be because democracy is their highest order goal, a goal adopted for a variety of reasons, of which several could be categorized as cultural or ideological. Postcommunist voters may also desire to further their individual material interests through the ballot, though in this very special and confused historical era inadequate information makes this kind of rational action problematic. The decision to vote may also be due to socialization in communist systems in which voting was required of all citizens. All of these motivations fit the rational actor model. They may also fit cultural explanations.

This brief review of turnout indicates a recurring problem in labeling the reasons for outcomes. With a rigorous conception of rational action of the Friedman variety, it is not necessary to inquire into people's motivations. It is enough that they act because of their preferences. But in political science it is often desirable to examine preferences themselves and how they arise. Few would deny that choice can be influenced by culture or religion or any number of ideational factors which could themselves, in turn, derive from formal or informal cognitive processes, childhood or adult socialization, behavioral conditioning, deprivation worries, or even fear of direct sanctions. While the mix of influences on turnout may not differ greatly in the advanced societies on which we concentrate, it is unwarranted to assume that they will be the same across all societies.

CHANGING PATTERNS IN THE MOBILIZATION OF PARTISANSHIP

The study of electoral behavior in comparative politics has benefited greatly from the importance of electoral choice for democratic political theory as well as for practical politics. Large sums have been invested both in the horse race aspects of electoral campaigns – who is winning – and also in scientific investigation into what appeals to voters and what motivates their choices. It is a useful area of focus for rigorous empirical work, as the vote is a discrete act and the actors are individuals.

A review of studies of partisan choice shows that the bases of electoral choice have varied according to space and time. An isomorphism seems to exist between theories of partisan choice and theories of changing patterns of the mobilization of mass publics in democracies.[5] Democratic mobilization has shifted from being based on *social* cleavages such as class, religion, ethnicity, and the like; to *politi-*

---

[5]This interpretation owes much to research on mass publics by several scholars. Russell Dalton pioneered the use of the concept of "cognitive mobilization" (1984). The review by Dalton and Wattenberg on "The Not So Simple Act of Voting" (1993) enriched the present chapter. The work of Franklin, Mackie, Valen et al. (1992), and of Ronald Inglehart (1977, 1990, and, with Abramson, 1995), was very valuable.

cal mobilization based on attachments to specific political objects; and, increasingly today, to *cognitive* mobilization reflecting individual decisions based on knowledge of issues, perceptions of interest, and preferences, including values. Such an interpretation assumes that in the earlier period attachment to groups defined by (societal) cleavages and institutions, of which unions and churches were the most significant, was the basis of partisan identity. In the second, it was attachment to particular political parties and movements that may have originated in the older cleavage structures but then acquired independent identities and loyalties. Advanced democracies today – with their highly educated populations, access to information through the media and elsewhere, and declining involvement in associational life – are moving toward cognitive mobilization.

Cognitive mobilization involves increasing individual processing of information, calculation of interests, and perhaps even the individual "construction" of political identities that were ascribed at birth in earlier times. Melucci (1989) argues that contemporary political identities may result largely from political action, from the exercise of choice among the wide variety of political movements and other outlets for political involvement. The grand political programs of the parties of the past, as well as the pragmatic adaptation to the party loyalties learned at home, carry little attraction for these citizens: One is what one militates in. This view has much in common with the widespread normative emphasis on participation as being good for the development of civic orientations, rather than being the consequence of their possession. The view also reflects emerging trends in advanced societies toward demassification, higher education, access to information, privatization, and rational egoism. It affects the importance of information processing, image manipulation, and the media for the study of partisan choice today, topics now at the leading edge of research.

Thus, paradoxically, in the age of cognitive mobilization, research on partisan choice needs to shift to the study of the processes through which elites provide the information available to the public, create the images, manage television, and interpret the culture for increasingly disparate publics. Several works underline this trend (see Graber 1993; Sniderman, 1993). Zaller argues that elites dominate opinion formation, and that it is primarily through division among elites that alternative views gain visibility. The public's response to information is affected by its level of cognitive engagement, or interest, with the issue; by its political predispositions; by how recently the issue has been thought about; and by the context of all the considerations that are salient or accessible (1992: 40-52).

In a work emphasizing "The Reasoning Voter," Popkin also stresses the role of information and how it is provided and received (1991). In a similar vein, Rosenstone and Hansen view electoral and other participation as largely a function of the efforts, or lack thereof, of elites to mobilize the public (1993). Budge and Farlie use a creative research design to demonstrate that, in 23 democracies, different parties are advantaged on different issues. Each party seeks to focus the electoral campaign on the issues that favor it; parties avoid confronting the same issues, so that the real electoral game is about defining the agenda, and the media play the critical role here (1983). These works all fit with a rich literature that is emerging on the role of the media and of information in general in campaigns. Comparative research on these topics is of quite recent vintage. Comparative studies of campaigns and the media are likely to become widespread.

There is strong empirical evidence for the progression described above, but research findings are not completely conclusive. Some components, such as a decline in the importance of many cleavages, the rise in educational levels, and the importance of the media – and television in particular – are noncontroversial.[6] The assumed decline in involvement in organizations and attachments to parties seems generally valid but not for all countries (see especially Kaase, Newton, and Scarbrough 1995). In this as in other areas of investigation on mass publics, attitudes and behaviors of the past are still quite apparent along with the harbingers of the future. Trends do not progress indefinitely. Diverse influences from the past linger, so that contemporary patterns reflect "priors" as well as influences of the present. As a result, no patterns are quite universal. What become critical are the size and consequences of shifts at the margins.[7]

A caveat is in order concerning the empirical basis for several aspects of this progression from social to political to cognitive mobilization. Very little hard survey data exist from before the post–World War II era, so we know little about the views of early social partisans. It is possible that what has changed is the quality of scientific inquiry rather than actual behavior, that had surveys existed earlier they would have revealed a much more sophisticated electorate in the old democracies than we currently suspect. But given the levels of education and methods of dissemination of information before the Second World War, this is highly unlikely. It is doubtful that the progression discussed above is the result of improvements in measurement.

PARTISAN IDENTIFICATION

The pioneering work in the study of electoral behavior through representative surveys was carried out largely in the United States (Lazarsfeld, Berelson, and Gaudet 1944; Berelson, Lazarsfeld, and McPhee 1954). Among advanced industrial democracies, it is the United States that always seems to be the outlier. Yet it is the United States that provided baseline measures on many aspects of mass attitudes and behavior, and this is a source of complications in comparative work. Early academic studies in the United States focused on sociological variables such

---

[6]The nature of the decline in cleavages is disputed. Dalton and Wattenberg (1993) argue that, while social class, religious, and some other cleavages have declined, many others based on different aspects of stratification survive. Franklin et al. (1992) celebrate the successful elimination of serious cleavages through generations of inclusiveness. See also Bartolini and Mair 1990.

[7]The debate is over interpretation as well as empirical questions: When are cleavages no longer important? One study noted the slow decline in their relevance combined with sudden changes in party systems: "… at 16 per cent or more of variance explained, cleavage politics appear durable. At 12 per cent or less they appear quite fragile." (van der Eijk et al. 1992:422.)

as occupation and group memberships as the most important predictor variables, and results were surprising to investigators in the United States when these variables proved not to be very important. But there is little doubt that social cleavages were important determinants of the vote in Europe.

Religion, class, and–in countries such as Spain and Belgium–region all fit into the category of social partisanship. While Marxist and leftist parties made extensive efforts at political education of their members – and also sought to create large membership organizations – many voters possessed little sense of a uniquely *political* identity. The vote was largely an expression of religious, class, and regional loyalties that for many if not most citizens were not necessarily primarily political. Unfortunately, few empirical data exist concerning the views and activities of the actors in this period.

The weakness of social partisanship in the United States led researchers at the University of Michigan in the 1950s, in a widely influential series of electoral studies and publications, to develop the concept of partisan identification (Campbell and Kahn 1952; Campbell, Gurin, and Miller 1954; Campbell et al. 1960, 1966). Underlying the concept is a learning model (Converse 1969) that has proved useful in explaining the relationship between age and participation, the strength of partisan attachments, volatility in voting patterns, perceived legitimacy of institutions, and other matters.[8] Partisanship is largely learned through socialization.

However, the Michigan model always conceived of the vote as a function of short-term factors such as campaign issues and the candidate's personal qualities as well as basic party orientations (Converse 1966; see also Anker 1990). The longer one has believed something, or done something, the more likely one is to continue to believe it or do it. Converse applied a learning model to the data from *The Civic Culture* (Almond and Verba 1963) and found an excellent fit: The level of stable partisanship in each country was a function of the amount of experience with democratic electoral politics.

The neat fit with data found in *The Civic Culture* has been hard to find elsewhere. The learning model has flaws. Early socialization may prove especially inadequate in periods of change, in which the past is a poor guide to the present. The early success of the learning model probably owed a great deal to the anchoring of partisanship in the cleavage structures of the past. Its application to recently expanded electorates, including Swiss women, Blacks from the American South, and Mexican women, showed these groups entering the electorate with higher than expected levels of partisanship (Niemi et al. 1985). Yet, proponents of a learning model would argue that one should not assume that just because they could not vote earlier, they were not developing partisan preferences.

Other studies have questioned whether dealignment is compatible with the learning model. Abramson showed that in Britain, a country with seemingly

---

[8]Despite the focus of the learning model on acculturation, Jackman (1993) and others place the learning model within a rational choice framework through an emphasis on "priors," a rational choice device for building in the influence of past choices.

highly stable allegiances, partisanship had declined among all birth cohorts, a finding that provides no support for the model (1992). Time is not the only influence on partisanship, and what is learned can be lost.

On the other hand, there is considerable evidence that different age cohorts react differently to the same stimuli, and some evidence that they do so with issue and demographic effects controlled for (see Barnes 1972; Billingsley and Tucker 1987; Mattei, Niemi, and Powell, 1990; Russell, Johnston, and Pattie 1992). Inglehart has shown systematic differences in values among generations in numerous countries, and these seem, in turn, closely related to differences in partisan preferences (1977; 1990). In particular, these value differences are closely related to the rise of Green parties in Europe.

One would expect period effects to have an impact on behavior in all systems. Thus the intensity of the civil rights struggle or the debate on the franchisement of women in Switzerland, not to mention the impact of long exposure to democratic electoral systems even for those who can't vote in them (or who could vote in some but not all elections and regions, as in Switzerland) could accelerate the learning curve – a process anticipated by Converse (1969). Likewise, many factors could affect the reproduction of partisan identity across cohorts without discrediting a learning model.

More damaging to the learning model is the disintegration of major parties in established party systems: witness the Italian Christian Democrats and Socialists; in Japan, the Liberal Democratic Party; the decline of the UCD, the leading party of Spain during the transition; and the severe losses of the Canadian Conservatives. While there are undoubtedly idiosyncratic explanations for these phenomena, they fit uneasily into a model that focuses on explaining stability.

One weakness of the simple and parsimonious version of a learning model is that it does not build in intensity, strong affect, charismatic leadership, and similar factors that can accelerate or block change.[9] Beck posits an intensity model of socialization that may be helpful: Critical events provide a generation with intense partisanship that is passed on to succeeding generations, but with decreasing intensity, so that its strength in a population declines unless critical moments redirect or reinforce it (Beck 1974; see also Pierce 1995).

The learning model is central for cultural explanations of partisanship, and its fate shows the importance of critical events for partisan change and realignment. The long influence of the New Deal on American electoral behavior has been widely demonstrated (among others, Campbell et al. 1960). In a series of studies of Spanish publics and democracy, McDonough, Barnes, and Lopez Piña document the low levels of partisanship, organizational membership, and participation in Spain. They also emphasize the largely tranquil nature of the Spanish democratic transition and consolidation, the absence of critical moments and of strong emotional attachments to the new regime, as well as the marginality of

---

[9]Converse's formulation (1969) did note that special considerations such as these could speed up or retard the achievement of stable partisanship, but it did not explore the topic.

the "public philosophy" or "civil religion" of the new system (1996). Franklin and his colleagues (1992) emphasize the lingering of old cleavage structures in Italy and Germany compared with other European countries and attribute it to the intense experience of fascism.

This brief discussion points out a difficulty in evaluating theories across time and space. Many, perhaps most, empirical social science generalizations decay over time. Approaches suitable to an era of deep cleavages and zero-sum outcomes may give way in stable and tranquil polities to periods in which only abortion is a life or death issue, in which marginal economic gains or losses motivate choice, in which the rational pursuit of private goals is possible, in which socialization in and loyalty to larger units – including the nuclear family – can be bypassed. The advanced democracies may be in such an era at the present time. At least in these countries, interest politics in general and rational choice approaches in particular may be especially appropriate. It is an opportune moment to test their utility.

Given the central role of partisan identification in much electoral research, two points merit attention. One is the argument over whether the concept is as applicable to Europe and elsewhere as to the United States. Kaase demonstrated that in Europe, where vote and partisan identification tend to change together, there is little difference between indicators for the two concepts (1976). Discussion of the utility of the concept for comparative research has continued without resolution. The second point concerns the stability of partisan identification over time. There are strong indications that it is one of the most stable of individual characteristics, at least in the United States (Barnes et al. 1988). Recent methodological analyses that take measurement error into account suggest that it is even more stable than thought and that it is little affected by short-term forces (Green and Palmquist 1990, 1994).

According to many scholars, European partisanship has also been stable throughout most of the postwar period. Lipset and Rokkan (1967) argued that European party systems were frozen in patterns established in the 1920s, and while there is debate over how such a stability should be measured (see Mair 1993) the main outlines of European loyalties seem to have changed little until recent years. Stable partisanship has been demonstrated for Germany, the Netherlands, and Britain (Richardson 1991), and there is a rich literature – mostly inconclusive due to differences in operationalization of key concepts – covering many European countries.

However, there has been a general decline in identification in most countries over the past generation. The decline fits uneasily with arguments for essential stability, and it has given rise to an intense debate concerning what is going on. Is the decline due to dealignment, the loss of partisanship? Or is it realignment, a shift from one set of strong loyalties to another? (See Andeweg 1982; Crewe and Denver 1985; Dalton, Flanagan, and Beck 1984; Franklin, Mackie, and Valen 1992; Kornberg and Clarke 1992; Zelle 1995). The case for dealignment seems stronger than that for realignment and also fits the general thesis of this chapter concerning secular trends in patterns of mobilization.

The analyses in the *Beliefs in Government* project (see Klingeman and Fuchs 1995; Kaase, Newton, and Scarbrough 1995; van Deth and Scarbrough 1995) suggest caution concerning most generalizations about change in Europe. Knutsen, for example, found "trendless fluctuation, not steady decline, in the impact of class and religion on party choice" (1995a: 506). Parties representing the old cleavages, such as the socialists, labor, liberals, conservatives, Christian Democrats, are still dominant in Europe. But the fit with class and religious practice is not what it used to be. Knutsen shows the differing impact of religion, left–right self-placement, and materialism–postmaterialism on partisanship in different countries: They are "moderately to strongly correlated with party support" (1995a: 487). In the most economically advanced countries, materialism–postmaterialism is the most important predictor of electoral choice (1995a: 507). These results challenge those of Franklin et al. who found a "developmental process of declining effects of social structure on party choice, apparently occurring in all western countries" (1992: 407). They placed different countries at different stages of this process. Changes have accelerated in some countries since the analyses of the above two research projects. It was Germany and Italy that Franklin et al. found to reflect most strongly the effects of class and religious cleavages, which they attributed to the experience of fascism in those two countries. It is clear that the Italian system has changed dramatically in recent years. On the other hand, the German has withstood the union of West and East Germany without many changes yet apparent. But the long-term impact of unification is not yet clear.

THE INFLUENCE OF IDEAS AND CULTURE

Ideas influence politics in many ways. The ideological sophistication of the public has been a widely researched and debated subject for a generation. While there are differences among researchers concerning the marginals, as well as some differences among countries, all conclude that only a small portion of the public exhibits an ideological orientation toward politics. Elites may be tied to a particular ideology or philosophy or theology. But the impact of abstract ideas on mass publics is largely through elite influences on the public, or through the absorption of what perhaps began as abstract ideas into their culture. Ideologues would like nothing better than the incorporation of their beliefs into culture, the set of shared assumptions of particular groups. The study of ideas thus conceived should not be separated from the study of how people acquire and change these shared assumptions and, especially, the experiences, institutions, and networks that shape their learning. Whether individuals follow the norms of culture is dependent on many contextual factors, among which the ability to deviate from the norms without suffering sanctions is quite important. Thus the nature of sanctions and social and other controls is more important than the degree of internalization of the norms: A widely shared norm is "cheat if you can get away with it." In complex advanced industrial societies that facilitate cognitive mobilization, the group and societal control mechanisms common in earlier periods lose their effectiveness, and it is likely that rational egoism increasingly dominates over cultural demands. But ideas seem important in politics, perhaps independently of their absorption in the larger culture. What follows are two examples of how ideational factors have related to partisan choice.

VALUES AND CULTURE

In a remarkable series of books and articles, Ronald Inglehart has developed a theory of value change that has held up through two decades of empirical research and criticism (1977, 1990). His thesis is that people value most – place higher on their value hierarchy – that which they felt deprived of in their youth. The result is a shift from materialist values among those socialized in less secure times and places to postmaterialist values among those who did not suffer such insecurities. Note that he refers to the ranking of values, not to their absolute level: Postmaterialists are not antimaterialists. Rather, they take material well-being for granted and focus on other concerns. Inglehart's research shows that postmaterialism is associated with many important shifts in public opinions. Although his four-item battery deals only with the ranking of fighting inflation, providing a strong defense, freedom of speech, and the right to participate, it yields a measure that is strongly associated with proenvironmentalist views, the new left, a civic culture, and choice in lifestyles. Postmaterialism is also strongly associated with support for Green parties, which are among the few innovations on the party landscape in the last generation. The widespread applicability and predictive power of this simple measure is encouraging about the possibility of using surveys to study ideas and cultural concerns among mass publics.

There is, of course, far more to values and culture than postmaterialism. Religious beliefs and practices are obviously important. The current revival of concern with questions of identity – national, ethnic, and others – also stems from a renewal of concern for aspects of culture.

LEFT AND RIGHT IDENTIFICATIONS

Subjective left and right self-identification is an ideational variable with a close relationship to partisan choice. When one focuses on the general tendency of the voter rather than on the particular party, European preferences seem especially stable. One difference between the United States and European multiparty systems is that in the latter one can shift one's vote to a different party without necessarily voting for one whose "tendency" is contrary to one's own. This is not possible in a two-party plurality system. That is, in Europe there are likely to be several parties reasonably close to the citizen in a spatial sense, and he or she can switch among them without deep emotional involvement.

In Europe, tendency is expressed in terms of left and right, often on a ten-point scale; in the United States, the usual measure is a similar liberal–conservative scale (ignoring the fact that in the rest of the world both of these positions fall on the right!). In France, where the Communist party is the only one to keep the same name over the postwar period, tendency is quite stable though party vote is labile (Converse and Pierce 1986). A panel study in Spain in 1978 and 1980 demonstrated that citizens in a new democracy quickly acquired a left–right identification and that it was very stable over time (Barnes, McDonough, and Lopez Piña 1985). Another study of European cohorts using Eurobarometer data from 1975 to 1987 showed a secular shift to the left in left–right identification, despite the success of right and center-right candidates during the period (Barnes 1991). This study also demonstrated that all of the political families had moved to the left, so that they remained unchanged in their relationships with one another.

Left–right tendency seems to be relational, an empty container into which are poured the issues and dimensions of conflict of the day (Knutsen 1995b). Issues are ordered by the political debate in a manner that may render meaning different from country to country and from time to time. Left–right is a useful device for voters to organize a confusing and complex political space. In electoral terms, it has no enduring substantive political meaning outside of particular political contexts and times.

The meaning of left and right changes over time, and we are witnessing an important cleavage emerging in Europe between the old left and the new left. The old is based on the group loyalties and interests associated with the working class, with its concern with mass parties, jobs, economic security, and the welfare state. The new left places greater value on such issues as the environment, peace, individual and group rights, and direct action.

A new right is emerging in Europe as well, one that, in separate countries, shares a concern with political and economic nationalism, opposition to immigrants, and populism (Billiet and de Witte 1995). The European right has hitherto been essentially more status quo oriented than ideological, but in recent decades innovation has been as likely to come from the right as from the left – witness Thatcher, DeGaulle, Berlusconi – while the working class, fearful of the new age of globalization of economies and the threat to the welfare state, seems resistant to change. These changes have contributed to the decline in the strength of the relationship between electoral choice and social class and create confusion in the contemporary meaning of left and right.

ECONOMIC APPROACHES TO PARTISAN CHOICE

In all times and places, the relevance of economic and other interests to politics and partisan choice has been acknowledged. The influence of groups defined in various ways has likewise been largely taken for granted. It is the way in which interests get to be understood and defined and how and why they are translated into political action and partisan choices that are the primary concerns in the study of electoral behavior.

Although rational choice approaches have made substantial contributions to many different areas of political science and comparative politics, their impact has not been as great on the latter as on the former. And many aspects of rational choice thinking blend with other approaches. The focus on the role of issues in electoral choice, for example, has benefited from rational choice concerns with individual goals and is often juxtaposed to the previous concern with partisan identification based on socialization. But students of "the old school" never neglected the role of issues. They merely did not ascribe (or find) as strong a role as later scholars did. As has been remarked earlier, given information costs, it may be quite rational to identify with a party and to use that party's leaders and pronouncements as guides as to what are the voter's best interests. The main shift in paradigms seems to concern the relative salience of issues as opposed to psychological identification and position in cleavage structures.

The publication of Downs's *An Economic Theory of Democracy* (1957) began the slow growth of rational choice theory in political science. Downs was the stimulus in political science for the shift in the evaluation of economic influences from groups to the rational actor, and he introduced spatial models into the study of voting. Spatial modeling has received considerable attention in political science and has produced an impressive body of writings (Enelow and Hinich 1984; Enelow and Hinich 1990; Grofman 1993; Stokes 1963). Much of the work on spatial models is purely formal; some is experimental; some is also empirical. Spatial modeling has as much to say about elite as about mass goal seeking, as it also deals with how parties should locate themselves in political space in order to minimize the distance between themselves and an electoral majority. It also implies that voters hold policy preferences and that they support the party, or parties, that have in the past been and promise in the future to be situated closest to these preferences.

Spatial models continue to hold an important place in theories of electoral choice as they do in coalition theory and other rational choice approaches. Their importance and relevance are unlikely to diminish with time. However, they continue to be modified and refined. A critique of spatial theory emerges from the research of MacDonald, Rabinowitz, and Listhaug (Rabinowitz and MacDonald 1989; MacDonald, Listhaug, and Rabinowitz1991; Listhaug, MacDonald, and Rabinowitz 1994; MacDonald, Rabinowitz, and Listhaug 1995). They argue for the superiority of directional over spatial models, saying that the concern of spatial models for minimizing issue space between parties and their voters misses the stimulus and attractiveness of intensity provided by parties with more extreme viewpoints. The centrism valued in spatial theory becomes a weakness rather than a strength. Directional theory is being tested in new environments, with the results suggestive of its strength but as yet not conclusive (Iversen 1994a, 1994b; Maddens 1996).

The traditional conceptualization of partisan identification assumed that there was nothing incompatible between loyalty to a party and voting for the party whose policies one favored. Given information costs and the marginality of politics for many people, continuing to vote for a particular party that had supported one's interests in the past was a rational form of decision making. But this view also recognized that partisanship entered into the voter's understanding of his or her interests, that voters might look to parties for guidance as to what were their interests. That policy preferences played an independent and major role in partisan choice was argued by Fiorina. In an important reinterpretation of American electoral behavior, Fiorina showed that partisan identification is greatly influenced by people's "past political events and experiences," by the performance of parties in office, and by their retrospective evaluations (1981: 200). Rather than being a permanent childhood acquisition, party loyalty is based on continual evaluation of how well the party is defending the interests of the individual critical voter, a running accounting of the fit between the party's actions and the voter's preferences. Retrospective vs. prospective (what the candidate promises to do) is now a recurring theme in electoral research. In Fiorina's work, the rational actor merges with the cognitively mobilized voter.

Although it is clear that economic concerns play a major role in electoral behavior, the state of the economy operates in an unusual manner in the voting decision. To the surprise of many, it has proved difficult to demonstrate a close relationship between the vote and change in the impact on the individual voter of economic conditions. Rather than their impact on the individual voter, it is the state of the economy as a whole that seems to affect voting choice, that is, the evidence shows that politicians are evaluated on their management of the economy rather than on how their policies affect the individual (Eulau and Lewis-Beck 1985; Jacobson and Kernell 1983; Kiewiet 1983; Lewis-Beck 1988). Kinder and Kiewiet (1981) labeled this phenomenon "sociotropic" voting, and it has been shown to be widespread in Europe as well (Lewis-Beck 1988; Middendorp and Tanke 1990; Rattinger 1986; for an example of pocketbook voting see Nannestad and Paldam 1995). Whether this is economic egoism or altruism is open to debate, but it certainly suggests a complicated relationship between economic conditions and individual choices.

THEORY AND THE STUDY OF MASS PUBLICS

In a seminal work of more than two decades ago, Przeworski and Teune wrote that the goal of comparative politics is to substitute the names of variables for proper names, a focus especially relevant in the study of mass publics (1970). Comparativists should look for similar patterns of attitudes and behavior across diverse political systems. If variables interact with one another in a similar fashion even if at different magnitudes, one can say that system is not important. They label this the most different system approach. Great progress has been made in the search for generalizations. Comparative research has identified numerous patterns of attitudes and behavior that reflect similar causes and relationships across a wide variety of systems. This is especially true in the study of mass publics where a rich comparative literature is developing in areas such as political participation, social movements, values, and, as demonstrated in the present chapter, electoral behavior.

But despite a generation of effort, country remains the most common proper name/explanatory variable in comparative politics: We can hardly do without it (see van Deth 1995). There are at least two possible reasons for this claim. One is that the unexplained variance exists because of measurement error, inadequate model specification and creativity on the part of researchers, and the sparse resources and attention devoted to systematic comparative research. The proper name of "country" is thus merely the label for what is not yet known. Increased effort will remedy the situation.

The other reason for the continued importance of country is that choices made in the past lead to particular paths of development. Different positions in economic, demographic, and other cycles have consequences. Geographic position, natural resources, religious and cultural heritages are destiny. As recent theoretical developments suggest, even the fluttering of butterfly wings far away may have consequences. These reasons too are amenable to scholarly analysis, though they probably require different tools from those discussed in this chapter.

It would be imprudent to predict how much of the differences among countries can be explained with universal generalizations. Considerable progress has been made. The search has led to some valuable findings. The previous pages have documented some of these for electoral behavior. It is important to know what is quasi-universal and what is particular, and for both theoretical and practical reasons. Comparativists need to develop a general, theoretically coherent, and empirically based understanding of the field; comparativists also need to understand the politics of particular areas by whatever sources of information seem to be relevant.

Previous "grand theories" in comparative politics owed much to varieties of structural-functionalism, an approach that quickly proved inadequate for the high expectations evoked. No contender received wide support as its replacement until the rise of rational choice approaches. Note that the search for generalizations in comparative politics does not require their incorporation into a single grand theory. Neither culturalist nor institutionalist theories hold much promise as grand theories. While "nothing is as practical as a good theory," as Karl Deutsch supposedly said, there are not enough of them around. Perhaps only rational choice is still a serious contender as a general theory, though it too is meeting substantial resistance (see, for example, Cook and Levi 1990; Green and Shapiro 1994).

Rather than all-purpose grand theories, it is islands of theory, theories of the middle range, that have largely emerged inductively in such areas as electoral behavior, participation, values and culture, and have thus far proved most useful in the study of mass behavior. Some of this success may be due to their ties to survey research and to the large investment in this area made possible by its many practical applications. Certainly, the practical value of understanding electoral behavior makes the study of particular elections in particular regions important, in addition to the search for general theory.

The development of general, cross-national, and elegant theories should be pursued. But this should not lead to the exclusion of regional and country studies, for such theories will be of little use if they don't contribute to understanding the politics of particular areas of the world. The inductive islands of theory approach should not be abandoned until something demonstrably superior comes along. Some rational choice scholars see their theory as the only promising unifying approach, and argue that *it* should be accepted until something demonstrably better comes along. To follow this advice would limit the comparative field's potential: The island of theory that is contemporary comparative research on electoral behavior can incorporate the achievements of rational choice theory without abandoning insights from other traditions. If rational choice lives up to its promise, it will be widely adopted.

Until this happens, the study of mass publics in comparative politics should continue to benefit from the knowledge of attitudes and behavior developed in particular areas by a generation of researchers, at first largely American but now European and international. Research on voting, political involvement, values, and related topics has benefited tremendously from insights coming from all of the approaches featured in this volume, from culture, rational choice, and institutions. Research has been problem-driven. This is especially suitable to a field that extends across many time zones, both geographically and temporally. While it is probably a good science strategy for some scholars to concentrate on model building devoid of empirical data and unconcerned with questions of verisimilitude, it is an unwise strategy if it results in a loss of concern for the idiosyncracies of the real world.

Rational choice approaches may prove to be more useful for the study of some regions and eras than others. Rational action or even choice are not equally available to diverse populations, whether due to cultural expectations, low levels of economic alternatives, or political authoritarianism. Models that focus on low levels of information may not resolve this problem. Moreover, in societies with civil wars, widespread brigandage, erratic law enforcement, and inadequate financial institutions, lack of predictability renders pursuit of long-range goals problematic. How useful rational choice assumptions will be in such situations remains to be determined.

On the other hand, the patterns of change in the nature of electoral choice discussed in this chapter suggest that aspects of electoral choice in advanced industrial societies may become increasingly amenable to explanations that focus on the individual's rational pursuit of his or her goals. These goals are likely to be increasingly complex, involving a trade-off between material and nonmaterial goals as information levels increase, opportunities expand, and resources and postmaterialists proliferate. For researchers, understanding the dynamics of choosing among these often conflicting and always complex goals is likely to be at least as interesting as the study of how they are pursued. The language may remain that of rational choice, but it must increasingly incorporate cultural and institutional variables into its models.

This brief recounting of some major insights of electoral research should be sufficient to indicate the multiplicity of influences on voting choices. Institutions are clearly important, in that electoral laws, party systems, and the internal lives of parties have a large influence in mediating between the individual voter and his or her ties to particular parties. Furthermore, the move to cognitive mobilization lessens the direct ties between the individual and the party as an institution and its leaders. Party organizations remain strong everywhere but in ways that are different from the past. City machines in the United States have virtually disappeared. United States elections are primarily candidate rather than party oriented, and this tendency is increasingly visible in other advanced democracies. The European mass party of mobilization/integration of the first three-quarters of this century, whether of the left or of a Christian Democratic orientation, seems in fatal decline. Elections are capital-intensive rather than labor-intensive. Television replaces rallies and demonstrations; it also places more emphasis on the image of the party leader. Electoral politics rather than internal party activity looms larger and larger, as party programs overlap and efforts are directed at voters as much as at party militants. Parties are primarily machines for winning elections, not for mobilizing true believers.

Although elections are still in part about interests, interests are as likely to be nonmaterial as narrowly economic. Interests of all kinds can be analyzed from the perspective of rational choice, but such a point of view does not seem to possess theoretical advantages over eclectic approaches that view interests as formed in part by socialization, in part by moral and intellectual choices, and in part by the context within which political action takes place. The search for generalizations should not be abandoned. But neither should the effort to understand particular situations. It is more than an act of faith to say that the former contributes to the latter.

REFERENCES

Abramson, Paul R. 1992. "Of Time and Partisan Instability in Britain." *British Journal of Political Science* 22:381-95.

Abramson, Paul R., and Ronald Inglehart. 1995. *Value Change in Global Perspective.* Ann Arbor: University of Michigan Press.

Aldrich, John A. 1993. "Rational Choice and Turnout." *American Journal of Political Science* 37:246-78.

Almond, Gabriel A., and Verba, Sidney. 1963. *The Civic Culture.* Princeton: Princeton University Press.

Andeweg, Rudy B. 1982. *Dutch Voters Adrift: On Explanations of Electoral Change 1963–1977.* The Netherlands: Krips Repro Meppel.

Anker, Hans. 1990. "Drawing Aggregate Inferences from Individual Level Data: The Utility of the Notion of a Normal Vote." *European Journal of Political Research* 18:373-87.

Baker, K. L., R. J. Dalton, and K. Hildebrandt. 1981. *Germany Transformed.* Cambridge: Harvard University Press.

Barnes, Samuel H. 1972. "The Legacy of Fascism: Generational Differences in Italian Political Attitudes and Behavior." *Comparative Political Studies.* 5:41-57.

———. 1991. "On the Electoral Persistence of Parties of the Right." In Karlheinz Reif and Ronald Inglehart, eds., *Eurobarometer.* London: Macmillan.

———. 1994. "Politics and Culture." In Frederick D. Weil, ed., *Research on Democracy and Society,* Vol. 2. Greenwich, CT: JAI Press Inc.

Barnes, Samuel H., Barbara Farah, Ronald Inglehart, and Kent Jennings. 1988. "Party Identification and Party Closeness in Comparative Perspective." *Political Behavior* 10:215-31.

Barnes, Samuel H., Peter McDonough, and Antonio Lopez Piña. 1985. "The Development of Partisanship in New Democracies: The Case of Spain." *American Journal of Political Science* 29:695-721.

Bartolini, Stefano, and Peter Mair. 1990. *Identity, Competition and Electoral Availability: The Stabilization of European Electorates, 1985–1995.* Cambridge: Cambridge University Press.

Barzel, Yoram, and Eugene Silberberg. 1973. "Is the Act of Voting Rational?" *Public Choice* 16:51-8.

Beck, Paul Allen. 1974. "A Socialization Theory of Partisan Realignment." In Richard G. Niemi, ed., *The Politics of Future Citizens: New Dimensions in the Political Socialization of Children.* San Francisco: Jossey-Bass.

Berelson, Bernard R., Paul F. Lazarsfeld, and William N. McPhee. 1954. *Voting.* Chicago: University of Chicago Press.

Billiet, Jaak, and Hans De Witte. 1995. "Attitudinal Dispositions to Vote for a 'New' Extreme Right-Wing Party: The Case of 'Vlaams Blok'." *European Journal of Political Research* 27:181-202.

Billingsley, Keith R., and Clyde Tucker. 1987. "Generations, Status and Party Identification: A Theory of Operant Conditioning." *Political Behavior* 9:305-22.

Borg, Sami. 1995. "Electoral Participation." In Jan van Deth and Elinor Scarbrough, eds., *The Impact of Values.* Oxford: Oxford University Press.

Brunk, Gregory G. 1980. "The Impact of Rational Participation Models on Voting Attitudes." *Public Choice* 35:549-64.

Budge, Ian, and Dennis J. Farlie. 1983. *Explaining and Predicting Elections.* London: George Allen and Unwin.

Campbell, Angus, Philip E. Converse, Warren E. Miller, and Donald E. Stokes. 1960. *The American Voter.* New York: John Wiley and Sons.

———. 1966. *Elections and the Political Order.* New York: John Wiley and Sons.

Campbell, Angus, Gerald Gurin, and Warren E. Miller. 1954. *The Voter Decides.* Evanston, IL: Row, Peterson, and Co.

Campbell, Angus, and Robert L. Kahn. 1952. *The People Elect a President.* Ann Arbor: University of Michigan.

Converse, Philip E. 1966. "The Concept of a Normal Vote." In Angus Campbell, Philip E. Converse, Warren E. Miller, and Donald E. Stokes, eds., *Elections and the Political Order.* New York: John Wiley and Sons.

———. 1969. "Of Time and Partisan Stability." *Comparative Political Studies.* 2:139-71.

———. "Politicization of the Electorate in the U.S. and France." *Public Opinion Quarerly* 26:1-23.

Converse, Philip E., and Roy Pierce. 1986. *Political Representation in France.* Cambridge: Belknap Press of Harvard University Press.

Cook, Karen Schweers, and Margaret Levi, eds. 1990. *The Limits of Rationality.* Chicago: University of Chicago Press.

Crepaz, Markus M. L. 1990. "The Impact of Party Polarization and Postmaterialism on Voter Turnout." *European Journal of Political Research* 18:183-205.

Crewe, Ivor, and David Denver. 1985. *Electoral Change in Western Democracies.* London: Croom Helm.

Dalton, Russell J. 1984. "Cognitive Mobilization and Partisan Dealignment in Advanced Industrial Democracies." *Journal of Politics* 46:264-84.

Dalton, Russell J., Scott Flanagan, and Paul Beck, eds. 1984. *Electoral Change in Advanced Industrial Democracies.* Princeton: Princeton University Press.

Dalton, Russell J., and Martin P. Wattenberg. 1993. "The Not So Simple Act of Voting." In Ada W. Finifter, ed., *Political Science: The State of the Discipline II.* Washington, D.C.: The American Political Science Association.

Downs, Anthony. 1957. *An Economic Theory of Democracy.* New York: Harper.

Enelow, James M., and Melvin J. Hinich. 1984. *The Spatial Theory of Voting: An Introduction.* Cambridge: Cambridge University Press.

————, eds. 1990. *Advances in the Spatial Theory of Voting.* Cambridge: Cambridge University Press.

Eulau, Heinz, and M. S. Lewis-Beck, eds. 1985. *Economic Conditions and Electoral Outcomes: The United States and Europe.* New York: Agathon Press.

Fiorina, Morris. 1981. *Retrospective Voting in American National Elections.* New Haven: Yale University Press.

Franklin, M., T. Mackie, and H. Valen et al. 1992. *Electoral Change: Responses to Evolving Social and Attitudinal Structures in Western Countries.* Cambridge: Cambridge University Press.

Friedman, Milton. 1953. "The Methodology of Positive Economics." In *Essays in Positive Economics,* ed. Milton Friedman. Chicago: University of Chicago Press.

Graber, Doris. 1993. "Political Communication: Scope, Progress, Promise." In Ada W. Finifter, ed., *Political Science: The State of the Discipline II.* Washington, D.C.: American Political Science Association.

Green, Donald P., and Bradley Palmquist. 1990. "Of Artifacts and Partisan Instability." *American Journal of Political Science* 34:872-902.

————. 1994. "How Stable Is Party Identification?" *Political Behavior* 16:437-66.

Green, Donald P., and Ian Shapiro. 1994. *Pathologies of Rational Choice Theory.* New Haven: Yale University Press.

Grofman, Bernard, ed. 1993. *Information, Participation, and Choice: An Economic Theory of Democracy in Perspective.* Ann Arbor: University of Michigan Press.

————. 1996. "Political Economy: Downsian Perspectives." In Robert E. Goodin and Hans-Dieter Klingemann, eds., *A New Handbook of Political Science.* New York: Oxford University Press.

Inglehart, Ronald. 1977. *The Silent Revolution.* Princeton: Princeton University Press.

————. 1990. *Culture Shift in Advanced Industrial Societies.* Princeton: Princeton University Press.

Iversen, Torben. 1994a. "The Logics of Electoral Politics: Spatial, Directional, and Mobilizational Effects." *Comparative Political Studies* 27:155-89.

————. 1994b. "Political Leadership and Representation in West European Democracies: A Test of Three Models of Voting." *American Journal of Political Science* 38:45-74.

Jackman, Robert W. 1987. "Political Institutions and Voter Turnout in the Industrial Democracies." *American Political Science Review* 81:405-23.

————. 1993. "Rationality and Political Participation." *American Journal of Political Science* 37:279-90.

Jackman, Robert W., and Ross A. Miller. 1995. "Voter Turnout in the Industrial Democracies During the 1980s." *Comparative Political Studies* 27:467-92.

Jacobson, Gary C., and Kernell, Samuel. 1983. *Strategy and Choice in Congressional Elections*. New Haven: Yale University Press.

Kaase, Max. 1976. "Party Identification and Voting Behavior in the West-German Election of 1969." In Ian Budge, Ivor Crewe, and Dennis Farlie, eds., *Party Identification and Beyond*. London: Wiley.

Kaase, Max, Kenneth Newton, Elinor Scarbrough, eds. 1995. *Beliefs in Government*. Oxford: Oxford University Press.

Kiewiet, D. R. 1983. *Macroeconomics and Micropolitics*. Chicago: University of Chicago Press.

Kinder, Donald, and D. R. Kiewiet. 1981. "Sociotropic Politics." *British Journal of Political Science* 11:129-61.

Klingemann, Hans-Dieter, and Dieter Fuchs, eds. 1995. *Citizens and the State*. Oxford: Oxford University Press.

Knutsen, Oddbjorn. 1995a. "Party Choice." In Jan van Deth and Elinor Scarbrough, eds., *The Impact of Values*. Oxford: Oxford University Press.

————. 1995b. "Value Orientations, Political Conflicts and Left-Wing Identification: A Comparative Study." *European Journal of Political Research* 28:63-93.

Kornberg, Allan, and Harold D. Clarke. 1992. *Citizens and Community: Political Support in a Representative Democracy*. New York: Cambridge University Press.

Lane, Jan-Erik, and Svante Ersson. 1990. "Macro and Micro Understanding in Political Science: What Explains Electoral Participation?" *European Journal of Political Research* 18:457-65.

Lazarsfeld, Paul F., Bernard R. Berelson, and Hazel Gaudet. 1944. *The People's Choice*. New York: Duell, Sloan and Pearce.

Lewis-Beck, Michael. 1988. *Economics and Elections: The Major Western Democracies*. Ann Arbor: University of Michigan Press.

Lipset, M. S., and Stein Rokkan, eds. 1967. *Party Systems and Voter Alignments: Cross-National Perspectives*. London: Macmillan.

Listhaug, Ola, Stuart Elaine MacDonald, and George Rabinowitz. 1994. "Ideology and Party Support in Comparative Perspective." *European Journal of Political Research* 25:111-49.

Lohmann, Susanne. 1993. "A Signaling Model of Informative and Manipulative Political Action." *American Political Science Review* 87:319-33.

MacDonald, Stuart Elaine, Ola Listhaug, and George Rabinowitz. 1991. "Issues and Party Support in Multiparty Systems." *American Political Science Review* 85:1107-32.

MacDonald, Stuart Elaine, George Rabinowitz, and Ola Listhaug. 1995. "Political Sophistication and Models of Issue Voting." *British Journal of Political Science* 25:453-83.

Maddens, Bart. 1996. "Directional Theory of Issue Voting: The Case of the 1991 Parliamentary Elections in Flanders." *Electoral Studies* 15:53-70.

Mair, Peter. 1993. "Myths of Electoral Change and the Survival of Traditional Parties." *European Journal of Political Research* 24:121-33.

Mattei, Franco, Nienni, Richard G., and G. Bingham Powell. 1990. "On the Depth and Persistence of Generational Change: Evidence from Italy." *Comparative Political Studies* 23:334-54.

McDonough, Peter, Samuel H. Barnes, and Antonio Lopez Piña. 1996. Mss. "Democratization and the Culture of Mass Politics: Spain in Comparative Perspective."

Melucci, Alberto. 1989. *Nomads of the Present: Social Movements and Individual Needs in Contemporary Society.* Philadelphia: Temple University Press.

Middendorp, C. P. and P. R. Kolkhuis Tanke. 1990. "Economic Voting in the Netherlands." *European Journal of Political Research* 18:535-55.

Mohler, Peter. 1987. "Cycles of Value Change." *European Journal of Political Research* 15:155-65.

Moon, David. 1992. "The Determinants of Turnout in Presidential Elections: An Integrative Model Accounting for Information." *Political Behavior* 14:123-40.

Morton, Rebecca B. 1991. "Groups in Rational Turnout Models." *American Journal of Political Science* 35:758-76.

Nannestad, Peter, and Martin Paldam. 1995. "It's the Government's Fault! A Cross-Section Study of Economic Voting in Denmark, 1990/1993." *European Journal of Political Research* 28:33-62.

Niemi, Richard G., G. Bingham Powell Jr., Harold W. Stanley, and C. Lawrence Evans. 1985. "Testing the Converse Partisanship Model with New Electorates." *Comparative Political Studies* 18:300-22.

Olson, Mancur. 1965. *The Logic of Collective Action: Public Goods and the Theory of Groups.* Cambridge: Harvard University Press.

Ott, J. S. 1989. *The Organizational Culture Perspective.* Chicago: Chicago University Press.

Overbye, Einar. 1995. "Making a Case for the Rational, Self-Regarding, 'Ethical' Voter ... and Solving the 'Paradox of Not Voting' in the Process." *European Journal of Political Research* 27:369-96.

Pierce, Roy. 1995. *Choosing the Chief: Presidential Elections in France and the United States.* Ann Arbor: University of Michigan Press.

Popkin, Samuel. 1991. *The Reasoning Voter.* Chicago: University of Chicago Press.

Powell, G. Bingham, Jr. 1986. "American Voting Turnout in Comparative Perspective." *American Political Science Review* 80:17-44.

Przeworski, Adam, and Henry Teune. 1970. *The Logic of Comparative Social Inquiry.* New York: Wiley-Interscience.

Rabinowitz, George, and MacDonald, Stuart Elaine. 1989. "A Directional Theory of Issue Voting." *American Political Science Review* 83:93-121.

Rattinger, Hans. 1986. "Collective and Individual Economic Judgements and Voting in West Germany, 1961–1984." *European Journal of Political Research* 14:393-419.

Richardson, Bradley M. 1991. "European Party Loyalties Revisited." *American Political Science Review* 85:751-75.

Riker, William H., and Peter C. Ordeshook. 1968. "A Theory of the Calculus of Voting." *American Political Science Review* 62:25-42.

Rosenstone, Steven J. 1996. "Data Collection Begins for the Comparative Study of Electoral Systems." In *ICORE News* Newsletter, Number 5, February.

Rosenstone, Steven J., and John Mark Hansen. 1993. *Mobilization, Participation, and Democracy in America.* New York: Macmillan.

Russell, A. T., R. J. Johnston, and C. J. Pattie. 1992. "Thatcher's Children: Exploring the Links between Age and Political Attitudes." *Political Studies* 40:742-56.

Schein, E. 1985. *Organizational Culture and Leadership.* San Francisco: Jossey-Bass.

Sniderman, Paul M. 1993. "The New Look in Public Opinion Research." In Ada W. Finifter, ed., *Political Science: The State of the Discipline II.* Washington D.C.: American Political Science Association.

Stokes, D. E. 1963. "Spatial Models of Party Competition." *American Political Science Review* 57:368-77.

Teixeira, Ruy. 1987. *Why Americans Don't Vote: Turnout Decline in the United States, 1960–1984.* New York: Greenwood Press.

———. 1992. *The Disappearing American Voter.* Washington, D.C.: Brookings Institution.

Uhlaner, Carole J. 1989. "Rational Turnout: The Neglected Role of Groups." *American Journal of Political Science* 33:390-422.

van der Eijk, Cees, Mark Franklin, Tom Mackie, and Henry Valen. 1992. "Cleavages, Conflict Resolution, and Democracy." In M. Franklin, T. Mackie, and H. Valen, eds., *Electoral Change: Responses to Evolving Social and Attitudinal Structures in Western Countries.* Chicago: University of Chicago Press.

van Deth, Jan W. 1995. "Comparative Politics and the Decline of the Nation-State in Western Europe." *European Journal of Political Research* 27:443-62.

van Deth, Jan W. and Elinor Scarbrough, eds. 1995. *The Impact of Values.* Oxford: Oxford University Press.

Wolfinger, Raymond E., and Steven J. Rosenstone. 1980. *Who Votes?* New Haven: Yale University Press.

Zaller, John R. 1992. *The Nature and Origins of Mass Opinion.* Cambridge: Cambridge University Press.

Zelle, Carsten. 1995. "Social Dealignment Versus Political Frustration: Contrasting Explanations of the Floating Vote in Germany." *European Journal of Political Research* 27:319-45.

6

TOWARD AN INTEGRATED PERSPECTIVE ON SOCIAL MOVEMENTS AND REVOLUTION

Doug McAdam, Sidney Tarrow, and Charles Tilly

The aim of this chapter is to evaluate the contributions of the rationalist, structuralist and culturalist traditions to the present state of empirical work in comparative politics. As students of "contentious politics," we have been asked to offer such an evaluation in regard to comparative work on social movements and revolutions. We are immediately faced with three major problems, as well as with an opportunity. The problems are: (1) theoretical multivocality; (2) a gap between studies of movements in liberal democratic systems and those in the rest of the world; and (3) that students of social movements and revolutions focus on different "phases" of the dynamics of contentious politics. The opportunity is that there are currently rich traditions of structuralist, rationalist, and culturalist work in the field of contentious politics that cry out for theoretical synthesis. The confrontation and synthesis of structuralist, rationalist, and culturalist perspectives raises serious metatheoretical issues: the nature of culture, its relationship to social structure, the general viability of rational choice explanations, the character of agency, and much more. Although shadows of those issues fall across the discussion repeatedly, our analysis focuses on treatments of contentious politics as they have developed over recent years.

PROBLEMS AND OPPORTUNITIES

At its most general, the study of contentious politics includes all situations in which actors make collective claims on other actors, claims which, if realized would affect the actors' interests, when some government is somehow party to the claims. In these terms, wars, revolutions, rebellions, (most) social movements, industrial conflict, feuds, riots, banditry, shaming ceremonies, and many more forms of collective struggle usually qualify as contentious politics. Although from time to time, a heroic synthesizer such as Kenneth Boulding (1962) lays out a general theory of conflict, the study of contentious politics has not proceeded as a unified field. Instead, specialists in different kinds of political contention have created sui generis models of their subject matter, often ignoring powerful analogies with neighboring phenomena. As a result, each group of practitioners has emphasized a different set of concepts, theoretical issues, and comparisons.[1]

A related problem for gathering comparative knowledge arises from the fact that the core of the current theoretical corpus of work on contentious politics focuses on Western reform movements, while specialists outside the domain of recent Western democratic experience (e. g., students of previous centuries and/or China, Latin America, Africa, the Middle East, or Eastern Europe) have often borrowed the ideas and apparatus of social movement specialists but have not established a genuine dialogue with analysts of contemporary Western European and North American movements. Differences inherent in these settings have all too frequently been dealt with by culturalist proclamation – or by assuming the universality of certain models – rather than by parsing differences into variables that can be integrated into systematic comparisons with movements in various parts of the world. As a result, scholars of Western democratic and Third World movements frequently use different vocabularies, sometimes lapsing into interpretative particularism and sometimes imagining they are theorizing broadly when their empirical bases exclude vast parts of the globe.

Finally, social movement analysts have stressed the origins, social bases, and organization and dynamics of the phenomena they study but usually neglect their outcomes, whereas analysts of revolution love origins and outcomes but often neglect organization and dynamics, and sometimes even agency. Thus we are faced with the problem that studies of social movements and revolutions focus on opposite ends of the scale of contentious politics; have developed a different language; and focus on different sectors of their processes of development.

What of the opportunity? In his essay in this volume, Mark Lichbach says of the "socially embedded unit act" that

> actors have goals. The situation in which they find themselves is pared into
> two parts – conditions and means. *Conditions* are the material elements that

---

[1] We have laid out this point of view and illustrated it copiously in a related paper, "To Map Contentious Politics," *Mobilization* 1. For an earlier mapping attempt, see Tilly (1978: ch. 1).

cannot be molded to the actor's purposes; they are the obstacles that constrain agency.... *Means* are the choices or actions undertaken by the actor
that enable agency. Finally, actors approach the situation with certain *norms*
(261, italics added).

Lichbach's "conditions, means, and norms" translate roughly into the three
main approaches that have divided the study of contentious politics since the
1960s: the study of *conditions,* the political institutions and processes that shape
collective mobilization; the study of *means,* the mobilizing structures supporting
collective action; and the study of *norms,* or, more broadly, the framing processes
around which collective action is conceived and acted out.

Given the origins of this field in political struggle, it is not surprising
that institutional conditions and structures have generally predominated
within it. Only recently have rational choice approaches begun to make much
headway, although these have long been prominent in the study of industrial
conflict.[2] As for cultural approaches, they have been most present in the study
of Third World peasants (Scott 1976, 1985) and peasant-based revolutions
(Wolf 1969; Colburn 1994). Their impact in the West has been most often
framed as criticism of prevailing structural and rational choice models.[3] But
"culture" is a multifaceted and a contested concept – intersecting with mentalities, strategic framing, and political ideologies (Tarrow 1992); without a
solid rational base and a relationship to structural constraints, culturalism
risks broadening conflict until, in Hegelian fashion, all politics becomes enmeshed in meaning.

Thus, in the long run, the analysis of contentious politics promises to be a
fruitful enterprise for the confrontation of institutionalist, rational choice, and
culturalist approaches. In the shorter run, we begin the topic cautiously, as if
we were lifting the lid of Pandora's box. In part one, we sketch the evolution
of what we regard as the main core of recent social movement research in western democracies. In parts two to four, we describe our three main orienting concepts – political opportunities, mobilizing structures, and framing processes –
and suggest convergences and intersections among them. We will then turn to
the study of the dynamics of the political process, which we argue is the terrain on which these three approaches may best be integrated. We will close
with the expansion of this dynamic perspective to include the comparative
study of revolutions.

---

[2]Recent work on revolutions (Taylor et al. 1988), on social movements and rebellion (Lichbach 1994,
1995), and on democratization (Opp, Voss, and Gern 1995) is changing this situation. For the application
of rational choice to industrial relations, see Golden (1997). But as will be argued below, the most successful versions of rationalist approaches to the study of contentious politics ultimately lean on structural
and cultural buttresses.

[3]Recently, anthropological perspectives (Wasserstrom 1994) and approaches from cultural history
(Sewell 1990, 1994) and identity politics (Brysk 1995; Melucci 1989) have been trained on contentious
politics, suggesting that change is occurring here as well – especially with respect to the "new" social
movements of the 1970s and 1980s (Larana, Johnston, and Gusfield 1994).

FROM THE SIXTIES TO THE NINETIES

The starting point for the current state of study of contentious politics was the Western social movement cycle of the 1960s. These provided empirical roots for all three of the approaches to social movements we sketch below, though not in equal proportions for different groups of scholars. A rapid look at the evolution of the main schools of thought in social movement studies since the 1960s will show how these developed and will help to outline the foundations for the synthesis we hope to advance.

STARTING FROM STRUCTURE

True to their traditions and led by the precocious rise of contentious politics there in the early part of the 1960s, American scholars were first off the mark with a largely structural approach to movements that centered on several versions of the concept that has come to be known as "political opportunity structure."[4] Even when they focused on Western Europe, American scholars like the Tillys (1975) and Tarrow (1983, 1989) saw collective action gravitating around the political struggle. Western European scholars, starting from a different empirical base, developed a different kind of structuralism – post-Marxism. The student movements of the late 1960s led some to infer a new class basis for social movements (Touraine 1971), while others tried to reframe structuralism around the study of objective life-chance coalitions (Habermas 1981; Offe 1985). This eventually developed into what was called in the 1980s the "new social movement" approach —a variety of macrostructuralism minus the obsessive preoccupation with class that had hamstrung classical Marxist approaches.[5]

Both the American and the European approaches were resolutely structural (that is, in Lichbach's terms, they focused on conditions that cannot be molded to the actors' purposes). However, given its grounding in political studies, the American version was more sensitive to the nuances of the political process, while the Europeans took from their native sociological tradition a broader macrosociological perspective.[6] Gradually, however, American scholars became more aware of the European approaches, while the Europeans–despite their distaste for American inductivism – were forced to focus on political institutions, since the movements they studied were soon involved in a "long march within the institutions." This led even the most resolutely abstract of the new social movement scholars to come to grips with political institutions (compare Offe 1985 with Offe 1990), while the more empirically inclined joined their American col-

---

[4]See Eisinger 1973, Kitschelt 1986, McAdam 1982, Piven and Cloward 1977, Tarrow 1989, and Tilly 1978, 1995, for some of the main benchmarks in the development and use of this concept.

[5]But note that very early on, culturalist insights entered the study of these movements, especially in Italy, where Francesco Alberoni (1968) and Alberto Melucci (1980, 1985, 1988) emphasized the personal and interpersonal elements in these movements.

[6]See the synthesis in the introduction to Klandermans et al. 1988 and Rucht 1991.

leagues in tracing the impact of different national political opportunities on social movements (Kitschelt 1986; Kriesi et al. 1995). This was the start of a promising comparative interaction between West European and American scholars coming from both sociology and political science that has resulted in a number of recent books (Klandermans et al 1988, and see the review in Tarrow 1996b).

Meanwhile, the study of revolutions was progressing along an equally structuralist track. In the deep historical investigations of Moore (1966), the anthropological-historical case studies of Wolf (1969), and the systematic agrarian comparisons of Paige (1975), both Western and nonwestern revolutions were examined in relation to their macrostructural underpinnings. More politically oriented analyses of Third World revolutions were carried out by Joel Migdal (1974). Migdal and others were influenced by the growing statist persuasion in political science that reached its culmination in the comparative-historical structuralism of Theda Skocpol.

Skocpol on Revolutions

Part of the enduring popularity of Skocpol's work on revolutions is due to the fact that it combined macrosociological and political structuralism (1979, 1994). In explaining the origins of three great social revolutions, Skocpol combined an emphasis on class relations (but not those of the urban proletariat) with an acute attention to states' fiscal crises, in interaction with their international vulnerability. When she turned to revolutionary outcomes, state structure loomed even larger while international factors receded into the background (cf. Walt 1996). As for the revolutionary political process – the dynamic of political culture, coalition building, and agency – Skocpol's stalwart statism left little space for it, a lacuna that her critics were quick to observe.[7]

In her later work on revolutions, Skocpol softened this elemental statism, added the relevance of urban classes and interclass coalitions to the overworked peasantry, and grudgingly admitted that professional revolutionaries and ideologies help to "make" revolutions within broad structural parameters. But even in the 1990s, her work remained innocent of cross-fertilization with the "softer" structuralism that was developing in the social movement field; with the growing emphasis on events and their contingencies that was advancing the study of revolutions (Sewell 1996); with the cultural approaches pioneered by Lynn Hunt (1984); with the rational choice approaches to revolution of Popkin (1977) or Taylor (1988); or with the ambitious syncretism of Goldstone (1991) or Wickham-Crowley (1992). These intersections with "softer," political process variables were far more advanced in the study of social movements.

---

[7]The corpus of criticism of Skocpol's book would fill a review article on its own. For her encyclopedic, and sometimes acerbic, reply to some of her critics, see her *Social Revolutions in the Modern World*, Conclusion (1994).

ENTER RATIONAL CHOICE

No sooner had political scientists and sociologists, so to speak, divided up the emerging field of contentious politics between varieties of structuralism than a new set of insights, based on a strong version of rational choice theory, entered the field from a surprising direction: economics, and particularly from the version of collective action theory contributed by American economist Mancur Olson (1965). Olson's work would have gone unnoticed during the pre-1960s period, when it was often assumed that grievances are largely sufficient to explain collective action. But in the 1960s, it converged with dissatisfaction with the "hearts and minds" approach in sociology (McAdam 1982: ch. 2) and with the growing conviction of social movement scholars that interests alone cannot explain mobilization. Indeed, Olson argued that rational people guided by individual interest might very well *avoid* taking action when they see that others are willing to take it for them – the now well-known "free rider problem."

Olson's reception into the study of contentious politics was slow and uneven. This is in part because, during a decade in which contentious politics was buzzing and blooming, he chose to focus his attention on explaining why it is unlikely to occur (Hirschman 1982)! Moreover, he seemed to limit the motivations for collective action to material incentives; but what of the thousands of people who struck, marched, rioted, and demonstrated on behalf of interests other than their own in the 1960s and later? Finally, though he named his theory *"collective* action," Olson had little to say beyond the individual level of motivation and aggregation. How could rational choice be reconciled with the movement cycle of the sixties? Two sociologists proposed an answer.

McCarthy and Zald on Movement Organization

The answer they proposed took off from the observation of the concrete empirical conditions of American society in the 1960s and 1970s, already an advance on Olson's ahistorical deductions (McCarthy and Zald 1973), and focused on the changing resources that were increasingly available to collective actors in advanced industrial societies (1977). McCarthy and Zald agreed that the collective action problem was real, but argued that the expanded personal resources, professionalization, and external financial support available to movements in advanced industrial societies provided them with an answer – *professional movement organizations.*[8]

While their European counterparts were focusing on the "why" of collective action, McCarthy and Zald's theory – resource mobilization – focused on the means available to collective actors, or on its "how" (Melucci 1988). This em-

---

[8]Zald's dissertation and first book (1970), unsurprisingly, dealt with the formation, transformation, and politics of the YMCA.

phasis on means was a source of disappointment to critics looking for explanations of the structural origins of movements, but it lent a refreshing concreteness to the study of movements that had previously been seen as the expression of ideological abstractions. For McCarthy and Zald, there was a rational answer to Olson's paradox of the free rider, and it lay in organization.

By the early 1980s, their theory of resource mobilization had become a dominant background paradigm for sociologists studying social movements, but paradoxically, it was more often criticized than embraced. Why was this? For one thing, McCarthy and Zald's adoption of the language of economics (e.g., movement "entrepreneurs," movement "industries," movement "sectors") left many scholars who had come out of the movements of the 1960s cold. What, the critics asked, had happened to ideology, commitment, values? For another, McCarthy and Zald's movement organizations (SMOs) were often difficult to distinguish from interest groups; particularly, European scholars wondered how their theory would survive in the rough-and-ready world of European contention. And third, their emphasis on the "solution" of the collective action program through professional movement organizations ignored an apparently contrary innovation of the 1960s: the grassroots antibureaucratic movements that many scholars began to see as the fundamental source of movement mobilization. Particularly as grassroots groups arose around issues of the environment, the bomb, gender, and sexual choice, an alternative model, emphasizing informal participation and internal democracy, arose (Evans and Boyte 1987; Fantasia 1988; Rosenthal and Schwartz 1989). In the hands of some scholars, this perspective hearkened back to Marxism, and thus to structural approaches; but in the general disillusionment with Marxism of the 1970s and 1980s, others found a new paradigmatic alternative in cultural approaches, which soon emerged as counter-models to resource mobilization, particularly in the United States.

THE CULTURES OF CONTENTION

Strangely enough, the earliest hint of a paradigm shift came from abroad – and from a Marxist! – from E. P. Thompson's enculturation of the concept of class (1966). Thompson did not want to throw social class out the window but only to substitute for the productivist Marxism of his forebears a focus on class self-creation. This led him to move the advent of the working class further back in British history (for if it was measured by self-awareness and not by structural factors, there were already signs of a self-conscious working class in the eighteenth-century workshop). And it brought him far afield from the factory floor, to factors like custom, grain seizures, and consumer mentalities. In a field that had previously been obsessed with class conflict, Thompson brought to the study of English crowds a sensitivity to interclass reciprocity, a factor that he labeled, somewhat ambiguously, the "moral economy" (1971).

Without anyone's intending it, and long before the fall of Marxism–Lenin-ism as a metanarrative, social class was unobtrusively receding as the moving force of history. For some, structure was even giving way to culture, a shift that was reinforced by the failure of the working class to rise to the challenge of the 1960s' student movements and by the rise of a new wave of theories coming from Europe in the form of Foucaultian social constructivism, Deridian deconstruc-tion, and a cultural misreading of Gramsci. As the 1980s dawned, scholars of both social movements and revolutions began to partake of a cultural "turn" without, in some cases, conceptual self-consciousness of the meaning and param-eters of "culture."[9]

With this new emphasis on culture, the reaction against resource mobiliza-tion ripened into a substantially new paradigm, one that emphasized the impor-tance of political culture and the construction of new collective identities through collective action (Melucci 1989). In this constructivist perspective, grievances were not "natural" and neither were identities – anything less would smack of "essentialism" (Somers and Gibson 1994). Social movements had to shape reality for their potential supporters, identifying injustices and attributing them to the system or to antagonistic others and providing positive symbols around which ordinary, and often timid, people could come together (Gamson 1988; Brysk 1995).

In its more empirical versions, this new emphasis on construction led to an emphasis on "framing" and to the revival of interest in Goffmann's (1974) book. And for some scholars, the process of attribution of injustice wore an in-strumental face (e.g., "How do leaders frame their movements so as to increase their appeal?"), linking the culture of social movements to the older resource mobilization tradition (Klandermans 1992). But for others, movements had an indissoluble cultural substratum; these scholars asked what the cultural norms, the ideal standards, and the societal expectations are to which move-ments appeal, thereby linking the study of movements to popular culture, to indigenous norms, and to the hegemonic cultural symbols and mentalities of their societies (Kertzer 1988). For a growing school of "constructionists," so-cial movements were *both* carriers of meanings and makers of meaning, that, by *naming* grievances and expressing new identities, constructed new realities and made these identities collective (Snow et al. 1986; Snow and Benford 1992).

These intersections between mass culture and movement framing were often restricted to the "identity" movements that developed out of the 1960s, and especially to the women's and gay and lesbian movements; or to national-ism, where the idea of "imagining" nations was diffused by the popularity of

---

[9]Thus, culture could mean everything from the reading groups of French prerevolutionary intellec-tuals (Chartier 1991), to native place associations of Shanghai workers (Perry 1993), to the collective iden-tity formation of participants in new social movements (Melucci 1988).

Benedict Anderson's remarkable book (1990). But to more systematic innova-tors, *all* movements construct meanings and meaning construction is move-ments' primary function (Eyerman and Jamison 1991). In some hands – for example, Anderson's – the cultural turn was an accretion to an underlying structuralism that pointed logically to the agents of movement diffusion. (What, after all, is Anderson's "print capitalism" but a structural category?) But for others, culture hovered high above the ground where it was difficult to see how it could trigger collective action from some social actors and not from others and why waves of collective action developed in some eras and not others.

Even in the study of revolutions–heretofore the domain of state-centered structuralism – cultural approaches have begun to gain ground (Foran 1993, 1997; Hunt 1984; Selbin 1993). The initial impetus for this was a real-world revolution – Iran's – that could not easily be explained through classical struc-turalist models and in which religion played a crucial role (Moaddel 1992); a sec-ond was the influence of anthropology, and especially of post-Vietnam anthro-pologists who saw the villages whose customs they had studied in the past ripped apart by napalm (Wolf 1969); and a third was the transfer of Thompsonian moral economy thinking from the villages of England to the fields and farms of the Third World.

Scott or the Culture of "Resistance"

In the work of James Scott, many of these trends came together. In the 1970s, after a conventional Yale political science training, Scott (1976) discov-ered and applied E. P. Thompson's "moral economy" concept to the movements of a class fragment – subsistence peasants in Southeast Asia. For this move, Scott earned the ire of a rationalist, Samuel Popkin (1977) but remained connected to the structuralist paradigm that still dominated the study of Third World peas-antries. For it was the structure of subsistence land tenure relations that produced the culture of reciprocity between landlords and peasants that Scott called the moral economy, an equilibrium that was upended when colonialism and capital-ist agriculture removed landlords' incentives to hew to obligations of social in-surance. If, in transporting Thompson's concept of the moral economy to South-east Asia, Scott transformed it from the problem of dearth to that of land, and if he failed to distinguish between elements of social insurance that were redistrib-utive and those that were merely ameliorative (Little 1989), this was barely no-ticed in the enthusiasm with which his thinking was greeted in the thus-far athe-oretical corpus of most work on Third World peasantries.

By the 1980s, though still focusing on the same class fragment of subsis-tence peasants, Scott had departed from structural constraints altogether, de-riving an ethnographic method from Geertzian interpretative theory (Geertz 1973) and focusing on individual behavioral reactions to the imposition of new agricultural technologies (Scott 1985). His earlier focus on the factors that produced collective movements now gave way to a concentration on individual "resistance," a term that covered everything from surliness to malingering, cheating landlords, and machine breaking, but provided little purchase on the question of when these low-level resentments would lead to mobilization and collective action and when they would remain at the level of individual ressentiment.[10]

THE NEED FOR SYNTHESIS

For some scholars, these various approaches to social movements provided a battleground on which to fight out the differences between structural, rational choice, and cultural approaches. But while many graduate students cut their theoretical teeth on these debates over the "correct" approach, little has been gained in the race for possession of the field and much ink has been spilled. For example, consider the debate about whether religious ideology was the cause of the Iranian revolution. Moaddel (1992) argues that it was the single "ideological mode" of that revolution; but Foran, in reply, points to the roots of Islamic radicalism in social and economic structure (1994), as well as in mass culture, and Parsa demonstrates how class and coalition building were the framework in which the Islamic revolutionaries eventually triumphed (1995). By elevating religious ideology as the single key to the Iranian revolution, Moaddel makes the same error for Iran that his model, Furet, made for the French Revolution with respect to republican ideology (1981): reifying it while suspending the pull and tug of both underlying structural conditions and the struggle for political power.

More challenging, because more productive of new knowledge, are the growing number of "crossovers," or scholars schooled in one or another of these approaches who attempt to integrate insights from the others. The first step in such a synthesis is to review the three major approaches as they are reflected in the study of contentious politics and demonstrate their openings to one another. The second is to explore how an emphasis on the political process can provide a terrain for their integration. And the third is to try to bridge the gap between the study of Western reform movements and other forms of contentious politics, cycles of protest, and revolutions. This we attempt to do in the next three sections.

---

[10]Some enthusiastic followers broadened Scott's concept still further, including under the alluring label of "everyday resistance" forms of collective action for which an adequate vocabulary already existed (Colburn 1989). By the 1990s, Scott had moved from sensitive ethnographic observation in an area of the globe that he knew well to the analysis of texts from everywhere in the world, and from individual phenomenology to inferred consciousness: "hidden transcripts" is his new term, which he studies from a variety of secondary sources, many of them literary (1990). In this latest phase of Scott's career, "interpretation" – from Geertz's meaning of the description of the meaning of an event for its participants – has shifted to the interpretation of actors' behavior by the sensitive outside observer. Just as the critic has displaced the author in poststructural literary studies, the observer was coming to replace the subject in poststructural studies of resistance.

POLITICAL OPPORTUNITIES

Writing in 1970, Michael Lipsky (p. 14) urged political analysts to direct their attention away from system characterizations presumably true for all times and all places:

> We are accustomed to describing communist political systems as "experiencing a thaw" or "going through a process of retrenchment." [This was in 1970!] Should it not at least be an open question as to whether the American system experiences such stages and fluctuations? Similarly, is it not sensible to assume that the system will be more or less open to specific groups at different times and at different places?

Lipsky clearly felt that the answer to both questions was affirmative. He assumed that the ebb and flow of protest activity was a function of changes that left the broader political system more vulnerable or more receptive to the demands of particular groups. Three years later, Peter Eisinger (1973: 1) used the term "structure of political opportunities" to help account for variations in the "riot behavior" of 43 American cities in the 1960s. Consistent with Lipsky's view, Eisinger (p. 25) found that "the incidence of protest is ... related to the nature of a city's political opportunity structure," which he defined as "the degree to which groups are likely to be able to gain access to power and to manipulate the system."

Within a decade, the key premise informing the work of Lipsky and Eisinger had been appropriated as the central tenet in an alternative "political process" model of social movements. Some proponents of the model saw the timing and fate of movements as largely dependent upon the opportunities afforded insurgents by the shifting institutional structure and ideological disposition of those in power (among others, see Jenkins and Perrow 1977; McAdam 1982; Tarrow 1983, 1989). Others (Kitschelt 1986) turned political opportunity into a structured way of comparing the influence of different state structures on collective mobilization. Still others integrated opportunity/threat into broader models of collective action (Tilly 1978), distinguishing this range of variables theoretically from the facilitation/repression of movements by the state. By the 1990s, the concept of political opportunity had become an analytical linchpin, even for authors who, like Hanspeter Kriesi and his collaborators, had cut their teeth on the study of "new" social movements (Kriesi et al. 1992, 1995).

Since that time, the central assumptions and the concept of "political opportunities" have become staples in social movement inquiry. The rise of movements as diverse as the American women's movement (Costain 1992; Katzenstein and Mueller 1987), liberation theology (Smith 1991), peasant mobilization in Central America (Brockett 1991), the peace movements of the United States and Europe (Meyer 1993; Rochon 1988), the homeless movement in Chile (Hipsher 1996), the American civil rights movement (McAdam 1982), and the Italian movements of the 1960s and 1970s (Tarrow 1989) have been attributed to the expansion of political opportunities. Related to this is the concept of cycles of protest, largely specified as the result of opportunity expansion and contraction (Koopmans 1993; Tarrow 1994: ch. 9). So broad has the concept become that there is danger of its confusion with the political environment in general and with post hoc "explanations" that find opportunities only after movements have had success.

THE INTEGRATION OF RATIONALIST AND POLITICAL PROCESS PERSPECTIVES

The contemporary stress on the role of political opportunities in shaping the emergence, development, and impact of contentious politics is largely true to its structuralist origins. Movements, in this view, are set in motion by changes in institutional rules, political alignments, or alliance structures that grant more leverage to aggrieved groups with which to press their claims. But even this most structural of concepts has a family resemblance to rationalism.[11] In other words, expanding opportunities derive their causal force by changing the cost-benefit calculus of insurgents and antagonists alike.

But if this is the case, why has no synthesis developed between the political process and rational choice paradigms? In the political process tradition, the guiding assumption is that movements arise, change, and succeed or fail as a function of changes in opportunities. However operationalized (and this is a source of some contention), a focus on opportunities produces a rich focus on political rules and institutions, strategic choice, and changes over time in the forms of contention. This gives an inherently comparative, historical, and inductive foundation to most work in the political process tradition.

In the form in which Mancur Olson bequeathed rational choice theory to the study of contentious politics, this focus on the variable and changing interaction between movements and their environments is radically foreshortened.[12] For most writers in the collective action tradition, collective action remains a generic term, which has the virtue of allowing its users to subsume a variety of kinds of action under a general theoretical rubric (Hardin 1982; DiNardo 1985), but whose subcategories are seldom distinguished from one another or related to different social actors or sites of contention. Individuals calculate the costs, risks,

---

[11]So, for example, in explaining how favorable shifts in the structure of political opportunities increase the likelihood of successful insurgent action in the civil rights movement, McAdam (1982:42-3) offered the following argument:

> [First] such shifts improve the chances for successful social protest by reducing the power discrepancy between insurgent groups and their opponents.... The practical effect of this development is to increase the likelihood that insurgent groups will prevail.... Second, an improved bargaining position for the aggrieved population raises significantly the costs of insurgent action.

For an exploration of the interfaces between rationalist and political opportunity structure approaches, see Tarrow (1996b).

[12]For notable exceptions, see Chong (1991) and Lichbach (1995).

and constraints on something called collective action based on the nature of the goods they want to maximize and on their incentives and constraints to seek them, but seldom take into account the incentives and constraints offered by particular learned traditions of collective action, like the strike, the *charivari,* or the protest demonstration.

Recent efforts have relaxed the microeconomic assumptions of the original model, focusing, for example, on the differential tendency to participate of people who are facing losses vs. gains (Berejikian 1992); on the effect that the probability that a campaign will succeed has on people's tendency to participate (Klandermans 1992); on the incentives to collective action that arise within communities (Taylor 1988); and on differentiating the incentives to collective action into markets, communities, hierarchies, and contracts (Lichbach 1994, 1995). While political process writers continue to focus on opportunities and rational choice theorists on mobilization, the elaboration of different forms of mobilization by rational choice scholars is beginning to bring the two traditions closer together.

CULTURE AND OPPORTUNITY

There are also plausible reasons to hope for a synthesis between the political process model and cultural approaches. After all, no reference to the *perceived* costs and benefits of collective action can omit the cultural influences on the motivations of potential participants. Indeed, in stressing the central importance of expanding opportunities, some theorists have been explicit about the necessary role of social construction and collective attribution in the mobilization process (McAdam 1982: 48). Others, like Laitin (1988), have argued that while mobilization processes are based on cultural understandings, these imply the presence of cultural *agents,* or entrepreneurs, who select identities out of a cultural repertoire. Some go so far as to argue that decisive framing processes may occur in the absence of any objective shifts in political opportunities. This creates the possibility that insurgents can *will* a movement into existence, as Charles Kurzman argued in the case of the Iranian revolution (1996).[13]

The study of comparative revolutions has produced some interesting syntheses between structural and cultural models. In the wake of the Iranian revolution, no less a structuralist than Theda Skocpol had to admit ideology into the circle of variables with which she explained social revolutions (1982). Recently, Timothy Wickham-Crowley has worked the concept of "rebellious cultures" into his synthetic, though mainly structuralist, model of Central American revolutions (1992: ch. 7).

---

[13]To quote Kurzman:

> ... the Iranian state was not particularly vulnerable to revolution in 1978, according to several indicators.... This finding suggests that social-movement theory should reconsider the relation between "objective" and "subjective" definitions of political opportunity. If opportunity is like a door, then social-movement theory generally examines cases in which people realize the door is open and walk on through. The Iranian revolution may be a case in which people saw the door as closed but felt the opposition was powerful enough to open it (164-5).

In summary, while the origins of political opportunity theory were decidedly structuralist, scholarship on the opportunity/action link has also explored the rationalist and culturalist dimensions of this relationship. We see nothing contradictory in this blending of theoretical influences. Indeed, in our view, one of the virtues of contemporary movement theory is its consistent openness to nominally antagonistic theoretical perspectives. While the theoretical foundation of political process models is structuralist, its conceptual edifice is stronger for the rationalist and cultural influences that are brought to bear on it. We will see a similar strengthening when we turn to the second of our theoretical concepts, mobilizing structures.

MOBILIZING STRUCTURES

As argued earlier, the emphasis on means in the study of how people mobilize had a dual origin in recent studies of social movements: in the organization theory tradition that McCarthy and Zald brought to the study of social movements and in the rational choice assumptions of Olsonian collective action. Rationalism pointed to the powerful mix of solidary incentives and sanctioning mechanisms employed to overcome the free rider problem; resource mobilization theory brought this somewhat abstract concern down to the level of established organizations or associational networks (Friedman and McAdam 1992; Hechter 1987). Thus, although movement organizations are structures in the most concrete sense, it was as a solution to the collective action problem posed by rational choice theorists that their study became central to resource mobilization theory. But resource mobilization theory has itself evolved a great deal since the 1970s, from formal movement organizations (SMOs) to mobilizing structures in general.

FROM MOVEMENT ORGANIZATIONS TO POLITICAL CONTENTION

By "mobilizing structures," we mean *those collective vehicles, both formal and informal, through which people come together and engage in collective action.* This focus on meso-level groups, organizations, and informal networks led resource mobilization theorists initially to focus uniquely on social movement organizations and on movement entrepreneurs. But over the two decades since McCarthy and Zald first applied their theory to social movements, even their focus has broadened to include political contention in general. First, Zald himself began to emphasize what he called "the social movement sector" instead of individual movement organizations, including in this category interest groups, political parties, and currents of opinion (Garner and Zald 1985); second, together with collaborators, John McCarthy shifted his attention from an almost exclusive focus on organizations to the analysis of contentious collective action;[14] third, as scholars began to explore the associations, indigenous institutions, and social networks that shape mobilization, more and more obvious links between the political process and movement mobilization began to emerge.

For example, in her work on the demobilization of the Chilean squatters' movement after the transition to democracy, Patricia Hipsher has shown that the homeless of Santiago (whom no one would accuse of possessing powerful resources!) responded to democratization with a decided shift in strategy from confrontation to lobbying and electoral mobilization (1996). Respondents in her study were clearly reacting to a change in opportunity. The study of mobilization was enriched by its marriage to a political process perspective.

CULTURE AND MOBILIZATION

The study of mobilizing structures has also been enriched by the cultural turn in the social and historical sciences. Culturalists see national traditions of ritual and symbolism as important in shaping the repertoires of insurgents (Kertzer 1988). They also see contentious episodes, especially great ones, reshaping political culture. Thus, William Sewell shows how the taking of the Bastille provided an impetus for the transformation of the French concept of revolution and for movement mobilization for decades to come (Sewell 1996). And Jeffrey Wasserstrom has explored how traditions of Chinese political theater influenced the staging of the Tiananmen Square rebellion (1994).

A particular intersection between culture and mobilization has been explored through the concept of the repertoire of contention (Tilly 1995; Traugott 1995). Forms of mobilization are learned routines that are rooted in particular cultural traditions. For example, French people who inherited the *charivari* as a means of shaming neighbors who have trespassed on community norms had it available when more broadly political struggles erupted (Aminzade 1993). And forms of collective action that develop in major contentious episodes, like the barricades in France, become part of the repertoire of future generations (Traugott 1995).

Community settings are also important for the role they play in encouraging system-critical framings as a prerequisite for collective action. This hinges on the strength of communities and of the social networks within them. The attribution of blame to oneself is more likely to occur under conditions of personal isolation than integration in communities;[15] and if we regard communities as integrated by cultural norms, then no understanding of collective action is possible without understanding culture.

[14]Thus, together with Clark McPhail and other collaborators, John McCarthy himself has been studying how practices of policing and channeling of protest affect movement organizations' strategies and prospects. See McCarthy, McPhail, and Smith (1994) and McCarthy, McPhail, and Crist (1995).

[15]Following Ferree and Miller (1977: 34), to the question of which social circumstances produce critical system framings, the likely answer is "among extremely homogeneous people who are in intense regular contact with one another" – in other words, in communities.

Rational choice theorists have not been insensitive to the importance of communities for motivating collective action. For example, as Michael Taylor (1988) argues, successful revolutionary action is more likely under conditions of "community ... not just because individual behavior can more easily be monitored [in communities], but because a strong community has at its disposal an array of powerful positive and negative social sanctions." Even as determined a rationalist as Samuel Popkin, studying the mobilization of Vietnamese peasants, had to admit that "the only successful organizations [were] those which included in their goals either nationalism or religion," in other words, cultural appeals (1977: 15). And in his recent apotheosis of the rational choice tradition, Mark Lichbach explicitly includes "community," alongside markets, hierarchies, and contracts, as one of the four main solutions to the collective action problem (1994: 15-16; 1995: ch. 4).

In other words, well-established organizations or associational networks represent the attempts of rational claims-makers to achieve their aims; but they become effective mobilizing structures because they can draw on shared beliefs and worldviews that motivate and legitimize protest activity. Social movement scholars interested in the solution to the collective action problem must attend to cultural variables as well as to mobilizing structures and to political opportunities. This leads to the third pillar of the conceptual framework we wish to elaborate.

FRAMING PROCESSES

If the combination of political opportunities and mobilizing structures affords groups a structural potential for action, these variables remain, in the absence of one other factor, insufficient to account for collective action. Mediating between opportunity, organization, and action are the shared meanings that people bring to their situations. At a minimum, they need to feel both aggrieved about some aspect of their lives and optimistic that, by acting collectively, they can redress the problem. Lacking either one or both of these perceptions, it is unlikely that they will mobilize even when afforded the opportunity to do so. Conditioning the presence or absence of these perceptions is that complex of social-psychological dynamics – collective attribution and social construction – that David Snow and some of his colleagues have referred to as *framing processes*.[16] Indeed, not only did Snow and his collaborators modify and apply Erving Goffman's term to the study of social movements; in doing so, they helped to crystallize and articulate a growing discontent among movement scholars at the lack of significance attached to ideas and sentiments in movement scholarship.

The recent resurgence of work on the framing dimensions of social movements draws much of its inspiration from culturalist sources (although social psychology has played an important role as well). These sources – ranging from Victor Turner (1969) to Clifford Geertz (1973) and Jurgen Habermas (1981), among

---

[16]See Snow et al. (1986); Snow and Benford (1992).

others – assert the fundamentally constructed nature of social life and, by implication, of collective action. For all the importance attributed to political opportunities, mobilizing structures, and organizational resources by the structuralists, social movements, in the culturalist view, depend in the final analysis on processes of social construction and framing.

LINKING CULTURE TO STRUCTURE

Even this starkly culturalist account of social movements, however, admits in actual scholarship of numerous points of convergence with the more structural accounts of collective action. Two of these have been noted previously. Both concern structural conditions that would seem to increase the likelihood of system-critical framing processes. The first is that system attributions are most likely to be produced in stable structural settings, rather than in conditions of personal isolation (Ferree and Miller 1977); the second is that insurgent framings often follow from, or are cued by, objective structural shifts that render established orders more vulnerable to challenge. The first of these observations can be illustrated in Skocpol's analysis of peasant revolutions, which she claims occur most often in autonomous peasant communities (1979), the second by Benedict Anderson's analysis of the rise of nationalism. Though sometimes counted as a prophet of the culturalist assault on structuralism, what gives Anderson's (1990) account its analytical edge is that the culture of nationalism was diffused through an exquisitely structural process – what he calls "print capitalism."

Two other points of structuralist/culturalist convergence can be noted as well. The first is the important role of formal *non*-movement organizations in even the most cultural of movements. This was illustrated in Leila Rupp and Verta Taylor's important work on the survival of the American women's movement in the middle decades of the twentieth century, when the fashioning of "abeyance structures" preserved the traditions of feminist struggle that the 1960s activists were to draw upon (1987). The second is the role of social networks in constructing collective action. Its importance can be shown by the explicit attempt of Emirbayer and Goodwin (1994) to integrate culturalist and structuralist perspectives. While offering a trenchant critique of the structural bias in much of the network literature on social movements, these authors nonetheless recognize that the cultural construction of collective action is invariably a network, that is to say, a structural, process.

RATIONAL CULTURES AND THE CULTURE OF RATIONAL ACTION

Culturalists have not been as willing to integrate rationalist assumptions into their work as they have the heritage of structuralism. This may be due as much to the tendency of early rational choice theorists to dismiss cultural variables as "soft," as to the antipathy among culturalists for considering pragmatic, maximizing variables as plausible explanations for the behavior they study. Cultural-ists rightly point out that the material incentives that are central to rational choice explanations of behavior are themselves cultural constructs; but by the same token, the cultural factors that they wish to focus on may be pragmatically invoked by movement entrepreneurs who "choose" a particular set of cultural identities over others for largely strategic reasons, which suggests a focus on agency and entrepreneurship (Laitin 1988).

Unless such choices are regarded deterministically, in which case culture be-comes as much of a cage as vulgar Marxism was in the past, or are seen as purely random, in which case social scientific analysis slips into pure phenomenology, then the rules according to which some actors choose to identify with one col-lective action frame, while others identify with another, may depend a great deal on which identity best maximizes their claims. This identity is what the rational choice perspective proposes to supply.

In summary, we think it fair to say that a theoretical blending of structural-ist, rationalist, and culturalist perspectives is both possible and desirable. Ad-mittedly, the initial impulse behind the paradigm shift occasioned by the 1960s was largely structural. Moreover, structuralist assumptions probably still consti-tute the conceptual fulcrum on which most movement research rests. But over the past twenty-five years, two new theoretical perspectives have developed, and more recently lines of convergent theory and research have appeared that can serve to integrate the three perspectives under review here. The blendings are by no means perfect or themselves free of contention; but they are no less real or con-ceptually important for their imperfections. In our view, it is at their intersec-tions that the most interesting and potentially groundbreaking work in the study of contentious politics is taking place.

But how will we find a framework for the integration of these approaches to contentious politics? Second, is it possible to build bridges between the two major empirical poles of research in this field – the study of social movements and the analysis of revolutions?[17] In the remainder of this chapter, we propose linked so-lutions, both of them tentative and contentious, to these two challenges. We want to argue that the integration of structural, rationalist, and cultural variables can best be effected with a process-oriented approach to contentious politics.

INTEGRATING STRUCTURE, MOBILIZATION, AND CULTURE: DEFINING A PROCESS APPROACH

Up to this point, we have remained resolutely static in illustrating the three ap-proaches to contentious politics and calling for their integration. This integration

---

[17]A third and even larger challenge – the application of social movement theory from its heartland in the liberal democracies of the West to nondemocratic and non-western countries – we will not attempt here but hope to turn to subsequently.

cannot simply take the form of aggregation of variables drawn from different traditions but can best occur in the context of a dynamic approach to processes of contention. A well-crafted, dynamic analysis identifies recurrent large-scale structures and sequences such as the common properties of social movement cycles, but only as a first step. The genuine payoff from process-oriented analysis arrives with the specification of recurrent smaller-scale causal mechanisms that concatenate differently in contrasting historical settings. Thus, in the long run, we hope to specify exactly how the prevailing collective action frame that constrains a given set of actors changes under the impact of struggle and alterations in the local political opportunity structure. We will illustrate these points through the well-studied case of the American civil rights movement.

THE EMERGENCE OF THE CIVIL RIGHTS MOVEMENT

The key to understanding the direct action phase of the civil rights movement in the mid-1950s does not rest in any one of the three broad approaches noted above, but in their confluence. From a stucturalist perspective, the main story line is clear: Beginning in the early years of the century, a series of long-term economic, demographic, and political processes served to weaken the set of elite alliances on which the country's racial status quo had been based. The three most important were the slow collapse of the cotton economy between roughly 1915 and 1935; the demographic move of black Americans from rural villages to cities and towns; and the radical change in U.S. foreign policy in the cold war period.[18] Together, these various trends combined to render certain elements within the national state more receptive to civil rights activity than at any time since radical reconstruction.

But these structural changes occurred not only at the level of national political opportunities: As national leaders were becoming more hostile to Jim Crow, the rural to urban shift of the black population in the South was transforming life within the region and expanding the organizational means available to African Americans there. At the heart of this process were three institutions whose growth was nothing short of remarkable: the black church, historically black colleges and universities, and the system of local NAACP chapters in the region. In these settings, self-confidence was mutually reinforced, cross-local networks were formed, and political entrepreneurs gained organizing skills (Chong 1991). To the structural potential of demographic, economic, and political change, a network of social institutions and organizations added a mobilizing potential that was to serve as the organizational nucleus for the civil rights movement.

---

[18]The gradual decline of King Cotton not only undermined the economic power of the landowning elite and those who depended on it; it also set African Americans in motion, fueling a massive migration that had effectively transformed the black vote by mid-century into one of the acknowledged keys to victory in close presidential elections (see McAdam 1982). Simultaneously, the onset of the cold war and the intense competition it fueled for influence among the emerging independent nations of the Third World undermined the "understanding" that had prevailed among national and Southern elites on the race issue. On this history, see Layton (1995).

But while important, these expanding opportunities and mobilizing structures did not produce the modern civil rights movement on their own. Together they only offered insurgents the structural conditions and the incentives and means for collective action. Mediating between opportunity and action were the actors and the subjective meanings they brought to the situation. This takes us to the concept of norms and to the changing cultural understandings that inform collective action, and this in two senses:

First, although there was clearly an opportunist rationale for the changing strategy of national political leaders toward Southern racism and racist-biased institutions (Piven and Cloward 1977: ch. 4), the general public's cultural perception was changing as well and was in some ways in advance of the electorally driven politics of Washington decision makers, who were often reluctant to intervene in the South on behalf of beleaguered civil rights groups. Although racism persists in the present in both North and South, few Northern whites could remain unmoved by the spectacle of black children blocked by state police at the schoolhouse door. Part of the change was due to the intervention of a new cultural institution – television – which broadcast local changes to a national audience in particularly foreshortened images; but a broad shift in public opinion was detectable as well.

Second, although a rationalist calculus correctly senses that the perceived costs of collective action were reduced as the perceived benefits were increasing (Chong 1991), this fails to explain the specific frames that served to mobilize people in the early phase of the movement or how these changed over time. That is, the calculus was available to many in the black community, but it wasn't the community as a whole that mobilized; it was actors like Martin Luther King and other church leaders whose distinctive framing of mobilizing appeals catalyzed the struggle. It is in the specific frames developed by these leaders that the analytic tools of the culturalists are important in accounting for the dynamics that accompanied the birth of the movement.

One change that helped to account for the success of the movement in its early phases was the transformation of the quietist, largely middle-class churchgoers of the Southern black church into the main support base of the civil rights movement. Black churchmen had traditionally accepted the subaltern role of African Americans in Southern society. Faced with new political opportunities and by increasing church membership, some – but by no means a majority – responded by calling for more activism. But had they done so with a call for direct confrontation they would have suffered not only the full force of the repression of the white power structure, they would also have faced rejection from their largely middle-class parishioners. Their strategic response was to mount forms of civil, nonviolent resistance that could draw on the pacific instincts of their constituents and highlight the contrast between peaceful civil rights marchers and the brutal violence of their opponents. The supremely cultural development of national television newscasting helped them to bring this tactic to a new level of sophistication.

In this development of the repertoire of contention can be seen the intersection of political opportunities, the strategic savvy of the leaders, and their capacity to design a strategy that would resonate with the culture of the black middle class. Each time the authorities responded with a larger or more cleverly deployed repressive force, the sites of contention were moved, the repertoire was expanded, and goals were shifted (McAdam 1983). This was in part to maintain the excitement and energy of the movement; but it was also aimed at seizing political opportunities and creating new ones (Tarrow 1994: ch. 5).

THE DECLINE OF THE CIVIL RIGHTS CYCLE

But once this dynamic was launched, the leaders of the movement were never wholly in possession of it and certainly exercised no control over their adversaries or over the national political contest. While they managed to contain their supporters' reactions to the first church burnings and to the murders of black activists, the killing of Martin Luther King, Jr. and other enormities unleashed a powerful wave of rage in the black community, one which, when it spread to the North, helped to trigger a wave of urban riots that led to a negative turn in both elite and mass white opinion. It was one thing to stand up peacefully on TV to the official bullies of the Southern white power structure; it was quite another to burn white stores in Harlem or Watts or to brandish guns and radical slogans on the streets of Oakland.

Another effect that helps to explain why this movement cycle described a tipping point in the mid-1960s is best explained through cultural analysis. As its older leadership became involved in political negotiation, a new generation of militants, imbued with racial resentment, adhering to an ideology of Black Power, and impatient with the limited goals of their elders, came into the limelight (here too, television coverage was crucial). As the politics of equal opportunity gave way to the politics of identity, the ambivalent role of white liberal support groups in the movement was spotlighted, and racial tensions developed within the movement that had the ultimate effect of alienating white liberal support. (The independent, but simultaneous, targeting of Jewish-owned stores in the ghetto riots had a parallel effect.)

Moreover, with the passage of the Civil Rights Acts of 1964 and 1965, the central political goal of the early phase of the movement had been achieved – the promise, if not the reality, of electoral representation. The Reverend King and other activists might call for a shift from voting rights to economic equality in the mid-1960s, but these new goals were both threatening and divisive. They were in part intended to appeal to the Northern black ghetto dwellers whose support was also being sought by the new generation of leaders, but they could not maintain the coalition of black Southern middle-class churchgoers and college students with Northern white liberals that had carried the movement in the previous decade. In the decline of the movement, as in its emergence, political opportunities, mobilizing structures, and cultural frames converged.

LESSONS FOR RESEARCH STRATEGY

We hope we have said enough above to indicate how we think a process-oriented approach to contentious politics could proceed. Let us summarize these suggestions briefly before moving on to the issue of integrating the study of social movements and revolutions.

First, we hope we have shown that taking a single tack through the events just summarized – whether structural, rationalist, or cultural – would have provided only a very partial and even a deceptive account of the cycle we have briefly traced: It is through the intersection of the three broad sets of factors that we think the rise and decline of the civil rights movement must be explained.

Second, these effects were mutually reinforcing at each stage of the civil rights cycle rather than stratified over time. That is, we cannot identify one set of variables with one phase of the process and then move on to the next set of variables for the next stage, and we will certainly make little progress if we direct our accounts to proving which sets of variables are important and which are absent at different stages. There is no substitute for relating all phases of a movement cycle to the three broad classes of factors outlined above, and this means the larder of social movement methodology must be stocked with cultural, political, and organizational victuals.

Third, whatever else it does, an adequate methodology must, at a minimum, trace the relevant sequence of events in a movement cycle, and not merely provide a still photograph of its high points.[19] Whatever methodology we adopt will have to be both time-specific and time-series based. It must provide information on all aspects of contentious politics, and not only on concrete movement organizations. It must also make it possible to relate these events with relevant covariates (e.g., electoral realignments) and with non-eventful policies like demographic change, migration, and the shift from King Cotton. Some researchers have experimented with time-series sensitive "event histories" (Olzak 1992); others have argued for theorized narratives (Sewell 1996); still others have looked at "short rhythms" or "protest cycles" within longer historical frameworks (Tilly 1995). Whether statistically structured or narratively organized, we argue that the best way to study contentious politics as a whole – and not only social movements, protest, or revolutions – must be carried by the enumeration and analysis of contentious events.[20]

This call for a dynamic approach to contentious politics raises a more difficult and even more intriguing question: If, as we have argued, social movements cannot be isolated from contentious politics as a whole, and if they must be embedded in a time-series analysis of entire sequences of contention, is it possible to examine social movements and other forms of contention, for example, revo-

---

[19]This is one reason why, in our empirical research, we have privileged the more or less systematic assembly of events data, although we readily admit its inability to get inside the heads of participants. On this point, see Tilly (1995:ch.2) and Tarrow (1996a).

[20]See Tarrow (1996a) for a review of these approaches.

lutions, with the same analytical grammar? As we pointed out at the outset, the traditions of these two fields argue for the distinctiveness of movement politics and revolutionary politics and for the separation of both from routine contention. In our final section we will argue the contrary case.

MOVEMENTS, CYCLES, AND REVOLUTIONS

Because of substantive specialization, students of social movements and of revolutions have failed to recognize that both of these belong on the same causal continuum. Note, for example, the parallels between social movement cycles and revolutionary situations (Cattacin and Passy 1993; Fillieule 1993; Goodwin 1994; Hoerder 1977; Joppke 1991; Koopmans 1993; Meyer 1993; Traugott 1995). In both movement cycles and revolutions, a successful challenge by one previously disadvantaged actor simultaneously:

1. advertises the vulnerability of authorities,
2. provides a model for effective claim-making,
3. identifies possible allies for other challengers,
4. alters the existing relationships of challengers and powerholders to each other (at the extreme, turning challengers into powerholders), and
5. thereby threatens the interests of yet other political actors who have stakes in the status quo, thus activating them as well.

Such an open situation becomes a revolutionary cycle if and when some challengers gain power, then league to fortify their positions against new challengers, a process that eventually splits mobilized actors between regime members and outsiders, demobilizes some outsiders, then drives the remainder toward increasingly risky actions until repression, cooptation, and fragmentation terminate the cycle. Such cycles recur in both social movements and revolutions. We can surely identify equivalent sequences in war, industrial conflict, and other forms of contentious politics as well (see Botz 1976, 1987; Cohn 1993; Cruz 1992–1993; Franzosi 1995; Kriesi et al. 1981; Most and Starr 1983; Porter 1994; Shorter and Tilly 1974; Starr 1994; Stevenson 1992).

These cyclical processes result from essentially the same causal relations as operate in the nexus of democracy opportunity or expansion contention: Up to a point, openings in a polity, demonstration effects, and competitive effects activate contention. Beyond that point – no doubt defined in part by both the government's capacity and current levels of democracy – saturation of available niches divides claim-makers into haves and have-nots. Haves move toward defense of their own positions and noncontentious means of claim-making, and have-nots split further into those who demobilize and those who adopt increasingly risky means of pressing their claims. Finally, cooptation and repression end the cycle.

In the case of social movement cycles, claimants who gain position and/or new advantages interpret their experience as hard-earned victory by forces of good followed by extremists' dangerous attempts to destroy the system. Losers, in contrast, interpret the whole process as a betrayal confirming the system's corruptness. At the end, nevertheless, a similar polity remains in place.

Parallels between social movement cycles and revolutionary processes abound. To see them, we need a distinction between revolutionary **situations** and revolutionary **outcomes**. Revolutionary situations are moments of deep fragmentation in state power; revolutionary outcomes are effective transfers of state power to new sets of actors. A full-fledged revolution combines the two. Great revolutions typically fall into several phases: situation–outcome–new situation–outcome, and so on until some set of political actors consolidates its hold over the state and beats down the next round of challengers.

Revolutionary situations, then, resemble the opening of new social movement challenges to the existing polity. One becomes the other to the extent that challenges multiply and put at risk the stakes of all existing potential actors in the existing system. Revolutionary outcomes resemble social movement actors' acquisition of recognition and/or advantages. One becomes the other to the extent that challengers' gains displace previous powerholders. In short, social movement cycles and revolutions fall on the same continuum, the difference in position being to what extent challenges put the existing structure of power at risk.

To say this is to identify a crucial difference between democratic and other polities. The combination of broad citizenship, equal citizenship, binding consultation, and protection promotes contentious claim-making up to a point, but it also contains that claim-making within established forms of voice. In Western democratic polities since 1815 or so, those forms have typically included associations, parties, electoral campaigns, public meetings, petitions, demonstrations, and a set of related means establishing that a given political actor or its constituency is worthy, unified, numerous, and committed.

To participate in politics on these terms, challengers implicitly or explicitly accept major restrictions on claims and forms of action. They agree, by and large, not to engage in direct physical attacks on the persons or property of other challengers, powerholders, or the state. They also agree, implicitly or explicitly, to abide by the outcomes of current political decision making, including movement-driven decision making, to wait their turns until they have been able to demonstrate worthiness, unity, numbers, and commitment with sufficient conviction to gain them advantages and recognition.

CONCLUSIONS

The comparative study of contentious politics has its work cut out for it. Three kinds of comparative work cry out for attention: first, comparisons across different varieties of contention, social movements, cycles of protest, and revolutions;

second, across the range of nondemocratic to democratic polities; and, third, among particular national histories of contentious politics. (And within this third category, there is still another distinction to be explicated – between short-term sequences of struggle and the long-term shaping of cultures and repertoires of contention).

In this chapter, we hope we have shown three things:

First, we have argued that a synthesis of the three major strands of research emerging from the main core of social movement research holds much more promise for theoretical progress than an endless disputation between rival schools. Along with our colleagues[21] and others thinking along similar lines, we hope to contribute to such a synthesis in our future work.

Second, we believe that no serious attempt at a comparative politics of contentious politics will be possible without a more self-conscious attention to a methodology that can encompass the often engaging, but frequently dispersed, case studies of individual movements that have dominated the field until now. One potential unifying methodology – the systematic cross-time and cross-sectional comparison of contentious events – holds great promise in this regard; other methodologies, for example the comparison of how objectively similar movements frame their programs in different states (Rucht 1996) or the narrative tracing of specific revolutionary cycles (Sewell 1996), hold similar promise.

Third, we call for a cautious and anti-imperialist enlargement of attention from what we know about particular forms of contention in democratic polities to a broader scope and more types of contentious politics. We recognize that a serious effort of respecification and operationalization of the stock-in-trade variables from the theoretical core of social movement theory are necessary to accomplish this, and we hope to contribute to it in our future work. We call for collaboration, criticism, and confrontation of research results to help bring this about.

REFERENCES

Alberoni, Francesco. 1968. *Statu nascenti.* Bologna: Il Mulino.

Aminzade, Ronald. 1993. *Ballots and Barricades: Class Formation and Republican Politics in France, 1830–1871.* Princeton: Princeton University Press.

Anderson, Benedict. 1990. *Imagined Communities. Reflections on the Origin and Spread of Nationalism.* London: Verso.

Berijikian, Jeffrey. 1992. "Revolutionary Collective Action and the Agent-Structure Problem." *American Political Science Review* 86:647-57.

Botz, Gerhard. 1976. *Gewalt in der Politik. Attentäte, Zusammenstösse, Putschversuche, Unruhen in Österreich 1918 bis 1934.* Munich: Wilhelm Fink.

———. 1987. *Krisenzonen einer Demokratie. Gewalt, Streik und Konfliktunderdrückung in Österreich seit 1918.* Frankfurt: Campus Verlag.

---

[21]We refer to the work of the Mellon/CASBS Contentious Politics Group started in 1995. For a description, see McAdam, Tarrow, and Tilly (1996).

Boulding, Kenneth E. 1962. *Conflict and Defense: A General Theory.* New York: Harper.

Brockett, Charles D. 1991. "The Structure of Political Opportunities and Peasant Mobilization in Central America." *Comparative Politics* 23:253-74.

Brysk, Alison. 1995. "'Hearts and Minds': Bringing Symbols Back In." *Polity* 27:559-86.

Carson, Clayborne. 1981. *In Struggle: SNCC and the Black Awakening of the 1960s.* Cambridge: Harvard University Press.

Cattacin, Sandro, and Florence Passy. 1993. "Der Niedergang von Bewegungsorganisationen. Zur Analyse von organisatorischen Laufbahnen." *Kölner Zeitschrift für Soziologie und Sozialpsychologie* 45:419-38.

Chartier, Roger. 1991. *The Cultural Origins of the French Revolution.* Durham: Duke University Press.

Chong, Dennis. 1991. *Collective Action and the Civil Rights Movement.* Chicago: University of Chicago Press.

Cohn, Samuel R. 1993. *When Strikes Make Sense — And Why.* New York: Plenum.

Colburn, Forrest, ed. 1989. *Everyday Forms of Peasant Resistance.* New York: M. E. Sharpe.

————. 1994. *The Vogue of Revolution in Poor Countries.* Princeton: Princeton University Press.

Costain, Anne N. 1992. *Inviting Women's Rebellion: A Political Process Interpretation of the Women's Movement.* Baltimore: Johns Hopkins University Press.

Cruz, Rafael. 1992–1993. "La Lógica de la Guerra. Ejército, Estado y Revolución en la España Contemporánea." *Studia HistoricaHistoria Contemporánea* 10-11:207-22.

DiNardo, James. 1985. *Power in Numbers. The Political Strategy of Protest and Rebellion.* Princeton: Princeton University Press.

Eisinger, Peter K. 1973. "The Conditions of Protest Behavior in American Cities." *American Political Science Review* 67:11-28.

Emirbayer, Mustafa, and Jeff Goodwin. 1994. "Network Analysis, Culture and the Problem of Agency." *American Journal of Sociology* 99:1411-55.

Evans, Sara M., and Harry C. Boyte. 1986. *Free Spaces: The Sources of Democratic Change in America.* New York, Cambridge, Philadelphia: Harper & Row.

Eyerman, Ron, and Andrew Jamison. 1991. *Social Movements. A Cognitive Approach.* University Park: Pennsylvania State University Press.

Fantasia, Rick 1988. *Cultures of Solidarity.* Berkeley: University of California Press.

Ferree, Myra Marx, and Frederick D. Miller. 1977. "Winning Hearts and Minds: Some Psychological Contributions to the Resource Mobilization Perspective of Social Movements." Unpublished paper.

Fillieule, Olivier, ed. 1993. *Sociologie de la protestation. Les formes de l'action collective dans la France contemporaine.* Paris: L'Harmattan.

Foran, John. 1993. *Fragile Resistance: Social Transformation in Iran from 1500 to the Revolution.* Boulder, CO: Westview.

————. 1994. "The Iranian Revolution and the Study of Discourses: A Reply to Moaddel." *Critique,* Spring.

————. 1997. *Theorizing Revolutions: New Approaches from Across the Disciplines.* London and New York: Routledge.

Franzosi, Roberto. 1995. *The Puzzle of Strikes. Class and State Strategies in Postwar Italy.* Cambridge: Cambridge University Press.

Friedman, Debra, and Doug McAdam. 1992. "Collective Identity and Activism: Networks, Choices and the Life of a Social Movement." In Aldon D. Morris and Carol McClurg Muller, eds., *Frontiers in Social Movement Theory.* New Haven and London: Yale University Press.

Furet, François. 1981. *Interpreting the French Revolution.* Cambridge: Cambridge University Press.

Gamson, William. 1988. "Political Discourse and Collective Action." In Bert Klandermans et al., *From Structure to Action: Comparing Social Movement Research Across Cultures.* International Social Movement Research I. Greenwich, CT: JAI, 219-44.

Garner, Roberta Ash, and Mayer N. Zald. 1985. "The Political Economy of Social Movement Sectors." In Gerald Suttles and Mayer N. Zald, eds., *The Challenge of Social Control. Citizenship and Institution Building in Modern Society.* Essays in Honor of Morris Janowitz. Norwood, NJ: ABLEX.

Geertz, Clifford. 1973. *The Interpretation of Cultures: Selected Essays.* New York: Basic Books.

Goffman, Erving. 1974. *Frame Analysis: An Essay on the Organization of Experience.* New York: Harper Colophon.

Golden, Miriam. 1997. *Heroic Defeats: The Politics of Job Loss.* New York and Cambridge: Cambridge University Press.

Goldstone, Jack A. 1991. *Revolution and Rebellion in the Early Modern World.* Berkeley: University of California Press.

Goodwin, Jeff. 1994. "Toward a New Sociology of Revolutions." *Theory and Society* 23:731-66.

Habermas, Jurgen. 1981. "New Social Movements." *Telos* 49:33-7.

Hardin, Russell. 1982. *Collective Action.* Baltimore: Johns Hopkins University Press for Resources for the Future.

Hechter, Michael. 1987. *Principles of Group Solidarity.* Berkeley: University of California Press.

Hipsher, Patricia. 1996. "Is Movement Demobilization Good for Democratization? Some Evidence from the Shantytown Dwellers' Movement in Chile." *Politics and Society,* Spring.

Hirschman, Albert O. 1982. *Shifting Involvements, Private Interest and Public Action.* Princeton: Princeton University Press.

Hoerder, Dirk. 1977. *Crowd Action in a Revolutionary Society: Massachusetts, 1765–1780.* New York: Academic Press.

Hunt, Lynn. 1984. *Politics, Culture, and Class in the French Revolution.* Berkeley and Los Angeles: University of California Press.

Jenkins, J. Craig, and Charles Perrow. 1977. "Insurgency of the Powerless: Farm Worker Movements 1946–1972." *American Sociological Review* 42:249-68.

Joppke, Christian. 1991. "Social Movements during Cycles of Issue Attention: The Decline of the Anti-Nuclear Energy Movements in West Germany and the USA." *British Journal of Sociology* 42:43-60.

Katzenstein, Mary Fainsod, and Carol McClurg Mueller, eds. 1987. *The Women's Movements of the United States and Western Europe: Consciousness, Political Opportunity and Public Policy.* Philadelphia: Temple University Press.

Kertzer, David. 1988. *Ritual, Politics and Power.* New Haven and London: Yale University Press.

Kitschelt, Herbert. 1986. "Political Opportunity Structures and Political Protest: Anti-Nuclear Movements in Four Democracies." *British Journal of Political Science* 16:57-85.

Klandermans, Bert. 1992. "The Social Construction of Protest and Multiorganizational Fields." In Aldon Morris and Carol McClurg Mueller, eds., *Frontiers in Social Movement Theory.* New Haven and London: Yale University Press.

Klandermans, Bert, Hanspeter Kriesi, and Sidney Tarrow, eds. 1988. *From Structure to Action: Comparing Social Movement Research Across Cultures.* Greenwich, CT: JAI Press. International Social Movement Research, vol. I.

Koopmans, Ruud. 1993. "The Dynamics of Protest Waves: West Germany, 1965 to 1989." *American Sociological Review* 58:637-58.

Kriesi, Hanspeter, René Levy, Gilbert Ganguillet, and Heinz Zwicky. 1981. *Politische Aktivierung in der Schweiz, 1945-1978.* Diessenhofen: Verlag Ruegger.

Kriesi, Hanspeter, Ruud Koopmans, Jan Willem Duyvendak, and Marco G. Giugni. 1992. "New Social Movements and Political Opportunities in Western Europe." *European Journal of Political Research* 22:219-44.

———. 1995. *The Politics of New Social Movements in Western Europe. A Comparative Analysis.* Minneapolis and St. Paul: University of Minnesota Press.

Kurzman, Charles. 1996. "Structural Opportunity and Perceived Opportunity in Social-Movement Theory: The Iranian Revolution of 1979." *American Sociological Review* 61:153-70.

Laitin, David D. 1988. "Political Culture and Political Preferences." *American Political Science Review* 82:589-97.

Laraña, Enrique, Hank Johnston, and Joseph R. Gusfield, eds. 1994. *New Social Movements: From Ideology to Identity.* Philadelphia: Temple University Press.

Layton, Azza Salama. 1995. "The International Context of the U.S. Civil Rights Movement: The Dynamics between Racial Policies and International Politics, 1941-1960." Ph.D. Dissertation, Department of Government, University of Texas, Austin.

Lichbach, Mark Irving. 1994. "Rethinking Rationality and Rebellion: Theories of Collective Action and Problems of Collective Dissent." *Rationality and Society* 6, January:8-39.

———. 1995. *The Rebel's Dilemma.* Ann Arbor: University of Michigan Press.

Lipsky, Michael. 1970. *Protest in City Politics.* Chicago: Rand McNally.

Little, Daniel. 1989. *Understanding Peasant China: Case Studies in the Philosophy of Social Science.* New Haven: Yale University Press.

McAdam, Doug 1982. *Political Process and the Development of Black Insurgency, 1930-1970.* Chicago: University of Chicago Press.

———. 1983. "Tactical Innovation and the Pace of Insurgency." *American Sociological Review* 92:64-90.

McAdam, Doug, Sidney Tarrow, and Charles Tilly. 1996. "To Map Contentious Politics." *Mobilization* 1:14-28.

McCarthy, John D., Clark McPhail, and John Crist. 1995. "The Emergence and Diffusion of Public Order Management Systems: Protest Cycles and Police Responses." Unpublished manuscript.

McCarthy, John D., Clark McPhail, and Jackie Smith. 1994. "The Institutional Channeling of Protest. The Emergence and Development of U.S. Protest Management Systems." Unpublished manuscript.

McCarthy, John D., and Mayer N. Zald. 1973. *The Trend of Social Movements in America: Professionalization and Resource Mobilization.* Morristown, NJ: General Learning Press.

———. 1977. "Resource Mobilization and Social Movements: A Partial Theory." *American Journal of Sociology* 82:1212-41.

Melucci, Alberto. 1980. "The New Social Movements: A Theoretical Approach." *Social Science Information* 19:199-226.

———. 1985. "The Symbolic Challenge of Contemporary Movements." *Social Research* 52:789-815.

———. 1988. "Getting Involved." In Klandermans, Kriesi, and Tarrow, eds. *From Structure to Action. Comparing Social Movement Research Across Cultures. International Social Movement Research I.* Greenwich, CT: JAI.

———. 1989. *Nomads of the Present. Social Movements and Individual Need in Contemporary Society.* Philadelphia: Temple University Press.

Meyer, David S. 1993. "Institutionalizing Dissent: The United States Structure of Political Opportunity and the End of the Nuclear Freeze Movement." *Sociological Forum* 8:157-79.

Migdal, Joel. 1974. *Peasants, Politics, and Revolution.* Princeton: Princeton University Press.

Moaddel, Mansoor. 1992. "Ideology As Episodic Discourse: The Case of the Iranian Revolution." *American Sociological Review* 57:353-79.

Moore, Barrington Jr. 1966. *The Social Origins of Dictatorship and Democracy: Lord and Peasant in the Modern World.* Boston: Beacon.

Most, Benjamin A., and Harvey Starr. 1983. "Conceptualizing 'War.' Consequences for Theory and Research." *Journal of Conflict Resolution* 27:137-59.

Offe, Claus. 1985. "New Social Movements: Challenging the Boundaries of Institutional Politics." *Social Research* 52:817-68.

———. 1990. "Reflections on the Institutional Self-Transformation of Movement Politics: A Tentative Stage Model." In Russell Dalton and Manfred Kuechler, eds., *Challenging the Political Order.* Oxford and New York: Oxford University Press.

Olson, Mancur, Jr. 1965. *The Logic of Collective Action.* Cambridge: Harvard University Press.

Olzak, Susan. 1989. "The Analysis of Events in the Study of Collective Action." *Annual Review of Sociology* 15:119-86.

———. 1992. *The Dynamics of Ethnic Competition and Conflict.* Stanford: Stanford University Press.

Opp, Karl-Dieter, Peter Voss, and Christiane Gern. 1995. *Origins of a Spontaneous Revolution: East Germany, 1989.* Ann Arbor: University of Michigan Press.

Paige, Jeffrey. 1975. *Agrarian Revolution: Social Movements and Export Agriculture in the Underdeveloped World.* London, New York: The Free Press.

Parsa, Misagh. 1995. "Conversion or Coalition? Ideology in the Iranian and Nicaraguan Revolutions." *Political Power and Social Theory* 9:23-60.

Perry, Elizabeth. 1993. *Shanghai on Strike: The Politics of Chinese Labor.* Stanford: Stanford University Press.

Piven, Frances Fox, and Richard A. Cloward. 1977. *Poor People's Movements; How They Succeed; Why They Fail.* New York: Vintage.

Popkin, Samuel. 1977. *The Rational Peasant. The Political Economy of Rural Society in Vietnam.* Berkeley: University of California Press.

Porter, Bruce. 1994. *War and the Rise of the State.* New York: Free Press.

Rochon, Thomas R. 1988. *Mobilizing for Peace. The Antinuclear Movements in Western Europe.* Princeton: Princeton University Press.

Rosenthal, Naomi, and Michael Schwartz. 1989. "Spontaneity and Democracy in Social Movements." In Bert Klandermans, ed., *Organizing for Change: Social Movement Organizations in Europe and the United States.* Greenwich, CT: JAI Press. International Social Movement Research, Vol. II.

Rucht, Dieter. 1996. "The Impact of National Contexts on Social Movement Structures: A Cross-movement and Cross-national Comparison." In Doug McAdam, John McCarthy, and Mayer Zald, eds. *Comparative Perspectives on Social Movements.* Cambridge: Cambridge University Press.

———, ed. 1991. *Research on Social Movements: The State of the Art in Western Europe and the USA.* Frankfurt am Main and Boulder, CO: Campus Verlag and Westview Press.

Rupp, Leila J., and Verta A. Taylor. 1987. *Survival in the Doldrums: The American Women's Rights Movement, 1945 to the 1960s.* Oxford and New York: Oxford University Press.

Scott, James 1976. *The Moral Economy of the Peasant, Rebellion and Subsistence in Southeast Asia.* New Haven and London: Yale University Press.

———. 1985. *Weapons of the Weak: Everyday Forms of Peasant Resistance.* New Haven: Yale University Press.

———. 1990. *Domination and the Arts of Resistance: Hidden Transcripts.* New Haven: Yale University Press.

Selbin, Eric. 1993. *Modern Latin American Revolutions.* Boulder, CO: Westview.

Sewell, William. 1990. "Collective Violence and Collective Loyalties in France: Why the French Revolution Made a Difference." *Politics and Society* 18:527-52.

———. 1994. *A Rhetoric of Bourgeois Revolution: The Abbé Sieyes and What Is the Third Estate?* Durham: Duke University Press.

Shorter, Edward, and Charles Tilly. 1974. *Strikes in France, 1830 to 1968.* Cambridge: Cambridge University Press.

Skocpol, Theda. 1979. *States and Social Revolutions. A Comparative Analysis of France, Russia, and China.* Cambridge: Cambridge University Press.

———. 1982. "Rentier State and Shi'a Islam in the Iranian Revolution." *Theory and Society* 11:265-83.

———. 1994. *Social Revolutions in the Modern World.* New York and Cambridge: Cambridge University Press.

Smith, Christian. 1991. *The Emergence of Liberation Theology.* Chicago: University of Chicago Press.

Snow, David A., and Robert D. Benford. 1992. "Master Frames and Cycles of Protest." In Aldon D. Morris and Carol McClurg Mueller, eds., *Frontiers in Social Movement Theory.* New Haven and London: Yale University Press.

Snow, David A., E. Burke Rochford, Jr., Steven K. Worden, and Robert D. Benford. 1986. "Frame Alignment Processes, Micromobilization, and Movement Participation." *American Sociological Review* 51:464-81.

Somers, Margaret R., and Gloria D. Gibson. 1994. "Reclaiming the Epistemological 'Other': Narrative and the Social Constitution of Identity." In Craig Calhoun, ed., *Social Theory and the Politics of Identity*. Oxford and Cambridge: Blackwell.

Starr, Harvey. 1994. "Revolution and War: Rethinking the Linkage Between Internal and External Conflict." *Political Research Quarterly* 47:481-507.

Stevenson, John. 1992. *Popular Disturbances in England, 1700–1832*. London: Longman. 2nd ed.

Tarrow, Sidney. 1983. *Struggling to Reform: Social Movements and Policy Change During Cycles of Protest*. Western Societies Program Occasional Paper No. 15. New York Center for International Studies, Cornell University, Ithaca, NY.

———. 1989. *Democracy and Disorder: Social Conflict, Political Protest and Democracy in Italy, 1965–1975*. New York: Oxford University Press.

———. 1992. "Mentalities, Political Cultures and Collective Action Frames: Constructing Meanings through Action." In Aldon Morris and Carol M. Mueller, eds., *Frontiers of Social Movement Research*. New Haven: Yale University Press.

———. 1994. *Power in Movement*. Cambridge: Cambridge University Press.

———. 1996a. "Studying Contentious Politics: From Eventful History to Cycles of Collective Action." Unpublished paper.

———. 1996b. "Social Movements and Contentious Politics: A Review Article." *American Political Science Review* 90:312-26.

Taylor, Michael. 1988. "Rationality and Revolutionary Collective Action." In Michael Taylor, ed., *Rationality and Revolution*. Cambridge: Cambridge University Press.

Thompson, E. P. 1966. *The Making of the English Working Class*. New York: Vintage Books.

———. 1971. "The Moral Economy of the English Crowd in the Eighteenth Century." *Past and Present* 50:76-136.

Tilly, Charles. 1978. *From Mobilization to Revolution*. Reading, MA: Addison-Wesley.

———. 1995. *Popular Contention in Great Britain, 1758–1834*. Cambridge: Harvard University Press.

Tilly, Charles, Louise Tilly, and Richard Tilly. 1975. *The Rebellious Century*. Cambridge: Harvard University Press.

Touraine, Alain. 1971. *The May Movement: Revolt and Reform*. New York: Random House.

———. 1985. "An Introduction to the Study of Social Movements." *Social Research* 52:749-88.

Traugott, Mark. 1995. "Barricades as Repertoire: Continuities and Discontinuities in the History of French Contention." In Traugott, ed., *Repertoires and Cycles of Collective Action*. Durham: Duke University Press.

Turner, Victor. 1969. *The Ritual Process: Structure and Anti-Structure*. Ithaca: Cornell University Press.

Walt, Steven. 1996. *Revolution and War*. Ithaca: Cornell University Press.

Wasserstrom, Jeffrey. 1994. "History, Myth, and the Tales of Tiananmen." In Jeffrey Wasserstrom and Elizabeth J. Perry, eds., *Popular Protest and Political Culture in Modern China*. Boulder, San Francisco, and Oxford: Westview Press. 2nd. ed.

Wickham-Crowley, Timothy. 1992. *Guerrillas and Revolution in Latin America. A Comparative Study of Insurgents and Regimes since 1956.* Princeton: Princeton University Press.

Wolf, Eric R. 1969. *Peasant Wars of the Twentieth Century.* New York: Harper & Row.

Zald, Mayer N. 1970. *Organizational Change: The Political Economy of the YMCA.* Chicago: University of Chicago Press.

7

THE ROLE OF INTERESTS, INSTITUTIONS, AND IDEAS IN THE COMPARATIVE POLITICAL ECONOMY OF THE INDUSTRIALIZED NATIONS*

Peter A. Hall

The field of political economy was born in the late eighteenth century when scholars such as Adam Smith began to ask how nations prosper and what kind of policies ensure their wealth.[1] It is surely not coincidental that the inception of the field coincides with the birth of the modern state and industrial capitalism. The state and the market represent two different ways of organizing human endeavor, and the relationship between them has always been one of the central themes of political economy.

Initially the field was coterminous with the study of economics but, when the marginalist revolution transformed economics into a discipline of its own, increasingly focused on the elaboration of neoclassical models of the economy, it fell to political economists to inquire more deeply into the relationship between politics and economics. That inquiry has taken many turns over the

*While absolving them of responsibility for any of its contents, I am grateful to Barbara Geddes, Ron Rogowski, Sven Steinmo, Rosemary C. R. Taylor, the other contributors to this volume, and especially to Mark Lichbach and Alan Zuckerman for comments on earlier versions of this chapter. I would also like to thank David Soskice and the Wissenschaftszentrum in Berlin for providing a hospitable and stimulating setting for its completion.

[1]For broader reviews, see Blaug (1983); Caldwell (1982); Roll (1956); and Staniland (1985).

past century but, by and large, political economy has been distinguished from economics by a profound interest in three kinds of issues.

First, political economists have been especially concerned about issues of power. They are inclined to ask: Whose interests are being served by any given set of economic arrangements and how do the latter distribute power and resources across social groups? Reflected in this stance is a salutary skepticism about the distributive efficiency of markets that has long distinguished political economy from neoclassical economics, which tends to celebrate the Pareto-optimality of market mechanisms.

Second, political economists have traditionally evinced a strong interest in the institutional arrangements that underpin the operation of market mechanisms. In some cases, this inspires them to study variation in the institutional structure of markets across nations, sectors, or time. In others, it leads them to emphasize the degree to which the operation of markets is affected by nonmarket institutions, including both the state and other sorts of social relationships.

Third, one of the long-standing strengths of political economy lies in its insistence that even our most basic conceptions of the economy are ultimately artificial constructs, devised to model something that cannot be perceived by the naked eye. Accordingly, many political economists ask: Where do these conceptions come from and how do they become influential? They often question what others see as the "constraints" facing governments or the "iron laws" of economics and tend to emphasize the primacy of politics in situations that might otherwise seem to be socioeconomically determined.

Such concerns are reflected in work as early as that of Adam Smith, who wrote *The Theory of Moral Sentiments* alongside *The Wealth of Nations*. They animate the arguments of Karl Marx and his followers about the distributive effects of capitalist markets and the power relations underlying them (cf. Kalecki 1943). In more recent decades, they form the basis for Karl Polanyi's (1946) magisterial analysis of the relationship between markets, states, and social institutions and Joseph Schumpeter's (1947) rumination about the effectiveness of capitalism and democracy. Andrew Shonfield (1969) pursued similar questions in his influential investigation of the social and political conditions that underpin different varieties of capitalism.

In the years since these scholars wrote, the body of work that examines the comparative political economy of the industrialized nations has grown substantially.[2] Like many fields of comparative politics, it encompasses analysts who approach the world from somewhat different perspectives and, in keeping with the themes of the volume, the object of this essay is to compare several of these perspectives, stressing the distinctiveness of those that attach special importance to

---

[2]Only a small portion of the literature can be discussed here since a full review of the field would require a volume in itself. Because my object is to consider the way in which institutions, interests, and ideas figure in contemporary analysis, I can touch on only a few of the many substantial works in the field. For other reviews, see Staniland (1985) and Hall (1998).

interests, institutions, or ideas in the analysis of the political economy. In broad terms at least, this division reflects the three primordial questions that animate the field.

Of course, the approaches considered here are not ironclad divisions: Some scholars have written from more than one of them; and interests, institutions, and ideas figure to some degree in all analyses of the political economy. However, this categorization is useful for illuminating some of the principal lines of inquiry in the field and the issues they confront. I begin by discussing a number of works that exemplify each approach with a view to revealing the insights and dilemmas inherent in them. Then, I ask how the approaches mesh with one other, considering both the potential for drawing more integrated insights from them and some differences in methodological perspective that limit the potential for full integration. I conclude by examining some of the developments taking place at the boundaries between these schools of thought and the challenges the field as a whole confronts.

INTEREST-BASED APPROACHES TO POLITICAL ECONOMY

Interest-based approaches characterize some of the most important literature in the field of comparative political economy. Interests, understood as the real, material interests of the principal actors, whether conceived as individuals or as groups, figure in all of the work in the field. But they assume particular importance in two bodies of literature.

The first of these are analyses that focus on "producer group coalitions." By and large, its contributors concentrate on explaining variation over time and across nations in patterns of economic policy. Their unit of analysis is usually the nation–state, and the central actors are producer groups. In general, such accounts suggest that we can explain the trajectory of economic policy (and sometimes further outcomes) by tracing the way in which the material interests of producer groups change so as to dissolve the support coalitions for past patterns of policy and to make possible the formation of more powerful coalitions in support of new patterns of policy.

Although remarkably similar, individual analyses in this group can be distinguished by reference, first, to how they define the central political actors and, second, to how they define or derive the material interests of those actors. In general, the key groups may be defined as broad social units, largely defined in terms of their relationships to the means of production (workers, capitalists, landowners), or in terms that are sector-specific according to the level of international competition they face (tradables vs. nontradables), their asset specificity (fixed vs. mobile assets), the capital/labor ratios associated with production there (capital or labor intensive), or the main site of their markets (domestic vs. foreign).

Building on earlier work by scholars like Schattschneider (1935), Gerschenkron (1943), and Moore (1966), the pioneers of this approach were Gourevitch (1977, 1986), Kurth (1979), and Ferguson (1984), who argued that subsets of producers in the economy were positioned quite differently relative to the international and domestic economies and thus would have quite different interests in policies bearing on tariff levels, the stimulation of domestic demand, and the like. Moreover, these interests would shift as conditions in the international economy change or firms move into later stages of their product cycle, allowing politicians, operating as entrepreneurs, to put together new coalitions behind particular mixtures of policy.

It should be apparent that the definition of the actors in these analyses usually follows from a more general theory specifying their material interests and, more precisely, how a particular kind of economic policy affects the material interests of groups that are differently positioned within the economy. This is a process nicely described by Gourevitch (1989) as "the political sociology of political economy."

Subsequent work in this vein has concentrated on specifying more formally the general theory from which the interests of producers are to be derived. Rogowski (1989) does so by applying a Samuelson-Stolper model of comparative advantage to argue that shifts in the terms of trade of a nation, of the sort generated by falling transport costs or a new tariff regime, shift the interests and (more ambiguously) the power of large groups defined as laborers, owners of capital, and landowners, thereby making new coalitions possible. As transportation costs fell in the late nineteenth century, for instance, labor and capital in Britain gained comparative advantage on international markets and so were likely to form a powerful political coalition in favor of free trade against landowners, who lost comparative advantage and favored protection. Rogowski claims to be able to explain tariff policy, the character of political coalitions, and associated regime changes with this sort of analysis. In large measure, his is a class-oriented analysis, not unlike that of Marx, albeit built on neoclassical foundations.

Frieden (1991a), by contrast, approaches such issues using a different economic theory, based on a Ricardo-Viner model, which predicts that the effects of a shift in the terms of trade will be distributed, not across broad social classes, but across specific sectors according to the competitiveness of the sector and the specificity of its assets (i.e., the ease with which they can be converted to other, more competitive uses). With it he gets somewhat different predictions. In further analyses (1991b), Frieden takes a similar approach to the problem of explaining another set of policies, namely, those bearing on the character of the exchange rate regime and the level of the exchange rate. Here he posits that sectors will take different positions according to the degree to which their products are traded vs. nontraded, their markets domestic vs. international, and their assets specific or mobile.

Much of this work has moved beyond traditional class analysis to draw our attention to the role that different kinds of business interests play in the formation of policy and to the importance of cross-class coalitions, uniting some segments of business with segments of labor. Swenson (1989, 1991), for instance, explains both the rise and fall of neocorporatist systems of wage bargaining by reference to the way in which employers in key export sectors make common cause with the workers there against workers or employers in the sheltered sectors of the economy, in the interest of preserving wage rates or skill differentials crucial to export success (cf. Fulcher 1991; Pontusson and Swenson 1996). Other scholars are beginning to explain developments in social policy in similar terms (Martin 1995; Pierson 1995).

This is a powerful approach with three distinctive strengths. First, it speaks directly to the widespread intuition that, if a pattern of policy is to be sustained, it must advance the interests of broad segments of society. Second, it highlights the degree to which policies tend to benefit some groups and disadvantage others, thereby tapping into the respects in which politics really is a struggle for control over scarce resources. Third, many of these analyses provide us with a powerful way for understanding how changes in the international political economy can affect the domestic politics and policies of a nation. They supply a nice bridge between comparative politics and international relations, perhaps best represented in Gourevitch's (1986) effort to show how changes in the international environment shift the interests of key groups in the support coalitions for particular policies (cf. Milner 1988).

However, these kinds of analyses also have some characteristic limitations. The results are highly sensitive to the economic theories used to specify the material interests of the relevant actors, and those theories can be controversial even among economists. The approach reflects an economic determinism that tends to see changes in the international economy as the driving force behind politics.[3] It attributes great importance to producer-group politics, assuming either that the extraparliamentary lobbying of producers is determinative of policy or that electoral coalitions turn on producer-group participation. Despite the centrality of coalitions to this perspective, it pays little attention to the collective action problems associated with coalition formation and the acquisition of influence.

A second body of work, which might be said to reflect the "electoral approach" to the subject, can also be subsumed under interest-based approaches to political economy. However, it is quite different from the producer-group approach in that individuals, rather than producer groups, are seen as the central actors and the focus of attention is on the electoral arena. Its core insight is that the politicians who make economic policy must also secure reelection and thus try to manipulate the economy to this end. The driving force in such analyses is the interest of politicians in reelection.

Central to this subschool is the literature on the "political business cycle" whose object is to explain fluctuations in the economy by reference to the way

---

[3]Gourevitch (1986) is the most sensitive to this problem and especially concerned to explore the way in which politicians exploit state structures and economic ideologies to construct coalitions.

politicians manipulate economic policy so as to enhance their prospects for re-election. The early literature argued that incumbent politicians would pump up the economy immediately prior to elections so that the benefits would accrue before the vote and the costs only afterwards (Nordhaus 1975; Tufte 1978). The premise was that voters would be myopic enough not to see the long-term effects of policy or inclined to discount the future so heavily as to be won over by its short-term benefits. However, the result is suboptimal economic performance in the long term.

Several modifications of the political business cycle theory have gained currency in recent years. Some suggest that left- and right-wing governments will behave differently, since the former seek support from a working class that fears unemployment and the latter from middle-class voters who are more averse to inflation. The implication is that left-wing governance should result in higher rates of inflation and lower rates of unemployment than would right-wing governance (Hibbs 1977; Schmidt 1982). Others also stress the difference between left- and right-wing governments but posit an expectations-augmented model of the economy that holds that real economic effects will follow only from policy moves that are unanticipated by economic actors (Alesina 1989). Thus, this rational partisan theory argues that the extent of the economic stimulus observed in the real economy will vary by party since voters expect more of a stimulus from left governments.

Others operating from the same broad approach seek to explain, not the course of the economy, but the outcome of elections. In past decades, voting behavior has been explained by reference to social cleavages, party identification, and issue voting. However, political economists have entered the field with "retrospective voting" theories, which argue that electorates will vote in such a way as to reward or punish the incumbent party for the performance of the economy (Fiorina 1981). As usual, the topic engenders controversy about which aggregates matter most to the electorate (real disposable income, inflation, unemployment, etc.), whether personal or national well-being has more impact on the vote, and whether past or expected future performance has more electoral salience (Kiewit 1983).

The most ambitious theorists have joined the two sides of this approach to construct overall politicoeconomic models designed to explain the kind of economic policies that politicians seek under a range of different institutional conditions and the impact of those policies on their chances for reelection (Alesina and Rosenthal 1995; Frey 1980). The result is a set of models built on neoclassical economic theory that effectively endogenizes vote-seeking politicians.

This approach has some significant strengths. First, if one has to attribute a single interest to politicians, it seems reasonable to define that as an interest in reelection. Second, there is considerable evidence in support of the contention that retrospective voting has an impact on electoral outcomes and much less, but still some, evidence that politicians often stimulate the economy prior to elections (Alt and Crystal 1983; Alesina et al. 1993). Models that contain politicians seem to predict the course of the economy better than those that do not; and there is much value in the way this work restores the electoral arena to a central position in the analysis.

However, there are also clear-cut limitations to the approach. The range of motivations it ascribes to politicians is severely circumscribed. Only occasionally are they said to seek more than reelection. The image of the electorate commonly purveyed here is that of a homogeneous mass undifferentiated by more specific economic interests and dominated by the mythical "median voter." While some fascinating work has been done on the effects that follow when the electorate has different discount rates or expectations structures, by and large, it is said to vote entirely on the basis of material interests; and the assumption is that voters readily perceive those interests. Thus, such analyses pay little attention to the factors that might lead voters with similar economic positions toward different interpretations of their interests.

INSTITUTION-ORIENTED APPROACHES TO POLITICAL ECONOMY

Institution-oriented approaches generally locate the primary causal factors behind economic policy or performance in the organizational structures of the political economy. Their principal unit of analysis is again the nation–state, although some scholars emphasize the importance of organizational differences at the sectoral or regional levels. The principal actors in the analysis are usually organizations representing key collectivities in the economy, such as employer associations or trade unions and, more recently, firms. By and large, the logic whereby institutional structures are said to influence the behavior of actors is a rational one, as in many neoclassical analyses. Unlike standard neoclassical accounts, which assume competitive markets and homogeneous institutions across nations, however, those who take this approach emphasize institutional differences across nations and their persistence over time. These institutional differences are said to result in distinctive patterns of economic performance and policy.

The literature that initially advanced this approach most forcefully was that on neocorporatism (Cameron 1984; Cawson 1985; Goldthorpe 1984; Hicks 1988; Katzenstein 1985; Schmitter 1974; Schmitter and Lehmbruch 1978). It emphasized the contrast between nations where wage bargaining is decentralized and those in which it is accomplished by a trade union movement and employers' associations that are centralized or concentrated such that responsibility for various aspects of economic policy could be devolved onto them. The general argument was that organizations representing the bulk of producers in the economy could effectively resist the inflationary pressures that result from leapfrogging under decentralized bargaining, internalize the overall economic impacts of wage settlements, and thereby secure wage settlements that attained maximum rates of employment at minimum rates of inflation. In some cases, it was also argued that the state could secure wage concessions from or negotiate more effectively with centralized producer groups (Lange 1984; Offe 1985; Przeworski and Wallerstein 1982).

Over time, scholars proposed a variety of modifications to this central argument. Some emphasized that economic coordination of this sort could be accomplished as effectively by employer organizations as by trade unions (Soskice 1990a; Thelen, 1995). Others argued that these arrangements are most associated with the small states that are most vulnerable to the international economy and least capable of tolerating internal conflict (Cameron 1978; Katzenstein 1985). Still others argued that the relationship between trade union organization and superior economic outcomes is not monotonic but that good economic performance can be achieved where trade unions are either highly encompassing or extremely weak (Calmfors and Driffill 1988). Finally, some argued that the effectiveness of trade union organization depends heavily on the party in power, the best performance being achieved by centralized trade unions under left-wing governance and highly decentralized trade unions under right-wing governments (Alvarez et al. 1991; Garrett and Lange 1988, 1991).

During the 1980s, a second group of scholars, using what might be termed "neoinstitutional analysis," built on these insights to develop expanded models of the way in which the organization of the political economy affects economic policy and performance. In the first instance, they added the structure of the financial system to the analysis, arguing that financial systems structured so as to provide long-term capital to industry made possible a different range of firm behaviors than systems that provided finance mainly on the basis of short-term profitability. With regard to policy, they argued that financial sectors oriented toward long-term finance supported patterns of policy quite different from those based on short-term finance (Cox 1986; Hall 1986; Scharpf 1991; Zysman 1983).

In recent years, this work has led to more extensive models in which a variety of features of the organization of the political economy are highlighted and said to interact (Finegold and Soskice 1988; Franzese 1994; Hall 1994; Soskice 1990b, 1991). These include: the structure of the industrial relations system, the structure of the financial system, the structure of the vocational training system, and the character of inter- and intra-firm relations more generally. The contention is that these structures interact to present most firms with a distinctive national matrix of sanctions and incentives that militate toward some kinds of behavior and away from others. The result is said to be nationally distinctive patterns of firm strategies that lead to particular patterns of aggregate economic performance and distinctive patterns of policy, as firms seek policies supportive of their long-standing strategies (Deretouzos et al. 1986; Hall and Franzese 1996; King and Wood 1998; Soskice 1990b, 1991, 1994).

The argument may be clearer if I provide a simple example. In it, the dependent variable is firm strategy, and the more precise issue is: How do the exporting firms of a nation respond when faced with an appreciation of the currency that makes their goods more expensive in foreign markets? There are good empirical data to show that British firms and German firms have responded quite differently. British firms refused to lower their prices in order to protect short-term profits. As a result, over the long term, they lost market share. German firms, by contrast, generally responded by reducing their prices in order to preserve market share even at the cost of lowering short-term profits (Knetter 1989).

The institutional model explains this difference by reference to the incentives that the different financial and industrial relations systems of the two nations present to their firms. In Britain, the financial system is organized in such a way that access to capital generally depends on short-term profitability. Thus, firms seek to maintain profits even if they have to lay off workers to do so. They can do so because the industrial relations system makes it relatively easy to fire workers. In Germany, the industrial relations system is organized in such a way that it is relatively difficult and disadvantageous to fire workers. Thus, firms are inclined to try to retain market share in order to avoid layoffs. What enables them to do so is a financial system that provides access to capital dependent not on short-term profitability but on a variety of indicators of long-term economic viability.[4]

There are fruitful points of tangency between this work and the efforts of a growing number of economists to incorporate institutional variables into their analyses. For some time, the most significant overlap was with economists working within the "regulation school" or on national innovation systems (cf. Boyer 1990; Nelson 1993). In more recent years, however, economists have made significant advances on two other fronts. The first focuses on central bank independence, when many scholars have examined the economic impact of making the central bank more independent from government (Alesina and Summers 1993; Cukierman 1992; Goodman 1992; Grilli et al. 1991). In general, they have tended to argue that this will lower rates of inflation by insulating monetary policy from political influence and altering the inflation expectations of wage and price contractors. More recently, however, political economists have noted that such effects may depend on other institutions in the economy, such as those that organize wage bargaining (Garrett and Way 1995; Hall and Franzese 1996; Iversen 1994). Second, several economists have begun to explore how the structure of the state and the party system can affect a nation's levels of debt and deficits, generally finding that it is more difficult to attain low levels of debt when the state and party system are fragmented (Alesina and Perotti 1994; Roubini and Sachs 1989).

Institutionalist studies of this sort have made major contributions to our understanding of economic policy and performance. First, they move beyond the tendency of conventional economic analysis to treat all developed economies as if they were institutionally identical, toward a fuller sense that there may be varieties of capitalism with distinctive trajectories of policy and performance. Second, they restore the firm to a central position in the analysis, generating a new

---

[4] I am indebted to David Soskice for drawing this case to my attention.

firm-centered political economy. Third, they draw our attention to the way in which diverse institutional structures in the political economy interact with one another to produce distinctive patterns of economic policy and performance and to the key role that strategic interaction plays in the economy. Finally, to the extent that these analyses posit rational actors operating within the matrix of sanctions and incentives posed by institutions, they build on a set of microfoundations that provides fruitful points of tangency with contemporary work in mainstream economics.

However, analyses of this sort are not without their dilemmas. As the range of institutions deemed important increases and further interaction effects among them are discovered, it becomes increasingly difficult to test such models through comparative analysis, since the number of potentially important independent variables soon exceeds the number of available national cases. Political economists may have to turn to simultaneous-equation models to solve such problems, but getting accurate measures of institutional configurations or firm-level strategies to feed into such models can be very difficult. In conceptual terms, there is some danger that we may end up with as many models of national capitalism as there are nations.

Similarly, the bite of such analyses turns on the resilience of institutions, and institutions are not immutable. To the degree that the core institutions of the political economy are subject to change, the focus of the analysis must shift toward the socioeconomic or political coalitions that underpin them and toward more dynamic theories of institutional determination. At a minimum, analysts who take this approach must develop fuller theories designed to account for continuity or change in the organization of the political economy.

Finally, all such analyses are potentially vulnerable to the charge that they have not identified the right institutions or those most important to the outcomes at hand. Here, the principal line of criticism comes from those who argue that it is not national-level institutions that most affect economic policy or performance but sectoral or regional-level institutions (Campbell et al. 1991; Hollingsworth et al. 1994). In large measure, this is an empirical question, but it is one that has not yet been much studied or resolved.

IDEA-ORIENTED APPROACHES TO POLITICAL ECONOMY

In the field of comparative political economy, approaches that emphasize the role of ideas or the importance of cultural variables to economic policy and performance are less developed than those that place more stress on interests or institutions. However, they have been far from unimportant. The literature that accords a prominent role to such ideas or culture can be divided into three groups, distinguished by the importance each attaches to such variables relative to other causal factors.

One group of scholars acknowledges that ideas may be important but stress that other kinds of variables should be given preeminence in the causal analysis. Goldstein and Keohane (1994: 26-7) lay out the basic heuristic behind this approach quite well. They argue that ideas should be imported into the analysis only after interest-based explanations for the outcomes have proved inadequate. This approach has been especially attractive to a number of rational choice analysts confronted with the problem of explaining how one equilibrium results from situations in which multiple equilibria are feasible. In such cases, some have argued that ideas supply the "focal points" toward which coordinated action can converge. Thus, Garrett and Weingast (1993) employ such an analysis to explain how the nations of the European Community converged on a particular kind of integration process and others apply it more widely (cf. Bates and Weingast 1995; Schelling 1980).

A second group of scholars assigns higher causal priority to ideas. They argue that the economic policies chosen by governments or the strategies chosen by firms are strongly influenced by the ideas about appropriate policy or best practice dominant within the relevant professional community. Experts and epistemic communities figure prominently in such analyses (cf. Haas 1992). Thus, Sikkink (1991) attributes the movement from one economic strategy to another to the growing popularity of new ideas within the economics profession and the international agencies that transmit such doctrines transnationally. Fligstein (1990) explains changes in the strategy of American firms by reference to the ideas promulgated in the forums of an increasingly professional managerial class; and Goldstein (1993) explains American trade policy by reference to the way in which successive waves of ideas about trade become institutionalized in various parts of the policy apparatus.

Many such analyses have a characteristic structure. They proceed by identifying the distinctive worldviews of a crucial set of actors and then tracing the way in which these actors secure positions of power from which to translate their ideas into policy. Economists figure prominently in such analyses along with the international institutions that transmit the latest economic theories across national borders (Lee 1989; Salant 1989; Sikkink 1991). In some cases, however, politicians are said to be equally influential and the influence of economic ideas is traced not only to their prominence with a community of experts but also to the broader political appeal they have for the partisans of particular political ideologies and potential supporters within the electorate (Hall 1989, 1993; Weir 1992b). In such cases, ideas are assigned causal force because they make new kinds of social or political coalitions possible (cf. Hall 1989; Jenson 1989; Rosanvallon 1989). By and large, the impact of new ideas is only fully realized when they become institutionalized into the standard operating procedures of key organizations and absorbed into the worldviews of those who manage them.

Finally, a third group of scholars goes even further to suggest that ideas or cultural variables more broadly defined should be assigned causal primacy because they are constitutive of the most basic meaning systems that make individual or collective action possible (Johnson 1994). Although it is not theorized in precisely these terms, Shonfield's (1969) magisterial work might be seen as a precursor to such analyses since he explains differences in the economic policies of the industrialized nations largely in terms of the broad stance that a variety of national actors take to the economy, which in turn is based on culturally specific orientations deeply rooted in national history. Those who argue for distinctive national "policy styles" follow in his footsteps (Hayward 1976; Richardson and Jordan 1982); and, more recently, Ziegler (1997) accounts for French and German industrial policies by reference to the worldviews implicit in the way that different kinds of knowledge have been distributed across the organizations responsible for technological and industrial advance.

More recently, a number of scholars seeking to identify the roots of regional or sectoral economic innovation have put renewed emphasis on the contribution that dense networks of social organization, extending in some cases to deeply embedded cultural practices, can make to such processes (Campbell et al. 1991; Herrigel 1995; Hollingsworth and Boyer 1997; Locke 1995; Salais and Storper 1993; Sabel and Zeitlin 1985). The most radical of such formulations emphasize how new templates for the organization of economic endeavor can arise from local efforts at experimentation and assert the creative power of ideas over and against existing institutional infrastructures (Sabel 1992, 1995).

Ideas-oriented approaches to political economy have real value in that they capture dimensions of human interaction normally lost in other perspectives. However, those working on this topic face an especially challenging intellectual task since it can be very difficult to disentangle ideological or cultural factors from other kinds of variables. In some respects, the positions taken by the various groups working within this approach reflect something of a trade-off. The cautious approach of those in the first group, who privilege interests and incorporate ideas into their analyses only in relatively restricted roles, allows for a clear causal analysis but tends to miss many of the respects in which ideas may influence economic behavior. By contrast, those at the other end of the spectrum, who refuse to identify interests independently of the ideas used to interpret them, may have more profound insights about the role of ideas in economic life, but they experience more difficulty in establishing the precise causal links between ideas and other factors driving developments in the political economy. Various scholars working in the epistemic communities tradition have found a middle ground, but even they sometimes find themselves drawn toward relatively mechanistic analyses that put great stress on the bearers of the ideas and how they secure power rather than on the way in which the ideas themselves have an impact on economic action.

The challenges facing those working with such approaches are clear but not easy to meet. First, they need to develop more sophisticated theories about how ideas can be persuasive in themselves, which is to say, at least partially independently of the power of their proponents. By and large, that demands better conceptualization of the way in which new ideas interact with ideas that are already influential within what Jenson (1989) calls the existing "universe of political discourse." A new set of ideas is more likely to flourish when planted on some kinds of ideological terrain than on others (cf. Hall 1989: ch. 14). Similarly, if the reception given a new set of ideas depends on the response of the cultural authorities who act as key gatekeepers within business or policy communities, we need a better understanding of who these cultural authorities are and of what motivates their behavior. Finally, if ideas only become truly influential when they are embedded in social contexts or institutionalized in the operating procedures of key organizations, we need to know more about how such institutionalization takes place, what initiates it, and how differences in the structure of the existing institutions affect the process.

THE THREE APPROACHES COMPARED

It should be apparent that these three approaches, as defined here, are distinguished from each other primarily by the kinds of variables on which they focus. Each tends to assign more or less importance to socioeconomic interests, institutions, or ideas in the political economy. The result is three sets of significantly different causal propositions based to some extent on different models of the political economy.

The significance of these differences can be seen most clearly if we compare the way each approach treats issues of interest to all of them. I will briefly consider two such issues, beginning with the problem of explaining why Keynesian policies of aggregate demand management were adopted with different degrees of enthusiasm, in different forms, and at different times across nations.[5]

Interest-based analysts have approached this problem as one of explaining how political coalitions in support of such policies were assembled from a diverse range of social groups. Thus, Gourevitch (1986) observes that, where Keynesian policies were adopted in the 1930s, it was invariably by regimes that sought and found support from coalitions formed from two groups whose interests had hitherto often seemed to diverge – farmers and industrial workers – sometimes joined by internationally oriented sectors of business. He finds this commonality among regimes otherwise as different as those of the United States, Sweden, and Germany in the 1930s. With the "cow trade" of 1936 engineered by the Swedish Social Democrats, the electoral realignment of 1932 under Franklin D. Roosevelt in the United States, and the rearmament program under Hitler in Germany, similar coalitions were assembled for a similar set of policies (cf. Ferguson 1984; Martin 1979; Rogowski 1988). In Britain, the political insignificance of the farmers made such a coalition difficult, and similar policies were pursued relatively late in France only after Leon Blum assembled just this sort of supportive political base.

[5]For a more extended discussion of this issue, see Hall 1989.

Institutionally oriented scholars have approached the same problem from a different perspective that emphasizes the structural capacities of the state and lessons drawn from past lines of policy. Accordingly, Weir and Skocpol (1985) explain Sweden's willingness to use public works to expand demand in the 1930s by reference to the legacies left by past programs of public works, and the hesitation of British governments to pursue similar policies by reference to the presence of an unemployment insurance scheme oriented away from public works and the central role of a Treasury structurally biased against such programs.

Ideas-oriented scholars, by contrast, explain these outcomes by reference to the progress that Keynesian ideas made among the relevant professional community in each nation, namely among economists, noting that the more open structure of that community in Britain and the United States led to rapid acceptance there, while nations with less developed professional communities of economists or more hierarchical communities proved more resistant (Furner and Supple 1992; Salant 1989). They also observe that the reception given to Keynes's ideas depended in some measure on the preexisting character of economic and political discourse. Where others with similar ideas had already acquired popularity, the reception was more rapid than in nations where economic thinking was still dominated by the classical tradition or political concerns about state intervention were more intense (de Cecco 1989; Lee 1989; Rosanvallon 1989).

There is a similar contrast in the way that scholars operating from each of these three approaches tackle an issue of current interest to the field, namely the problem of explaining how increasing flows of goods and capital across national boundaries affect the policies and institutions of the industrialized nations.

Interest-based analysts suggest that intensified international integration shifts the interests of firms away from traditional regulatory regimes and modes of organizing production, leading them to initiate changes in firm strategies and to demand changes in institutional frameworks or policies that can be enforced by the additional power that firms gain vis-à-vis labor and the state when freer trade flows and the removal of exchange controls allow them to threaten to move production abroad (cf. Pontusson 1995; Pontusson and Swenson 1996). Many also emphasize the way in which increased openness shifts the comparative advantage of various kinds of producers or intensifies cleavages between those in the traded and nontraded sectors in such a way as to erode old political coalitions and make new ones feasible (Frieden and Rogowski 1996). The general implication of such approaches is that we should see increasing convergence of firm strategies, institutional frameworks, and policies across nations, as each comes under similar socioeconomic pressure.

Another set of analysts resists such convergence hypotheses, arguing instead that national institutional frameworks have considerable resilience in the face of socioeconomic pressures. Some stress the importance of national political frameworks. From this point of view, while shifting economic conditions may open up possibilities for new social coalitions, their achievement will depend heavily on the character of the national electoral system and the structure of the state (Garrett and Lange 1996). Others stress the mediating effect of the institutional structure of the political economy in each nation (Fioretis 1996; King and Wood 1998; Soskice 1994). They argue that, while firms and policy makers may seek adjustments in the face of changing economic circumstances, those will vary from nation to nation according to the way in which the political economy is organized there. Thus, the British and Americans may seek widespread deregulation to compete more effectively on cost terms, in line with their existing firm strategies, but the Germans and Japanese are likely to eschew deregulation of this kind in favor of improvements to the dense network of social institutions that make more effective the kind of quality-oriented competition in which they have long specialized.

Finally, although they are not yet as strongly represented in this debate, those who emphasize the impact of ideas also have a distinctive perspective on globalization. At the firm level, they stress that widespread changes in the organization of work derive as much from the diffusion of particular models of management, often pioneered by the Japanese, as from technological or economic imperatives (Cole 1989; Sabel 1991). At the political level, they question whether contemporary shifts in policy away from Keynesian demand management toward deregulation have really been forced on governments by economic circumstances. Instead, they suggest politicians have more room for maneuver than this kind of economic determinism acknowledges and that such changes in policy are often driven by the doctrinal fashions that sweep across policy communities or by the efforts of politicians to construct political ideologies that will appeal more effectively to the electorate (Hall 1993; Notermans 1993). The intensive efforts now underway to explain why the famous "Swedish model" has collapsed provide a fascinating case study of such debates. Some argue that the exhaustion of the Fordist model of production and efforts by Swedish firms to embrace flexible specialization drove the key developments. Others put more emphasis on the way in which the institutional infrastructure for collective bargaining permuted over time in such a way as to inspire employers to seek its reform. Still others emphasize the efforts of Swedish politicians to borrow ideas widely embraced elsewhere to respond to the concerns of the electorate about the growing bureaucratization of the welfare state and to reassemble a political coalition that was fraying at the edges (Iversen 1996; Notermans 1993; Pontusson and Swenson 1996; Rothstein 1996).

THE POTENTIAL FOR AND LIMITS TO INTEGRATION IN THE FIELD

As this account suggests, much of the richness in the field of comparative political economy stems from the presence of more than one approach to the same topic. At times, however, this can be frustrating, and it is arguable that faster progress could be made if we had a unified theory of political economy. Therefore, it is worthwhile asking: How much potential is there for a fuller integration among the perspectives currently represented in the field?

Some such potential certainly exists. Except in their most extreme versions, these three approaches are not entirely incommensurable with each other. It is often possible to incorporate insights from each into a single analysis. Moreover, some of the most exciting conceptual developments in the field are those taking place at the margins of each approach where it interfaces with the others. Work that builds from these interfaces can borrow strengths from both sides and avoid the excessive monism that occasionally afflicts those in one school or another. The challenge is to capture some of the complexity of the political world without altogether forsaking the parsimony on which good social science depends.

One example of the inherent possibilites for integration can be found in Weir's work on the development of American economic policy (1989, 1992a, 1992b). She begins in the realm of ideas, focused on the problem of explaining the fate of Keynesian ideas in the United States, but incorporates into her arguments a nice sense for the importance of political coalitions to this outcome and a real appreciation for how the structure of the American polity militated in favor of some coalitions and against others.

Returning to one of the examples cited above, there may also be some potential for integration in the growing body of work about the impact of intensified international integration on the domestic political economy (cf. Berger and Dore 1996; Boyer and Drache 1996; Keohane and Milner 1996). An integrated analysis might begin by observing that changes in the international economy shift the material interests of key groups located across the traded and nontraded sectors in such a way as to erode historic compromises and dissolve long-standing political coalitions. However, it could also recognize that the interests of such groups are not identical across nations because they are affected by nationally distinctive firm strategies and institutional infrastructures. Thus, the same pressures might lead similar groups toward different responses across nations. Moreover, the ability of any one group to formulate a coherent strategy, form a coalition, and influence policy might depend on the capacities that existing organizational frameworks provide for collective action. The ensuing political struggle could even be analyzed with some sensitivity to the way in which the formation of new economic ideologies makes new political coalitions possible.[6]

To consider models of this sort is to import a certain amount of complexity into the analysis. However, this need not be crippling if the causal chain is made relatively clear, as in a recursive network of equations, and the analysis is concentrated on particular pieces of it. In any one study, some variables might be treated as exogenous (for instance, economic developments and institutional structures) while others are deemed endogenous (e.g., interests, coalitions, and policies). Other analyses could then expand the range of variables treated as endogenous. In an era when models of the economy are highly complex, it does not make sense for our models of the political economy to be exceedingly simple.

[6]For one effort to outline at least some components of such an integrated view, see Hall 1998.

However, to put the problem in these terms slightly overstates the potential for integration in the field, in part because it neglects a methodological divide that cuts across the three approaches to political economy outlined in this essay. In some respects, this division mirrors the distinction between rationalists and culturalists developed elsewhere in this volume, but the correspondence is not perfect and, in the field of comparative political economy at least, the difference is often more a matter of emphasis than a profound philosophical difference. There are multiple dimensions to this divide, but it might loosely be described as one that separates those who seek what is sometimes termed a "positive political economy" from those who emphasize the "primacy of politics."

On one side stand those who tend to view political economy as an enterprise that seeks to apply the theories and methods of economics to politics. By virtue of this, they adopt a methodology built largely on rational choice assumptions about human behavior that sees "homo politicus" in largely the same terms as "homo economicus." Where institutions figure in the analysis, they are conceptualized as a matrix of sanctions and incentives to which rational actors respond and their presence is often explained largely in functional terms. In many cases, such work posits a causal dynamic in which socioeconomic developments figure as the prime movers behind political events.[7]

On the other side of the divide stands a group of scholars who tend to see political economy in quite different terms, as a mode of inquiry that resists the socioeconomic determinism of economic models in favor of arguments that assert the causal primacy of other factors, and notably of politics. Those who take such an approach to the subject often resist seeing human agents as entirely rational actors in favor of an emphasis on the degree to which their rationality is "bounded" or their self-interest tempered by broader bonds of sociability and considerations of social justice. Institutions are seen as complex constructs, which reflect pieces of larger cultural systems and tend to link the actors within them to distinct worldviews. They are said to derive from path-dependent processes of historical development that rarely respond entirely to functional imperatives. Thus, scholars inclined toward this approach see politics as relatively open-ended and emphasize the ways in which noneconomic factors, associated with politics or culture, influence the course of events that others might attempt to explain in entirely economic or rationalst terms.[8]

Both of these portraits are stylized and no single scholar need subscribe to all the tenets I have associated with each of them. They are what the French would call *tendances* rather than completely coherent epistemologies. However, they display several dimensions along which work in the field tends to vary, at least some of which are unlikely to be bridged in any single analysis. On the contrary, interchange between the two sides has long generated a contrapuntal rhythm that accounts for much of the liveliness in the field.

---

[7] At least some of these dimensions are well displayed in Alt and Shepsle 1990.

[8] For work that shares some, if not all, of these perspectives, see: Berger and Piore 1980, Sabel 1995, 1997; and Zysman 1977.

In general, enthusiasm for "positive political economy" is strongest among those who take what I have called an interest-based approach to political economy, while "primacy of politics" arguments are more prominently represented among those who operate from ideas-oriented approaches. Scholars who adopt an institutions-oriented approach to the subject tend to find themselves in the middle of such debates, because institutions can be modeled in rational choice terms or with more emphasis on their cultural embeddedness and path-dependent origins.

Partly as a result, some of the most exciting conceptual developments in the field today are taking place at the boundaries of the institutional approach, where it interfaces with interests-based or ideas-oriented work. In some cases, these developments constitute potential bridges for integrating work across several orientations in the field. In other cases, they provide new sites for dialogue between the partisans of different methodological perspectives or orientations. I will touch briefly on four such developments.

Two of these are advances in economic theory that hold out special promise for more fruitful interaction between those taking interests-based and institutions-oriented approaches to the discipline. They are: the growing body of work associated with the "new economics of organization" and the elaboration of what is often termed "endogenous growth theory."

The new economics of organization is important in this context because it begins from the sort of rationalist premises that are widely accepted among economists and interests-based analysts of the political economy but, building on game theory, it develops a framework for understanding how institutional frameworks can affect behavior that can be seen as an alternative to the traditional marginalist analysis of market-oriented economics (cf. Aoki 1988, 1990; Milgrom and Roberts 1992; Putterman 1986; Williamson 1985). It provides an increasingly elaborate set of concepts for understanding how firm behavior, conceptualized in terms that neoclassical economists can appreciate, may be affected by the institutional structures that underpin the organization of the political economy (cf. Finegold and Soskice 1988; Soskice 1994). Thus, the new economics of organization offers economists and interest-based analysts an opening to institutional analysis; and for institutional analysts, it offers a basis for more systematic theorizing about the impact of institutions.

Such theorizing provides a firm grounding for comparative analysis. The capacity of national financial systems to provide "patient capital" can be understood in terms of the kind of monitoring mechanisms that their institutional frameworks provide (cf. Hancke and Soskice 1996). Industrial relations systems can be compared with regard to the capacities they provide for employers and unions to coordinate their behavior; and the character of the interaction between central banks and wage contractors can be linked to the organization of wage bargaining (cf. Hall and Franzese 1996; Iversen 1996; Thelen 1991). Moreover, the recent interest that political scientists have displayed in these theories suggests that they may also be used to describe at least some of the overall political context for economic relations (cf. Moe 1984; Weingast and Marshall 1988).

Another advance in economics, the development of endogenous growth theory, also has real potential for linking interests-based and institution-oriented approaches to the economy. Proponents of the latter have long argued that the organization of the political economy creates a new kind of comparative advantage that is not based solely on factor endowments but is institutionally created (cf. Zysman 1996). Neoclassical economists have often been skeptical about this contention. However, endogenous growth theory now gives them a systematic basis for understanding why it might be true. In a nutshell, endogenous growth theory explains the residual productivity growth of an economic unit that is left over after appropriate increments in productivity have been assigned to changes in the inputs of capital or labor to that unit (cf. Grossman and Helpman 1994; Krugman 1990; Romer 1991). It does so in terms of learning effects and network externalities that can be related directly to the institutional structure of the political economy by virtue of the way the latter contributes to the up-skilling of the workforce or the kind of communication between firms and their employees that fosters learning-based improvements to productivity (cf. Porter 1990). Thus, endogenous growth theory provides a systematic basis for understanding how the organization of the political economy can contribute to productivity and economic growth.

In addition, endogenous growth theory provides a potential bridge between the coalitional analyses prominent among interests-based approaches to political economy and more institutions-oriented approaches. As we have seen, it has become conventional for coalition theories to suggest that international economic developments erode old political coalitions and create the potential for new ones primarily by altering the comparative advantage enjoyed by different groups in the economy. To date, most such theories turn on traditional concepts of comparative advantage oriented around factor endowments and ignore the institutional structure of the political economy.

However, the notion of institutionally created comparative advantage implicit in endogenous growth theory suggests that the effects of international economic developments on any one group of firms or workers may depend on whether that group draws its comparative advantage from relative factor endowments or from a particular set of institutional structures. When a group depends primarily on institutionally created comparative advantage, its interests and political posture may not be heavily affected by changes in the international economy that operate primarily through the relative scarcity of factor endowments. However, developments in the international economy that threaten the institutional infrastructure surrounding such a group could deeply affect its interests and political posture. In other words, endogenous growth theory has the potential to link coalitional analysis in political economy to perspectives that emphasize the institutional infrastructure of the political economy (cf. Frieden and Rogowski 1996).

Turning to the other boundary where institution-oriented approaches to political economy meet ideas-oriented approaches, two other spheres of theoretical development offer sites for potentially fruitful interchange between those with structural and cultural perspectives on the field. These center on the theories now being developed with regard to "social capital" and the "new institutionalism in organization theory."

I use the term "social capital" in a broad sense to refer to those characteristics of society that facilitate the operation of the economy and the implementation, in this case, of economic policy.[9] After some years in which the field conceptualized economic organization largely in terms of a dualism between markets and hierarchies, both at the level of ordinary economic transactions, where firms were seen as hierarchies devised to cope with tasks at which market relations were inefficient, and at the level of public regulation, where the operation of the market was juxtaposed to the hierarchy of the state, a growing number of scholars have been trying to identify a third set of relationships central to the organization and coordination of economic relations. As yet, there is no consensus about what this third pillar should be called: It is variously termed a constitutional order, sectoral governance mechanism, social regime of production, coordinating capacity, or regional order (Hollingsworth et al. 1994; Hollingsworth and Boyer 1997; Sabel 1997; Schmitter and Streeck 1990; Soskice 1994). However, there is wide agreement that a set of institutional relationships, either more or less formal, operating alongside market relations and hierarchical relationships, is indispensable to the effective operation of the economy and the implementation of economic policy in most settings (cf. Granovetter 1985; Levy 1994; Swedberg 1994; Zukin and DiMaggio 1994).

Thus, we now have the basis for a wide-ranging and potentially very interesting debate about precisely how this third pillar is constituted and why it affects economic performance or policy. Some scholars construe it as a broad network of associational ties that create norms of reciprocity that can serve multiple purposes (Coleman 1990; Culpepper 1996; Putnam 1993). Others understand it as a set of organizational structures purpose-built to facilitate certain kinds of coordination, akin to neocorporatist relations (Smyrl 1996; Soskice 1991), while still others see it as a more culturally constructed web of social relations, which can take multiple forms provided they build the kinds of trust essential for economic cooperation (Herrigel 1995; Locke 1995; Ostrum 1990; Sabel 1992).

As they are expressed, there is some overlap among these views and we need a more precise specification of how the institutions central to each kind of analysis affect economic development or the implementation of various kinds of economic policy, but this is a promising line of inquiry and one that that will almost certainly draw institutionally oriented analysts into dialogue with those who argue for more culturally-oriented variables.

A second body of work, often referred to as the "new institutionalism in organization theory," also opens up new avenues for thinking about the relationship between culture or ideas and institutional development (cf. Hall and Taylor

---

[9]Of course, Putnam (1993) and Coleman (1990) use this term in a somewhat more specific sense, but I see them here as part of a wider debate.

1996; March and Olsen 1989; Powell and DiMaggio 1991). The new institutionalists begin by challenging the distinction conventionally drawn between rationally motivated action (in the sense of means–ends rationality) and culturally driven action (in the sense of normative behavior). To do so, they make two broad analytical moves.

First, they argue that many of the features of human action and, especially, modern organizations that are normally attributed to the drive for greater efficiency, actually derive from a search for legitimacy or culturally appropriate forms of endeavor. Thus, corporations producing diverse product ranges are said to develop homogeneous organizational structures, not necessarily because those are most efficient, but because they come to be seen as appropriate for such corporations (Fligstein 1990).

Second, these analysts challenge the traditional view of culture as a set of prescriptive norms internalized by the incumbents of particular social roles (cf. Parsons and Shils 1951). Instead, they conceptualize culture, in more cognitive terms, as a repertoire of strategies for action or commonly accepted ideas about how one **can** behave that influence behavior, not by prescribing or proscribing particular acts but by providing the basic templates through which the world and its possibilities are construed, much like the social scripts to which symbolic interactionists refer (March and Olsen 1989; Powell and DiMaggio 1991; Swidler 1986). Thus, culture is seen not as a set of values but as a set of institutions, understood as cognitive templates, and policy makers are said to initiate policies or organizational reforms because the latter have been validated by the relevant cultural authorities or in the forums that are indispensable reference points for their spheres of endeavor (Scott 1995; Scott and Meyer 1994).

Fligstein (1990) employs this kind of analysis to explain how institutional innovations were rapidly diffused through American corporations in the early decades of the century. Tolbert and Zucker (1983) use it to explain the force behind the "good government" movement of the same period; and Dobbin (1994) takes a similar approach toward explaining differences in the economic policies of France and the United States.

In this context, the significance of the approach lies in the dialogue it opens up with institutionally oriented scholars of political economy, who are more inclined to treat the behavior of firms or governments as rational responses to environmental pressures without substantial reference to the range of ideas that might be canvassed by the relevant decision makers or the cultural cachet of those ideas. From such dialogue, there may well be room for synthetic theories to emerge, which recognize the pressure that market relations put on firms or governments to adopt new strategies but also accord importance to the way in which transnational cultural processes make model strategies available or attractive. By interpreting culture in more cognitive terms, the new institutionalists in organization studies have made it easier for institutionalists in political economy to incorporate such factors into their theories.

In sum, some of the most exciting intellectual developments in the field of comparative political economy are taking place at the margins of one of its principal schools of thought, where at least four evolving bodies of theory promise fruitful interaction among proponents of ideas-oriented, interests-based, and institutions-oriented work.

THE CONTEMPORARY CHALLENGE

Lest we congratulate ourselves too soon about the accomplishments of the field, however, it is important to note the areas in which it is still not living up to its full potential. In recent years, the field has concentrated, above all, on explaining cross-national differences in economic policies and performance. This is an important endeavor, which should not be neglected.[10] In some respects, however, it has drawn contemporary political economists away from some of the overarching issues that absorbed many of the greatest political economists in years past. By and large, these were issues about the relationship between the state, seen as the custodian of a general interest, and the market, seen as a mechanism for interchange among private interests, and the consequences of this interaction for the overall distribution of well-being in society.

Such issues are returning to the agenda of political economy in response to the intensified international integration that has taken place in recent decades. Greater flows of goods, capital, and labor across national borders now challenge the national policy regimes of many states and have begun to raise questions about the capacity of governments to regulate increasingly international markets. As a result, growing numbers of scholars are asking whether international integration will enforce a new convergence in behavior and institutions across nations, and some have begun to ask whether democratic states can still play a constructive role in the face of more globalized markets (cf. Berger and Dore 1996; Boyer and Drache 1996).

However, there are still some significant lacunae in the literature, and by way of conclusion, I want to emphasize three of the most significant of these.

First, the field as a whole has paid relatively little attention to distributive issues, by which I mean the way in which national patterns of economic policy and performance give rise to multiple inequalities in the distribution of resources and life-chances. It is paradoxical that political economy has neglected such issues since political scientists should be more attuned to them than economists.[11] Perhaps thirty years of unprecedented growth after World War II drew attention

---

[10]The sincerity of this statement is reflected in my own work (cf. Hall 1986, 1989).

[11]I am grateful to Andrew Glyn for pointing this out to me. For some notable exceptions, see Glyn and Sutcliffe (1968) and Marglin and Schor (1990).

away from such issues. However, they are hard to ignore today, after two decades in which inequalities of wealth and income have widened in most of the industrialized nations. Precisely for this reason, we can expect more political economists to turn their attention to such issues.

One of the routes into the problem will be to examine the relationship between the character of a nation's social policy or welfare state and the organization of its political economy. Research has generated various models of national welfare states, whether liberal, conservative, or social democratic, and different models of national capitalism, whether coordinated and liberal or Fordist and flexibly specialized (cf. Albert 1992; Esping-Andersen 1990; Soskice 1990b). As yet, however, we do not have a clear understanding of how these different kinds of welfare states interact with different models of the economy. In particular, we might ask why some combinations are more common than others and whether they produce distinctive distributions of life-chances across subgroups in the population. Similarly, we know relatively little about how the performance of the economy affects the development of social policy or vice versa. There is an emerging research agenda here that is only now being explored (cf. Iversen and Wren 1996; Mares 1996).

Second, the study of political economy has largely been divorced from the study of representation in recent years. This is surprising. On the one hand, one of the central issues in political science has always been: Whose voices are being heard in the political process (cf. Beer 1982)? On the other hand, the outcomes that political economists study are some of the most consequential in politics. Yet few have asked: Who gets represented in the decision-making processes that produce specific patterns of economic policy and performance?

Once again, merely to mention the topic is to evoke multiple intuitions. Electoral theories yield some insights, as do institutional analyses that emphasize the positional power of various actors. However, these kinds of analyses are rarely linked to theories of representation; and few efforts have been made to consider the long decision chain through which significant economic outcomes are generated. While it is a start, a focus on the process of economic policy making alone is not sufficient, since economic outcomes follow from a long chain of decisions that involve key organizations in the economy, such as firms and unions, as well as governments. The issue was broached ten years ago in debates about neocorporatism, but it is time to revisit it today (cf. Berger 1982; Offe 1985).

Finally, all three of the approaches surveyed in this chapter suffer from a heuristic limitation of considerable significance. None captures very well the contribution that political conflict and political debate make to the construction of interests and the formation of coalitions. The vast majority of analyses produced by political economists take the same general form, which is to say that they identify a fixed set of variables, whether composed of interests, institutions, or ideas, given exogenously to the process of political conflict, and then show how these structure the situation so as to produce the relevant outcomes. This kind of analysis can have real value, but what it misses is the extent to which the outcomes may be created via processes of political conflict and not generated entirely by the antecedents to that conflict.[12]

The problem is clearest in the case of many interest-based approaches to political economy. On the one hand, analyses of this sort often have the most potential for considering the construction of interests because they model politics as a clash between groups with conflicting interests. On the other hand, most such analyses assume that the perceived interests of the relevant groups are fixed by a set of socioeconomic conditions prevailing in the domestic and international economy. In some cases, they may be. But it takes only a moment's reflection to realize that most people have multiple interests, often associated with the multiple roles they play in the world, some of which conflict with each other, and many of which are subject to multiple interpretations. Faced with a given issue, then, the actors may have trouble identifying their interests clearly, especially with regard to macroeconomic issues, which are frequently difficult to understand. Thus, on many of the most important economic questions of the day, it cannot always be said that the interests of a group or individual are "given" by their socioeconomic position. On the contrary, those interests have to be derived via a process of interpretation.

Politics is fundamental to this process of interpretation. Much of what goes on in the political arena is, in fact, a struggle among political entrepreneurs to define the way in which the electorate or potential followers within it interpret their interests. Nineteenth-century British politics, for instance, was dominated by the efforts of competing leaders to persuade potential followers that free trade was either in their interest or inimical to it (Kindleberger 1975; Rohrlich 1987). Many recent contests between candidates for the American presidency have turned on debates about what sort of economic policies would truly be in the interest of the middle class. European politicians and interest-group leaders have recently been locked in debate about whether a European Monetary Union will or will not serve the interests of their nations (Berger 1995).

In short, politics is not only a contest for power. It is also a struggle for the interpretation of interests (cf. Gourevitch 1977). To treat it, even in the most sophisticated way, as a process in which socioeconomic change immediately shifts perceived interests or in which institutions confer power on some groups rather than others, with a set of interests given in advance of the process, is to neglect the creative contribution that political contention can make to the definition of interests and, thus, mispecifies the political process quite fundamentally. Interests must be seen not as givens, but as objects of contestation. Politics is more open than most political economists see it.[13]

---

[12]On this point, my thinking has been significantly influenced by many discussions with Suzanne Berger.

[13]In slightly different terms, this is a point well made by Sabel (1995, 1997).

One of the principal challenges facing the field, then, is to model the political dynamic more effectively so as to capture the process whereby political contention contributes to the development of particular interpretations of interest among key social groups. This is undeniably difficult. Even those accustomed to focusing on the role of ideas in politics find it hard to say why some ideas win out over others. The results seem to emerge from an iterated process of interaction between potentially new interpretations of interest and existing ones, mediated by the institutions that structure political competition and allocate cultural authority within the relevant communities (cf. Hall 1989: ch. 14). However challenging this task may be, to ignore it and specify interests entirely ex ante is hardly a solution.

In sum, those who study the comparative political economy of the industrialized nations can look back on considerable accomplishments in recent years, to which scholars with a focus on interests, institutions and ideas have all contributed. While some might lament the failure of the field to embrace a single paradigm, its diversity has provided real stimulation, and some of the most interesting developments today are occurring on the boundaries where one approach meets the others. These developments and contemporary economic events, which have generated rising levels of inequality and new challenges for states confronted with global markets, are again drawing the attention of the field to some of the overarching themes that inspired its founders.

REFERENCES

Albert, Michel. 1992. *Capitalism Against Capitalism.* London: Whurr.

Alesina, Alberto. 1989. "Politics and Business Cycles in Industrial Democracies." *Economic Policy* 8:58-98.

Alesina, Alberto, and Roberto Perotti. 1994. "The Political Economy of Budget Deficits." NBER Working Paper, No. 4637.

Alesina, Alberto, G. Cohen, and N. Roubini. 1993. "Electoral Business Cycles in Industrial Democracies." *European Journal of Political Economy* 23:1-25.

Alesina, Alberto, and Lawrence Summers. 1993. "Bank Independence and Macroeconomic Performance: Some Comparative Evidence." *Journal of Money, Credit and Banking* 2456:151-62.

Alt, James, and K. Chrystal. 1983. *Political Economics.* Berkeley: University of California Press.

Alt, James, and Kenneth Shepsle, eds. 1990. *Perspectives on Political Economy.* Berkeley: University of California Press.

Alvarez, Michael, Geoffrey Garrett, and Peter Lange. 1991. "Government Partisanship, Labor Organization and Macroeconomic Performance." *American Political Science Review* 85:2.

Aoiki, Masahiko. 1988. *Information, Incentives and Bargaining in the Japanese Economy.* New York: Cambridge University Press.

———. 1990. "Toward an Economic Model of the Japanese Firm." *Journal of Economic Literature* 28.

Bates, Robert H., and Barry Weingast. 1995. "A New Comparative Politics: Integrating Interpretive and Rational Choice Perspectives." *Center for American Political Studies Working Paper,* Harvard University.

Beer, Samuel. 1982. *Modern British Politics.* New York: Norton.

Berger, Suzanne, ed. 1982. *Organizing Interests in Western Europe.* New York: Cambridge University Press.

———. 1995. "Trade and Identity: The Coming Protectionism." In Gregory Flynn, ed., *Remaking the Hexagon.* Boulder: Westview.

Berger, Suzanne, and Ronald Dore, eds. 1996. *National Diversity and Global Capitalism.* Ithaca: Cornell University Press.

Berger, Suzanne, and Michael Piore. 1980. *Dualism and Discontinuity in Industrial Societies.* Cambridge: Cambridge University Press.

Blaug, Mark. 1983. *Economic Theory in Retrospect.* New York: Cambridge University Press.

Boyer, Robert. 1990. *The Regulation School: A Critical Introduction.* New York: Columbia University Press.

Boyer, Robert, and Daniel Drache, eds. 1996. *States Against Markets.* New York: Routledge.

Caldwell, Bruce. 1982. *Beyond Positivism: Economic Methodology in the Twentieth Century.* London: Allen and Unwin.

Calmfors, Lars, and John Driffill. 1988. "Centralization of Wage Bargaining." *Economic Policy* 6:13-61.

Cameron, David. 1978. "The Expansion of the Political Economy: A Comparative Analysis." *American Political Science Review* 72:1243-61.

———. 1984. "Social Democracy, Corporatism, Labor Quiescence and the Representation of Economic Interest in Advanced Capitalist Society." In John Goldthorpe, *Order and Conflict in Contemporary Capitalism.* New York: Oxford University Press.

Campbell, John L., J. Rogers Hollingsworth, and Leon N. Lindberg, eds. 1991. *Governance of the American Economy.* New York: Cambridge University Press.

Cawson, Alan, ed. 1985. *Organized Interests and the State.* Beverly Hills: Sage.

Cawson, Alan, and J. Ballard. 1984. *A Bibliography of Corporatism.* European University Institute Working Paper.

Cole, Robert A. 1989. *Strategies for Industry.* Berkeley: University of California Press.

Coleman, James. 1990. *Foundations of Social Theory.* Chicago: University of Chicago Press.

Cox, Andrew, ed. 1986. *The State, Finance and Industry.* Brighton: Wheatsheaf.

Cukierman, Alex. 1992. *Central Bank Strategy, Credibility and Independence.* Cambridge: MIT Press.

Culpepper, Pepper D. 1996. "Employers' Organizations and the Politics of Vocational Training in France and Germany." Paper presented to the American Political Science Association.

de Cecco, Marcello. 1989. "Keynes and Italian Economics." In Peter A. Hall, ed., *The Political Power of Economic Ideas.* Princeton: Princton University Press.

Dertouzos, John, Richard Lester, and Robert Solow. 1986. *Made in America.* Cambridge: MIT Press.

DiMaggio, Paul, and Walter Powell. 1991. "Introduction." In Walter Powell and Paul DiMaggio, eds., *The New Institutionalism in Organizational Analysis.* Chicago: University of Chicago Press.

Dobbin, Frank. 1994. *Forging Industrial Policy.* Cambridge: Cambridge University Press.

Esping-Andersen, Gosta. 1990. *Three Worlds of Welfare Capitalism.* Princeton: Princeton University Press.

Ferguson, Thomas. 1984. "From Normalcy to New Deal: Industrial Structure, Party Competition and American Public Policy in the Great Depression." *International Organization* 38:41-94.

Finegold, David, and David Soskice. 1988. "The Failure of Training in Britain: Analysis and Prescription." *Oxford Review of Economic Policy* 4:3.

Fioretos, Karl-Orfeo. 1996. "Globalization, National Production Regimes and Multilateral Institution-Building: The Case of Britain and Sweden." Paper presented to the American Political Science Association, 1996.

Fiorina, Morris. 1986. *Retrospective Voting in American National Elections.* New Haven: Yale University Press.

Fligstein, Neil. 1990. *The Transformation of Corporate Control.* Cambridge: Harvard University Press.

Franzese, Robert. 1994. "Central Bank Independence, Sectoral Interest and the Wage Bargain." Harvard Center for European Studies Working Paper.

Frey, Bruno. 1978. *Modern Political Economys.* New York: Wiley.

Frieden, Jeffry A. 1991a. *Debt, Development and Democracy.* Princeton: Princeton University Press.

———. 1991b. "Invested Interests: The Politics of National Economic Policies in a World of Global Finance." *International Organization* 45:4.

Frieden, Jeffry A., and Ronald Rogowski. 1996. "The Impact of the International Economy on National Policies: An Analytical Overview." In Robert Keohane and Helen Milner, eds., *Internationalization and Domestic Politics.* New York: Cambridge University Press.

Fulcher, James. 1991. *Labour Movements, Employers and the State.* Oxford: Clarendon Press.

Furner, Mary, and Barry Supple. 1992. *Economists in Government.* New York: Cambridge University Press.

Garrett, Geoffrey, and Peter Lange. 1986. "Performance in a Hostile World." *World Politics* 38:517-45.

———. 1991 "Political Responses to Interdependence: What's Left for the Left." *International Organization* 45:4.

———. 1996. "Internationalization, Institutions and Political Change." In Robert Keohane and Helen Milner, *Internationalization and Domestic Politics.* New York: Cambridge University Press.

Garrett, Geoffrey, and Christopher Way. 1995. "Labor Market Institutions and the Economic Consequences of Central Bank Independence." Paper presented to the American Political Science Association.

Garrett, Geoffrey, and Barry Weingast. 1993. "Ideas, Interests and Institutions: Constructing the European Community's Internal Market." In Judith Goldstein and Robert Keohane, eds., *Ideas and Foreign Policy.* Ithaca: Cornell University Press.

Gerschenkron, Alexander. 1943. *Bread and Democracy in Germany.* New York: Fertig.

Glyn, Andrew, and Bob Sutcliffe. 1968. *The Profits Squeeze.* Harmondsworth, U.K.: Penguin.

Golden, Miriam, and Jonas Pontusson, eds. 1992. *Bargaining for Change.* Ithaca: Cornell University Press.

Goldstein, Judith. 1993. *Ideas, Interests and American Trade Policy.* Ithaca: Cornell University Press.

Goldstein, Judith, and Robert Keohane, eds. 1993. *Ideas and Foreign Policy.* Ithaca: Cornell University Press.

Goldthorpe, John A., ed. 1984. *Order and Conflict in Contemporary Capitalism.* New York: Oxford University Press.

Goodman, John. 1992. *Monetary Sovereignty.* Ithaca: Cornell University Press.

Gourevitch, Peter A. 1977. "International Trade, Domestic Coalitions and Liberty." *Journal of Interdisciplinary History* 8:281-313.

———. 1986. *Politics in Hard Times.* Ithaca: Cornell University Press.

———. 1989. "Keynesian Politics: The Political Sources of Economic Policy Choices." In Peter A. Hall, ed., *The Political Power of Economic Ideas.* Princeton: Princeton University Press.

Granovetter, Mark. 1985. "Economic Action and Social Structure: The Problem of Embeddedness." *American Journal of Sociology* 91:481-510.

Grilli, Vittorio, Donato Masciandaro, and Guido Tabellini. 1991. "Political and Monetary Institutions and Public Financial Policies in the Industrialized Countries." *Economic Policy* 13:42-92.

Grossman, Gene M., and Elhanan Helpman. 1994. "Endogenous Innovation in the Theory of Growth." *Journal of Economic Perspectives* 8:23-44.

Haas, Peter M. 1992. "Introduction: Epistemic Communities and International Policy Coordination." *International Organization* 46:1-35.

Hall, Peter A. 1986. *Governing the Economy.* New York: Oxford University Press.

———, ed. 1989. *The Political Power of Economic Ideas: Keynesianism across Nations.* Princeton: Princeton University Press.

———. 1993. "Policy Paradigms, Social Learning and the State." *Comparative Politics* 23:275-96.

———. 1994. "Central Bank Independence and Coordinated Wage Bargaining: Their Interaction in New York and Europe." *German Politics and Society* 31:1-23.

———. 1998. "The Political Economy of Europe in an Era of Interdependence." In Herbert Kitschelt et al., eds., *Change and Continuity in Contemporary Capitalism.* New York: Cambridge University Press.

Hall, Peter A., and Robert Franzese, Jr. 1996. "Mixed Signals: Central Bank Independence, Coordinated Wage Bargaining and European Monetary Union." Discussion paper of the Wissenschaftszentrum, Berlin.

Hall, Peter A., and Rosemary C. R. Taylor. 1996. "Political Science and the Three New Institutionalisms." *Political Studies* 44:936-57.

Hancke, Bob, and David Soskice. 1996. "Coordination and Restructuring in Large French Firms: The Evolution of French Industry in the 1980s." Discussion Paper of the Wissenschaftszentrum, Berlin.

Hayward, Jack. 1976. "Institutional Inertia and Political Impetus in France and Britain." *European Journal of Political Research* 4:341-59.

Hayward, Jack, and Michael Watson, eds. 1975. *Planning, Politics and Public Policy.* Cambridge: Cambridge University Press.

Herrigel, Gary. 1995. *Industrial Constructions.* New York: Cambridge University Press.

Hibbs, Douglas. 1977. "Political Parties and Macroeconomic Policy." *American Political Science Review* 71:1467-87.

Hicks, Alexander. 1988. "Social Democratic Corporatism and Economic Performance." *Journal of Politics* 50:677-704.

Hollingsworth, J. Rogers, and Robert Boyer, eds. 1997. *Contemporary Capitalism: The Embeddedness of Institutions.* New York: Cambridge University Press.

Hollingsworth, J. Rogers, Philippe Schmitter, and Wolfgang Streeck, eds. 1994. *Governing Capitalist Economies.* New York: Oxford University Press.

Iversen, Torben. 1996. "Power, Flexibility and the Breakdown of Centralized Wage Bargaining: The Cases of Denmark and Sweden in Comparative Perspective." *Comparative Politics* 28:399-438.

———. 1994. "Wage Bargaining, Monetary Regimes and Economic Performance in Organized Market Economies: Theory and Evidence." Paper presented to the Annual Meeting of the American Political Science Association.

Iversen, Torben, and Anne Wren. 1996 "Equality, Employment and Fiscal Discipline: The Trilemma of the Service Economy." Paper presented to the American Political Science Association.

Jenson, Jane. 1989. "'Different' but Not 'Exceptional': Canada's Permeable Fordism." *Canadian Review of Sociology and Anthropology* 26:69-126.

———. 1989. "Paradigms and Political Discourse: Protective Legislation in France and the United States before 1914." *Canadian Journal of Political Science* 22:235-58.

Johnson, James. 1994. "Symbolic Dimensions of Social Order." Paper presented to a conference on "What Is Institutionalism Now?" University of Maryland.

Kalecki, M. 1943. "Political Aspects of Full Employment." *Political Quarterly* 14:322-30.

Katzenstein, Peter J. 1978. *Corporatism and Change.* Ithaca: Cornell University Press.

———. 1985. *Small States in World Markets.* Ithaca: Cornell University Press.

Keohane, Robert O., and Helen V. Milner, eds. 1996. *Internationalization and Domestic Politics.* New York: Cambridge University Press.

Kern, Horst, and Michael Schumann. 1989. "New Concepts of Production in West German Plants." In Peter Katzenstein, ed., *Industry and Politics in West Germany.* Ithaca: Cornell University Press.

Kiewit, Roderick. 1983. *Macroeconomics and Micropolitics.* Chicago: University of Chicago Press.

Kindleberger, Charles. 1975. "The Rise of Free Trade in Western Europe, 1820–1875." *Journal of Economic History* 35:20-55.

King, Desmond, and Stewart Wood. 1998. "Neo-Liberalism and the Conservative Offensive: Britain and the United States in the 1980s." In Herbert Kitschelt et al., eds., *Change and Continuity in Contemporary Capitalism.* New York: Cambridge University Press.

Knetter, M. 1989. "Price Discrimination by US and German Exporters." *American Economic Review* 79:198-210.

Krugman, Paul. 1990. *Rethinking International Trade.* Cambridge: MIT Press.

Kurth, James. 1979. "Political Consequences of the Product Cycle." *International Organization* 33:1-34.

Kurzer, Paulette. 1993. *Business and Banking.* Ithaca: Cornell University Press.

Lane, Christel. 1989. *Management and Labour in Europe.* London: Edward Elgar.

Lange, Peter. 1984. "Unions, Workers and Wage Regulation." In John A. Goldthorpe, ed., *Order and Conflict in Contemporary Capitalism.* New York: Oxford University Press.

Lazonick, William. 1991. *Business Organization and the Myth of the Market Economy.* New York: Cambridge University Press.

Lee, Bradford A. 1989. "The Miscarriage of Necessity and Invention: Proto-Keynesianism and Democratic States in the 1930s." In Peter A. Hall, ed., *The Political Power of Economic Ideas.* Princeton: Princeton University Press.

Lehmbruch, Gerhard, and Philippe Schmitter, eds. 1982. *Patterns of Corporatist Policy-Making.* Beverly Hills: Sage.

Levy, Jonah. 1994. *Tocqueville's Revenge: Dilemmas of Institutional Reform in Post-Dirigiste France.* Ph.D. Dissertation, MIT.

Locke, Richard. 1995. *Remaking the Italian Economy.* Ithaca: Cornell University Press.

Locke, Richard, and Kathleen Thelen. 1995. "Apples and Oranges Revisited: Contextualized Comparisons and the Study of Comparative Labor Politics." *Politics and Society* 23:337-67.

March, James, and Johan P. Olsen. 1989. *Rediscovering Institutions.* New York: Free Press.

Mares, Isabela. 1996. "Is Unemployment Insurable? Employers and the Institutionalization of the Risk of Unemployment." Discussion Paper of the Wissenschaftszentrum, Berlin.

Marglin, Stephen, and Juliet Schor, eds. 1990. *The Golden Age of Capitalism.* Oxford: Clarendon Press.

Martin, Andrew. 1979 "The Dynamics of Change in a Keynesian Political Economy: The Swedish Case and Its Implications." In Colin Crouch, ed., *State and Economy in Contemporary Capitalism.* London: Croom Helm.

Martin, Cathie Jo. 1995. "Nature or Nurture? Sources of Film Preferences for National Health Reform." *American Political Science Review* 89:898-913.

Matzner, Egon, and Wolfgang Streeck, eds. 1991. *Beyond Keynesianism.* London: Edward Elgar.

Maurice, Marc, Francois Sellier, and Jean-Jacques Silvestre. 1986. *The Social Foundations of Industrial Power.* Cambridge: MIT Press.

Milgrom, Paul, and John Roberts. 1992. *Economics, Organization and Management.* Englewood Cliffs, NJ: Prentice Hall.

Milner, Helen. 1988. *Resisting Protectionism.* Princeton: Princeton University Press.

Moe, Terry. 1984. "The New Economics of Organization." *American Journal of Political Science* 28:739-77.

Moore, Barrington, Jr. 1966. *The Social Origins of Dictatorship and Democracy.* Boston: Beacon Press.

Nelson, Richard R. 1993. *National Innovation Systems.* New York: Oxford University Press.

Nordhaus, William D. 1975. "The Political Business Cycle." *Review of Economic Studies* 42:169-90.

Notermans, Ton. 1993. "The Abdication from National Policy Autonomy." *Politics and Society* 21:133-67.

Offe, Claus. 1985. *Disorganized Capitalism.* Cambridge: MIT Press.

Ostrum, Elinor. 1990. *Governing the Commons.* New York: Cambridge University Press.

Parsons, Talcott, and Edward Shils, eds. 1951. *Towards a General Theory of Action.* Cambridge: Harvard University Press.

Pierson, Paul. 1995. "The Scope and Nature of Business Power." Paper presented to the Annual Meeting of the American Political Science Association.

Piore, Michael, and Charles Sabel. 1984. *The Second Industrial Divide.* New York: Basic.

Polanyi, Karl. 1946. *The Great Transformation.* Boston: Beacon Press.

Pontusson, Jonas. 1995. "From Comparative Public Policy to Political Economy: Putting Institutions in Their Place and Taking Interests Seriously." *Comparative Political Studies* 28:117-47.

Pontusson, Jonas, and Peter Swenson. 1996. "Labor Markets, Production Strategies and Wage-Bargaining Institutions." *Comparative Political Studies* 29:223-50.

Porter, Michael. 1990. *The Competitive Advantage of Nations.* London: Macmillan.

Powell, Walter, and Paul DiMaggio, eds. 1991. *The New Institutionalism in Organizational Analysis.* Chicago: University of Chicago Press.

Przeworski, Adam, and Michael Wallerstein. 1982. "The Structure of Class Conflict in Democratic Capitalist Societies." *American Political Science Review* 76:215-38.

Putnam, Robert D. 1993. *Making Democracy Work.* Princeton: Princeton University Press.

Putterman, Louis, ed. 1986. *The Economic Nature of the Firm.* Cambridge: Cambridge University Press.

Richardson, Jeremy, and W. Jordan, eds. 1982. *Policy Styles in Western Europe.* Boston: Allen and Unwin.

Rogowski, Ronald. 1989. *Commerce and Coalitions.* Princeton: Princeton University Press.

Rohrlich, Paul Egon. 1987. "Economic Culture and Foreign Policy: The Cognitive Analysis of Economic Policy Making." *International Organization* 41:61-92.

Roll, Eric. 1956. *History of Economic Thought.* Englewood Cliffs, NJ: Prentice Hall.

Romer, Paul. 1991. "Increasing Returns and Long-Run Growth." *Journal of Political Economy* 99:500-21.

Rosanvallon, Pierre. 1989. "The Development of Keynesianism in France." In Peter A. Hall, ed., *The Political Power of Economic Ideas.* Princeton: Princeton University Press.

Rothstein, Bo. 1996. *The Corporatist State.* Pittsburgh: University of Pittsburgh Press.

Roubini, Nouriel, and Jeffrey Sachs. 1989. "Government Spending and Budget Deficits in the Industrialized Societies." *Economic Policy* 8:99-132.

Sabel, Charles F. 1991. "Moebius-Strip Organizations and Open Labor Markets: Some Consequences of the Reintegration of Conception and Execution in a Volatile Economy." In Pierre Bourdieu and James S. Coleman, eds., *Social Theory for a Changing Society.* Boulder, CO: Westview.

———. 1992. "Studied Trust: Building New Forms of Cooperation in a Volatile Economy." In Frank Pyke and Werner Sengenberger, eds., *Industrial Districts and Local Economic Regeneration.* Geneva: International Institute for Labor Studies.

———. 1995. "Learning by Monitoring: The Institutions of Economic Development." In Neil Smelser and Richard Swedberg, eds., *Handbook of Economic Sociology.* Princeton: Princeton University Press.

————. 1997. "Constitutional Orders: Trust-Building and Response to Change." In
　　J. Rogers Hollingsworth and Robert Boyer, eds., *Contemporary Capitalism.*
　　New York: Cambridge University Press.

Sabel, Charles F., and Jonathon Zeitlin. 1985. "Historical Alternatives to Mass Pro-
　　duction." *Past and Present* 108:103-76.

Salais, Robert, and Michael Storper. 1993. *Les Mondes de Production.* Paris: Ecole des
　　Hautes Etudes en Sciences Sociales.

Salant, Walter S. 1989. "The Spread of Keynesian Doctrines and Practices in the
　　United States." In Peter A. Hall, ed., *The Political Power of Economic Ideas.*
　　Princeton: Princeton University Press.

Scharpf, Fritz W. 1988. "Game-Theoretical Interpretations of Inflation and Unem-
　　ployment in Western Europe." *Journal of Public Policy* 7:227-57.

————. 1991. *Crisis and Choice in European Social Democracy.* Ithaca: Cornell Univer-
　　sity Press.

Schatschneider, Elmer E. 1935. *Politics, Pressures and the Tariff.* New York: Prentice-
　　Hall.

Schelling, Thomas. 1980. *The Strategy of Conflict.* Cambridge: Harvard University Press.

Schmidt, Manfred. 1982. "The Role of the Parties in Shaping Macroeconomic Poli-
　　cy." In Francis Castles, ed., *The Impact of Parties.* Beverly Hills: Sage.

Schmitter, Philippe. 1974. "Still the Century of Corporatism." *Review of Politics*
　　36:85-131.

————. 1990. "Sectors in Modern Capitalism: Modes of Governance and Variations
　　in Performance." In P. Brunetta and C. Dell'Aringa, eds., *Labour Relations
　　and Economic Performance.* London: Macmillan.

Schmitter, Philippe C., and Gerhard Lehbruch, eds. 1979. *Trends Toward Corporatist
　　Intermediation.* Beverly Hills: Sage.

Schmitter, Philippe, and Wolfgang Streeck, eds. 1990. *Private Interest Government.*
　　Beverly Hills: Sage.

Schumpeter, Joseph. 1947. *Capitalism, Socialism and Democracy.* New York: Harper &
　　Row.

Scott, W. Richard. 1995. *Institutions and Organizations.* Thousand Oaks, CA: Sage.

Scott, W. Richard, and John W. Meyer. 1994. *Institutional Environments and Organi-
　　zations.* Thousand Oaks, CA: Sage.

Shonfield, Andrew. 1969. *Modern Capitalism.* New York: Oxford University Press.

Sikkink, Kathryn. 1991. *Ideas and Institutions: Developmentalism in Brazil and Argenti-
　　na.* Ithaca: Cornell University Press.

Smyrl, Marc. 1996. *European Programs, Regional Projects, Local Politics: Implementing Eu-
　　ropean Community Regional Policy, 1985–1994.* Ph.D. Dissertation, Harvard
　　University.

Soskice, David. 1990a. "Wage Determination: The Changing Role of Institutions in
　　Advanced Industrialized Countries." *Oxford Review of Economic Policy* 6:36-61.

————. 1990b. "Reinterpreting Corporatism and Explaining Unemployment: Co-
　　ordinated and Non-coordinated Market Economies." In R. Brunetta and C.
　　Dell'Aringa, eds., *Labour Relations and Economic Performance.* London:
　　Macmillan.

————. 1991. "The Institutional Infrastructure for International Competitiveness:
　　A Comparative Analysis of the UK and Germany." In A. B. Atkinson and
　　R. Brunetta, eds., *The Economics of the New Europe.* London: Macmillan.

————. 1994. "Innovation Strategies of Companies: A Comparative Institutional Analysis of Some Cross-Country Differences." In Wolfgang Zapf, ed., *Institutionenvergliech un Institutionendynamik.* Berlin: WZB.

Sorge, Arndt, and Wolfgang Streeck. 1988. "Industrial Relations and Technological Change." In Richard Hyman and Wolfgang Streeck, eds., *New Technology and Industrial Relations.* Oxford: Blackwell.

Staniland, Martin. 1985. *What Is Political Economy?* New Haven: Yale University Press.

Streeck, Wolfgang. 1994. "Corporatist Industrial Relations and the Economic Crisis in West Germany." In John Goldthorpe, ed., *Order and Conflict in Contemporary Capitalism.* New York: Oxford University Press.

————. 1992. *Social Institutions and Economic Performance.* Beverly Hills: Sage.

Streeck, Wolfgang, and Philippe Schmitter. 1985. *Private Interest Government.* Beverly Hills: Sage.

Swedberg, Richard. 1994. "Markets as Societies." In Neil J. Smelser and Richard Swedberg, eds., *The Handbook of Economic Sociology.* Princeton: Princeton University Press.

Swenson, Peter. 1989. *Fair Shares.* Ithaca: Cornell University Press.

————. 1991. "Bringing Capital Back In, or Social Democracy Reconsidered." *World Politics* 43:513-34.

Swidler, Ann. 1986. "Culture in Action: Symbols and Strategies." *American Sociological Review* 51:273-86.

Thelen, Kathleen. 1991. *Union of Parts.* Ithaca: Cornell University Press.

————. 1995. "Beyond Corporatism: Toward a New Framework for the Study of Labor in Advanced Capitalism." *Comparative Politics.*

Tolbert, Pamela S., and Lynne G. Zucker. 1983. "Institutional Sources of Change in the Formal Structure of Organizations: The Diffusion of Civil Service Reform 1880–1935." *Administrative Science Quarterly* 28:22-39.

Tufte, Edward R. 1978. *Political Control of the Economy.* Princeton: Princeton University Press.

Weingast, Barry, and William Marshall. 1988. "The Industrial Organization of Congress." *Journal of Political Economy* 96:132-63.

Weir, Margaret,. 1989. "Ideas and Politics: The Acceptance of Keynesianism in Britain and the United States." In Peter A. Hall, ed., *The Political Power of Economic Ideas.* Princeton: Princton University Press.

————. 1992a. *Politics and Jobs.* Princeton: Princeton University Press,.

————. 1992b. "Ideas and the Politics of Bounded Innovation." In Sven Steinmo et al., eds., *Structuring Politics.* New York: Cambridge University Press.

Weir, Margaret, and Theda Skocpol. 1985. "State Structures, the Possibilities for Keynesian Response to the Great Depression in Sweden, Britain and the United States." In Peter Evans et al., eds., *Bringing the State Back In.* New York: Cambridge University Press.

Williamson, Oliver. 1985. *The Economic Institutions of Capitalism.* New York: Free Press.

Ziegler, Nicholas. 1997. *Governing Ideas: Strategies for Innovation in France and Germany.* Ithaca: Cornell University Press.

Zukin, Sharon, and Paul DiMaggio, eds. 1994. *Structures of Capital.* New York: Cambridge University Press.

Zysman, John. 1977. *Political Strategies for Industrial Order.* Berkeley: University of California Press.

———. 1983. *Governments, Markets and Growth.* Ithaca: Cornell University Press.

———. 1996. "How Institutions Create Historically-Rooted Trajectories of Growth." *Industrial and Corporate Change* 3:243-83.

8

STUDYING THE STATE*

Joel S. Migdal

Over the course of the twentieth century, comparative political scientists' core questions have changed very little. From Weber (1964) and Gramsci (1971) to Almond and Verba (1963) and Skocpol (1979), their concerns have centered on why people obey and on what sorts of structures and cultures facilitate obedience and conformist behavior. The elements that political scientists have singled out for investigation as the key to understanding obedience and conformity have included the usual suspects: parliaments, bureaucracies, governmental leadership, courts and law, and police and military. These form the constituent parts and parameters of that complex and somewhat elusive structure called the modern state – the mountain that all political scientists sooner or later must climb.

In the pages ahead, as we look at how the perspectives framed in Lichbach's article have been used to study the state, I will make several central points. First, in the next section, I will argue that, despite the assault on the state from a number of directions, it will remain central to the study of comparative politics well into the twenty-first century. Second, in part due to the overwhelming influence of Weber on the study of the state, all the various perspectives – culturalist, rationalist, and institutionalist alike – have tended to isolate it as a subject of study, peering into its innards and poring over its organization in order to understand how it succeeds in gaining obedience and conformity from its population. This sort of analytic isolation of the state, I will claim, has led to a mystification of its capabilities and power. Finally, if we are to develop a more useful way to approach the state, we will need to recognize it as the "limited state." To accomplish that will mean blending the largely ignored culturalist

*I would like to thank Gad Barzilay, Tom Lewis, and Marc Ross for their suggestions on an earlier draft of this paper and Tamir Moustafa for his research assistance.

perspective with the more dominant institutionalist approach as well as shifting the analytic focus from the state as a freestanding organization to a process-oriented view of the state-in-society.

RHETORIC AND REALITY OF MODERN STATES

That the state became so central to the study of comparative politics in the nineteenth and twentieth centuries is not so surprising. While global and transnational challenges to state authority have been evident throughout this period, particularly at the end of the twentieth century, the state – that sprawling organization claiming territorial sovereignty – has been the dominant form for organizing political power. Certainly, by the beginning of the nineteenth century, states had become "the sole constitutive elements of the international system at the exclusion of others" (Spruyt 1994: 3), and that is still largely true today (Jackson and James 1993: 6-11). The state's very existence was part and parcel of the great transformation bringing modernity, which preoccupied Marx, Weber, and so many other major thinkers.

What makes the modern state modern? Serving both the ideals of the Enlightenment and the needs of modern capitalism, the modern state has been constructed to create a uniformity or universality to life within its borders. Weber fretted about just that dimension of states in his lament on the iron cage. Unlike most premodern political structures, the state has aimed to impose uniform and ultimate conformity on social life within far-reaching (but still circumscribed) boundaries: Its leaders have sought obedience in even the most personal realms of social interaction, from whom one might sleep with to how one must bury the dead. Compliance to these sorts of social norms was not new, but the claims of a single centralized organization to enforce such norms over huge territorial expanses were novel almost everywhere they were made. And, indeed, one can point to real cases in which this kind of microregulation has been successfully achieved. Astonishingly, some states have been able to garner from people's yearly earnings a share equivalent to all their work performed through April or May or, sometimes, even June of that year and to sequester their children for 30 or so hours a week in a state institution. Premodern political leaders could not have imagined such audacious goals.

Now, whether one feels high taxes and compulsory public education are justified or not, the ability of some states to accomplish these acts over expansive territories in fairly uniform ways is truly remarkable. For that reason alone, states should remain centerpieces in the study of comparative politics well into the twenty-first century. Other important factors also suggest that scrutiny of the state will continue to hold sway in the decades ahead but most likely with a different sort of research agenda. In Western Europe, the very birthplace of the state, debates have raged over the proper distribution of powers between long-standing states and the European Union. Elsewhere, in what used to be the Third World and the communist bloc, the late 1980s and the 1990s have brought the simultaneous disintegration of existing states and the birth of new ones.

The demise of old states has included rock solid ones, as in the case of the Soviet Union, as well as flimsy reeds, such as Somalia, Liberia, and Afghanistan. The last decade has been the first time in more than half a century that some states have simply disappeared from the world map. At the same time, we have witnessed the creation of a gaggle of new states, the most proclamations of independence since the end of the colonial era about 35 years ago. From Kyrgyzstan to Croatia, from Eritrea to Palestine, new states and state wannabes have imposed themselves on the existing international system. The leaders of new states have made the same claims of territoriality, sovereignty, autonomy, and independence that marked the rhetoric of earlier states. And they have made similar calls for the obedience of their populations, for governing the minutiae of personal life, as did their forerunners.

At the very moment that officials have been proclaiming the inviolability of their new states' sovereignty, however, global forces have cut into the prerogatives of even the well-established ones (Elkins 1995). From the formal constraints imposed by the International Monetary Fund or international environmental conventions to the subtle (or sometimes not-so-subtle) pressures stemming from the vast increases in capital flows, new forces have emerged that have given the word sovereignty a shopworn look (Camilleri and Falk 1992; Duchacek, Latouche, and Stevenson 1988; Erfani 1995; Gottlieb 1993; Keller and Rothchild 1996; Kuehls 1996; Lyons and Mastanduno 1995; Shapiro and Alker 1996).

All these late twentieth-century changes will force political scientists to look much more closely at states.[1] Old definitions of states as having a monopoly over coercive means or as shaping the public domain or as coherent actors with vast autonomy will come under close scrutiny. One certain conclusion is that most states, if not all, have failed to live up to earlier promises or even to scholars' characterizations of them. The grand rhetoric of states, even the most unsteady ones, as well as the expectations about state capabilities generated in the scholarly literature, have obscured the failures of public institutions and policies. The presumptions of political leaders, and even of political science theories – that states could impose a uniform and universal law, induce economic development, deal with abuse of women and children, shape the everyday behavior of those in society through public policies, and much, much more – have simply not eliminated the problem of achieving conformity and obedience. If anything, by setting the bar so high in terms of what states should and could properly demand of those they rule, leaders and scholars have succeeded in bringing the disparity between state goals and state accomplishments into sharp relief.

That gap is the scab that comparative political scientists will pick at as they explore subjects ranging from economic liberalization policies to regulating im-

---

[1] Philosophers, too, have come back to the question of the state. See Sanders and Narveson (1996).

migration to the prevalence of civic attitudes in a given population. As the twentieth century draws to a close, the state will remain center stage, but increasingly it will be the state's difficulties in achieving conformity and obedience that should attract the interest of comparative political scientists. If we are to understand the yawning gap between state rhetoric and performance, our old ideal-typical images of states as successfully imposing uniformity, as building an iron cage, need to be replaced by theories that start with the limitations of actual states.

For two decades now, political scientists have isolated the state as a subject of inquiry.[2] Through a variety of lenses and approaches, they have studied this distinctive structure of the modern age intensively. The literature has been most prominent in research on the non-Western world, in large part because of the appearance of so many new states in Asia and Africa after World War II. Much of the research has been on what some political scientists have called the developmental state, looking especially at state-building or state capabilities. But books like Krasner's *Defending the National Interest* (1978) mined the field for North American and European cases, as well.

My contention in the coming pages is that these sorts of inquiry – ones that isolate the state as a subject of study, focusing on its structure first and only then on how it fits in a world of other structures – have led too often to a mystification of the state and its capabilities. In the next section, I will review how political scientists using a variety of perspectives have approached the structure of the state. I will note here how the culturalists' and rationalists' approaches were fairly marginal to the study of state structure, as it emerged in the late 1970s and early 1980s. Rather, it was the system-dominant structural perspective that swept political scientists off their feet two decades ago. But the gap between rhetoric and reality, between an image of powerful states and the diversity of actual states, has led to disillusionment with this approach, as well. Increasingly, comparativists have moved to an "institutions" perspective on the state that is much less deterministic and more open to a diversity of outcomes.

I will go on to argue in the following section that a focus on structure, on the state in isolation, is insufficient. If we are to understand the inherent limitations of states we must develop a focus on *process,* one that starts with the web of relationships between them and their societies. At the heart of the modern state's successes and failures, especially its ability to gain obedience, is the nature of its relationship to those it claims to rule. The battering of states by global economic and information systems, by the challenges of supranational organizations like the European Union, by the disintegrative effects of virulent ethnic and tribal forces, all have deeply affected the relationship between states and their populations.

---

[2]In this regard, they have been influenced heavily by Weber who emphasized repeatedly the need to study the "power of command." In his discussion of Weber, Barker (1990: 50) notes that "authority stems from an author who is both its possessor and its source." It was the authority of the state, as seen through its structure and practices, toward which Weber pointed us.

The point of departure in looking at process in this essay is the engagement of the contemporary state with those people within its boundaries. Again using different colored lenses, particularly those of culturalists and institutionalists, I will review how scholars have conceived states and their relationship to their populations. The argument will center on how a basic paradox in that relationship demands we move toward a different understanding of the state, one that starts with its hamstrung and limited qualities. Only by adding a culturalist approach to the prevailing "institutions" perspective can the study of states move in the twenty-first century to theories that explain the varieties of limited sovereignty and capabilities that we find in actual cases.

EXPLAINING HOW THE STATE IS CONSTITUTED

THE CULTURALIST PERSPECTIVE

Of the three lenses, the culturalist perspective has had, by far, the smallest impact on the study of why states turn out as they do. Only a limited number of political science works have used this approach in research on state-building or state capabilities. As one researcher put it, "In every way 'culture' is the poor relation of 'structure'" (Archer 1985: 333). Another stated, "The systematic study of politics and culture is moribund" (Laitin 1986: 171). In Ross's survey of politics and culture in this volume, too, one finds very little mention of the state. None of the five contributions he sets out in which culture has contributed to comparative political analysis tackles the issue of the construction of the state. Indeed, the most interesting cultural approaches to studying the state have come from outside the discipline of political science.

Despite its marginality in previous political science research on the construction of the state, I want to spend a bit of time on this perspective now because of its potential to help us move toward a new agenda for research in the twenty-first century. Three related points coming out of this literature are very important for the study of the state. The first, often an implicit point, is that everything else being equal, organizations (especially complex organizations like states) tend to disintegrate because their parts are pulled in so many different directions. Second, culture offers a centripetal antidote to those centrifugal tendencies. And, third, the rituals associated with the state, often undertaken as ends in themselves rather than simply as means to increase power, represent much of that cohesive power that culture offers.

Outside of political science, the work of the renowned anthropologist, Clifford Geertz, has been the most influential. While much of Geertz's thought on the topic stems from his research on the Balinese state of precolonial Indonesia, others have extended his work into the contemporary period. Geertz's specific case, Negara, differed from modern states most notably in its leaders' indifference to actual governing, in their hesitancy in regulating people's everyday actions, and in their lack of interest in territorial sovereignty.

Their attention pointed "toward spectacle, toward ceremony, toward the public dramatization of the ruling obsessions of Balinese culture: social inequality and status pride. It was a theatre state in which the kings and princes were the impresarios, the priests the directors, and the peasants the supporting cast, stage crew, and audience" (Geertz 1980: 13). Geertz's culturalist perspective turned the study of the state on its head – "power served pomp, not pomp power" (Geertz 1980: 13). All the elaborate ceremonies that we associate with states – from inaugurations to press conferences – might not be, as we always thought, means toward an end. They might, as in the Balinese case, be ends in themselves.[3]

In this view the court-and-capital "is not just the nucleus, the engine, or the pivot of the state, it *is* the state.... It is a statement of a controlling political idea – namely, that by the mere act of providing a model, a paragon, a faultless image of civilized existence, the court shapes the world around it into at least a rough approximation of its own excellence" (Geertz 1980: 13). Geertz does not hide from interests and institutions. He sees a constant tension between the integrative effects of the state provided by ideals or the master narrative, what he calls the "controlling political idea," and the disintegrative forces of the "power system composed as it was of dozens of independent, semi-independent, and quarter-independent rulers" (Geertz 1980: 19).

Implicitly, Geertz's notion takes issue with political scientists who simply assume the coherence that rationality or structure and institutions provide, or to those who pay lip service to the role of "values and norms" while actually devoting themselves to studying the ins and outs of the organization of the state. His assumption is the opposite: We cannot look at the bricks of the state without understanding the mortar. We should expect that a complex of organizations would be pulled in a hundred different directions; only a controlling idea, a cultural glue, could keep them from doing that. A century ago Mosca (1939: 70-2) made reference to a similar notion in his analysis of the "political formula," the legal and moral principle that sustains the ruling class. A comment made by one writer on Geertz concerning rulers and ruled might serve as a yellow flag for political scientists: Master narratives "operate as the unchallenged first principles of a political order, making any given hierarchy appear natural and just to rulers and ruled" (Wilentz 1985: 4).

A political scientist, David Laitin, modified Geertz's insights and adapted them to political science. He also tried to break down the notion of master narratives to more workable subunits, what he called shared "points of concern." Here is how Laitin (1986: 175) interpreted Geertz:

> Social systems are not rigid. Subsystems have their own internal dynamics that influence the wider social system. Exogenous change puts pressures on different subsystems and ultimately the social system as well. Social systems are therefore adaptive; they accommodate change as subsystems mutually adjust their values so that there will be a homeostatic equilibrium in the society.

[3]Similar attention to the ceremony of the state is made by other anthropologists. Richards (1964), for example, notes the deference paid in Buganda to the Kabaka, or king. "Loyalty had to be expressed formally and constantly..." (274).

Laitin allows for more discord than Geertz in saying that the points of concern, rather than simply values or preferences, represent sets of values that people share on what is worth worrying about. "A symbol system will provide a clue to what is worth fighting about and also to what is so commonsensical that attempts to change it seem pointless" (175). In other words, the cultural glue does not necessarily mean the existence of a broad consensus about some master narrative but can refer to common understandings about what the agenda should be and agreement on how and when to disagree.

Even in cases in which we are not talking about precolonial entities, Geertz's prescription resonates. Modern states are made up of multiple agencies and bureaus, with widely different tasks and interests. The forces pulling them in different directions – regional demands, interest group leverage, international pressures – are tremendous. A focus on culture, whether it refers to some master narrative or simply to points of concern, directs researchers toward the beliefs and shared meanings that prevent institutional chaos. Geertz's understanding of culture and the state differs from some of the more common cultural approaches in sociology, which zero in on the integration and disintegration of *society* as a sort of indirect path toward applying the notion of culture to the state (Archer 1985; Schudson 1994; Shils 1972) or focus on the interaction of culture and the state, including the manipulation of culture by the state (where the state is seen largely in structural or institutional terms) (Joseph and Nugent 1994; Siu 1989). Geertz also goes beyond common cultural approaches found in political science, such as that in an influential book like *The Civic Culture* (Almond and Verba 1963), in which the actual construction of the state plays a negligible role and the focus, instead, is on how broadly held values affect politics. His focus is directly on the "concrete social institution" (Geertz 1980: 19) of the state, and he devises a cultural explanation for its ability to stay together and shape its society.

Thompson (1974), who seemingly came to the idea of the state as theater independently of Geertz, ended up at much the same point, although in the end he gave even more credence to the bricks that make up the state than Geertz. "A great part of politics and law," Thompson observed, "is always theater; once a social system has become 'set,' it does not need to be endorsed daily by exhibitions of power...; what matters more is a continuing theatrical style" (Thompson 1974: 389). To note that control is "cultural," he wrote, "is not to say that it was immaterial, too fragile for analysis, insubstantial. To define control in terms of cultural hegemony is not to give up attempts at analysis, but to prepare for analysis at the points at which it should be made: into the images of power and authority, the popular mentalities of subordination" (Thompson 1974: 387).[4]

Others have picked up on the idea of theater states and have tried to apply it to more contemporary cases (e.g., Esherick and Wasserstrom 1990). Even Geertz makes no secret of his belief that an approach stressing theater and master narratives should be applied to modern examples, too. In another essay, he

---

[4]Thompson borrowed the concept of cultural hegemony from Gramsci (1971).

wrote, "Now, the easy reaction to all this talk of monarchs, their trappings, and their peregrinations is that it has to do with a closed past, a time in Huizinga's famous phrase, when the world was half-a-thousand years younger and every-thing was clearer.... Thrones may be out of fashion, and pageantry too," he con-tinued, "but political authority still requires a cultural frame in which to define itself and advance its claims, and so does opposition to it" (Geertz 1983: 142-3).

Culture for Geertz is not the cults and customs but the master narratives that give shape to people's experience. The problem for him and for others seeking to apply this approach to the study of today's states is how to do that. Geertz him-self notes, "One of the things that everyone knows but no one can quite think how to demonstrate is that a country's politics reflect the design of its culture" (Geertz 1973: 310). Perhaps that is why the flurry of excitement with Geertz's approach that rippled through the scholarly community in the 1970s and early 1980s could not sustain itself (e.g., see Wilentz 1985). We know that culture is important, that the state is more than a configuration of roles or an interchange-able structure; we just cannot quite figure out how to study it comparatively, how to make it much more than a giant residual category.

THE SYSTEM-DOMINANT STRUCTURALIST PERSPECTIVE

While those who viewed the state from the culturalist perspective remained on the margins of political science, the structuralist approach swept comparativists by storm in the 1970s. In part, they were affected by the rebirth of realism (now as neorealism) in international relations. Many, too, were influenced by the reemer-gence of comparative historical sociology, led by key figures who spanned the dis-ciplines of sociology and political science (Mann 1986; Moore 1966; Skocpol 1979; and Wallerstein 1974), and by the rush to "bring the state back in" (Evans, Rueschemeyer, and Skocpol 1985). Most commonly, this approach treated states as integral, coherent units whose actions could be understood by looking at the align-ment of forces (domestic or international) in their environment. This is a system-dominant perspective in which structuralists see states as interchangeable to the de-gree that they expect them to act similarly if facing the same array of forces (the systemic element). Researchers could, then, understand state actions based on the state's interests as an integral unit within a configuration of other forces.

In assuming the coherence of the state in following its own set of interests, political scientists, such as Nordlinger (1981) and Krasner (1978), touted its au-tonomy. Indeed, autonomy became a kind of buzzword in the state-building lit-erature, especially with growing numbers of studies on the success stories of East Asia (Woo-Cumings 1991; Haggard 1990). The oddity, from our perspective at the end of the century, is how quickly the system-dominant structuralist ap-proach faded, becoming nearly as rare as cultural interpretations of the state. As Katznelson indicates in his chapter in this book, this approach has lost its ener-gy, imagination, and leadership.

One of the last monumental works on the state from the system-dominant structuralist perspective was Goldstone's *Revolution and Rebellion in the Early Modern World* (1991). His direct concern is not with state-building as much as with state breakdown. While attentive to a variety of historical forces, Goldstone's powerful theory allows him to treat a multiplicity of states across several centuries as interchangeable parts in his equation. The theory is so attractive because it is both simple and general.

States crack when they are hit simultaneously by three sorts of crises – a state financial emergency, severe elite divisions, and a potential and propensity for popular groups to mobilize. What is the underlying structural condition that leads to these crises occurring simultaneously in different places and in varying periods? The answer can be found in demographic patterns – worsening in the ratio of resources to population size sets the stage for the problems that undermine the state.

What attracts us in such theories is also what repels us. The general, abstract quality of the argument is spellbinding. Goldstone does nothing less than give us a grand narrative plan for understanding history. But the theory is troubling nonetheless. Culture rears its head but as a mere byproduct of the three crises. Once those occur, he argues, we will see an increase in heterodox cultural and religious ideas. The actual content of these ideas does not seem to matter much at all. Nor do the different institutional paths that widely varying states and societies have taken. His theory has removed agency, the power of people to affect the course of history, from both state and society. In the end, we remain with an overly determined portrait in which the differing institutional histories, contrasting systems of meaning, and the initiatives of groups or individuals count for very little in the unfolding of history.

THE RATIONALIST PERSPECTIVE

At the same time that system-dominant structuralist theories were in their glory, some rational choice writers also turned their attention to the state, although that subject was certainly not central to the emerging rational choice paradigm. No book was more influential here than *Markets and States in Tropical Africa* (Bates 1981). Bates begins his inquiry by noting a fundamental paradox: African state rulers knew quite well what sorts of economic policies were needed to spur economic success, yet they pointedly avoided those policies and chose pathological others. The resolution he comes to in his research starts with the interests of these leaders. Their precarious political stand dictated to them a path of behavior that left their economies in shambles. Through an examination of the actions and choices of key individuals, Bates could tell us about the pathologies of entire states.

In a subsequent book, *Beyond the Miracle of the Market,* Bates (1989) extends his rational choice analysis by stressing the importance of institutions, particularly political institutions. Drawing on North (1981) and others working on new

institutional theories in economics, he notes that the particular institutional milieu within which policy makers find themselves creates the incentive structure
that guides their choices. In other words, the preferences that politicians hold
and that establish the goals they rationally aim to achieve are not simply random.
His implication is that such preferences cannot remain exogenous to rational
choice theory but must be endogenized, that is, theoretically accounted for.

Bates's clear aim is to contribute to the growing literature on the state by
giving the rationale for the choices made by "autonomous" states. Or, in his
words, his theory "provides the microfoundations for the macrothemes dominating the statist literature" (Bates 1989: 6). Those microfoundations derive from
interests – "interested actions of private parties who bring their resources to bear
upon politically ambitious politicians and the political process" (5). In the case
of Kenya, the subject of Bates's research, the dominance of a social class geared
toward accumulation rather than redistribution explains that country's policy
choices and consequently its higher economic growth rates compared to its
neighbors. We can explain the Kenyan outcome on the basis of its "structure of
political institutions and the incentives they generate for politicians" (149). He
goes on,

> People see clearly where their interests lie. They invest in the creation of in-
> stitutions in order to structure economic and political life so as better to de-
> fend their position within them. They invest in institutions so as to vest
> their interests.... Institutions influence subsequent actions. They may have
> been created for economic reasons; or they may have been founded as to en-
> hance the fortunes of particular economic interests. But once created, they
> generate positions of political power and systems of political incentives.
> They define strategic possibilities and impose constraints (151-2).

The rationalist approach merged nicely with the reemergence of the state as
a subject of study. It moved political scientists away from exclusive concern with
extremely broad, often slippery macrostructures or master narratives to a much
more manageable level of research. As Levi notes in her chapter here, rational
choice theory drew on its experience with voting and electoral politics to provide
a grounded, empirical approach to broad comparative questions. This orientation
led to a concern with hard evidence, too often sloughed off in the structuralist or
culturalist perspectives.

By specifying leaders' goals clearly, it allowed researchers to deduce their actions – and, as a result, political outcomes – from those goals and from the specific configuration of circumstances that the rulers faced. In that sense, like structuralism, one could treat the units of study as largely coherent actors that were
theoretically interchangeable. It lent great parsimony to the study of states, even
if it threatened the understanding of the state with an unbending reductionism.
Bates went beyond system-dominant structuralism by putting politics squarely
back into the analysis of the state. By incorporating institutions into the analysis, Bates succeeded in contextualizing interests (the dominant interests in Kenya

differed from those in nearby countries) while still using a universal method (all politicians use the same rational calculations to deal with those varying interests). As Levi writes in this volume, "As comparative and historical rational choice develops, it has increasingly become a form of institutional analysis."

But, again, as with the structuralists, culture plays an entirely derivative role. Unlike the structuralists, the rationalists did try to account for different institutional paths. But Bates' effort to endogenize the institutional dimension was problematic. While his discussion of the historical development of social structure in Kenya through an analysis of class formation is very well informed, it takes place outside the parameters of the theory itself. The rationalists have not yet found a way to incorporate the institutional configuration, the particular array of interests that dominate in Kenya or elsewhere, within the elements of their theories. And, while the rational actor is the agent of change (unlike in the system-dominant structuralist theories), his or her agency, as Katznelson notes in this volume, is entirely utilitarian, predicted and determined by exogenous forces.

THE HISTORICAL INSTITUTIONALIST PERSPECTIVE

It would be a gross exaggeration to say that culturalist, system-dominant structuralist and rationalist perspectives on state-building have disappeared in the 1990s. Indeed, the rationalist orientation has prospered in many subfields of political science, and the comparative study of the state is no exception. Nonetheless, in surveying literature on the state presently, one comes away with the feeling that comparative political science has been left with a kind of default approach to the study of states, that of institutionalism. Or, more precisely, as Katznelson discusses in his chapter, the study of states has been subsumed under the heading of historical institutionalism. This perspective is a close kin to structuralist, culturalist, and rationalist perspectives, and it absorbs elements from all of these. Like system-dominant structuralism, it is interested in how the parts are put together so as to channel the choices available to individuals. But, as it has emerged in the late 1980s and the 1990s, institutionalism's central premise is that the distinctive ways of doing things today will matter tomorrow, as well; states facing the same circumstances will not behave similarly, as the system-dominant structuralists would have it. In other words, the particular configurations of institutions determine, modify, and order individual motives (March and Olsen 1989: 4). Distinctive roles, relations, and procedures that mark how the parts of the state interact with one another and how they tie into groups in society and outside are critical for understanding state actions.

While culture plays an important role in coming to terms with institutional ties – after all, those roles, relations, and procedures are underwritten by shared subjective interpretations of how to behave – the emphasis by most institutionalist political scientists has been less on symbols and meanings than on the ordering of relations and the understanding of political institutions "as acting autonomously in terms of institutional interests" (March and Olsen 1989: 4). Similarly, as we shall see, rationality is key to institutionalism, as individuals' choices are made within a socially formed context and, as in the case of Bates's policy makers, are understood by the interests that stand behind them. Indeed, the newer rational choice writings on the state, such as Levi's (1988) highly regarded book or that of Geddes (1994) or, as we have seen, Bates's (1989) more recent work, have in effect merged rationalism with North's (1981) theories of institutionalism. These works have had a significant impact on yet another type of institutionalism, historical institutionalism.

An early work that used this approach was Polanyi's monumental *The Great Transformation* (1957), a work that has greatly influenced me and a fair number of others.[5] The book provided a model of scholarship for those who were dissatisfied with behavioralist and (mostly Marxist) system-dominant approaches and who were interested in developing a historically grounded perspective. Behavioralists' concerns with the characteristics, attitudes, and behavior of individuals and groups tended to minimize historical factors and miss the important impact that varying forms of organization could have. At the same time, Marxism's determinism seemed to deny the importance of institutional diversity.

The subtitle of Polanyi's book, "The Political and Economic Origins of Our Time," hints not only at Polanyi's own ambition but at a more general belief that such an approach need not devolve into small-scale idiographic studies and explanations. While Polanyi wove numerous threads through his narrative, in the end his preoccupation was with that demon that had turned his own world on its head, fascism. In dealing with that dreaded political form, he had to come to terms with the material interests approach that had so influenced his thinking and still to find a way to steer clear of Marx's propensity to overdetermine outcomes. Note the fine line that Polanyi walks:

> If ever there was a political movement that responded to the needs of an objective situation and was not a result of fortuitous causes it was fascism. At the same time, the degenerative character of the fascist solution was evident. It offered an escape from an institutional deadlock which was essentially alike in a number of countries, and yet, if the remedy were tried, it would everywhere produce sickness unto death. This is the manner in which civilizations perish (Polanyi 1957: 237).

The deadlock to which he refers stemmed from the uneasy cohabitation in the liberal state of the needs of capitalism (institutionally expressed through the self-regulating market and adherence to the gold standard) and democracy. Here, as in Geertz, Goldstone, and Bates, the emphasis is first on the essential character of the state, on its make-up and decision making, and only then on the environment within which that structure operates. On one side, for Polanyi, the state served capitalism and the market, which subordinated society's expression of

---

[5]Thelen and Steinmo (1992: 7-10) have distinguished historical institutionalism from rational choice institutionalism. Another key formative figure in historical institutionalism, who will not be discussed here, is Gerschenkron (1962).

multiple needs and desires – as he writes, "It means no less than the running of society as an adjunct to the market" (Polanyi 1957: 57). The market, that "satanic mill," mercilessly disposed of the physical, psychological, and moral qualities of human beings and left them with no safety net into which to fall.

At the same time, the state, through the pressure put on it by labor groups in parliament, became the basis for "paternalistic regulationism" (Polanyi 1957: 125). Groups organized a countermovement, "a reaction against a dislocation which attacked the fabric of society ..." (Polanyi 1957: 130). This bundle of contradictions in the state, the clash of economic liberalism and social protection, caused deadlock. The Alexander who could cut this Gordian knot was a new institutional configuration, fascism. Its solution was both to transform the market and to eliminate democracy.

Polanyi's goal was a delicate one. He, at once, wanted to show how a particular array of forces could explain the emergence of the fascist state (just as a good system-dominant structuralist would) and to leave open the possibility of other outcomes. Neither Britain nor the United States, where he sat writing his book during the dark days of World War II, had succumbed to the fascist solution. Institutions adapt to the real environment within which they are embedded – for Polanyi that environment was a world economy marked by the gold standard and a system of states within a balance of power. But that is not an infinitely replicable process. Different states and societies could respond in varying ways.

In the postwar era, Huntington (1968) stressed the same lesson: Different sorts of political actions and varying types of engagement by social groups with the state produce disparate political results. His immediate attention was with the proliferation of new states that came out of the decolonization process and with the fond hopes that they would lead their societies to the promised land of modernity and prosperity. He observed rather dourly that political decay and instability were as likely outcomes as political development.

Huntington did not use the word state – it was not fashionable yet – but it was very much present in his analysis. In fact, if anyone could be credited with bringing the state back in, it is Huntington; without the word at hand to encompass it, he described how the actions and characteristics of the array of public institutions in a country (the state) made a vast difference for society. He returned public institutions to center stage. Indeed, his theory implies that if we focused exclusively on how well the state developed its institutions, we would not have to look much farther. His thesis is simple: Only where the level of political institutionalization outstrips the level of political participation can there emerge stable politics working in the public interest. Although his conservative outlook regarding United States foreign policy induced many to minimize his theory's impact on them, I would venture to say that no work surpassed Huntington's in its influence on a generation of comparative political scientists studying the state.

Huntington's impact went beyond academics. One former high-level Ethiopian official told me of the military coup against Emperor Haile Selassie in

1973. When the young officers burst into the room where the Emperor's aides ran the affairs of state, one political official looked up and asked, "Where did we fail?" At that point, an army officer took a copy of Huntington's book and slid it across the table. "You should have read this." Now, whether that story is apocryphal or not, it gives some glimpse of how influential the work has been.

A host of important publications in the 1990s have fed off the insights of Polanyi and Huntington. The same balancing of environmental pressures and the variety of responses to those factors that one finds in Polanyi and the attention to political capacity and autonomy of Huntington mark the best of the contemporary works on the state by historical institutionalists doing cross-national studies (e.g., Collier and Collier 1991; Evans 1995; Jackman 1993; Waterbury, 1993) and by those doing in-depth country studies (e.g., Boone 1992; Hagopian 1996; Kohli 1990; Shue 1988; Vitalis 1995). Evans, for example, attempts to unravel why some states have so successfully tweaked industrial transformations of their societies while others' records have been so abysmal. The answer lies in the particularity of institutional arrangements. "States are not generic. They vary dramatically in their internal structures and relations to society. Different kinds of state structures create different capacities for state action" (Evans 1995: 11). This statement comes a long way in allowing for the diversity of actual states. But like the works of those using the culturalist, structuralist, and rationalist perspectives, it still reflects the emphasis on looking first and foremost at the state as a free-standing structure, as an entity that can be isolated in inquiry.

THE LIMITED STATE: ENGAGEMENT OF STATE AND SOCIETY

The modern state has posed itself as the ultimate authority, standing above society and demanding wide-ranging obedience and conformity. But the engagement of social groups with the state, and the mutual transformation that entails, have tempered those broad claims to be the ultimate authority. Appearances to the contrary, states may be badly fractured and weakened through the particular nature of their encounters with other social forces. By understanding how the state's sails have been trimmed through its engagement with such social forces, we begin to build a basis for a twenty-first century research agenda, one that starts with process rather than structure, a blueprint that focuses on a limited state. Such an agenda will allow us to escape from the stifling effects on clear thinking of national ideologies stressing the complete sovereignty of the state and from academic theories, beginning with Weber's ideal-typical state, that underscore the monopoly over coercive means and legitimate authority.

National ideologies create master narratives that may well be suited to dealing with issues such as the consolidation of power or the collective expression of identity. They are far less useful as guides to the capabilities and limitations of actual states. Theories, such as those of Weber and political scientists following in his footsteps, create different sorts of problems. Their understanding of the state as a stand-alone organization with firm boundaries between it and other social forces leads to inquiries that zero in on its makeup, into how it is constructed. The effect is to essentialize the state and overstate its capabilities. An approach that focuses on the state-in-society (Migdal, Kohli, and Shue 1994), on the process of state engagement with other social forces, highlights the mutual transformation of the state and other social groups, as well as the limitations of the state. Mitchell (1991) elaborates on this point very well. He writes,

> Statist approaches to political explanation present the state as an autonomous entity whose actions are not reducible to or determined by forces in society.... The customary Weberian definition of the state, as an organization that claims a monopoly over the legitimate use of violence, is only a residual characterization. It does not tell us how the actual contours of this amorphous organization are to be drawn.... The state appears to stand apart from society in [an] unproblematic way ... (82).

The twenty-first century state, buffeted by the winds of globalization, supranational entities, and divisive ethnic conflict, must be stripped of its myths of unity and omnipotence. With new states abounding and old states struggling with disintegrative challenges, more than ever political scientists will need ways of unraveling the relationship between states and those within their borders. They will need ways of studying the fractious process of redrawing social boundaries, of creating coalitions with some and excluding others.

That is a tall order. It will mean avoiding structural views that portray the state as largely determined by a grand historical narrative and/or present it as a gargantuan coherent and unified "actor" in history (see Mitchell 1991). It will entail improving the institutionalist tools for analyzing the states that have proliferated in the last decade, focusing increasingly on the institutional junctures of state and society, even where the boundary between them is blurred beyond recognition. And it will involve serious attention to cultural understandings of the state, which have made little headway so far in the political science literature.

The connection between the state and its population has been particularly complex, if for no other reason, as noted earlier, than that the modern state in its rules and laws has demanded so much from people. If, in premodern empires, rulers might have aimed for little more than revenue from many peasants, modern officials have devised legal codes, specifications of what individuals can and cannot do, whose volumes take up endless shelves. And they have constructed centralized bureaucracies to press their regulations on large populations. Of course, coercion and the threat of coercion, by most definitions, lie at the center of the meaning of the state and its demands for compliance by its population. Both Marx (1963) and Weber (1964) made that clear a century ago, and others, such as Cover (Minow, Ryan, and Sarat 1993: 211-14) and Tilly (1985), have regularly restated it.

But it is simply impossible for a state to achieve tractability by relying ex-clusively on its judges and jailers.[6] No matter how vaunted the bureaucracy, po-lice, and military, officers of the state cannot stand on every corner ensuring that each person stop at the red light, drive on the right side of the road, cross at the crosswalk, refrain from stealing and drug dealing, and so on. Modern state lead-ers could easily find their institutions quickly overwhelmed by the enormity of the task of enforcement, even with vast bureaucracies.[7]

What have modern states done to ensure that each subject toes the line, even without a police officer at every corner? Their response has come on two addi-tional levels, one addressed most cogently by those using an institutionalist out-look with strong rationalist overtones, and the other by researchers using a cul-turalist perspective. Both indicate a process-oriented approach in which states and societies are in a mutually transformative relationship.

For historical institutionalists the emphasis has been on rules and proce-dures, on routine. Those same weighty code books that spell out the do's and don'ts for individuals also implicitly address people's needs to have a road map on how to navigate an increasingly convoluted world. State rules have insured the viability of agreements into which one enters, protected the water one drinks, as-sured the terms for receiving credit, provided schools as a means of mobility for one's children, and much, much more. As the division of labor has become more and more elaborated, state laws have given assurance to the individual concern-ing products and services about which one has meager knowledge or skills. Far more than in the premodern era, states have gone beyond defense of the realm to offer a large chunk of the *strategies of survival* that people construct for themselves (Migdal 1988). Obedience and conformity, then, have been trade-offs by indi-viduals who see the state as a large piece of their personal life puzzles.

In their inquiries into the state, historical institutionalists have tended to em-phasize this sort of calculation, merging their interest in structure with a ratio-nalist perspective. But they have also gone to some lengths to differentiate them-selves from rational choice theories. The emphasis in historical institutionalism has been on the organizational milieu in which people do such reckoning (Robert-son 1993). In other words, scholars using this approach favor looking at habit in any given situation more than utility maximization. Koelble (1995: 233) notes,

> When making decisions, individuals do not ask the question "how do I maximize my interests in this situation?" but instead "what is the appro-priate response to this situation given my position and responsibilities?" In

---

[6]"Political life centers on the exercise of power, and that, unlike physical force, power is intrinsical-ly relational. Although all states have the capability to inflict physical sanctions, their ability to exercise power is the key element of their political capacity. In this context, the prolonged use of force reflects a loss of power and is fundamentally apolitical, because it indicates a deterioration in the relationship be-tween rulers and ruled" (Jackman 1993: 156).

[7]In fact, the *overburdened state* (as seen, for example, in the mushrooming prison population in the United States) is one important part of the puzzle explaining the disparity between state goals and achievements.

the majority of situations, rules and procedures (that is, institutions) are clearly established, and individuals follow routines. They follow well-worn paths and do what they think is expected of them.

Historical institutionalist works note that those paths are forged through the engagement of groups, such as labor or merchants or capitalists from certain sectors, with parts of the state. Indeed the nature of that engagement often underpins those writers' analyses. For Evans (1995), the kinds of connections that states have had to certain industrial sectors and firms have determined whether they could induce sustained industrial growth. While Evans focuses on the rosy question of state-led development, Vitalis (1995) hones in on a far seamier side of state action, the creation of rent havens. His inventive book challenges the grand narrative that places late (or failed) industrialization – in his case, in Egypt – in "an overarching struggle between imperialism and the nation ..." (Vitalis 1995: 5). Rather, it is the variety of alliances between specific business groups and fractions of the state that explain Egypt's (and others') path. Indeed, one of the great advantages of Vitalis's work is his willingness to go beyond analyzing the state as a single coherent actor (or as represented entirely by one of its agencies) to a view in which parts of the state operate quite differently, often in conflict with one another.

Other important works analyze different dimensions of the engagement of states with social groups. Hagopian's innovative work (1996) examines the ironic reliance of Brazil's military leaders on traditional oligarchic elites. These soldiers took over the state in 1964 and professed a belief in technocratic rule rather than reliance on the old politicians but ended up depending on those they had spurned. In Collier and Collier's (1991) research on Latin America, the key is the variety of ways in which labor was incorporated by states. Senegal's state is seen by Boone (1992) as consisting of key political actors whose standing comes from their individual patron–client ties with constituencies in the country. Her aim is to explain the impotence of the state despite all the trappings of power. Like Vitalis (1995), her analysis does not presume the state to be a single actor. In fact, one could understand the Senegalese state only by taking account of its fractured core. She writes,

> Regime consolidation was a political process that involved not only creating new structures and relations of power, but also tying existing structures of societally based power to the state. Modes of governance and exploitation were shaped by social forces that could subvert or strengthen these underpinnings of state authority, as well as by societally based competition for advantage within and through the institutions of government (Boone 1994: 133).

The engagement of the state, or parts of it, with individuals and groups in society, so aptly emphasized by the historical institutionalists, has been not a static process but a mutually transformative one. One criticism of the rational choice institutionalists' approach, made by Zuckerman in this volume and by others (Thelen and Steinmo 1992: 9), has been its acceptance of goals, strategies, and preferences as given (and often fixed) rather than as changing over time in meaningful ways. We might add that the very process of interaction of ruler and ruled, looked at so convincingly by a rational choice institutionalist such as Levi (1988), substantially changes both. This mutual transformation may limit the usefulness of rational choice methodology. The engagement of state and society involves the creation of alliances and coalitions and, for each side of the bargain, the incorporation of a new material basis as well as new ideas and values into its constitution. That process of incorporation of new constituencies and their ideas transforms the preferences and bases for action of the original actor. What rational choice theorists assume is fixed may very well be a moving target.

Beyond coercion, then, why have people obeyed state rules and dictates? The historical institutionalists, as we saw, respond by pointing to the calculation of individuals within the confines of rules and procedures and the routinization of their behavior within the possibilities that existing institutions afford. They picture the actions of the state's subjects as running on a treadmill to create viable strategies of *survival* (not maximization) – or to "satisfice," in March and Olsen's (1989) terms. Institutions create routines, and, even with coercion only a distant threat, those routines ensure significant obedience (Lane 1997: 114-22).

Another answer as to why and how states can avoid stationing police every 50 meters is much trickier. To understand it fully, comparative political scientists must turn to the culturalist approach and develop new tools within that genre. The answer rests on the premise that in individuals, as Shils wrote, there is a "state of consciousness which includes an awareness of a self residing in them, including them, and transcending them" (Shils 1972: vii). That is, humans are not only animals who run in packs, creating institutions for themselves. They also have conceptions about themselves as members of the pack and of the pack as something with a life beyond their personal existence. Those "packs" are societies, which in human history have come in all shapes and sizes – that is, with different institutional configurations.[8]

How have societies taken form? Berlant (1991) wrote that "the accident of birth within a geographical/political boundary transforms individuals into subjects of a collectively held history. Its traditional icons, its metaphors, its heroes, its rituals, and its narratives provide an alphabet for a collective consciousness ..." (Berlant 1991: 20). That shared alphabet imposes a discipline upon people, molding their discourse and action. Like Geertz's theater state, Berlant's subjects are drawn into props and pomp, into stories and metaphors, which mark them off from others outside. The formation of societies leads, again in Shils' words, to some degree of "authority and the maintenance of order," or, in our terms, to some modicum of obedience and conformity (Shils 1972: vii).

This understanding of society, Shils noted, "could not be reduced to a marketlike equilibrium of interests or to a product of coercion" (Shils 1972: xii). In

---

[8]"There is no sense in asking how individuals come to be associated. They exist and operate in association" (Dewey 1927: 23).

other words, neither police at every intersection nor trade-offs by calculating individuals, who are figuring out their strategies of survival, can fully explain obedience and conformity. For Shils, a big part of the explanation lies in people's internalization of society, their "collective self-consciousness." People obey, in this view, because their personal identities are inextricably tied to the existence of a bigger unit; their identities depend on the viability of the rules, written and unwritten, that maintain that larger group.[9]

Submission to the group's rules thus supports not only the collectivity but the individual whose identity rests on the continuing existence of the group; obedience and conformity are integral to establishing and maintaining one's identity. In society, any number of groups or organizations could insure continuing compliance – "the household, the kinship group, the neighborhood association, the market community, and other loose associations formed for some specific purpose" (Weber 1954: 342). One's identity rests upon the continuing viability of one's family (or some other group) so individuals conform in ways that keep that group alive and thriving. In the twentieth century and for several centuries before that, it has been the state that has demanded such compliance, taking the lead in authority and the maintenance of order.

But the state has created some special problems in this regard. One key distinction of the modern era, as I noted, has been the broad claims of state leaders and officials – if not to demand all obedience and conformity directly, then at least for the state to be the umbrella under which other groups or organizations may gain and insure their authority. Yes, families can exercise authority over their members, especially children and (often) women, or businesses can make rules for their workers. But they must do so, state leaders assert, within the parameters set by the state. If a family exercises its authority by abusing its children or a business sets discriminatory rules, the state steps in, even to the point of disbanding the family. In a fundamental sense, then, the state appears to stand above and apart from the rest of society. Even if the actual image of states standing above society is flawed, as Mitchell notes, at the very least state leaders aim for a "ghost-like effect" (Mitchell 1991: 91), where the state appears to be standing above society, with a finger in every pot. In Breuilly's terms (1994: 390), there exists a "distinction, peculiar to the modern world, between state and society."

But, as important as the private–public marking (or its appearance) is in establishing the special status of state authority, it also has created enormous problems for state officials in demanding obedience. The appearance of a gulf separating the state from the rest of society makes it difficult for its leaders to tap into a basis of authority beyond coercion or "a marketlike equilibrium of interests" for calculating individuals. As an entity appearing to stand *apart* from society and its individuals, it has difficulty gaining conformity through individuals' tying their

---

[9]"Identities ... produce societal boundaries allowing individual members as groups and collectivities, in actual or desired, existing or imaginary communities, to make sense of 'us' versus 'them.'" (Moore and Kimmerling 1995: 387).

personal identities to a collective of which they self-consciously feel *a part.* This is the paradox of the modern state, one that theoretically and practically leads us to the conception of the limited state.

The challenge for political leaders has been how to remain *apart* from society – the state as the ultimate authority – while somehow still benefiting from people's "collective self-consciousness," their sense of belonging to something bigger than themselves of which they are an integral *part.*[10] Or, to pose the problem differently, state leaders and their agencies have sought ways to change those they rule from disconnected *subjects* of state rule to some other status that would connect their personal identities to the continued existence and vitality of the state. And it has wanted to establish this connection while all the while remaining the ultimate authority and arbiter, standing in a continuing object–subject relationship with them.

States have dealt with the paradox of their being above society but needing to seem an integral component of society in a number of ways, each of which aims to transform society. One has been the Communist path, to abolish society entirely. In that case, the individual's new status is that of state functionary, a role reserved not for a select subset of the population (public officials) but applicable to everyone. The population is not a society, in the sense that its parts have been largely stripped of authority and it does not play an active role in people's collective consciousness. Those who by dint of class background are deemed unworthy of the new status may be re-socialized into it during a transition period or, at worst, eliminated altogether. The new identity of individuals (such as the "new Soviet man and woman") indicates a collective self-consciousness revolving entirely around the state; no separate society, characterized by its own "authority and the maintenance of order," exists. Through raw power and through an impressive array of theatrical symbols, Communist leaders sought the extraordinarily ambitious goal of making the state the single authoritative entity and thus the only one with which people could ground their own identities.

A far more common route of transforming society involves, as Breuilly (1994: 390) puts it, abolishing the distinction between state and society altogether through the use of nationalism. In that case, the transformation of society comes by creating a subset of it, the *nation,* and a special status for those defined as nationals. Nationalist state leaders have aimed to eliminate the perception that the state stands above society and to foster an alternative view, that the state and the society are indistinguishable in purpose, if not in form.

---

[10]The problem for states is related to that posed by Habermas (1975: 68-73) regarding the legitimation crisis of the state. He writes, "The state must preserve for itself a residue of unconsciousness in order that there accrue to it from its planning functions no responsibilities that it cannot honor without overdrawing its accounts.... This end is served by the separation of instrumental functions of the administration from expressive symbols that release an unspecific readiness to follow" (69-70). But in the end he notes, "The state cannot simply take over the cultural system ..." (73). The administrative (authoritative) role of the state does not sit easily with a cultural role, no matter how much theater is employed. (As examples of such theater, Habermas offers symbolic use of hearings, juridical incantations, and others.)

This is not the place to review the voluminous and growing literature on nationalism. But it is important to note that nationalism has been used to nibble at the state–society divide; states have sought added obedience and conformity through the merging of personal identity first and foremost with the collective self-consciousness of the nation. As the expression of the nation's sovereignty, the state has aimed to gain compliance beyond what it could expect from coercion and appealing to the calculations of individuals working out their strategies of survival (Stern 1995). Its authority can be accepted willingly if it is an extension or source of one's identity. The state, then, becomes the embodiment of the nation, and people who identify themselves primarily as nationals see their well-being and the well-being of the state as indistinguishable.

This perspective comes out strongly in culturalists' analyses of nationalism. Writers as opposed as Smith (1988) and Anderson (1991) note how nationalist myths have bound individuals to each other and to the *nation*–state. "Nationalism's peculiar myth of the nation," writes Smith (1988: 2) "may be seen as a particularly potent and appealing dramatic narrative, which links past, present and future through the character and role of the national community." While Smith minimizes modernity as a formative influence in the creation of the nation, Anderson sees the nation as integrally related to the modern rise of capitalism. But Anderson, too, emphasizes the same cultural links. "The members of even the smallest nation will never know most of their fellow-members, meet them, or even hear of them, yet in the minds of each lives the image of their communion" (Anderson 1991: 6). And that communion is related to the state. "Nations dream of being free.... The gage and emblem of this freedom is the sovereign state" (Anderson 1991: 7). As Guibernau and Montserrat (1996: 70) indicate, "The state favours nationalism as a means to increase the links existing among its citizens." And, it can be added, to link them to the state itself.

Perhaps the preceding paragraph makes the entire enterprise of creating the nation–state seem all too manipulative. The deep interpenetrations of state officials and certain social groups and the assimilation of icons, narratives, and metaphors into the theatrics of governing transform both rulers and ruled. The resultant political culture, which melds individual identities into a collective, state-focused identity, may become an unquestioned set of assumptions (a cultural hegemony) for state officials as much as for others in society. The notion of conscious manipulation of such culture by state officials may lend too rationalist a perspective to this phenomenon.

Neither Communist states' attempts to abolish society nor nationalism's purported effect of eliminating the state–society distinction have freed the state from its paradoxical bind. Nowhere, not even in Stalin's Soviet Union, has a society with its own authority disappeared entirely (Jowitt 1992: 54). And the total elimination of the boundary between state and society through nationalism has been impossible, as well.

Certainly states have reshaped societies with some success, refashioning societal boundaries to conform to the borders of the state (or to its desired borders).

As Schudson (1994, 64) wrote, "The modern nation–state self-consciously uses language policy, formal education, collective rituals, and mass media to integrate citizens and ensure their loyalty." Those using a culturalist perspective have pointed out how state leaders have used ritual and other means to blur the distinction between state and society and to have individuals develop a stake in the well-being of the state. Rituals have linked individuals to society and each other (Durkheim 1965; Kertzer 1988; 10), and to the state as the putative representation of society (Wilentz 1985; Siu 1989). Kertzer, an anthropologist, sees this connection as essentially nonrational: "Political reality is defined for us in the first place through ritual, and our beliefs are subsequently reaffirmed through regular collective expression" (Kertzer 1988: 95). We can add that the nonrational dimension may apply to state officials, too; they may be expressing deeply inculcated cultural mores of their own as much as a well-defined plan to use symbols as the route to effective social control.

In short, the culturalists – from Geertz to those writing on nationalism – provide us with an image of the state as using and representing a master narrative. This narrative has multiple functions in their formulations. First, it serves as the basis to hold the state together, from having its multiple parts fly off in different directions. Second, it links citizens to each other and to the state, subverting other narratives and thus the possibility of other autonomous, authoritative structures. And, third, the master narrative creates the limits and possibilities of the institutions involved in social control.

This image of the master narrative, however, needs modification. It, too, looks first and foremost at the state and its construction as stand-alone phenomena (rather than at the state in society) and consequently tends to overstate the power of the state or even the appearance of that power. Master narratives that eliminate other narratives are impossible to sustain as Cover (Minow, Ryan, and Sarat 1993) has argued. At best, at a moment of epiphany, such uniformity can exist. But that quickly gives way to the creation of alternative and dissenting narratives. Perhaps in ancient societies, such dissonance could be handled by exile, secession, or death. But modern societies cannot avoid the existence of multiple narratives; they are irrevocably multicultural.

Some culturalists have noted this process of the creation of multiple narratives. They argue that the distinction between state and society – the state's aim to stand apart, as the ultimate authority – does quite the opposite from strengthening social control. It creates openings for opposition and distinction. Dirks (1994: 487-8) makes this point powerfully: "Because of the centrality of authority to the ritual process, ritual has always been a crucial site of struggle, involving both claims about authority and struggles against (and within) it…. Resistance to authority can be seen to occur precisely when and where it is least expected." He adds, "At the same time that representation, in discourse or event, makes ritual claims about order, representation itself becomes the object of struggle" (502).

Dirks writes on India. Others writing theoretically or about different countries also take issue with the notion of the cultural unity implied in the works of

Durkheim and Shils (Archer 1985; Schudson 1994; Siu 1989). In Mexico, Joseph and Nugent (1994: 13) note, "the power of the state, especially the capitalist state, has been of signal importance in providing some of the idioms in terms of which subordinated groups have initiated their struggles for emancipation, particularly in the twentieth century." Roseberry (1994: 365) refers in Mexico to "the problematic relationship between the talking state and the distracted audience." The uniformity or universality that underlies an image of the absence of a distinction between state and society falls victim to all sorts of refraction and diversity "as the laws, dictates, programs, and procedures of the central state are applied in particular regions, each of which is characterized by distinct patterns of inequality and domination ..." (365).

CONCLUSION

Returning to our earlier question – what makes the modern state modern? – we can now add that it has not been only the sheer magnitude of the state's claims upon individuals it governs in terms of taxes, personal and social behavior, and the like. It also has been the effect of states through their practices to lay claim above all others to collective consciousness, that is, to the identity of the nation. Again, in Berlant's (1991) terms, the state has been at the center of struggles for people's collectively held history, "its traditional icons, its metaphors, its heroes, its rituals, and its narratives." In so doing, state leaders and agencies have been at the center of redrawing societal boundaries to coincide with the actual or desired political borders, a process as exclusive (in separating out those outside the physical or metaphorical boundaries) as it is inclusive (in creating an overarching collective self-consciousness). In short, through symbols and institutions states have been at the core of the reinvention of society.

But even where states have successfully sequestered youth for 30 hours a week, they have by no means guaranteed victory in the ambitious endeavor of defining collective consciousness. Both global factors outside the state's control and internal elements of the society have worked to thwart or modify the emergence of a state-drawn collective consciousness. Because so much of the ability to get people to do what one wants them to do rests on the authority deriving from collective consciousness, it is not surprising that tremendous contestation has existed over who defines and taps into it. Those struggles within states and between states and other social forces, and their different outcomes in various places and times, are of primary interest to political scientists. At times, those struggles can lead to social and political disintegration, even uncontrolled slaughter of the population. In other instances, while no master narrative can be said to exist, Laitin's (1986) notion of shared "points of concern" indicates that some cultural glue does exist. We must analyze those instances if we are to understand the continuing existence of state and society and their particular patterns of interpenetration.

In the contemporary world, individuals have inhabited a number of crucial social formations – nations, states, ethnic and other subnational groups, civil society, the global economy, and more. All of these have established authority, or at least have tried to, making powerful demands upon the behavior and psyches of people. Sometimes, those demands have been complementary, even reinforcing shared points of concern, and in other instances their stipulations have clashed head-on. In creating the categories of citizen or member of the nation, state leaders, in effect, have attempted to domesticate those other social formations, neutralizing their impact or subordinating their authority or eliminating them altogether. These state efforts are certainly not new; they have gone on for half a millennium and constitute the push by states to create sovereignty.

State sovereignty has been elusive, however. While the efforts at Westphalia in the seventeenth century acted to codify and institutionalize a continent of sovereign states in Europe, ever since then states have continued to face challenges along two paths. Both forces originating outside the boundaries that the state claims for itself and those within its borders have contested state efforts to monopolize the exercising of authority. The result has been the limited state.

States have been unable to transform societies sufficiently so as to solve the paradox of being simultaneously apart from society and a part of society. More than that, the engagement of the state with society, which has created sites of struggle and differences in society, subverting the state's efforts at uniformity, has also transformed the state. The mutual transformation of state and society has led to contending coalitions that have both cut across and blurred the lines between them. It is within these dynamic institutional arrangements that we must now approach the study of the state – an organization divided and limited in the sorts of obedience it can demand. We must abandon approaches that isolate the state as a unit of analysis. To do that, we must develop the means to forge the efforts of the historical institutionalists and culturalists, who until now have worked mostly in splendid isolation from one another.

REFERENCES

Almond, Gabriel A., and Sidney Verba. 1963. *The Civic Culture.* Princeton: Princeton University Press.

Anderson, Benedict. 1991. *Imagined Communities: Reflections on the Origin and Spread of Nationalism.* London: Verso.

Archer, Margaret S. 1985. "The Myth of Cultural Unity." *British Journal of Sociology* 36:333-53.

Barker, Rodney. 1990. *Political Legitimacy and the State.* New York: Oxford University Press.

Bates, Robert H. 1981. *Markets and States in Tropical Africa: The Political Basis of Agriculture Policies.* Berkeley: University of California Press.

————. 1989. *Beyond the Miracle of the Market: The Political Economy of Agrarian Development in Kenya.* Cambridge: Cambridge University Press.

Berlant, Lauren. 1991. *The Anatomy of National Fantasy: Hawthorne, Utopia, and Everyday Life.* Chicago: University of Chicago Press.

Boone, Catherine. 1992. *Merchant Capital and the Roots of State Power in Senegal, 1930–1985.* New York: Cambridge University Press.

————. 1994. "States and Ruling Classes in Postcolonial Africa: The Enduring Contradictions of Power." In Joel S. Migdal, Atul Kohli, and Vivienne Shue, eds., *State Power and Social Forces: Domination and Transformation in the Third World.* New York: Cambridge University Press.

Breuilly, John. 1994. *Nationalism and the State.* Chicago: University of Chicago Press.

Camillari, Joseph A., and Jim Falk. 1992. *The End of Sovereignty?: The Politics of a Shrinking and Fragmenting World.* Brookfield, VT: Edward Elgar.

Collier, Ruth B., and David Collier. 1991. *Shaping the Political Arena: Critical Junctures, the Labor Movement, and Regime Dynamics in Latin America.* Princeton: Princeton University Press.

Dewey, John. 1927. *The Public and Its Problems.* New York: Henry Holt.

Dirks, Nicholas B. 1994. "Ritual and Resistance: Subversion as a Social Fact." In Nicholas B. Dirks, Geoff Eley, and Sherry B. Ortner, eds., *Culture/Power/History: A Reader in Contemporary Social Theory.* Princeton: Princeton University Press.

Duchacek, Ivo D., Daniel Latouche, and Garth Stevenson. 1988. *Perforated Sovereignties and International Relations: Transsovereign Contacts of Subnational Governments.* New York: Greenwood Press.

Durkheim, Emile. 1965. *The Elementary Form of Religious Life.* Swain. New York: Free Press.

Elkins, David J. 1995. *Beyond Sovereignty: Territory and Political Economy in the Twenty-First Century.* Toronto: University of Toronto Press.

Erfani, Julie A. 1995. *The Paradox of the Mexican State: Rereading Sovereignty from Independence to NAFTA.* Boulder, CO: Lynne Rienner.

Esherick, Joseph W., and Jeffrey N. Wasserstrom. 1990. "Acting Out Democracy: Political Theater in Modern China." *Journal of Asian Studies* 49:835-65.

Evans, Peter B. 1995. *Embedded Autonomy: States and Industrial Transformation.* Princeton: Princeton University Press.

Evans, Peter B., Dietrich Rueschemeyer, and Theda Skocpol. 1985. *Bringing the State Back In.* Cambridge: Cambridge University Press.

Geddes, Barbara. 1994. *Politician's Dilemma: Building State Capacity in Latin America.* Berkeley: University of California Press.

Geertz, Clifford. 1973. *The Interpretation of Cultures: Selected Essays.* New York: Basic Books.

————. 1980. *Negara: The Theatre State in Nineteenth Century Bali.* Princeton: Princeton University Press.

————. 1983. *Local Knowledge: Further Essays in Interpretive Anthropology.* New York: Basic Books.

Gerschenkron, Alexander. 1962. *Economic Backwardness in Historical Perspective: A Book of Essays.* Cambridge: Harvard University Press.

Goldstone, Jack A. 1991. *Revolution and Rebellion in the Early Modern World.* Berkeley: University of California Press.

Gottlieb, Gidon. 1993. *Nations Against State: A New Approach to Ethnic Conflicts and the Decline of Sovereignty.* New York: Council on Foreign Relations Press.

Gramsci, Antonio. 1971. *Selections from the Prison Notebooks,* ed. Quitin Hoare and Geoffrey N. Smith. New York: International Publishers.

Guibernau, Berdun, and Maria Montserrat. 1996. *Nationalisms: The Nation-State and Nationalism in the Twentieth Century.* Cambridge, MA: Polity Press.

Habermas, Jurgen. 1975. *Legitimation Crisis.* Boston: Beacon Press.

Haggard, Stephan. 1990. *Pathways from the Periphery: The Politics of Growth in the Newly Industrializing Countries.* Ithaca: Cornell University Press.

Hagopian, Francis. 1996. *Traditional Politics and Regime Change in Brazil.* New York: Cambridge University Press.

Huntington, Samuel P. 1968. *Political Order in Changing Societies.* New Haven: Yale University Press.

Jackman, Robert. 1993. *Power Without Force: The Political Capacities of Nation-States.* Ann Arbor: University of Michigan Press.

Jackson, Robert H., and Alan James, eds. 1993. *States in a Changing World: A Contemporary Analysis.* Oxford: Clarendon Press.

Joseph, Gilbert M., and Daniel Nugent. 1994. "Popular Culture and State Formation." In Gilbert Joseph and Daniel Nugent, eds., *Everyday Forms of State Formation: Revolution and the Negotiation of Rule in Modern Mexico.* Durham: Duke University Press.

Jowitt, Kenneth. 1992. *New World Disorder: The Leninist Extinction.* Berkeley: University of California Press.

Keller, Edmond J., and Donald Rothchild. 1996. *Africa in the New International Order: Rethinking State Sovereignty and Regional Security.* Boulder, CO: Lynne Rienner.

Kertzer, David. 1988. *Ritual, Politics, and Power.* New Haven: Yale University Press.

Koelble, Thomas A. 1995. "The New Institutionalism in Political Science and Sociology." *Comparative Politics* 27:231-43.

Kohli, Atul. 1990. *Democracy and Discontent: India's Growing Crisis of Governability.* New York: Cambridge University Press.

Krasner, Stephen D. 1978. *Defending the National Interest: Raw Materials, Investments and U.S. Foreign Policy.* Princeton: Princeton University Press.

Kuehls, Thom. 1996. *Beyond Sovereign Territory: The Space of Ecopolitics.* Minneapolis: University of Minnesota Press.

Laitin, David D. 1986. *Hegemony and Culture: Politics and Religious Change among the Yoruba.* Chicago: University of Chicago Press.

Lane, Ruth. 1997. *The Art of Comparative Politics.* Boston: Allyn and Bacon.

Levi, Margaret. 1988. *Of Rule and Revenue.* Berkeley: University of California Press.

Lyons, Gene M., and Michael Mastanduno, eds. 1995. *Beyond Westphalia? State Sovereignty and International Intervention.* Baltimore: Johns Hopkins University Press.

Mann, Michael. 1986. *The Sources of Social Power.* New York: Cambridge University Press.

March, James G., and Johan P. Olsen. 1989. *Rediscovering Institutions: The Organizational Basis of Politics.* New York: Free Press.

Marx, Karl. 1963. *The Eighteenth Brumaire of Louis Bonaparte, with Explanatory Notes.* New York: International Publishers.

Migdal, Joel S. 1988. *Strong Societies and Weak States: State–Society Relations and State Capabilities in the Third World.* Princeton: Princeton University Press.

Migdal, Joel S., Atul Kohli, and Vivienne Shue, eds. 1994. *State Power and Social Forces: Domination and Transformation in the Third World.* New York: Cambridge University Press.

Minow, Martha, Michael Ryan, and Austin Sarat, eds. 1993. *Narrative, Violence, and the Law: The Essays of Robert Cover.* Ann Arbor: University of Michigan Press.

Mitchell, Timothy. 1991. "The Limits of the State: Beyond Statist Approaches and Their Critics." *American Political Science Review* 85:77-96.

Moore, Barrington. 1966. *Social Origins of Dictatorship and Democracy: Lord and Peasant in the Making of the Modern World.* Boston: Beacon Press.

Moore, Dahlia, and Baruch Kimmerling. 1995. "Individual Strategies of Adopting Collective Identities: The Israeli Case." *International Sociology* 10:387-407.

Mosca, Gaetano. 1939. *The Ruling Class.* New York: McGraw-Hill.

Nordlinger, Eric A. 1981. *On the Autonomy of the Democratic State.* Cambridge: Harvard University Press.

North, Douglas C. 1981. *Structure and Change in Economic History.* New York: Norton.

Polyani, Karl. 1957. *The Great Transformation.* Boston: Beacon Press.

Richards, A. I. 1964. "Authority Patterns in Traditional Buganda." In L. A. Fallers and A. I. Richards, eds., *The King's Men: Leadership and Status in Buganda on the Eve of Independence.* New York: Oxford University Press.

Robertson, David B. 1993. "The Return to History and the New Institutionalism in American Political Science." *Social Science History* 17:1-36.

Roseberry, William. 1994. "Hegemony and the Language of Contention." In Gilbert Joseph and Daniel Nugent, eds., *Everyday Forms of State Formation: Revolution and the Negotiation of Rule in Modern Mexico.* Durham: Duke University Press.

Sanders, John T., and Jan Narveson, eds. 1996. *For and Against the State: New Philosophical Readings.* Lanham, MD: Rowman and Littlefield.

Shapiro, Michael J., and Hayward R. Alker. 1996. *Changing Boundaries: Global Flows, Territorial Identities.* Minneapolis: University of Minnesota Press.

Shils, Edward. 1972. *The Constitution of Society.* Chicago: University of Chicago Press.

Schudson, Michael. 1994. "Culture and the Integration of National Societies." *International Social Science Journal* 46:63-82.

Shue, Vivienne. 1988. *The Reach of the State: Sketches of the Chinese Body Politic.* Stanford: Stanford University Press.

Siu, Helen F. 1989. "Recycling Rituals: Politics and Popular Culture in Contemporary Rural China." In Perry Link, Richard Madsen, and Paul G. Pickowicz, eds., *Unofficial China: Popular Culture and Thought in the People's Republic.* Boulder, CO: Westview Press.

Skocpol, Theda. 1979. *States and Social Revolutions: A Comparative Analysis of France, Russia, and China.* New York: Cambridge University Press.

Smith, Anthony D. 1988. "Myth of the 'Modern Nation' and the Myths of Nations." *Racial Studies* 11:1-26.

Spruyt, Hendrik. 1994. *The Sovereign State and Its Competitors: An Analysis of System Change.* Princeton: Princeton University Press.

Stern, Paul C. 1995. "Why Do People Sacrifice for Their Nations?" *Political Psychology* 16:217-35.

Thelen, Kathleen, and Sven Steinmo. 1992. "Historical Institutionalism in Comparative Politics." In Sven Steinmo, Kathleen Thelen, and Frank Longstreth, eds., *Structuring Politics: Historical Institutionalism in Comparative Analysis.* New York: Cambridge University Press.

Thompson, E. P. 1974. "Patrician Society, Plebian Culture." *Journal of Social History.* 7:382-405.

Tilly, Charles. 1985. "War Making and State Making as Organized Crime." In Peter Evans, Dietrich Rueschemeyer, and Theda Skocpol, eds., *Bringing the State Back In.* New York: Cambridge University Press.

Vitalis, Robert. 1995. *When Capitalists Collide: Business Conflict and the End of Empire in Egypt.* Berkeley: University of California Press.

Wallerstein, Immanuel M. 1974. *The Modern World System: Capitalist Agriculture and the Origins of the European World-Economy in the Sixteenth Century.* New York: Academic Press.

Waterbury, John. 1993. *Exposed to Innumerable Delusions: Public Enterprise and State Power in Egypt, India, Mexico, and Turkey.* New York: Cambridge University Press.

Weber, Max. 1954. *Max Weber on Law in Economy and Society.* Ed. Max Rheinstein. Cambridge: Harvard University Press.

———. 1964. *Theory of Social and Economic Organization.* New York: Free Press.

Wilentz, Sean., ed. 1985. *Rites of Power: Symbolism, Ritual, and Politics Since the Middle Ages.* Philadelphia: University of Pennsylvania Press.

Woo-Cumings, Meredith. 1991. *Race to the Swift: State and Finance in Korean Industrialization.* New York: Columbia University Press.

PART IV

SOCIAL THEORY AND EXPLANATIONS IN COMPARATIVE POLITICS: CONCLUSION

9

SOCIAL THEORY AND COMPARATIVE POLITICS

Mark I. Lichbach

It is not the "actual" interconnections of "things" but the *conceptual* interconnections of *problems* which define the scope of the various sciences.

Max Weber

For the believer there are no questions; for the nonbeliever there are no answers.

Rabbi Menachem Mendel

We live ... amid the debris of Reason.
Adam Seligman

INTRODUCTION

I begin where inquiry should always begin: an assessment of the problem situation toward which inquiry is directed (Popper 1965).[1] What is the current state of theory in comparative politics? Compared to twenty-five years ago, self-conscious theoretical reflection finds almost no home in our field. We do not take our theories or our theorists seriously.

[1] I want to thank Robert Bates, Jeffrey Kopstein, Peter Lange, David Mapel, Michael McGinnis, James Scarritt, James C. Scott, Adam Seligman, Sven Steinmo, Nina Tannenwald, and Alex Wendt; the participants in the May, 1996, Brown University conference on "Interests, Identities and Institutions in Comparative Politics – Samuel Barnes, Peter Hall, Ira Katznelson, Margaret Levi, Joel S. Migdal, Marc Howard Ross, Sidney Tarrow, and Alan Zuckerman; Barbara Geddes and the audience at the two panels on "Theory in Comparative Politics" at the 1996 Annual Meetings of the American Political Science Association, San Francisco, Californa; and the graduate students in my 5075 course – Introduction to Political Science – for their lively and provocative comments on earlier drafts of this chapter.

Evidence to support this harsh judgment comes from our leading journal's recent symposium on "The Role of Theory in Comparative Politics" (*World Politics,* October 1995). The participants minimized the value of deductive, a priori theorizing of the sort that is done within strongly defined research communities. While the symposium included widely acknowledged experts in specific research traditions, apparently no one viewed, for example, today's rationalist–culturalist divide as theoretically interesting, exciting, and productive. Structural or institutional analysis was not even recognized as a distinctive theoretical enterprise but rather was thought to be part of the field's "messy center." Most participants feared that comparative politics might return to the sort of Marxist–functionalist debate that characterized it in the 1950s and 1960s.Consequently, method – prediction, comparison, counterfactuals, history, quantitative and qualitative data, explanation, interpretation, causation, and generalization – was on everyone's mind. The "nomothetic" vs. "ideographic" divide was what really animated discussion. The consensus was that most comparativists are part of the consensus: Today's comparativists practice "theoretically informed empirical political analysis" and adopt "diverse conceptual lenses" (2) and "eclectic combinations" (5). They are interested in "questions" and "empirical puzzles" (10). Hence, "comparative politics is very much a problem-driven field of study" and comparativists are mostly interested in solving "real-world puzzles" (46).

The flaw of this pragmatist, means-oriented heaven is obvious: "If the problem orientation of the field tends to relegate the role of theory mainly to that of a tool of empirical research, the quest for causal generalizations, by contrast, moves its role to the forefront" (47). Similarly, the conclusion from a methods symposium on comparative (small-n) studies in another leading journal (*American Political Science Review,* June 1995) may be stated as paraphrase of Kant: Good theory without good research design is empty; good research design without good theory is blind (454). As Rogowski's (1995) important essay makes clear, one cannot begin inquiry with "evidence" derived from and used to test "theory"; one must begin with theoretically embedded observations. The inevitable conclusion is that researchers must eventually reflect on the nature of that theory – which leads to questions broadly defined as "social theory" or "philosophy of social science."[2]

World Politics's symposium did not contribute to the cause of theory in comparative politics because its picture of theory in our field as dominated by a "messy center" is inaccurate and self-defeating. This chapter seeks to refute that perspective and advance theory in comparative politics in three ways.

First, I recognize that three ideal-type research traditions – the rationalist, culturalist, and structuralist – are active in contemporary comparative politics,

---

[2] Actually, not so inevitable. *World Politics* rejected a version of this chapter with the comment, "Bottom line: the exclusive focus on theory is not for us...." Can a discipline mature if no one specializes in its ideas?

just as they are astir throughout the social sciences.[3] Section 1 thus begins the analysis with three exemplary comparativists. Each thinks of himself or herself as a member of a strong research community. Robert H. Bates (1989) argues that he is a rationalist, James C. Scott (1985) identifies with the culturalists, and Theda Skocpol's (1979) work is determined by structuralist principles. While each recognizes the value of synthesis and the cross-fertilization of ideas, each is principally concerned with advancing a particular intellectual tradition and theoretical agenda that transcend comparative politics. Section 2 deepens this analysis by dissecting each research community's ontology, methodology, comparative strategy, lacunae, and subtraditions.

Second, I set the dialogue among the schools within the historical context of the development of social theory. Section 3 thus attempts to understand the three research communities by tracing them back to Talcott Parsons's (1937) effort to systematize several classic social theorists and thereby integrate social theory. I have modified his approach to take account of the structure-action problem of reconciling individuals and collectivities. I call this modified approach the socially embedded unit act. Using this meta-framework to provide insight into the individual frameworks, I demonstrate the underlying unity and significance of the approaches for addressing questions of social theory.

Finally, I set the dialogue among the schools within the historical situation confronting today's comparativists. Section 4 thus seeks an underlying unity in rationalist, culturalist, and structuralist thought by delving even further back to Max Weber's master problem of a century ago. Weber studied the dialectic of modernity in world historical and comparative perspective: how reason and non-rationality manifest themselves at individual and societal levels with great normative and empirical significance. The dialectic is important to contemporary politics in the West. Due to the West's influence on the globe, the dialectic is equally important to the entire world community of nations.

Section 5 is a summary of my theme about the problem situation of contemporary comparative politics: There are fundamental difficulties with a field that consists only of a "messy center" and basic virtues in a field that embraces creative confrontations, which can include well-defined syntheses in particular research domains, among strongly defined research communities. Comparativists should explore the rationalist–culturalist–structuralist debate and thereby appreciate the different structure-action combinations of interests, identities, and institutions that guide inquiry. Even self-described "problem-oriented" comparativists – those who think of themselves as part of a "messy center" – should be aware of the competing research traditions that have historically been a part of the social sciences. We cannot remain theoretically challenged – a field of theoretical philistines – and actually solve substantive problems. Contemporary com-

---

[3]The current revival of interest in the philosophy of the social sciences, which has centered on the significance of rationality, culture, and structure for social theory, has become a mini-textbook industry. My graduate syllabus, which contains an up-to-date set of references, is available upon request.

parative politics therefore will be greatly enriched by a dialogue among the traditions, especially one that is informed by self-conscious reflection about the enduring issues of social theory.[4] Comparative politics needs strong and yet mutually sympathetic intellectual communities: believers who raise questions and nonbelievers who appreciate answers.

SECTION 1: THREE EXEMPLARS

In order to demonstrate that our field consists of more than a "messy center," it is necessary to examine comparativists who consciously specialize in specific research traditions. Consider three of the most widely cited and deeply respected works in contemporary comparative politics: Robert H. Bates's (1989) *Beyond the Miracle of the Market,* James C. Scott's (1985) *Weapons of the Weak,* and Theda Skocpol's (1979) *States and Social Revolutions.*

Bates explains how reason shapes the political economy of agrarian development in Kenya. He offers a materialistic theory of political preferences: An actor's location in Kenya's agrarian economy shapes his or her preferences about economic and political institutions. Bates also argues that institutions shape the calculations of political entrepreneurs and hence affect how material interests are defined, organized, and aggregated by vote-maximizing politicians. Interests, in other words, are both materially and politically determined. The tragedy is that these reasoning voters, politicians, consumers, and producers create the drought, famine, and subsistence crises that plague the people of Kenya. Bates's book is therefore a seminal study of "the impact of economic interests upon politics and the impact of institutions upon economic interests" (46), one that explores both the intended (and wanted) and unintended (and unwanted) consequences of reason.

Scott's study of the peasant village of Sedaka in Malaysia takes a very different perspective: "The peasants of Sedaka do not simply react to objective conditions per se but rather to the interpretation they place on those conditions as mediated by values embedded in concrete practices" (305). He argues that the discourses and practices of class conflict in Sedaka take the form of "everyday forms of peasant resistance" in which the poor and the well-to-do abide by different norms and rules. Scott's book is therefore a masterful analysis of the fragile ideological hegemony of the landed elite over the peasantry, one that traces the basis of a reasoning and nonrational class order to the creation of identities and communities.

---

[4]In the international relations field, the debate between neoliberals and neorealists helps structure inquiry and inform scholarly identities. Articles and books have thus evaluated the meaning and significance of the controversy (Baldwin 1993; Kegley 1995; Keohane 1986). Because they participate in this debate, our colleagues in the field of international relations are well aware of the value of social theory in sharpening theoretical lenses (Wendt, forthcoming). The underlying purpose of this chapter and volume is to create a similar concern with theoretical reflection in our field of comparative politics.

Skocpol, in a comment that could have been directed at Bates or Scott, rejects a "purposive image" of social causation that "suggests that revolutionary processes and outcomes can be understood in terms of the activity and initiation or interests of the key group(s) who launched the revolution in the first place" (17). Skocpol explains revolution by "rising above" the subjective viewpoints – the interests and identities – of the participants. She takes a structural perspective, or "an impersonal and nonsubjective viewpoint – one that emphasizes patterns of relationships among groups and societies" (18). Skocpol is especially interested in "the institutionally determined situations and relations of groups within society and upon the interrelations of societies within world-historically developing international structures" (18). Skocpol's book is therefore a classic comparative historical analysis of revolution in France, Russia, and China, one that traces the reason (e.g., the development of democracy, markets, and state bureaucracies) and irrationality (e.g., the blind violence and human costs) of revolution to an "iron cage" of forces[5] that operate behind the backs of individuals.

In sum, Bates offers a rational/social choice study of how interests produce the dialectic of reason and irrationality in Kenya's political economy, Scott a culturalist/interpretivist account of how communities and identities constitute the dialectic in Malaysia's class relations, and Skocpol a structuralist/institutionalist analysis of how social forces drive the dialectic in the French, Russian, and Chinese revolutions. Even a cursory examination of our recent journals and books reveals that comparativists today have indeed coalesced around these three competing research schools: Social choice theories, culturalist approaches, and structural analyses offer competing visions of the field. As in political science more generally and social science even more generally, interests, identities, and institutions contend for theoretical primacy in comparative politics (Garrett and Weingast 1993; Heclo 1994; Selznick 1992: 78)

This significance of the rationalist–culturalist–structuralist dialogue in comparative politics is also demonstrated by the contributions to this volume that examine substantive research areas. Peter A. Hall shows that the field of comparative political economy involves a lively and fairly equal struggle among interest-, idea-, and institution-oriented perspectives. Doug McAdam, Sidney Tarrow, and Charles Tilly indicate that the three main concepts used to explain contentious politics – political opportunities, mobilizing structures, and cultural frames – embody rationalist, culturalist, and structuralist elements. Joel S. Migdal maintains that rational choice and culturalist perspectives have been marginal to comparative studies of the state but are now challenging the hegemonic structuralist perspective. Finally, Samuel H. Barnes evinces that the survey research tradition in the study of voter turnout and partisan choice has been affected by all the perspectives but has come to rely recently on the (declining?) rationalist approach.

---

[5]Weber's ([1904-05] 1985: 181) used of the term actually corresponds to an iron cage that is originally produced by actors and their ideas but eventually becomes a set of material forces that externally constrain individuals.

If space permitted, the footprint of the rationalist–culturalist–structuralist dialogue could have been traced in comparative studies of democratization, globalization, modernization, and several other substantive domains.

The intellectual problem, of course, is that as one contemplates the three exemplars from the competing research schools, one is forced to recall a line from the old Monty Python show – "and now for something completely different." How are we to make sense of the fact that three such different theoretical perspectives coexist in the same field of comparative politics? Perhaps we should ask the question in ways that engage our three authors. Can rationalists, culturalists, and structuralists secure mutually profitably intellectual exchange, or is monopoly inevitable? What overall meaning can the three schools have, apart from a teleology toward ideological hegemony? How can a single discipline be structured such that the three perspectives coexist, or must one approach institutionalize its victory?

In the face of this disorienting pluralism, partialism, and perspectivism, admirers of Weber can take comfort in one of his memorable lines: "It is not the 'actual' interconnections of 'things' but the *conceptual* interconnections of *problems* which define the scope of the various sciences" ([1903-17] 1949: 68, emphasis in original). This nominalist proposition follows from the Kantian argument that concepts or theories without empirical intuition or observation are empty phrases; empirical intuition without concepts is blind. Kant thus stresses the ordering function of theory and the impotence of experience without the guidance of theory. Combining Weber and Kant, the message to comparativists is clear: The choice of a preconception or framework for ordering the chaos inherent in reality and hence for guiding empirical study is the fundamental analytical question. The rationalist–culturalist–structuralist dialogue indeed shapes inquiry. The question to be addressed now is how it does so.

SECTION 2: THE THREE RESEARCH SCHOOLS

Bates, Scott, and Skocpol can be best understood as exemplars of ideal-type research schools in the social sciences. Each tradition shares an ontology, a methodology, and a philosophy of science. Each also faces characteristic lacunae which account for its historical development into subschools. Similarities and differences among the approaches are summarized in Table 1.

This table can be used in two ways: working down the properties and comparing rationalist, culturalist, and structuralist thought; or working across the research communities and comparing properties. Comparative case studies of the rationalist, culturalist, and structuralist research programs appear in the chapters in this volume by, respectively, Margaret Levi, Marc Howard Ross, and Ira Katznelson. Rather than repeating their configurative discussions here, I will adopt the second approach. With apologies to Ira Katznelson (this volume), I will "slice and dice" my variables in order to draw explicit comparisons among the approaches.

Table 1. *Research Communities and Their Properties*

Property	Community		
	Rationalist	Culturalist	Structuralist
Ontology	Rational actors Intentional explanation Actions, beliefs, desires Methodological individualism	Rules among actors Intersubjectivity Common knowledge Common values	Relations among Actors Holism
Methodology	Comparative statics Irrational social consequences of individually rational action Unintended, unwanted, unavoidable, unexpected outcomes	Meaning and significance Culture as cause/constitutes reality, identity, action, order	Social types with causal powers Structures with laws of dynamics
Comparison	Positivism Generalization Explanation	Interpretivism Case study Understanding	Realism Comparative history Causality
Lacunae	Instrumental rationality Mechanical-behavioral view of subjectivity	Tautology, teleology in existence and causal impact on outcomes	Iron cage determinism Voluntarism absent
Subtraditions	Human nature rationalists Social situation rationalists	Subjectivists Intersubjectivists	State/society Pluralism-Marxism-statism
Exemplars	Robert H. Bates	James C. Scott	Theda Skocpol

ONTOLOGY

Each school is founded on certain presuppositions about the way the world is constructed. Each perspective, that is, assumes something about the nature of existence: the entities and their properties that populate our lives.

Rationalists like Bates are methodological individualists who argue that collectivities have no status apart from the individuals who comprise them: Only actors choose, prefer, believe, learn, and so on. All explanations of groups, rationalists argue, must therefore be understandable in terms of individuals. People, in turn, must be understood with intentional explanations of rational choice: Desires and beliefs direct action. In other words, if actions are taken for certain reasons, then the reasons motivate the actions. The concept of "interest" follows: If action A is in person P's interest, then P must be able to supply a reason for doing A. Rationalists are therefore concerned with the collective processes and outcomes that follow from intentionality, or the social consequences of individually rational action. Often these consequences are quite irrational: They are unintended, unwanted, unavoidable, and unexpected, albeit inevitable. For example, Bates's (1989: 1) first lines are: "This book is about the political economy of development. It is about the politics and economics of agriculture. And it is about Kenya." Bates then indicates that he will use the Coase Theorem, a microeconomic perspective that focuses on the transaction costs of individual exchange, to explore the efficiency of institutions, governments, and politics. In sum, rationalist ontology depicts a world populated by rational individuals and possibly irrational collectivities. The rational pursuit of individual interest explains the all-too-common occurrence of irrational social outcomes.

Culturalists are methodological holists who think of norms as intersubjective or transindividual: The members of a group or community have common, mutual, or shared ideas, orientations, or ways of looking at the world. These values are found in all of society's institutions – political, religious, economic, and social – and in society as a whole. Intersubjective consciousness is composed, more specifically, of two elements: cognitions and conscience. Culture involves common knowledge – is's and not should's – about the construction of reality. Culture also involves common understandings about the way the world should be. Common cognitions and conscience are constitutive of community. Hence, Scott (1985: 234) refers to "the moral logic of tradition" in which custom, ritual, and norms define a community's meaningful roles or expectations.

Culture and community – common cognition and common conscience – are in many ways the bases of social order. First, they are needed for the practical management of daily social life. Collective action and social coordination require mutuality of information and values. Second, culture and community underlie the affective and emotional symbolism of daily life. The world is constituted by social interactions and communicative acts endowed with meaning and significance. Third, culture and community are the bases of social control. Roles dictate standards of social respect, recognition, "reputation, status, and prestige" (Scott 1985: 234). These, in turn, provide social sanctions that restrain self-seeking individualism, "dog-eat-dog" competition, and "beggar-thy-neighbor" strategies of survival. As Scott (17) puts it, "For it is shame, the concern for the good opinion of one's neighbors and friends, which circumscribes behavior within the normal boundaries created by shared values." Fourth, culture and community provide standards of individual and collective obligation "that lie beyond immediate relations of production and serve both to create and to signify the existence of community – one that is more than just an aggregation of producers" (169). Hence, there is a "*collective* and *public* recognition that the village has an obligation to protect the livelihood of its members" (212, italics in original). Mutual expectations and preferences make the village, in effect, "one family" (196). Finally, culture and community underlie personal and group identities. The self is really a "communal self" developed in interactions with others. Culture is therefore *both* outside *and* inside individuals: external, in that it is materially real and transmitted from the past; internal, in that individuals are socialized into it.

While culture constitutes social order, Scott argues that it is contested. In contradistinction to the Parsonians, he (xviii) offers a "'meaning-centered account of class relations" in Sedaka in which class consciousness is constitutive of class relations and class conflict. Hence, there is a "public symbolic order" (25) that is based on a "symbolic balance of power" (22). Class conflict thus turns out to be "a struggle over the appropriation of symbols, a struggle over how the past and present shall be understood and labeled, a struggle to identify causes and assess blame, a contentious effort to give partisan meaning to local history" (xvii). For example, the breaking of accepted social conventions and behavioral norms leads to the symbols and exemplars of "the greedy rich" and "the grasping poor" (18).

Culture is therefore constitutive of both consensus and conflict. On the one hand, class struggle "requires a shared worldview ... [it only makes sense] unless there are shared standards of what is deviant, unworthy, impolite" (xvii). On the other hand, class struggle is contingent on shared values that are betrayed: "What is in dispute is not values but the facts to which those values might apply: who is rich, who is poor, how rich, how poor, is so-and-so stingy, does so-and-so shirk work?" (xvii).

In sum, culturalist ontology assumes that culturally embedded individuals follow social rules that are constitutive of their individual and group identities. In contrast to the rationalists, interests are not merely given and/or random; reason is not necessary and universal but conditional and contingent; and the categories of rational thought and the nature of rationality vary by culture.

Structuralists are also methodological holists. They study networks, linkages, interdependencies, and interactions among the parts of some system. A structural argument is therefore always concerned with the relationships – both static and dynamic – among individuals, collectivities, institutions, or organizations.[6] One can understand a thing, structuralists argue, only if it is related to other things of which it is a part. Hence, entities are defined in terms of relationships with other entities and not in terms of their own intrinsic properties. Waltz (1979: 81) thus argues that "in defining structures the first question to answer is this: What is the principle by which the parts are arranged?" He (74) offers the example of George and Martha in Albee's *Who's Afraid of Virginia Woolf?* George and Martha are a pair of individuals whose fortunes cannot be separated into individual-level components: Their fate is rooted in their (marital) relationship.

Structuralists thus focus on the political, social, and economic connections among people. Historically rooted and materially based processes of distribution,

---

[6]Higher-level structures can, of course, be composed of lower-level structures. For example, the state is a structure that can enter into a structural relationship with other states in the international system.

conflict, power, and domination, thought to drive social order and social change, are their particular concern. Skocpol (1979), for example, argues that state breakdown, peasant revolutions, and state reconstruction have structural causes. Her structure–conflict–change approach to state and revolution emphasizes five structures. First, the international context: Skocpol focuses on international structures and relations, or war and trade, and the world-historical circumstances in which states find themselves. Second, intranational class conflicts: Skocpol is concerned with *"historically specific institutional arrangements"* (116, emphasis in original), such as "agrarian class and local political structures" (117), that affect intraclass and interclass relations.[7] Third, the nature of the revolutionary crisis: The processes of state breakdown and of peasant revolts become the legacies of the Old Regime that affect state reconstruction. Fourth, the nature of states: Skocpol explores states as "administrative and coercive organizations" (14) that penetrate society and control people and territory. Finally, the relations of states and classes: Skocpol is particularly interested in "the potential autonomy of the state" from dominant and subordinate classes in society (24).[8]

In contrast to rationalists and subjective culturalists like survey researchers, structuralists reject an agential and reductionist focus on the actors themselves. Skocpol is very forceful on this point. She (14) argues that "an adequate understanding of social revolutions requires that the analyst take a nonvoluntarist, structural perspective on their causes and processes." Hence, "any valid explanation of revolution depends upon the analyst's 'rising above' the viewpoints of participants" (18) and taking "an impersonal and nonsubjective viewpoint" (18). Skocpol (29) thus prefers to "emphasize objective relationships and conflicts among variously situated groups and nations, rather than the interests, outlooks or ideologies of particular actors in revolutions." In other words, she focuses on the "structural contradictions and conjunctural occurrences beyond the deliberate control of avowed revolutionaries" (291)

Skocpol thus forcefully rejects a voluntarist approach to revolution based on mobilizable groups and "the emergence of a deliberate effort" (15).[9] She argues

[7]Intraclass relations include what she calls "peasant solidarity," or the peasantry's internal organization and resources. Hence, Skocpol (115) explores "the degrees and kinds of solidarity of peasant communities." Interclass relations include what she calls "peasant autonomy from direct day-to-day supervision and control by landlords and their agents" (115). Skocpol hypothesizes that rentier agrarian class relations, those with absentee nobles and a landed peasantry, beget numerous peasant conflicts, while large estates managed by nobles and worked by serfs or landless labor resist peasant rebellions. Part of her explanation also involves the political structures of local government and its relation to peasantry and national government: "Those vulnerable agrarian orders also had sanctioning machineries that were centrally and bureaucratically controlled" (117).

[8]She is thus concerned with the relations between the state and the dominant (rural) classes. In "statist societies" she suggests that the state was autonomous from the nobility and hence better able to push through needed reforms (e.g., prerevolutionary Russia modernized more than prerevolutionary China). Skocpol is also concerned with the relationship between the state and the dominated (rural) classes. Peasant rebellions are a function, first, of whether the state penetrated the peasantry and consequently did not rely on local elites for social control and, second, "the relaxation of state coercive sanctions against peasant revolts" (115).

that analysts should not assume self-conscious and purposive revolutionary van-
guards or movements whose members share grievances and goals. Hence, Skocpol
minimizes the ability of revolutionary leaderships backed by revolutionary ideologies (e.g., Jacobinism, Marxism-Leninism) to transform the state. She prefers
to focus on the structural conditions under which elites struggle to consolidate
and use state power, or the "specific possibilities and impossibilities within
which revolutionaries must operate as they try to consolidate the new regime"
(171). Revolutionaries thus do things they never intended, and preferences,
goals, and ideologies are not a valid guide to outcomes.[10]

In sum, structuralist ontology explores how relations among social agents are
concretely structured. Skocpol thus focuses on "objective structural conditions"
rather than on "politically manipulable subjective conditions" (16).

Rationalists therefore study how actors employ reason to satisfy their interests, culturalists study rules that constitute individual and group identities, and
structuralists explore relations among actors in an institutional context. Reasons,
rules, and relations are the various starting points of inquiry.

METHODOLOGY

Schools also have explanatory strategies. Each possesses a "positive heuristic" for
argumentation (Lakatos 1970).

Rationalists engage in vicarious problem solving. As Schelling (1978: 18) puts
it, "If we know what problem a person is trying to solve, and if we think he can actually solve it, and if we can solve it too, we can anticipate what our subject will
do by putting ourselves in his place and solving his problem as we think he sees
it." Once they place themselves in a problem situation, rationalists, as Bates (1989:
9-10) indicates, perform a *gedanken* or thought experiment that involves two time
periods. In the first period, their model is in equilibrium. The model is then per-
turbed by a series of exogenous shocks. In the second period, rationalists observe
the impact of the exogenous changes on the endogenous variables of concern.

What kind of exogenous shocks are possible in these comparative static exercises? Since rationalists are intentionalists, variations in action can only be explained by variations in desires and beliefs. Rationalists, moreover, gravitate to-

[9]She maintains, more specifically, that voluntaristic theories of revolution go wrong in four ways.
First, they get the process wrong: Revolutionary intentions develop in the course of revolution. Second,
they get the counterfactuals wrong: Such theories imply a voluntaristic conception of political order and
stability. Third, they get the causes wrong: Revolutionary crises simply occur and are historically nonvol-
untaristic, rather than being "made" by revolutionary movements. Finally, they get the outcomes wrong:
States are not constructed by the revolutionary agency of vanguard parties.

[10]Similar to the rationalists, Skocpol looks at revolutions as the unintended consequences of the interaction of rational actors or sets of actors: "Revolutionary conflicts have invariably given rise to outcomes
neither fully foreseen nor intended by – nor perfectly serving the interests of – any of the particular groups
involved" (1979: 18). The term she (298, fn. 44) uses here is "conjuncture": "the coming together of separately determined and not consciously coordinated (or deliberately revolutionary) processes and group efforts." Rather than focusing on explicitly formulated intergroup coalitions, she thus prefers to focus on
"the conjunctural, unfolding interactions of originally separately determined processes" (320, fn. 16).

ward materialist theories of preference and cognition. The material constraints of the "objective external world" are held to affect action because they influence the desires and beliefs of the "subjective internal world" of the actor. In other words, rationalists are positivists who restrict their comparative static exercises to hard or "objective" shocks because they wish to avoid studying fuzzy or "subjective" ones (Lichbach 1996: 233). Rationalists consequently explore the conditions of choice: the shadow, relative, or opportunity prices (in terms of forgone material opportunities) of action. For example, Bates (1989: 10) indicates that "in the early portions of this work, the shock is the colonial incursion. In the later portions, it is a failure of the rains. In the intermediate periods, the shocks include variations in access to land, cash crops, or productive ecological zones." While Bates certainly understands the culture of Kenya, and he certainly factors it into his equilibrium model, what ultimately drive his analysis are independent and exogenous material shocks and forces. As Bates (153) reluctantly and revealingly puts it, he "has been driven to a materialist conception of politics." In sum, empirically oriented rationalists are ultimately materialists in that they assume that material conditions drive subjective consciousness and ultimately rational choice. Rational actor theories are consequently parasitic on material structuralist ones.

Human actions are intentional: People express and act upon purposes. Culturalists like Scott (1985: 45) thus argue that the human sciences should concern themselves with the emotions, attitudes, and other subjective dispositions that allow researchers to evaluate the meaning and significance of human interaction. It is only by penetrating the frames of meaning used by actors that analysts can explore how culture causes and constitutes reality, identity, action, and social order. The methodology of interpretation, hermeneutics, or *verstehen* makes four fundamental assumptions. First, interpretive approaches are premised on the idea that participants' understandings might not be the same as scientists' understandings.[11] Interpretivists thus attempt to see things from the actor's point of view or in terms of his or her own self-understanding. Their goal is therefore to produce an empathetic awareness of the outlooks, feelings, motives, and experiences of another. Second, since the meaning of an action is comprehended in light of the agent's particular situation, the norms, forms, and practices of his or her society are relevant. Interpretation thus involves value relevance: Meaning is relative to culture. Third, interpretation involves a hermeneutic circle: The parts must be understood in terms of the whole and the whole must be understood in terms of its parts. Meaning, in other words, must be established holistically or by relating individual and society. Finally, comprehending the material world is not the same as comprehending the social world. The social world must be understood from within rather than explained from without. In fact, the analyst should limit himself or herself to comprehending the self-understanding of human beings. He or she must go beyond establishing the materialistic causal connections

---

[11]Weber (cited in Calhoun 1995: 48) offers a classic rejoinder to this perspectivism: "One does not need to be Caesar to understand Caesar."

sought by rationalist *gedanken*: Instead of seeking the external causes of behavior, analysts should seek the internal meaning of action. Understanding rather than explanation is therefore the goal: Positivists study cause-and-effect explanations, rooted in the nomothetic idea that recurrent law-like processes exist, and interpretivists seek interpretive understanding rooted in the ideographic idea that societies are unique. In sum, culturalists reject materialistically oriented positivism and adopt an interpretive philosophy of science. They study how reason and nonrationality are constitutive of individuals and societies.

Structuralists study structures and hence adopt a realist philosophy of science. Realism is characterized by two basic principles that are very compatible with structuralism.

First, realists adopt an entity- rather than an event-centered ontology: "Entities (ontology) condition theories (epistemology)" (Wendt forthcoming: 20). Realists thus assume that objects and entities – perhaps known only by their effects – exist in the world. For example, the state is real and is not simply a police car; similarly, the international state system is real and is not just the U.N. charter. Structures are thus real entities or objects. Realists assume that mature scientific theories typically refer directly to this real world of (perhaps unobservable) objects and hence provide knowledge of reality "out there." Scientific theories are therefore about the basic building blocks of the world, including their properties and interactions. Scientists search for these fundamental entities, called "natural kinds" in their particular domains of inquiry. Natural kinds have a differentiated structure and hence coherence and unity: They are forms or kinds of things with interconnected parts or elements. Hence, a natural kind is more than a heap of properties or an ad hoc collection of bundles of qualities. For example, a dog is a natural kind; a pile of sand or five randomly chosen objects on my desk are not.

The implications for social science are that social structures are real and that social scientists should search for "social kinds." Little (1993: 190) argues that "candidates for social kinds include 'riot,' 'revolution,' 'class,' 'religion,' 'share cropping land-tenure system,' 'constitutional monarchy,' market economy,' 'nationalist political movement,' 'international trading regime,' and 'labor union.'" Skocpol thus focuses on historically concrete types of cases: "This book does not, of course, analyze in depth all available historical cases of social revolution. Nor does it analyze a 'random' sample from the entire universe of possible cases. In fact, comparative historical analysis works best when applied to a set of a few cases that share certain basic features. Cases need to be carefully selected and the criteria of grouping them together made explicitly" (1979: 40). Hence, France, Russia, and China "have been grouped together as fundamentally *similar* cases of social revolution" (40, emphasis in original). Why? "It is the premise of this work that France, Russia, and China exhibited important similarities in their Old Regimes and revolutionary processes and outcomes – similarities more than sufficient to warrant their treatment together as one pattern calling for a coherent causal explanation" (41).

Second, these perhaps unobservable natural or social kinds – what I have termed structures – have, following Skocpol, causal powers. Wendt (forthcoming: 26) suggests that "the behavior of things is influenced by self-organizing or homeostatic internal structures, and the analysis of those structures should to that extent figure in explanations of behavior." Realists argue that scientists search for these real – albeit hidden – causal mechanisms. For example, chemistry looks for chemical elements and the laws of chemistry; physics looks for elementary particles and the laws of physics. Hence, structure, process, and outcome are linked: Natural bodies or kinds have natural proclivities or powers which produce natural laws of development. Piaget (cited in Lloyd 1986: 257, emphasis in original) thus maintains that *there is no structure apart from construction.* Structuralists thus follow Aristotle and assume that structures have actualities and potentialities and that form determines development. These law-like processes thus involve production and reproduction, stability and change, growth and development, and maintenance and transformation.

The implication for social science, as Ira Katznelson develops in his contribution to this volume, is that social structures must be analyzed in macro-historical and macrodevelopmental perspective. The substantive concerns include state-building, war, capitalism, industrialization, and urbanization. Structural mechanisms that produce these historical dynamics include competition, conflict, consensus, division of labor, differentiation, diversity, distribution, inequality, stratification, polarity, size, density, and hierarchy. Still other structural logics that produce dynamics involve contradictions, paradoxes, ironies, and unintended consequences. Examples abound. Adam Smith argues that in the pursuit of private gain society organizes itself and thereby produces a market governed by the laws of supply and demand. Karl Marx argues that capitalist societies have a different set of laws of development and ones that lead to their own demise. Max Weber argues that patriarchalism, domination by notables, political patrimonialism, feudalism, hierarchy, Caesaropapism, bureaucracy, charismatic community, church, sect, household, neighborhood, kin group, ethnic group, oikos, and enterprise have characteristic patterns of development.

Skocpol is thus concerned with the concrete historical dynamics of a certain type of state (1979: 304, fn. 1). What types of old-regime states that she studied were susceptible to social revolution? "Autocratic," "protobureaucratic," "imperial," "monarchies" that were "well-established," "wealthy," "politically ambitious," "historically autonomous," and in "noncolonial" states with "statist societies" and "agrarian" economies that faced "intense international military competition" from "economically developed military competitors" underwent social revolution (1979: 41; 161; 167; 285; 287-8; 304, fn. 4). What type of state was the outcome of the social revolutions she studied? Bureaucratic and mass-incorporating states – rationalized, autonomous, and powerful – were the products of revolution.

In sum, structuralists analyze real social types with causal powers and hence study the historical dynamics of structures. This implies that they are opposed to the rationalist's atomistic reductionism. Structuralists indeed reject the view that social life can be explained by particles of matter and their movement, which are subject only to the laws of motion and their own material nature. Skocpol thus opposes "strategies of analytic simplification" (294). She argues that analysts (5) should not concentrate "only upon one analytic feature (such as violence or political conflict" that characterizes major social revolutions. Rather, "we must look at the revolutions as wholes, in much of their complexity." Structuralists, moreover, view cause as natural necessity. This implies that they violate the rationalist's Hempelian deductive-nomological approach to explanation (see Alan Zuckerman's chapter in this volume). Structuralists indeed transgress a positivism that sees cause as entailing only logical necessity.

Rationalists therefore perform comparative static experiments, culturalists produce interpretive understanding, and structuralists study the historical dynamics of real social types. Positivism, interpretivism, and realism are the possible philosophies of social science.

COMPARISON

Given a school's ontology and methodology, each develops an approach to comparison. All take a stand on the ideographic-nomothetic debate and on the question of covering laws and causal accounts raised in Alan Zuckerman's essay in this volume.

Rationalist methodology involves the comparative-static experiments discussed earlier that link structure to action. This comparative static methodology sounds like the basis for generalization. It is indeed the ideal PGM – proposition generating machine. Rationalists see individuals as hardheaded scientists who ground their preferences and beliefs in the material world. Similarly, rationalists see themselves as hardheaded scientists who conduct *gedanken* and then evaluate their success. Rationalists are thus careful to specify what counts as decisive evidence against their experiments. They think in terms of observable implications that are falsifiable (i.e., rationalists suggest null hypotheses and counterfactuals). For example, Bates (1989: ch. 4) offers a series of regression equations that demonstrate that political institutions and public policies affect Kenya's food stocks and thus stand between drought and famine. Refuting theories of unregulated markets offered by neoconservative development economists and of benevolently regulated markets offered by neoliberal development economists, he presents statistical evidence of a "policy-induced food cycle" (111). Institutions, that is, "may generate pressures that convert abundance into dearth and therefore translate droughts into food crises." Bates considers these lessons generalizable to agrarian politics in other Third World countries. As he puts it, "this chapter has taught us about subsistence crises" (115). In sum, rationalists are led, as if by an invisible hand, to quantitative methodologies and a positivist philosophy of science. They attempt to account for an explanandum (irrational social action) by fitting it into a structure of knowledge: Initial conditions (about rational desires and beliefs) and general laws (about their operation) allow rationalists to deduce the anomalous (irrational) phenomenon in question.[12]

Culturalist methodology involves gaining interpretive understanding of meaning. Since meaning is peculiar to particular cultures, culturalists favor case studies. Moreover, they stress the uniqueness of cases. Individual cases are characterized by radical historical contingency. Individual developments are largely open-ended historical accidents in four ways. First, outcomes are paradoxical: They are unintended and unwanted. Second, outcomes are path-dependent: Critical events and tipping points shape history. Locally, cases are temporally ordered and historically connected sequences of events. Globally, cases are subject to spatial and temporal diffusion as each case changes the context within which subsequent cases operate. Third, outcomes are multifarious: Multiple equilibria are possible and counterfactuals are always relevant. Finally, outcomes are unstable and unpredictable: The forces that produce any one outcome are finely balanced, and hence short-run.

Culturalists are therefore suspicious of generalizing across cases. They reject the idea of nomothetic research conducted on random samples of the world's current population of states in order to develop generalizations that hold independently of space, time, and context. All universals, uniformities, and invariants are suspect. Norms, means, and averages are just that. Theories are never fulfilled precisely the same way in all situations. Cases are not merely instances of general things – lifeless variables, categories, and abstractions. Modifications, exceptions, and qualifications are the rule. Hence, comparativists should not think in terms of ideal-type theories and concepts. These do not exist, have never existed, and will never exist. In short, all grand historical narratives and totalizing universal histories must be deconstructed.

Rather than compare to establish vague similarities, culturalists believe that comparativists should compare to establish sharp differences. Comparativists should thus be historical relativists. They should positively value diversity and multiplicity; expect historical particularity, specificity, and locality; understand individuality, singularity, uniqueness, and distinctiveness; appreciate deviants, outliers, idiosyncrasies, unrepresentativeness, and anomalies; and hence study variation, heterogeneity, fragmentation, differentiation, and plurality.

For example, Scott (1985: xviii) states that "a certain amount of storytelling seems absolutely essential to convey the texture and conduct of class relations." Larger theoretical "considerations require, I think the flesh and blood of detailed instances to take on substance. An example is not only the most successful way of embodying a generalization but also has the advantage of always being richer and more complex that the principles that are drawn from it" (xviii). Hence, Scott opens his book with two wonderful stories of social outcasts: Razak, the

---

[12]Margaret Levi, in her contribution to this volume, indicates that some comparatively and historically oriented rationalists are moving away from positivist comparative-static exercises and toward "analytical narratives."

symbol of "the grasping poor," and "Haji 'Broom,'" the symbol of "the greedy rich" (18).

In sum, culturalists stress configurative paths – there are as many paths as there are cultures. Hence, comparativists should compare in order to establish the differences among a set of developments.[13] They should study phenomena in their local and concrete historical context, focusing on their origins and outcomes.

Now consider the structuralists. Structures are patterned objects. There are obviously systematic similarities and differences among these patterns. Structuralists thus divide objects into species and genera. Their theoretical generalizations and statements are confined to particular classes and categories of phenomena. Structuralists can therefore be located between the universalists (rationalists) and the particularists (culturalists): Between all and each lie some. Structuralists thus achieve generality by partitioning cases into subsets and establishing classificatory frameworks.

While structures come in types and structuralists are basically classifiers, the way things are grouped by kind is very important to structuralists. As realists, they argue that scientists must take note of the real and objective divisions in the world: Analysts should divide nature at its joints. They reject the idea of nominalist, artificial, or subjective classifications that are merely imposed by observers and arbitrarily given by language. Divisions, in other words, are discovered and not invented. This is why Skocpol (1979), for example, focuses on the historically concrete forms of the state mentioned earlier.

Structuralists thus classify cases into a number of categories, each fundamentally different from one another. They then investigate the historical dynamics associated with each class. Similar processes, sequences, and laws thus occur in similar structures; different processes, sequences, and laws occur in different structures. A small number of typical paths of development and change are thereby located. Structuralists therefore do comparative histories to discover the historical laws of structural development. State breakdown and peasant revolutions occur according to Skocpol (1979), for example, differently in agrarian bureaucracies than in postcolonial regimes. Because of differences in initial conditions, institutions, structures, groups, and contexts, similar causes or shocks (e.g., wars) produce dissimilar effects in different systems.[14] On the other hand, different contexts within a similar overall type produce similar outcomes.[15]

This typological approach limits the generalizability of one's findings to the type of cases examined. Hence, Skocpol (288) asks, "Can [these findings] be applied beyond the French, Russian, and Chinese cases? In a sense, the answer is unequivocally 'no': one cannot mechanically extend the specific causal arguments that have been developed for France, Russia, and China into a 'general theory of revolutions' applicable to all other modern social revolutions. There are two im-

---

[13]This was one of Weber's principal methodological themes (Lichbach 1995: 290-1).

[14]Examples include Brenner (1976, 1982) and Katzenstein (1978).

[15]Examples include Moore (1966) and Skocpol (1979).

portant reasons why such a strategy would be fruitless." First, new cases might have new causes: "The causes of revolutions (whether of individual cases, or sets of similar cases) necessarily vary according to the historical and international circumstances of the countries involved" (288). Second, new cases might interact with old causes: "Patterns of revolutionary causation and outcomes are affected by world-historical changes in the fundamental structures and bases of state power as such" (288). Skocpol (290) concludes that "other revolutions require analyses in their own right" because they occur in different types of structures (e.g., in different states and in different world-historical circumstances).

In sum, structuralist comparison involves three steps. The first step involves classification: Structuralists locate different configurations of bounded and patterned action and interactions. The second step involves morphology: The principles that structure the relationships among the parts, or the theme, logic, or rules that establish the functioning of a configuration or form, are specified. The final step involves dynamics: A structure's development, institutionalization, and change are studied. This involves a focus on origins, or how the structure comes into being; maintenance, or how the structure comes to be stable; and transformation, or how the structure changes.

Rationalists therefore generalize, culturalists particularize, and structuralists typologize. Comparativists can compare to establish similarities, differences, or both similarities and differences.

LACUNAE

A school's particular ontology, methodology, and approach to the ideographic-nomothetic problem produce characteristic strengths and weaknesses. A comparative analysis of the approaches illuminates these virtues and vices.

The rationalist perspective is "externalist," "behaviorist," or "throughput": Given that rational actors attempt to efficiently adapt to their environment, external conditions and not human consciousness are the focus of the theory. Rationalists thus tend toward a mechanical-behavioral view of subjectivity and adopt a particularly anemic or thin version of intentionality, rationality, and interests. Actors are thus left with an impoverished orientation to action: People are computing devices and mechanical robots who calculate their interests. Rationalists who explain action in terms of exogenously changing prices thus inevitably slight the individual and group identity-formation question: Personal and communal identities are treated as exogenous to rather than constitutive of stable and orderly social relationships and interactions. For example, Bates (1989: 150) suggests that people are concerned with efficiency and Pareto-optimality because it can help everyone including themselves: "In an almost Marxian manner, the theory contends that people devise institutions so as to unleash the full productive potential of their economies." While this materialism might seem to be the basis of mutual cooperation and social order, the problem is that people are even more concerned with distribution, power, and property rights because these can help them most of all: "People see clearly where their interests lie. They invest in the creation of institutions in order to structure economic and political life so as better to defend their position within them. They invest in institutions so as to vest their interests" (151). Hence, rationalists like Bates ultimately offer a materialist theory of preferences[16] under which interest is an obstacle rather than a basis for social order: Rationalists view ends as random in a positive sense and as equal in a normative sense, which means that values ultimately divide rather than unite people. In sum, rationalists sacrifice the subject and surrender the self, undoing the community and unmaking the collectivity[17]

Scott (1985: 27) asks, "Why are we here, in a village of no particular significance, examining the struggle of a handful of history's losers?" Evidently, "the big battalions of the state, of capitalist relations in agriculture and of demography itself," which beget the metanarratives of large-scale peasant rebellion and revolution, "are arrayed against them." His answer is that while the material dimensions of class conflict and social change are undeniable, conflict and change must ultimately be understood interpretively. Other culturalists go even further than Scott, adopt an all-embracing Hegelianism, and argue that it is "ideas all the way down." Whether they are moderates or extremists, culturalists face the problem that the existence and causal impact of culture is difficult if not impossible to investigate. There are major problems with testing arguments about the existence of norms because norms vary by people, context, time, integration, intensity, and completeness. For example, Samuel H. Barnes in this volume shows that partisan allegiance has temporal instabilities and comparative nonequivalences. Moreover, norms are not directly observable and are subject to the "owl of minerva" problem (i.e., they are easiest to discover when they are in decline). This leads to the second major problem faced by the culturalists: testing arguments about the consequences of norms. Do norms actually produce action and outcomes? When action and the material world are swept up into an all-embracing Hegelian idealism, teleology and tautology are inevitable. Hence, culturalists face the problem of eliminating plausible rival hypotheses. Their ideas are significant but nonfalsifiable. For example, while Scott (1985: 139) does suggests several "standards of evidence and inference" on which one interpretation is to be preferred to another, he does not pretend to offer a research design capable of separating idealist from materialist forces. In sum, culturalists do not attempt to separate the material from the ideal because they assume that material must always be interpreted in terms of the ideal.[18]

As indicated earlier, Skocpol (1979) minimizes the voluntarism of revolutionary masses and elites and slights the significance of their values, beliefs, and

---

[16]A related criticism is that they also have a materialist theory of beliefs.

[17]A related criticism thus challenges the rationalist's methodological individualism.

[18]Other critiques of cultural analyses of politics are developed by Marc Howard Ross in his contribution to this volume.

actions. Her purely structural theory emphasizes that structures, not actions, produce outcomes. She argues a rigid methodological holistic position: Structure is significant and individual actions, desires, and beliefs are not. In other words, individuals have no choices. They are all but eliminatable, overwhelmed by structure. People are merely "bearers," "carriers," or "supporters" of functions determined by objective structures.[19] Moreover, when structuralists consider individuals, they tend to homogenize them. All people within a category are the same, merely role players who lack individuality. Culturalists thus charge that strict structuralists study history without a subject. Human beings are made into mechanical robots and dupes who are forced to comply with the dictates of some system. Structural theories, in other words, lack people with agency: actors who have choices and take meaningful actions. Structuralists thus produce a bloodless social science: People are the victims of and silent witnesses to history. This bloodless social science means that structural theories miss politics: the strategic interaction among goal-seeking individuals. They also miss human activity, creativity, and ingenuity. Rationalists thus charge that strict structuralists miss collective action and coalitional processes. This bloodless social science also means that structural theories are deterministic: Given structure, outcomes follow. Structural causes are so powerful that everything becomes predictable: There are imperatives and not possibilities, dictates and not contingencies. To structuralists, in sum, structure is fate. This perspective leads to historical fatalism, an iron cage determinism, and the absence of voluntarism.

Rationalist thinking therefore culminates in materialism, culturalist thought in idealism, and structural tenets in determinism. Hard-core rationalists lose values and contexts, true-believer culturalists miss choice and constraint, and die-hard structuralists miss action and orientation. Bates (1989), Scott (1985), and Skocpol (1979) are well aware of these lacunae. In order to advance their research communities, they willingly make these trade-offs.

SUBTRADITIONS

Each tradition specializes: Rationalists concentrate on action, culturalists focus on norms, and structuralists center on conditions. "Thin" versions of programs stick closely to their traditional cores. Consequently, one can test the program in a very fundamental way. The problem, however, is that the program is easily fal-

---

[19]In practice, of course, the level of constraints varies from situation to situation and may produce more or less limited choices. Inglehart (1990: 18) wisely suggests that

> on one hand, one can conceive of situations so totally rigidly structured that virtually nothing the individual can do affects his or her fate. The situation of a prisoner in a concentration camp may be very near this extreme. On the other hand, one can also conceive of situations in which what happens mainly reflects the individual's behavior; a libertarian society with lavish and well-distributed resources might approach this ideal. In the real world, one is almost never at either extreme; outcomes reflect both internal orientations and external constraints.

Hence, action, as in the socially embedded unit act, is both subjective and conditional.

sified: Exclusivity slights a great deal of the complex empirical world and hence produces unsatisfactory explanations of the richness of social life. "Thick" versions of research programs therefore begin to look empirically attractive to the members of each research community. Pragmatic researchers willingly add on elements from the other approaches. Consequently, a single tradition can subsume many specific theories, and one can test the program but not in any basic way. The three research communities thus contain an internal struggle between the purists and the monopolists, or between those who wish to develop thin versions of the program and those who wish to develop thick ones.

Rationalists study individual action and social outcomes. Thin rationalists are pure intentionalists who see reasons as causes of action. They have a reductionist view of conditions and culture that understands them as individual beliefs and desires. For example, economists who do public choice (e.g., Becker 1976) focus on a supposedly universal human nature and its laws: diminishing marginal utility, irrelevance of fixed costs, substitutes and complements in choice, market equilibrium of supply and demand, etc. Hence, thin rationalists might be more accurately called "human-nature rationalists." One can extend the boundaries of the rationalist approach by deepening the micro, and hence studying culture, and exploring the macro, and hence examining institutions (Lichbach 1995: chap. 10). Thick rationalists like Bates thus move toward structure by looking at conditions as both causes and effects (although they do not go all the way to the structuralist position and explore how structure affects the constitution of actors themselves). Thick rationalists like Bates also move toward culture by looking at preferences (although they do not go all the way to study how actors are themselves constituted by values) and beliefs (although they do not go all the way and become cognitive psychologists) as both causes and effects. Hence, thick rationalists might be more accurately called "social-situation rationalists." Bates thus begins with the historically specific opportunity structure in Kenya which defines the desires, beliefs, and choices of Kenyans. In addition to exploring how the concrete situation in Kenya constrains or limits, and enables or empowers, individual Kenyans, Bates also examines how Kenyans determine their historically concrete situation: The economic, social, and political institutions and outcomes of Kenyan political economy are endogenous.

Culturalists study subjective and intersubjective values and beliefs. Thin culturalists include the survey researchers who maintain that actors make culturally informed choices. They also maintain that material structures must always be filtered through ideas – values and beliefs. Culturalists broaden their perimeter by analyzing how culture defines choices and structures. Thick culturalists thus explore the decision rules behind choice and how actors are constituted by culture. Intersubjective approaches that take a thick view of culture include Gramscian hegemonic culturalists and Parsonian functionalists. Subjective and intersubjective subtraditions is a very significant divide. Samuel H. Barnes in this volume refers to it as the "I/we problem: Culture is what *we* believe, not what *I* believe." Marc Howard Ross's essay in this volume surveys the many cultural analyses of politics that are variations on these two themes.

Structuralists study civil society, the state, and the international system of states. Structuralists include the pluralists, Marxists, and statists. Thin structuralists are materialists. They argue that a base or substructure drives a periphery or superstructure. They also minimize the significance of actors and their freedom to choose. Since they see choice and culture as derivative of structures, thin structuralists often do not even bother to examine them. Structuralists thicken their approach by studying how the reason and nonrationality contained in structures are manifested in actions and orientations. Thick structuralists thus explore the materially driven dynamics of structures of collective action and social norms.[20]

In sum, purists/traditionalists and monopolists/synthesizers pull their research programs in opposite directions. Purists keep the approaches close to their traditional roots; they therefore minimize within-tradition variance and maximize between-tradition variance. Their extensions are usually trivial and their arguments most often turn out to be wrong. Monopolists move their approaches beyond their traditional core to synthesize perspectives; they therefore maximize within-tradition variance and minimize between-tradition variance. Their extensions are usually more interesting, but it is usually hard to know whether the program is producing the really useful insights.

SECTION 3: THE SOCIALLY EMBEDDED UNIT ACT

These basic similarities and differences in rationalist, culturalist, and structuralist thought raise deeper interpretive questions: What is the meaning and significance of the three approaches? How can we understand and appreciate the dispute among the three research communities that characterize contemporary comparative politics? And why, after all, is today's battle of the paradigms taking place among rationalists, culturalists, and structuralists and, unlike the 1960s, not among functionalists, systems theorists, and Marxists?

Such questions are best approached by setting the dialogue among the schools within the historical context of the development of social theory. The origins of social thought provide clues to contemporary understandings and debates in comparative politics. More specifically, comparativists can begin to appreciate the similarities and differences and the connections and disjunctures among the research schools by exploring how the approaches can be traced to Parsons's unit act and Weber's paradox of modernity.

---

[20]Ira Katznelson's essay in this volume offers another way to parse structuralism: One tradition (e.g., Moore, Skocpol) develops grand macroanalytic narratives of world-historical importance while another "smaller-scale historical institutionalism" (e.g., the one described by Peter A. Hall in his essay in this volume) is more empirically and theoretically restrained and makes the relatively modest claim that histories and institutions matter.

Parsons (1937) used the conceptual device of the "unit act" to systematize or rationalize the ideas of several of the founders of social thought.[21] His purpose was to unite the rationalist, culturalist, and structuralist foci on interests, identities, and institutions into one framework. The "action frame of reference," part of his voluntaristic theory of action, was the first attempt to end the war of the schools and integrate the conflicting paradigms.[22]

Building on Weber's ([1924] 1968) idea of social action, one can say that both acts and contexts matter and hence that all acts are socially embedded. I have therefore extended the unit act to take account of the structure-action problem of reconciling individuals and collectivities.[23] The socially embedded unit act is represented in Figure 1. The diagram has three layers – an inner or individual layer, a middle or collective layer, and an outer or approach layer – which reveal important connections among the schools.

THE INNER OR INDIVIDUAL LAYER

The socially embedded unit act involves a hypothetical person in a situation in which the world is at least partially under his or her control. The actor thus has some agency: He or she manifests subjectivity, has purpose, possesses free will, uses reason, and acts. The presumed result is human creativity and personal responsibility.

Philosophical discussions of intentional explanation and technical discussions of individual decision making therefore stress that agents possess three important characteristics (Elster 1989). They have desires – goals, purposes, and ends – that they intend to satisfy. They have beliefs – information and knowledge – about their situation. Finally, they make choices – act, do, and perform – in order to reach their goals. In sum, at the individual level desires and beliefs direct action.

---

[21] For nearly two decades, Parsons's unit act and related conceptual schemes dominated a great deal of social science. Many of the paradigms that became popular during comparative politics's earlier flirtation with theory and generalization in the 1950s and 1960s were rooted in Parsons (e.g., structural functionalism).

[22] Parsons eventually moved from a general theory of action – a view of social order as resulting from the contingency of individualistic decision making and the voluntaristic interaction of isolated individuals in some larger framework of norms and values – to a structural-functional scheme – a systems theory of social order based on functional or systemic imperatives. This chapter does not consider the entirety of Parsons's thought, including the structure-function scheme and "general action complexes" that synthesize social, cultural, personality, and behavioral aspects of modern societies. For a review of Parsons's work, see Sculli and Gerstein (1985). An important recent contribution is Camic (1989).

[23] Parsons's (1937) presentation of the unit act in fact mixes the individual and collective levels. Actors have goals. The situation in which they find themselves is pared into two parts – conditions and means. Conditions are the material elements which cannot be molded to the actor's purposes; they are the obstacles that constrain agency about which actors develop beliefs. Means are the choices or actions undertaken by the actor that enable agency. Finally, actors approach the situation with certain norms. They use their own subjective judgments or standards to interpret or understand their situation. The pursuit of goals and the choice of means is therefore judged by normative considerations, ideal standards, or value expectations.

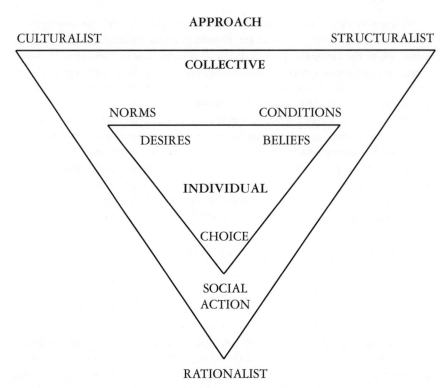

Figure 1.   *The Socially Embedded Unit Act: The Basic Diagram*

THE MIDDLE OR COLLECTIVE LAYER

The socially embedded unit act also involves sets of individuals who comprise some collectivity. People, in other words, are part of some social order.

   The structure-action or individual-collective problem involves linkages between the three properties of agency and three corresponding properties of society. Individual desires reflect and produce social norms. Individual beliefs correspond to and ultimately influence material conditions. Finally, individual action aggregates into and also responds to collective action. In sum, at the collective level cultural norms and environmental conditions affect social action.

THE OUTSIDE OR RESEARCH COMMUNITY LAYER

All grand syntheses, like Parsons's voluntaristic theory of action, become the object of close scrutiny. The intellectual division of labor takes its toll. Specialists have therefore appropriated each of the components of the socially embedded unit act and spawned a research community. There are now experts in action (the rationalists), norms (the culturalists), and conditions (the structuralists).

Hence, the outer layer of the diagram indicates that each of the schools concentrates on one vertex of the triangle. Culturalists specialize in individual desires and cultural norms, structuralists in individual beliefs and environmental conditions, and rationalists in individual choice and social action.[24]

THE CONNECTIONS AMONG THE LAYERS

The connections among these three layers problematize several important themes in social theory and hence reveal several significant relationships among the approaches. First, Figure 1 clarifies why the debate among Marxists, structural functionalists, systems theorists, etc., in the 1960s evolved into a debate among rationalists, culturalists, and structuralists in the 1990s. Theoretical thinking has sharpened and the issues are now crisper. Hence, there is now a certain symmetry among the competing positions, which is occurring throughout the social sciences,[25] that was missing from the earlier "war of the schools." Each contemporary school coalesces around a subject matter: Choice, culture, and context are the domains of study. Each adopts an ontology: Reasons, rules, and relations constitute the world. Each explores a key explanatory variable: Interests, identities, and institutions drive outcomes. Finally, each lends itself to a theory of social order: The intersection of strategies, symbols, and structures define society. In sum, our problem situations and research designs in comparative politics consist of three natural models and foils. The value in juxtaposing the approaches is that critical confrontations reveal the junctures where a school's lacunae are best addressed by the other schools.

Second, the socially embedded unit act clarifies the central issue in social thought: the structure-action problem of uniting micro, meso, and macro levels of analysis. The difficulty here is that human beings are the continually active subjects who make the eternally passive objects which limit their subjectivity.[26] Individuals are therefore more or less intentional agents who make history, society, conditions, and rules and yet history, society, conditions, and rules make individuals. We are both autonomous creators and dependent creatures, innovators and prisoners. The world is both fact and counterfactual, constraint and construct. Some examples will drive home the point:

> Taking and selling prisoners becomes the institution of slavery. Offering one's services to a soldier in return for his protection becomes feudalism. Organizing the control of an enlarged labour force on the basis of standardized rules becomes bureaucracy. And slavery, feudalism and bureaucracy be-

[24]There are several individualistic, micro, or action approaches to inquiry besides rational choice. When I considered culturalist approaches, for example, I briefly discussed subjectivist approaches (e.g., modern survey research) that offer a richer focus on the cognition, reasoning, motivation, and existential meaning the individual actor attaches to his or her action. There are also richer intersubjective approaches to consciousness that emphasize praxis or the enactment and performance of social acts.

[25]See footnote 3.

[26]This section draws upon Lichbach and Seligman (1996) and Seligman and Lichbach (1996).

come the fixed, eternal settings in which struggles for prosperity or survival or freedom are then pursued. By substituting cash payments for labour services the lord and peasant jointly embark on the dismantling of the feudal order their great grandparents had constructed. (Abrams 1982: 2-3)

The structure-action problem is concerned, more specifically, with interrelating the three aspects of the micro (individual), meso (group and institutional), and macro (societal) levels of analysis. The first is the aggregation problem: how unintended, unwanted, unexpected, unpredictable and yet seemingly inevitable collective outcomes result from a set of more or less purposeful individual actions. The second is the institutionalization problem: how these emergent properties solidify over time into structures. The third is the contextual problem: how this solidified social order comes to constrain and enable individual consciousness and action. Hence, the structure-action problem has important normative[27] and positive[28] implications, especially about freedom and determinism, and hence the possibilities of rationality and nonrationality.

A glance at the socially embedded unit act diagram shows how the framework goes beyond Parsons's individualistic unit act and clarifies these issues. Looking vertically, one discovers that there are actually two structure-action problems: culture and rational action, structure and rational action. Looking horizontally, there is one structure-structure problem: culture and structure. Legitimacy and social order thus rest on the harmonization of institutions and identities, identities and interests, and interests and institutions. In addition, the aggregation problem exists for all components of the socially embedded unit act – action (individual action and collective action), values (individual preferences and collective values), and beliefs (individual cognitions and institutional development). Rationalization thus occurs in the action sphere, where individual and collective action is reconciled through organization; in the ideal sphere, where the abstraction and systematization of values (substantive rationality) proceeds; and in the material sphere, where bureaucratization (functional rationality) develops. The parts of the inner or individual layer of the socially embedded unit act (desires, beliefs, and action) are thus associated with the middle layer of spheres of society (ideal culture, material structure, and group action), something

---

[27]The individual-society issue is important normatively. All societies must deal with value conflicts among individuals and harmonize social values. All societies must then establish principles of the good life and reconcile them with the principles of the good society. All societies must create an ethical totality in the face of possible fragmentation, polytheism, and a relativistic "everything goes" mentality. Societies must, in short, establish legitimacy. However, our western values lead us to wish to preserve agency, as did Weber. The individual-society issue therefore cuts to the core of the liberal agenda. It is intimately associated with an analyst's philosophical or value orientations.

[28]The individual-society problematique is related to all the major issues in positive political theory. Questions of personality (being, autonomy, existence, and alienation), culture (legitimacy, trust, morality, justice, and ethics), economics (market, socialism, equity, efficiency, and welfare), society (civil society, contract, corporatism, community), conflict and cooperation (peace, war), and politics (the state, democracy, and liberalism) grapple with the structure-action problem.

that was not clear in Parsons's individualistic unit act. Hence, an individual's desires are a reflection of his or her ideal culture; an individual's beliefs are founded on the material structure in which he or she exists; and an individual's actions are a part of the activities of some collectivity. There are also individual-collective connections across the parts of the socially embedded unit act. One may investigate, for example, how individual actions reflect collective values. Hence, one may explore connections at the collective level, at the individual level, and across the individual-collective divide, both within and between parts of the socially embedded unit act.

Third, the socially embedded unit act clarifies the competing perspectives on two other grand issues of social thought: social order and social change. Each school generates a theory of social order: Social order is based either on reason, common values, or a hierarchical structure's imposition of material rewards and punishments (Lichbach 1996). Each school also generates a theory of social change. Rationalists explore how individuals react to the unintended and unwanted social consequences of rational action and construct new institutions – which are, of course, subject to dysfunctions and hence institutional change. Culturalists focus on how culture institutionalizes structures and hence how cultural change renders situations obsolete. Institutionalists explore the historical dynamics of structures.

Finally, consider how the diagram relates to the nominalism vs. realism debate. I employ a Weberian nominalist rather than a structural realist orientation to the three research schools. Since Weber's "ideal types" address general methodological problems in comparative politics, and since the nature of ideal types sets the boundaries of this conceptual exercise, Weber's ideal-type analysis bears elaboration (Weber [1903-17] 1949).

One cannot study all the theories and approaches that exist in contemporary comparative politics in all of their complexity and flux. The chaos of the theoretical world is as severe as the chaos of the empirical world. Hence, we need orienting models and guiding frameworks that define and frame questions and problems. These are of necessity selective working heuristic tools rather than exhaustive and exact depictions of reality. They embody, in other words, a rather one-sided picture of the "reality" of the theories in comparative politics that exaggerates, accentuates, intensifies, highlights, and dramatizes certain features.

The socially embedded unit act is therefore a typology or classification scheme designed to juxtapose the three "ideal types" (not all possible types) of social theory now found in our most prominent research communities. What are the central and significant features of the theories that deserve emphasis in these ideal types? One must take account of the goals, perspectives, and ideas of the theorists themselves. I also have interests and values – what Weber calls value relevance – in exploring those features that I consider significant for contemporary social theory. The ideal types of rationalist, culturalist, and structuralist thought that I have developed mix both sets of concerns.

Each ideal type theory is thus logically coherent: ontology, methodology, comparison, lacunae, and subtraditions form a whole. This demonstrates that there is a certain internal logic to my interpretation of the value systems held by each set of theorists.

The set of ideal types – the classification scheme – reveals certain contrasts that allow the exploration of the alternatives and conflicts inherent in the differentiation among the types. More concretely, the typology can be used to generate four fruitful types of comparison among types (general theoretical traditions) and cases (particular theories). First, one can compare among the types to show their similarities and differences. Weber thus explores types and subtypes, sets and subsets, of cases. I have drawn numerous comparisons in rationalist, culturalist, and structuralist thought. Second, one can compare among cases. Weber thus argues that one needs clear concepts before one can show the similarities and (especially) the differences among cases. I have drawn numerous comparisons among the theories developed by Bates, Scott, and Skocpol. Third, one can compare a type with a case within its range (to show its applicability). Weber thus uses an ideal type as a yardstick to define individual cases: It is a standard against which empirical cases can be measured. By comparing the real with the ideal, Weber is able to throw a case into relief, highlighting errors and assessing deviations. I have drawn comparisons between rationalism and Bates, culturalism and Scott, and structuralism and Skocpol. Finally, one can examine a single case from the point of view of several ideal types. Weber thus tries to explain particular cases by applying a battery of ideal types and theories. Actual cases, in other words, are unique, specific, and distinctive combinations of the ideal types. The next section will therefore analyze Weber from rationalist, culturalist, and structuralist perspectives.

These four sets of contrasts, analogies, and juxtapositions allow comparativists to fruitfully mix the general and the specific, engaging theories and the cases. They allow Weber to place cases and situate developments within general contexts; they facilitate general comparative and typological explication of particular events and situations; and they enable him to focus his analysis on those cases that had great substantive and theoretical significance. Moreover, ideal type analysis makes comparativists aware of the pitfalls of moving from theory to case. Weber argues that ideal types are only useful fictions that do not exhaust and exactly depict reality. Hence, they should not be reified into something "real" rather than something "nominal": They cannot be used to "deduce" cases and therefore they are not "falsified" by locating deviations from real cases.

I have therefore combined various properties of social theories (e.g., ontology, methodology) to produce three types of social theories. The ideal-type rationalist, culturalist, and structuralist research communities developed here should be judged on pragmatic grounds: They are useful or not useful for this or that problem from this or that conceptual point of view; they should be displaced by another set of ideal types that highlight different and, from another point of view, more significant aspects of the reality of contemporary comparative politics.

In sum, a consideration of three ideal-type research schools forces comparativists to confront some fundamental issues in social theory: the nature of the competing paradigms and the structure–action, social order–social change, and nominalism-realism debates. The socially embedded unit act helps clarify, albeit not solve, these enduring issues.

SECTION 4: MAX WEBER, MODERNITY, AND COMPARATIVE POLITICS TODAY

Parsons's failed synthesis thus holds the key to a deeper understanding of the connections and disjunctures among the three research communities that dominate contemporary comparative politics. Any satisfactory substantive explanation in our field will employ one or more of these sets of "nuts and bolts" (Elster 1989). But what would be the purpose of such a theory? What is the historical situation in which social scientists find themselves that requires understanding?

Max Weber[29] argues that social scientists should begin inquiry by analyzing the value relevance of the problem situation in which they find themselves. Weber thus explores the world-historical significance of his own circumstances and then evaluates his state of affairs from the point of view of a normative theory of politics: how people ought to live, the definition and implementation of the common good, and what is the best or right life and regime. This reflection led Weber to identify his central problem, and surely the central problem of his age, as the dialectic of modernity, or how modernity emancipates and exploits.[30]

Medieval thought centered on the word of God as revealed through the teachings of the Roman Catholic Church. As Hawthorn (1976: 8), paraphrasing Hobbes, puts it, "Reason was always and necessarily subservient to revelation, which alone could reveal God's purpose." Weber's concerns, and indeed the concerns of all of the founders of social thought, can be traced to a process, begun in the Renaissance and continuing in the Enlightenment, that disputed medieval thinking. The rigid but stable old order of communities and hierarchies, based on ecclesiastical, feudal, and monarchical authority, was challenged by cognitively and morally reasoning individuals (Nisbet 1966). These individuals attempted to create a new rational order in all spheres of social life.

---

[29]It is fascinating to recall how much of the language of contemporary comparativists can be traced to Weber: ideal interests and material interests; ideal type and *verstehen*; class, status, and party; traditional, charismatic, and rational legitimacy; formal and substantive rationality; the iron cage of reason and the disenchantment of the world; bureaucracy and the modern state; the ethic of ultimate ends and the ethic of responsibility; and the Protestant ethic and a calling. Behind this vocabulary lie Weber's methodology and substantive theories which have also had a lasting impact on comparative politics.

[30]Weber's master problem has also been identified as the origins of capitalism and the West, the nature of domination and the state, and the science of culture (Hennis 1983; Nelson 1974; Schroeder 1992: chap. 1; Tembruck 1980).

Modernity thus involved the growth of reason that culminated in a series of macro changes involving the rationalization of social structures. In politics, liberal democracy, the rule of law, and state bureaucracy were created. In international relations, globalization and internationalism culminated in a world system. In the intellectual world, science and technology were founded. In the economic world, bourgeois capitalism – markets, industrialization, mass consumption, and manufacturing – were developed. In civil society, specialization, division of labor, complexity, and pluralism were fashioned. Finally, the culture sphere saw the growth of liberalism, individualism, universalism, egalitarianism, humanism, secularism, materialism, and the idea of progress.

The project of modernity thus involved reason at two levels. At the individual level, individual rationality and moral autonomy were to be constitutive of identities. At the societal level, the rationalization of structures and institutions were to be constitutive of social order.

Weber (1946: 117) is a rationalist in that he warns about the paradoxical consequences of this modernity: "The final result of political action often, no, even regularly, stands in completely inadequate and often even paradoxical relation to its original meaning." The macro transitions and transformations, in other words, produce new irrationalities, instabilities, inefficiencies, and contradictions that challenge social order. Modern western (occidental) rationality, he maintains, is concerned with means-ends calculations (formal rationality) rather than with reasoned judgments about the value of ends themselves (substantive rationality). The drive to control all aspects of the natural and human worlds has several structural consequences: imperialism and dependence, or the ruthless expansion and exploitation of the planet and all of its peoples, which inevitably produce destructive wars; the bureaucratization of everything, or the growth of rationalized and anonymous administrative systems that regulate all forms of modern life, which ultimately controls the body and sexuality; and the struggle by all peoples for nationalism and democracy, which finally cause intractable and deadly conflicts. The policy consequences are equally dramatic: Humans create an artificial world of irrationalities; this begets further rational means-ends calculations, which result in another round of policy interventions designed to rid the world of the first-order irrationalities; in the end, newer and deeper irrationalities result. The drive to control the natural and social worlds also has major consequences for values: the secularization of culture (what Weber calls the "disenchantment of the world," or the expulsion of magic, myths, and all forms of irrational social life) and the standardization of culture (what others have called massification and homogenization). Finally, the supposedly rational individuals suffer the most dire consequences of all: the loss of certainty about the meaning and purpose of their lives. Moral individualism, the radical isolation, separation, and divorce of individuals from all social ties, is responsible for several evils: The commodification and depersonalization of social relationships, and hence the deterioration of common values and the shrinking of a shared ethical space, are perhaps expected outcomes; the growth of feelings of alienation and powerlessness, and the resulting failure of the will to power (the drive to self-perfection and self-promotion, or the desire to perfect and extend the self by relying on personal creative power rather than depending on anything external), are perhaps paradoxical outcomes; solipsism, relativism, and perspectivism are perhaps logical outcomes; and since people need meaning, the rise of fundamentalisms, myths, and superstitions to replace the traditional values that have been lost is perhaps the inevitable outcome of moral individualism.

In the twentieth century, these structural, policy, cultural, and individual developments culminated in pathologies unimaginably worse than the greatest evils of the premodern world: two world wars and totalitarianism. The logical consequence of reason applied to means and not ends was the Holocaust: The trains ran on time but to a place inconceivable to all but moderns. Rational means had furthered irrational ends, and an unimaginably pathological and barbaric irrationality at that.[31]

Weber is also a culturalist in that he explores a fascinating paradox in the origins of modern rationality: how the irrational quest for meaning and salvation helped create the rational individuals and institutions of the modern world. He hypothesizes that "Calvin's doctrine of predestination resulted, among his followers, not in fatalism, not in a frantic search for earthly pleasures, but curiously and counterintuitively – in methodical activity informed by purpose and self-denial" (Hirschman 1977: 130). In other words, the Protestant Reformation produced ascetic Protestantism which, in turn, actualized the individualism that encouraged a rational social order: The spirit of capitalism motivated bourgeois capitalism; an inquisitive scientific outlook inspired the Cartesian-Newtonian scientific framework; moral individualism encouraged political liberalism; and methodical patterns of action galvanized state bureaucracies. Rationality, according to Weber, thus depends upon such irrational motivations as the Protestant doctrine of proof and the idea of a "calling." Swidler (1973: 41) concludes that "the values which motivate rationality, the control of ideas over action, must themselves be non-rational. There is always a sphere of social life which is non-rational, and it is on the preservation of this sphere that the rationality of the rest of the system depends." Only meaning, faith, and a calling can save us from the irrationalities of reason.[32]

Finally, Weber is also a structuralist in that he studies how the institutional dynamics of state and society cage individuals in the dialectic of reason and irrationality. He explores the institutionalization of three types or systems of domination or authority – rational, traditional, and charismatic legitimacy ([1924] 1968) – and the logics of three types or systems of stratification – class, status,

---

[31]The postmodernists challenge the "logic" of such grand historical narratives.

[32]Science, according to Weber, is perhaps the best example of how the basis of rationality is an irrational commitment to ultimate values. He suggests that values guide the choice of scientific problems and that the commitment to science is itself a value commitment based on the desire to shape the world. Hirschman (1977: 38) concludes that "unintended consequences flow from human thought (and from the shape it is given through language) no less than from human actions."

and party (1946). Weber also examines the development of the legal system ([1924] 1968), the dynamics of premodern and modern capitalisms ([1923] 1961, [1896] 1988), and the rationalization of religious belief systems (1951, 1952, [1904-05] 1985, [1958] 1992).

In sum, at the beginning of the century, Weber explores modernity's dialectic of reason and irrationality in individuals and collectivities. He conducts comparative and historical, positive and normative, analyses of the rationalization (reconciliation, harmonization, and development) of individual and society. He does so, moreover, in rationalist, culturalist, and structuralist terms.[33]

Weber's master problem of modernity is today, the dawn of the third millennium, still the master problem of comparative politics: "We live... amid the debris of Reason" (Seligman 1992: 1). Enlightenment trends engulf the state (e.g., the worldwide growth of democracy) and the economy (e.g., the global movement to markets). Counterenlightenment trends, however, overwhelm civil society (e.g., the growth of ethnic diversity and the consequent rise of intractable social conflicts) and cultural life (e.g., postmodernism, religious fundamentalisms, mysticisms, and relativisms of all sorts). While democracy and markets represent developments that continue to support reason, ethnic and cultural wars are developments that continue to challenge reason. The problems of modernity and postmodernity are on today's agenda in the liberal and market-oriented West. Due to the West's influence, they are also momentous issues facing the entire world community of nations.

To the true Enlightenment mind, the failings of modernity are simply problems to be solved. Moderns assume, after all, that the social world is open to human control. Truth and value can be rationally discovered (if not created): Through the universal scientific method, humans can conquer the natural world and social life. Descartes's self, in other words, can unlock Newton's mechanical universe and Plato's social world. The rational organization of society can end human bondage to physical nature and social institutions and bring moral progress, social justice, and human happiness. Moderns, in short, can create utopia: the perfect human society that enables a rationally managed life. An Enlightenment social science, rationally divided into several disciplines, is therefore needed to understand modernity and solve its problems. Today's students of comparative politics thus explore the dialectic of modernity in ways rooted in Weber: The deeper unity among the approaches is therefore that they offer critical commentaries on the emergent institutions of modernity.

The rationalist Weber examines status groups and social classes with material interests in order to explore the unintended negative consequences of reason. Contemporary rationalists also explore the modernity problematique by concentrating on reason: Instrumental rationality, after all, is the hegemonic mode of

---

[33]Weber's thought is complex and difficult to pigeonhole. For example, he did not manifest all the ideal-type properties of a structuralist: As a methodological individualist, he made no ontological commitment to the existence of collectivities.

thought in the modern world. Rationalists thus seek to understand how choice controls reason yet produces irrationality. Just as in Weber's studies of the paradoxical consequences of rationality, today's rationalists explore the intended and positive, as well as the unintended and negative, consequences of rationality. In Kenya, for example, Bates (1989) finds that reasoning voters and politicians, consumers and producers, create drought, famine, and subsistence crises. Rationalist solutions to the modern problems of democracy and capitalism tend to stress that more rationality is needed: A more efficient economic market, social contract, and political liberalism creates reason and hence overcomes many of the pathologies of modernity.

The culturalist Weber examines religious ethics and normative orders in order to explore the irrationality that drove the rationality that turned irrational. Contemporary culturalists also explore the modernity problematique by concentrating on the nonrational: Reason, after all, cannot accomplish everything because it is self-destructive and negates itself. Culturalists thus seek to understand the values which give reason and rationality their meaning and significance. Just as in Weber's studies of the nonrational origins of modern occidental rationality, today's culturalists explore how culture constitutes reason, or how culture contextualizes thought and establishes the boundaries of rationality. In Malaysia, for example, Scott (1985) analyses the fragile ideological hegemony of the landed elite over the peasantry and traces the basis of an irrational class order to the creation of identities and communities. Culturalist solutions to the modern problems of diversity and social conflict tend to stress the nonrational: The homogeneity of values and beliefs found in true communities allows the construction of more fully human identities that are the antidote to many of the pathologies of modernity.

The structuralist Weber examines patterns of stratification and systems of domination in order to explore the institutional logics of the forces that operate behind the backs of reasoning and nonrational individuals. Contemporary structuralists also explore the modernity problematique by concentrating on the containment or constraint of reason and rationality: The rational choice teleology, after all, is limited by the resiliency of society and power. Nature restricts man's powers, and not the reverse. Newton's mechanistic world strikes back at Descartes's autonomous self. The determinism of structuralist thought is also attractive to moderns.[34] Structuralists thus seek to understand the "iron cage" of forces[35] that results from and constrains rationality and nonrationality. Just as in

---

[34]Bloom (1987: 255) points out that Tocqueville warned against democracy's attraction to deterministic explanations: "Tocqueville explained this tendency as a consequence of the importance of the individual in egalitarian society. Curiously in democracy, the freest of societies, men turn out to be more willing to accept doctrines that tell them that they are determined, that is, not free. No one by himself seems to be able, or have the right, to control events, which appear to be moved by impersonal forces. In aristocracies, on the other hand, individuals born to high position have too great a sense of their control over what they appear to command, are sure of their freedom and despise everything that might seem to determine them."

[35]See footnote 5.

Weber's studies of institutional dynamics, today's structuralists explore the constraints of the concrete material world. In France, Russia, and China, for example, Skocpol (1979) argues that revolution resulted from the state being enmeshed in two sets of constraining structures: international relations, which consist of political and economic conflict among states, and domestic relations, which consist of conflict between dominant and subordinate classes. Structuralist solutions to the pathologies of modernity tend to stress institutions and organizations: Reformers need strong and rationalized state bureaucracies to cope with the economic and political competition that arises from the system of states and from the internal disorder that arises from conflicting social forces; radicals need an organized group of like-thinking individuals to destroy and eventually remake the state.

The question of modernity will remain our master problem well into the next century. Contemporary comparativists will grapple with its challenges by specializing in each of Weber's perspectives. Our historical situation offers us great theoretical leverage. On the one hand, understanding Weber's master problem helps us appreciate the significance of the approaches. Rationalist, culturalist, and structuralist thought have an underlying unity because they offer critical commentaries on the same central problem of modernity. On the other hand, understanding rationalist, culturalist, and structuralist thought helps us appreciate the significance of these challenges. The dialectic of reason and irrationality in individuals and collectivities can be understood and reconciled in three interrelated ways.

SECTION 5: CONCLUSION

My assumption throughout this chapter has been that all research is conducted within a framework of concepts and methods and hence that theoretical criticism assists concrete empirical work. Comparativists should reflect on the presuppositions that underpin their practices. Our theorists and theories need to be reflexive and self-critical, aware of their goals, assumptions, and limitations, and willing to publicly explicate and defend their commitments. Even problem-oriented comparativists cannot maintain a strict separation between theoretical and substantive concerns. They should recognize that a more critical understanding of theories is the best way to elaborate, reformulate, and extend substantive insights.

My goal has therefore been to move reflection about the nature of social theory onto the agenda of comparative politics. My means has been to elaborate three ideal-type research schools. I have shown, for example, that the structure/action, nominalism/realism, holism/individualism, materialism/idealism, rationality/culture, and subject/object debates are relevant to a sophisticated appreciation of the work of important comparativists such as Bates, Scott, and Skocpol.

The field of comparative politics is in a particularly good position to appreciate these issues of social theory that are embedded in the rationalist–culturist–structuralist dialogue. Comparativists, after all, study the macrotransformations of state and society and the microchanges in individuals and their identities associated with modernity. Comparative politics is the natural home of Mills's (1959) "sociological imagination." Hence, the battle of the paradigms contributes to comparative politics, and comparative politics contributes to the battle of the paradigms. The comparative and historical analysis of rationality, culture, and structure will be central to the agenda of comparative politics in the twenty-first century. Future comparativists will choose to work within one or more of these frameworks.

Comparativists who are engaged in such study should recall the words of Rabbi Menachem Mendel: "For the believer there are no questions; for the nonbeliever there are no answers." There is always the danger that proponents of a research community will become true believers and view their opponents as their bitter enemies. If this occurs, the "battle of the paradigms" or the "war of the schools" in contemporary comparative politics will take on the character of an interfaith disputation out of the Middle Ages. We must avoid this. Comparativists need a "dialogue of the hearing" in which believers ask searching questions and nonbelievers offer valuable answers.

Comparativists who are engaged in such study should also think about Weber. His case and comparative case studies remain unparalleled, by far the best exemplars for young comparativists. Weber had an uncanny eye for the central theoretical dilemma that confronts a particular problem area. Weber was successful because he, more than anyone else, realized that the key analytical issue underlying inquiry most often revolves around the rationalist, culturalist, and structuralist dialogue. After nearly a century, his work remains the most satisfactory resolution of this enduring issue of social thought. Weber was a rationalist, culturalist, and structuralist who produced the most creative synthesis – of structure and action, of individual and collectivity – that has ever been made. Given their roots in Weber, it is clear that rationalists, culturalists, and structuralists can make rich and exciting contributions to comparative politics. Bates, Scott, and Skocpol have proven that comparativists can legitimately and productively define their perspective as a positivist focus on explaining rational action and choice, an interpretive focus on understanding values and beliefs, a realist focus on comprehending structures and their dynamics, or, most enticingly, any combination thereof.[36]

In sum, I offer a four-part thesis about improving the state of theory in comparative politics. First, if we approach theory by believing that our field consists only of a "messy center," our search for better theory will end almost immediately. Second, if, on the other hand, we embrace creative confrontations, which

---

[36]The chapters by Peter A. Hall and by Doug McAdam, Sidney Tarrow, and Charles Tilly in this volume stress the value of fruitful interactions among the approaches.

can include well-defined syntheses, among the strongly defined research communities in our field, reflexive understandings of theorists of their theories will flourish. Third, contemporary comparativists can get the most out of such a dialogue by appreciating the historical context of the development of social theory. Finally, contemporary comparativists can also gain from such a dialogue by recognizing that the approaches offer a critical commentary on the challenges of modernity which, in turn, helps us appreciate the significance of rationalist, culturalist, and structuralist thought.

REFERENCES

Abrams, Philip. 1982. *Historical Sociology*. Ithaca: Cornell University Press.

American Political Science Review. 1995. Symposium on "The Qualitative-Quantitative Disputation." *American Political Science Review* 89:454-81.

Baldwin, David A., ed. 1993. *Neorealism and Neoliberalism: The Contemporary Debate*. New York: Columbia University Press.

Bates, Robert H. 1989. *Beyond the Miracle of the Market: The Political Economy of Agrarian Development in Kenya*. Cambridge: Cambridge University Press.

Becker, Gary S. 1976. *The Economic Approach to Human Behavior*. Chicago: University of Chicago Press.

Bloom, Allan. 1987. *The Closing of the American Mind*. New York: Touchstone

Brenner, Robert. 1976. "Agrarian Class Structure and Economic Development in Preindustrial Europe." *Past and Present* 70:30-75.

———. 1982. "The Agrarian Roots of European Capitalism." *Past and Present* 97:16-113.

Calhoun, Craig. 1995. *Critical Social Theory: Culture, History, and the Challenge of Difference*. Oxford: Blackwell.

Camic, Charles (1989). "Structure after 50 Years: The Anatomy of a Charter." *American Journal of Sociology* 95:38-107.

Elster, Jon. 1989. *Nuts and Bolts for the Social Sciences*. New York: Cambridge University Press.

Garrett, Geoffrey, and Barry R. Weingast. 1993. "Ideas, Interests, and Institutions: Constructing the European Community's Internal Market." In Judith Goldstein and Robert O. Keohane, eds., *Ideas and Foreign Policy: Beliefs, Institutions, and Political Change*. Ithaca: Cornell University Press.

Hawthorn, Geoffrey. 1976. *Enlightenment and Despair: A History of Sociology*. Cambridge: Cambridge University Press.

Heclo, Hugh. 1994. "Ideas, Interests, and Institutions." In Lawrence C. Dodd and Calvin Jillson, eds., *The Dynamics of American Politics: Approaches and Interpretations*. Boulder, CO: Westview.

Hennis, Wilhelm. 1983. "Max Weber's 'Central Question.'" *Economy and Society* 12:135-80.

Hirschman, Albert O. 1977. *The Passions and the Interests: Political Arguments for Capitalism Before Its Triumph*. Princeton: Princeton University Press.

Inglehart, Ronald. 1990. *Culture Shift in Advanced Industrial Society*. Princeton: Princeton University Press.

Katzenstein, Peter, ed. 1978. *Between Power and Plenty.* Madison: University of Wisconsin Press.

Kegley, Charles W., Jr., ed. 1995. *Controversies in International Relations Theory: Realism and the Neoliberal Challenge.* New York: St. Martin's Press.

Keohane, Robert O., ed. 1986. *Neorealism and Its Critics.* New York: Columbia University Press.

Lakatos, Imre. 1970. "Falsification and the Methodology of Scientific Research Programs." In Imre Lakatos and Alan Musgrave, eds., *Criticism and the Growth of Knowledge.* Cambridge: Cambridge University Press.

Lichbach, Mark Irving. 1995. *The Rebel's Dilemma.* Ann Arbor, MI: University of Michigan Press.

———. 1996. *The Cooperator's Dilemma.* Ann Arbor: University of Michigan Press.

Lichbach, Mark, and Adam Seligman. 1996. "Theories of Revolution and the Structure-Action Problem in the Social Sciences." Unpublished manuscript.

Little, Daniel. 1991. *Varieties of Social Explanation: An Introduction to the Philosophy of Science.* Boulder, CO: Westview.

———. 1993. "On the Scope and Limits of Generalization in the Social Sciences." *Synthese* 97 (November):183-207.

Lloyd, Christopher, 1986. *Explanation in Social History.* Oxford: Basil Blackwell.

Mills, C. Wright. 1959. *The Sociological Imagination.* London: Oxford University Press.

Moore, Barrington. 1966. *Social Origins of Dictatorship and Democracy: Lord and Peasant in the Making of the Modern World.* Boston: Beacon Press.

Nelson, Benjamin. 1974. "Max Weber's 'Author's Introduction' (1920): A Master Clue to His Main Aims." *Sociological Inquiry* 44 (No. 4):269-78.

Nisbet, Robert A. 1966. *The Sociological Tradition.* New York: Basic Books.

Parsons, Talcott. 1937. *The Structure of Social Action.* New York: Free Press.

Popper, Karl J. 1965. *Conjectures and Refutations: The Growth of Scientific Knowledge.* New York: Harper Torchbooks.

Rogowski, Ronald. 1995. "The Role of Theory and Anomaly in Social-Scientific Inference." *American Political Science Review* 89:467-70.

Schelling, Thomas C. 1978. *Micromotives and Macrobehavior.* New York: Norton.

Schroeder, Ralph. 1992. *Max Weber and the Sociology of Culture.* Newbury Park, CA: Sage.

Scott, James C. 1985. *Weapons of the Weak: Everyday Forms of Peasant Resistance.* New Haven: Yale University Press.

Sculli, David, and Dean Gerstein (1985). "Social Theory and Talcott Parsons in the 1980s." *Annual Review of Sociology* 11:369-87.

Seligman, Adam B. 1992. *The Idea of Civil Society.* New York: Free Press.

Seligman, Adam, and Mark Lichbach. 1996. "Revolution and Relegitimation: The Making of Social Order in France and the Netherlands." Unpublished manuscript.

Selznick, Philip. 1992. *The Moral Commonwealth: Social Theory and the Promise of Community.* Berkeley: University of California Press.

Skocpol, Theda. 1979. *States and Social Revolutions: A Comparative Analysis of France, Russia and China.* Cambridge: Cambridge University Press.

Swidler, Ann. 1973. "The Concept of Rationality in the Work of Max Weber." *Sociological Inquiry* 43 (No. 1):35-42.

Tembruck, Friedrich H. 1980. "The Problem of Thematic Unity in the Works of Max Weber." *British Journal of Sociology* 31:316-51.

Waltz, Kenneth N. (1979). *Theory of International Politics.* Reading, MA: Addison-Wesley.

Weber, Max. 1946. *From Max Weber: Essays in Sociology.* Trans. and ed. Hans H. Gerth and C. Wright Mills. New York: Oxford University Press.

———. 1949. *The Methodology of the Social Sciences.* Trans. and ed. Edward A. Shils and Henry A. Finch. New York: Free Press.

———. 1951. *The Religion of China: Confucianism and Taoism.* Trans. Hans H. Gerth. New York: Free Press.

———. 1952. *Ancient Judaism.* Trans. and ed. Hans H. Gerth and Don Martindale. New York: Free Press.

———. [1923] 1961. *General Economic History.* Trans. F. H. Knight. New York: Collier Books.

———. [1924] 1968. *Economy and Society.* Two Volumes. Berkeley: University of California Press.

———. [1904-05] 1985. *The Protestant Ethic and the Spirit of Capitalism.* Trans. Talcott Parsons. London: Unwin Paperbacks.

———. [1896] 1988. *The Agrarian Sociology of Ancient Civilizations.* Trans. R. I. Frank. London: Verso.

———. [1958] 1992. *The Religion of India: The Sociology of Hinduism and Buddhism.* Trans. and ed. Hans H. Gerth and Don Martindale. New Delhi: Munshiram Manoharlal Publishers.

Wendt, Alex. Forthcoming. *Social Theory of International Politics.*

World Politics. 1995. Symposium on "The Role of Theory in Comparative Politics." *World Politics* (October):1-49.

10

REFORMULATING EXPLANATORY STANDARDS AND ADVANCING THEORY IN COMPARATIVE POLITICS*

Alan S. Zuckerman

And if you ask me how, wherefore, for what reason? I will answer you: Why, by chance! By the merest chance, as things do happen, lucky and unlucky, terrible or tender, important, or unimportant; and even things which are neither, things so completely neutral in character that you would wonder why they do happen at all if you didn't know that they, too, carry in their insignificance the seeds of further incalculable chances (Joseph Conrad, cited in Kellert 1993: 49).

[U]nforeseen catastrophes are never the consequence of the effect, if you prefer, of a single motive, of *a* cause singular; but they are rather like a whirlpool, a cyclonic point of depression in the consciousness of the world, towards which a whole multitude of causes have contributed (Gadda [1957] 1984: 5).

The Danube does not exist, that is as clear as day. The Danube is not something, not the water, not the molecules, not the dangerous currents, but the *totality*: the Danube is the form. The form is not some mantle beneath which something still more serious lies hidden (Esterhazy 1994: 24).

*Earlier versions of this chapter benefited greatly from the critical comments of Mark Lichbach and and Marc Ross and the encouragement of Roger Cobb. I am very pleased to thank them and to free them of any responsibility for any of its flaws.

In comparative politics, theory seeks explanations for sets of political phenomena. The standard forms of explanation include covering laws and causal accounts. No matter their generalized acceptance within the field, each is characterized by significant deficiencies, so that together and separately they provide unreasonable standards for assessing explanations. Furthermore, nomological and causal explanations share an ontology that includes linear and frequently determined relationships among variables, clocklike patterns, parity in the size of cause and effect, and microprocesses as determinants of structures. Both utilize point predictions as the means of testing explanatory hypotheses. The successes of theories in comparative politics that share these conceptualizations of reality notwithstanding, there is strong reason to view the political world as containing nonlinear relationships among variables, probabilistic outcomes and structures, aperiodic systems, unpredictable phenomena, chance factors, and open-ended possibilities. There is reason, therefore, to propose standards for explanation in comparative politics that accommodate these complex patterns. As the explanatory requirements change, fresh combinations of ideas appear. Assumptions, modes, and levels of analysis, and theoretical principles may be drawn from more than one research school. Process models that apply to particular cases join cross-national comparisons; complex statistical techniques join methods that assume linear relationships among variables; analyses join individual and structural variables. New theories emerge, and the ability to explain political phenomena advances.

THE STANDARD FORMS OF EXPLANATION IN COMPARATIVE POLITICS: COVERING LAWS AND CAUSAL ACCOUNTS

Scientific understanding distinguishes between description and explanation and provides pride of place to efforts to know why the world works as it does, not the mere presentation of information about it. Consider Hempel's classic formulation of the difference:

> A scientific explanation may be regarded as an answer to a why question, such as "Why do the planets move in elliptical orbits with the sun at one focus?" "Why does the moon look much larger when it nears the horizon than when it is high in the sky?" ... "Why did Hitler go to war against Russia?" (Hempel 1965: 334).

"What" questions detail the case at hand, specifying that the planets move in elliptical orbits, the size of the moon varies by its location in the heavens, or that Hitler went to war against Russia. "Standard philosophical accounts characterize scientific understanding as arising from an accumulation of questions that answer 'Why questions' (sometimes expanded to include 'How possibly questions')" (Kellert 1993: 81). For those who seek scientific understanding, explanation trumps description.

Explanations in science require standards that assess their adequacy. During the past several decades, covering law and causal theories have defined the forms of acceptable explanations.[1] Nomological explanations utilize covering laws, demonstrating that the explanandum – the event or process under examination – had to occur, in the sense that it is a particular manifestation that follows logically from a general principle.[2] These general laws "cover" the particular events, phenomena, or decisions that are being explained. They may come in two forms: universal principles (general laws) that apply uniformly and statistical laws that adhere to a specified and high degree. In principle, these laws are not bound to particular domains; they are not limited by place or time. Note that no causal mechanism links explanandum and explanans. Rather, successful explanations subsume particular events and decisions under general principles. Causal accounts supply "knowledge of the hidden mechanism, causal or other, that produces the phenomena that we seek to explain" (Salmon 1989: 135).[3] Following a stream of criticism initiated by Hume, most causal arguments note the existence of factors that putatively stand for this relationship – constant conjunction, temporal precedence, and nonspuriousness. Here, dependent and independent or treatment variables, effects and causes, are related such that the latter bring about, influence, produce – to list several synonyms – the former. *"The paradigmatic assertion in causal relationships is that the manipulation of a cause will result in the manipulation of an effect"* (Cook and Campbell 1979: 36, italics in original). Variation in one or more factors causes change in the dependent phenomena. Explanations based on covering laws and causal accounts have long defined the set of acceptable forms of scientific understanding.

The established goals of comparative politics reflect these standards. As comparativists propose cross-national generalizations, they posit covering laws. As they test hypotheses, they seek to formalize explanatory claims as universal principles. Recall three well-known accounts that helped to establish the primary objective of comparative politics:

The pivotal assumption of this analysis is that social research, including comparative inquiry, should and can lead to general statements about social

---

[1] For recent surveys, see Kellert (1993); Kitcher (1989); Salmon (1989); Sklar (1993); Woodward (1989).

[2] In some forms, this logical implication is law-like but not determinative and in others the outcome is phrased as a determined result of the general principles. See Kellert (1993: 96-112) for a review of the distinction. Hempel formulates the general principle: "The explanation here outlined may be regarded as an argument to the effect that the phenomenon to be explained, *the explanandum phenomenon,* was to be expected in virtue of certain explanatory facts. These fall into two groups: (i) particular facts and (ii) uniformities expressible by means of general laws" (Hempel 1965: 336, italics in original).

[3] Sklar poses the questions whose affirmative answers justify causal explanations: "Isn't it the case, it is argued, that what makes one event explain another is the fact that the first event caused the other, or constituted part of the mechanism by which the other was made to occur? Mustn't we take some notion of causation or mechanism, then, as the core ingredient in explanation, and not the notion of the subsumption of events under patterns of lawlike or statistical regularity?" (1993: 141).

phenomena. This assumption implies that human or social behavior can be explained in terms of general laws established by observation (Przeworski and Teune 1970: 4).

[Propositions] that would be of explanatory and predictive importance would be based on the fundamental propositions that the state of the system at any time t_1 is determined by its state at some other time t_0 and by all the events which occur on the boundary during the time interval t_0-t_1. The state of the system is described in terms of the determinate sequence of structure-mechanism and process-functions (Holt and Richardson 1970: 29, citing Holt 1967: 86-7).

Why compare? ... [C]omparisons *control* – they control (verify or falsify) whether generalizations hold across the cases to which they apply (Sartori 1994: 15, reaffirming a principle established in Sartori 1970, italics in original).

This position defines comparative politics as the effort to establish the empirical bases of universal laws, or at least law-like propositions, of politics, which apply to a potentially unlimited set of precisely defined cases. King, Keohane, and Verba's recent methodological guide to comparative research in political science reflects a stream of research that affirms the centrality of causal explanations.[4]

Causal theories are designed to show the causes of a phenomenon or set of phenomena. Whether originally conceived as deductive or inductive, any theory includes an interrelated set of causal hypotheses. Each hypothesis specifies a posited relationship between variables that creates observable implications: if the specified explanatory variables take on certain values, other specified values are predicted for the dependent variable. Testing or evaluating any hypothesis requires causal inference (King, Keohane, and Verba 1994: 99-100, italics in original).

Here, causal inference seeks to specify the results of the absence or presence or variation in an amount of one or more explanatory factors on the outcome or dependent variable. Establishing a *"counterfactual* conditional is the essence behind this definition of causality" (1994: 77, italics in original). The two standards differ in the extent to which theories need to include universal principles, apply to large-scale domains, and include causal accounts.

Comparative politics enhances scientific understanding in political science in two ways. Analyzing across nations and points of time tests general propositions that stand as covering laws or law-like statements about political phenomena. Research helps to establish the boundaries of the general propositions and the theories from which the hypotheses derive. As comparativists examine different nations and points of time, they vary the settings, offering a mode of counterfactual

---

[4]King, Keohane, and Verba cite a stream of work in the philosophy of science on causal explanations. They omit discussion of the substantial body of scholarship that centers its debates around covering laws and the contrasts between the two forms of explanation. Here, and in many other of their assumptions and methodological recommendations, they resemble Cook and Campbell (1979).

analysis. It is not surprising that comparative politics developed within political science when nomological and causal accounts became the standards for explanation.

The centrality of covering law explanations and causal explanations shines through the research schools in comparative politics. Lichbach and Levi in this volume[5] associate rational choice theory and the search for covering laws. Riker, a founding father of the rationalist school, establishes the principle: "To explain an event is to subsume it under a covering law, that, in turn, is encased in theory." Insisting that causal accounts never adequately distinguish between the "necessary" and the "sufficient" and the "coincidental" and the "irrelevant," Riker emphasizes that, "explanation, just like prediction, needs a covering law" (Riker 1990: 167). As Lichbach's, Katznelson's, and Migdal's chapters in this volume affirm, classic structuralist accounts combine covering law and causal explanations. The realism inherent in structuralist analyses of revolution – from Marx through Skocpol (1979) and Goldstone (1991) – rests on a claim to have matched theoretical concepts with the elements of the political world, to have discovered natural types. Here, abstract concepts become political actors, justifying the merger of both forms of explanations. At the heart of the divisions among the culturalists is a fundamental disagreement over the nature of explanation. Even as Lichbach associates this research school with interpretive explanations, Ross's and Barnes's chapters survey culturalist studies that search for covering laws and causal accounts. Indeed, because some interpretivists seek only to understand an actor's goals, eschewing the need for theory or causal mechanisms, they move their scholarship outside the realm of scientific explanations (see Geertz [1973] for a classic example). In comparative politics, as in political science and all disciplines that claim to be science, covering law and causal explanations have long stood as the standards for scientific understanding.

No matter the formal acceptance of these requirments in comparative politics, covering laws and causal accounts provide inappropriate and inadequate standards for scientific understanding. The search for nomological explanations has bedeviled political scientists, leading some to suggest that scientific understanding is an illusion (see, for example, Almond and Genco [1977]). Efforts to establish universal principles and causal claims have forced comparativists to emphasize questions of methodology – especially sample size and case selection – rather than issues that relate more directly to theory and the standards of explanation. The relative dearth of covering laws and widely accepted causal explanations in comparative politics derive from more than the search for the right variables to be included in their theories, the appropriate measures for the variables, and the selection of the right cases for comparisons.[6] In order to advance the ability to explain political phenomena, there is reason to reformulate the standards for scientific understanding in comparative politics.

---

[5]Levi's essay also displays efforts by some rationalists to provide causal explanations, in the form of analytic narratives.

[6]Sartori (1994: 27, 31) maintains that the field has displayed too few examples of analytic successes, locating the field's problems with the misuse of the comparative method. Here, I present an argument that focuses on the standards for explanation and the nature of theory.

EXPANDING THE NATURE OF SCIENTIFIC UNDERSTANDING IN COMPARATIVE POLITICS

The widespread appreciation of nomological and causal explanations notwithstanding, there is reason to expand the models of scientific understanding used in comparative politics. Each of the standard forms of explanations has deficiencies. Some of these are long-standing, appearing in the work of philosophers of science. Recent work in various scientific disciplines uncovers additional deficiencies in the standard epistemology and ontology. Furthermore, and of direct relevance to the field of comparative politics, the slow development of theory in this area of political science derives in part from the gap between the formal goals of establishing causal accounts and covering laws and the need to describe and explain events, decisions, and processes that do not easily lend themselves to covering law and causal arguments.

FLAWS IN THE STANDARD FORMS OF SCIENTIFIC UNDERSTANDING

Philosophers of science have identified flaws in nomological explanations. Perhaps the most obvious problem, and for many the most telling, is the strong intuition that explanation requires establishing causal relationships. Covering laws, therefore, do not explain, because they eschew causal claims.[7] Kitcher (1989: 411-13) summarizes four additional objections:

1. In practice, scientists accept many statements as scientific explanations even though they do not meet the stated requirements.
2. No one has proposed a satisfactory analysis of the notion of a scientific law, especially the distinction between accidental generalizations and laws.
3. It is easy to provide examples of arguments that fit the form of the covering law but that cannot possibly explain the problem of asymmetry.
4. Hempel's account of statistical laws requires probabilities that are so high as to make them too exceptional to be useful.

Because this mode of scientific understanding displays significant deficiencies, explanations in science need not include covering laws.[8]

Philosophers of science have also laid bare weaknesses in causal explanations. Sklar (1993: 141-3) outlines the difficulties of specifying what is related in the causal claim. He asks whether they are "events, states of affairs, facts, or universals" and then draws attention to a host of long-standing problems. To those who defend the intuitive reality of causes, he returns attention to Hume's fundamental criticism.

---

[7]Salmon (especially 1984) develops the argument that scientific explanations require causal mechanisms. See also the essay published in 1989, in which he allows for other forms of scientific understanding.
[8]See Sklar (1993: 140-1) for a similar review.

> But the absence from phenomenal experience of "causation itself," as opposed to constant conjunction, spatio-temporal contiguity, temporal precedence, and so on – the absence that Hume so clearly noted – does present a group of puzzles that the causal primitivist must resolve (Sklar 1993: 143).

Stated more generally, all efforts to establish a causal relationship presuppose a theory that provides the conceptual language; without a theory there can be no causal explanation. At the same time, in the absence of randomly assigned control and treatment groups, there is no certain method to establish causal connections: "But, of course, the trouble with counterfactuals is that you cannot hold fixed *all* the circumstances of the antecedent while making the antecedent (which is actually false) come true" (Kitcher 1989: 473, italics in original). The absence of any one factor means that the control group and the test group differ with regard to other factors as well, confounding the search for the counterfactual condition. (Kitcher 1989: 473-5; see also Lieberson 1985: 42; Sklar 1993: 142; and Mohr 1996). Furthermore, the focus on a "microreductive causal theory" may stand in the way of developing explanatory theories that examine more macroscopic patterns and regularities (Woodward 1989: 365). Just as it may be possible to explain without covering laws, scientific understanding need not include causal propositions.

ALTERNATIVE FORMS OF SCIENTIFIC UNDERSTANDING

Recent work in chaos and complexity theory answers How questions, not the Why questions that structure nomological and causal arguments. In theories of complex dynamical systems,

> the central puzzling questions include How does extremely complicated behavior come to occur in nature? How does it happen that some physical behavior is completely unpredictable? How do orderly patterns persist amid apparent randomness? (Kellert 1993: 81)

Chaos theory offers process models in lieu of the standard forms of explanation. This approach provides scientific understanding, "by constructing, elaborating, and applying simple dynamical *models*" (Kellert 1993: 85, italics in original).

> [L]ooking at models better describes what chaos theory employs to provide understanding. Better, that is, than the philosophical accounts which portray science as proceeding by methods which are microreductionist, deductivist, and synchronic (Kellert 1993: 86).

> Chaos theory does not provide predictions of quantitative detail but of qualitative features; it does not reveal hidden causal processes but displays mechanisms; and it does not yield law-like necessity but reveals patterns (Kellert 1993: 96).

Process models explain by locating the underlying regularities displayed by the observed patterns. Indeed, as results are presented in graphical displays, the beauty of the patterns may sometimes represent the strength of the analysis (C. Brown 1995: 27). These regularities do not provide point predictions for any one event, and they do not refer to causal processes. Also, narratives do not suffice; analysis displays high levels of technical precision and mathematical sophistication (C. Brown 1995, T. Brown 1995, and the other essays in Kiel and Elliot 1995; Kellert 1993; Kontopolous 1993). Chaos theory and other efforts to analyze complex dynamical systems provide alternative standards for scientific understanding.

General principles that serve as universal propositions and the description of the specific instances to be explained require levels of precision that are so high as to deny the need for general laws in the explanation of complex changing systems:

> [C]overing law explanations could only be useful for experimental systems, or systems so simple that they approach experimental systems in the paucity of their dynamic interactions" (Dyke 1990: 379).

The prediction of future states is not an appropriate criterion for the adequacy of scientific understanding. Because relevant conditions necessarily differ across cases and because fundamental changes can occur at any point in time, the ability to control for the presence of alternative causal factors is limited. "The linear, billiard ball conception of 'causation' has to be re-examined, and its hegemony as explanatory pattern of choice reassessed" (Dyke 1990: 377). Because aggregate patterns may not be reduced to atomistic parts, explanations need also to examine holistic patterns and interactions. Processes are distinct from causal accounts and do not require covering laws; other forms of scientific understanding apply.

It follows that explanations in each and all of the sciences need include neither covering laws nor causal accounts. Both offer unreasonable standards. Note that the claim is *not* that nomological and causal explanations are inherently impossible. Rather, they offer criteria that are rarely met. Note too that the claim is *not* that in the absence of these standards, there are no criteria by which to assess explanations. In practice and in principle, scientific understanding requires and proceeds with other ways to determine the adequacy of an explanation. Scientific understanding requires "knowledge that brings some kind of credentials with it" (Meehl 1986: 317; see also Overman 1988; Zuckerman 1991). All explanations are assessed by the balance between reasons for certainty and doubt about their claims concerning theoretical scope, logical rigor, and empirical accuracy. Furthermore, if neither covering laws nor causal accounts serve as adequate models for scientific understanding, there is reason to expand the criteria that establish the adequacy of an explanatory account. In the next sections of this chapter, I will propose more useful standards for explanations in comparative politics.

EXPANDING ASSUMPTIONS ABOUT THE NATURE OF REALITY

Some of the deficiencies of the standard modes of explanation derive from their limited conception of reality. Causal and nomological explanations apply only to simple and determinate patterns, and they assume that reality rests on smaller, more basic phenomena. They envision a world composed of linear relationships among variables, parity in the size of cause and effect, recurrent patterns over time, and the fundamental insignificance of chance happenings. They share the principle that we live in a world of determined patterns, such that processes have defined ends. Analyses of complex dynamical systems, however, call attention to the limitations of this ontology.

> Chaos and quantum theory lead us to ... a vision of the universe as a con-
> geries of interrelated but open possibilities, foaming forth in its infinitude.
> Determinism is not so much proven false but rendered meaningless (Kellert
> 1993: 73-4).

These forms of explanation cannot easily serve as standards for the analysis of a world of nonlinear relationships among phenomena: no necessary parity between size and effect; sensitive dependence on initial conditions; the possibility of change at any point in time; open-ended processes; and the presence of chance as a substantive part of processes and their explanations–characteristics of an ontology associated with the chaos theory and other modes of analyzing complex dynamical systems (see especially Dyke 1990; Glass and Mackey 1988; Huckfeldt 1990; Kellert 1993; Kontopolous 1993; Lieberson 1985; Richter 1986; Waldrop 1992; Woodward 1989). The widespread acceptance of the metaphor that describes the world as a clock symbolizes research that examines recurrent patterns among atomistic phenomena, overlooking complex nonlinear formations.[9]

Although the precise utility of chaos and complexity theory in comparative politics still remains to be demonstrated, there are obvious parallels between political phenomena and the world described in these new fields of study.[10] Comparativists in particular, and political scientists in general, analyze a world of complex interactions among variables, in which historical patterns constrain subsequent decisions and events, simple direct and deterministic relations are infrequent, important phenomena are frequently unpredictable, and different levels of analysis stand independent of each other, so that theories of individuals and structures address different questions. In comparative politics, research explores a political world that is not encompassed by the simple ontology of causal and nomological explanations.

---

[9]The contrasting images of clocks and clouds are recurrent themes in the criticisms of the standard models of scientific understanding. Glass and Mackey's (1988) application of the metaphor to biological phenomena stands apart from Almond and Genco's (1977) presentation for political science. Both argue that much of what their fields study does not resemble the recurrent patterns of clocks. Whereas Glass and Mackey maintain that biology requires scientific understanding of new forms, Almond and Genco draw the conclusion that political phenomena are immune to scientific understanding. Archer (1995) details how ontology affects methodology and the mode of explanation.

[10]For discussions of this issue, see C. Brown 1995; T. Brown 1996; Dyke 1990; Huckfeldt 1990; Kontopolous 1993; McCloskey 1991; Reisch 1991, 1995; Roth 1992; Roth and Rickman 1995; Shermer 1995. See also Schofield (1995) for an effort that begins to explore the links between rational choice and chaos theories.

COMPLEX POLITICAL PHENOMENA

Research on political and social structures has uncovered fluid and complex patterns. Ethnicity, social class, and political diversity have characterized European and North American societies over the past century. Those who share location in divisions that cut wide swaths through a society, like occupation, language, religion, and ethnicity, vary in the extent to which they live near each other; go to the same schools; choose each other as friends and spouses; and join together to vote for the same party, to march, and to riot.[11] Sometimes, social class and ethnic ties reinforce each other, strengthening the likelihood that a set of persons will interact frequently and peacefully. Sometimes these ties intersect, dividing members of ethnic categories along lines of occupation, residence, and education, and separating members of class categories along lines of dialect, language, religion, and origin. Always directly influencing voting decisions, ties to political parties may also affect the ability to obtain jobs, educational opportunities, and friends. Frequently, these political ties cut additional lines through the social divisions, organizing subsets of persons into blocs of voters and activists while separating them from others in the ethnic and class categories who do not have these political ties. Sometimes, social class, ethnicity, and politics overlap; sometimes they do not; always the extent of the overlap varies (Zuckerman 1975, 1982; Zuckerman et al. 1994, 1995 elaborate these points).

Recent work in the study of political attitudes displays the stochastic nature of people's political cognitions and evaluations. People hold varying considerations about their political preferences. "[A]ttitudes are ambivalent; each of us carries around competing considerations. Each citizen has a range of views, depending upon which consideration is consulted, not a single fixed one, and that range tends to be large" (Stimson 1995: 183, drawing on the work of Zaller 1992 and Zaller and Feldman 1992; see also Alvarez and Franklin 1994; Kinder 1983). In a single survey, similar questions frequently elicit divergent responses, and views on political issues frequently do not match formal ideologies. Over time, people offer different responses to the same questions asked in surveys and posed on election ballots. "From Zaller's ambivalence notion we are nearly all part racist, part sexist, *and* nearly all part believers in equality. We carry around considerations that can push us in either direction, finally 'fixed' only in the grave. All of these views are genuine" (Stimson 1995: 183, italics in original). Political attitudes are complex, variable, and probabilistic. Hence, explanatory questions need to examine the probabilities that accompany phenomena.

Nonlinearities characterize interactions among citizens and the people around them. Encounters with other people and the individual's location in the

---

[11]The classic source for this position is Max Weber's criticism of Marx's concept of social class (Gerth and Mills 1958: 180-95). For recent examples that develop the theme that social class and ethnicity are best analyzed as variables, not concepts treated as natural types, see Brass (1985); Katznelson (1986); Kocka (1986); Reddy (1987); Yancey, Eriksen, and Juliani (1977); Zolberg (1986); Zuckerman (1982, 1989, 1995).

social structure strongly influence how people perceive, evaluate, and take part in politics. As the social contexts vary, so do the opinions held, the calculations made, and the behavior that derives from the interactions of individuals and their friends, families, workmates, and neighbors (see for example C. Brown 1995; T. Brown 1996; Huckfeldt and Sprague 1995).[12] These claims apply to the analysis of electoral decisions and political preferences over time. They imply:

1. The probability of displaying anchored political preferences – as measured by casting ballots for a political party at one election and in adjacent elections, presenting coherent policy preferences, and retaining the same views on a single issue or set of issues – is directly affected by the rate of interaction with persons who share the same political views and whether or not the citizen retains the same location in the social structure.
2. The effects of these structural variables on political preferences will hold, even after controlling for psychological variables that characterize each person (Zuckerman, Valentino, and Zuckerman 1994; Zuckerman, Kotler-Berkowitz, and Swaine in process).

The influence of social contexts and discussion networks is not simple and straightforward but complex and interactive. Interdependent citizens learn about politics from those with whom they discuss issues, candidates, and events, and they choose their discussion partners from a set of persons that is powerfully limited by how they live their lives. Citizens are rewarded and punished for political viewpoints that agree or disagree with the preferences and understandings of those whom they encounter. No matter the extent of interdependence and no matter the amount of bias and overlap in the sources of information, no structural determinism applies. People always screen, interpret, and apply the information. "Rational citizens rationally decide. Social and economic structures, accidentally but nevertheless systematically, mold homogeneity by repeatedly triggering individual reassessments of political beliefs" (Huckfeldt and Sprague 1995: 51). As a result, processes of preference formation and decisions about political behavior are doubly stochastic, as opportunities and structures that surround individuals vary for any one person over time and across persons, and as citizens select and accept the information that reaches them. Furthermore, because social contexts do not determine discussion networks, information and preferences move through communities, forming public opinion that is more than the sum of individual private views. The multiple levels of analysis uncover the interplay between voluntarism and structured opportunities that defines the paradox of democratic politics (see Huckfeldt and Sprague 1995 for a full statement; see also Huckfeldt and Sprague 1987, 1988, 1991, 1992, 1993; C. Brown 1995;

---

[12]Sniderman's (1993) review of the recent literature on public opinion displays the extent to which these studies examine isolated individuals, free of social context.

T. Brown, 1996). In turn, there is reason to deny the claim that explanation requires the reduction of aggregate processes to microphenomena. Rather, it requires multiple, independent, and interactive levels of analysis.

The principle of sensitive dependence on initial conditions finds its parallel in long-standing efforts in comparative politics to show how the formative characteristics of structures and decisions constrain subsequent processes and events. Lipset and Rokkan's generalization exemplifies this principle:

> {T}he party systems of the 1960's reflect, with but few significant exceptions, the cleavage structures of the 1920's. This is a crucial characteristic of Western competitive politics in the age of "high mass consumption": the party alternatives, and in remarkably many cases the party organizations, are older than the majorities of the national electorates (Lipset and Rokkan 1967: 50, italics in original).

Patterns formed at the start of competitive mass politics endure, they maintain, constraining electoral processes in each country. This claim has guided subsequent research (see for example Bartolini and Mair 1990; Dalton, Flanagan, and Beck 1984; Rokkan 1970; Rose and Urwin 1970; Shamir 1984). Panebianco applies the general principle to his theory of political parties:

> The underlying idea in this attempt was to reaffirm a classical intuition of sociology, in particular Weberian, concerning the importance of founding moments of institutions.... The organization will certainly undergo modifications and even profound changes in interacting throughout its life cycle with the continually changing environment. However, the crucial political choices made by its founding fathers, the first struggles for organizational control, and the way in which the organization was formed, will leave an indelible mark (Panebianco 1988: xiii).

Political patterns at any given point in time – whether aggregate results of elections or the organizational characteristics, ideological claims, and coalition strategies of political parties – are conditioned by forms established at the point of origin.

The confluence of recent work on the emergence of political protest and revolutions details the inherent unpredictability of some political phenomena. Lichbach offers a broad-scale answer composed of many precise solutions to the "rebel's dilemma," the problem of overcoming the calculations that make taking part in collective dissent nonrational. The unpredictability of critical aspects of collective political protests denies the possibility of a general theory of political protest and rebellion:

> The results of this book belie such a simple story. A general theory of why people rebel will fail for one simple reason: aggregate levels and particular outbreaks of collective dissent are largely unpredictable (Lichbach 1995: 281, italics in original).

Kuran surveys structural, interest based, and relative-deprivation theories as well as a host of historical and contemporary accounts of revolution, concluding that the initial outburst is always unpredictable.

[P]redictive failure is entirely consistent with calculated purposeful action. Underlying an explosive shift in public sentiment are multitudes of individual decisions to switch political allegiance, each undertaken in response to changing incentives. So just as a failure to predict a rainstorm does not imply that the clouds obey no physical laws, a failure to predict some revolution does not imply individual irrationality (Kuran 1991: 45).

Approaching the problem of political protest from a structuralist perspective, Tarrow too notes the frequent surprise associated with emergence of collective dissent: "Protest cycles are often touched off by unpredictable events" (Tarrow 1995: 93). Protest events are members of a set of political phenomenon, whose emergence is affected by chance occurrences.[13]

More generally, chance factors influence social and political patterns. Drawing on the implications of chaos theory, Ruelle states the general principle:

Historical determinism must thus be corrected (at least) by the remark that some historically unpredictable events or choices have important long-term consequences. I think that more in fact can be said. I think that *history systematically generates unpredictable events with important long-term consequences* (Ruelle 1991: 90, italics in original).

Boudon applies the Cournot Effect, "the convergence of two independent causal series" (Boudon 1986: 175), as he argues for the importance of chance in social analysis (see also Mandelbaum 1987). Here, the classic example is the falling slate that stuns the passer-by. However one may be able to account for each independent event, the slate slipping off the roof and heading for the ground and the person's decision to walk next to the building, the meeting of person and slate occurs by chance.[14] Scharpf echoes the principle claim:

For my own understanding, I find it useful to conceptualize real-world events as "intersections" of processes and factors whose separate "logics" may be captured by explanatory theories, but whose interaction may only be accessible to historical description (Scharpf 1987: 9, in Kontopolous 1993: 150).

Boudon develops the general point:

Chance is therefore not *nothing*. It is a particular *form* that sets of cause/effects linkings as *perceived by a real observer* can take on. Some of them have a total form of order (the match causes the fire that causes the fire brigade to arrive). Others have a partial form of order (the match causes a fire and also causes the person holding it to cry out in pain). Others contain contingent links (the series "A causes B, which causes C" occurs at the same time as "P causes Q, which

---

[13]The importance of unpredicted and unpredictable events appears as well in the analysis of cabinet coalitions. Browne, Frendreis, and Gleiber (1984; 1986a; 1986b) combine a stochastic factor into their analysis of cabinet stability and duration.

[14]See also Mohr's discussion of the relationship between "encounters" and explanation in political science (1996, especially pp. 25-7).

causes R") but it is impossible to decide whether the synchronization is really between B and P, B and Q or C and Q. It is therefore impossible to tell whether event BP, BQ or CQ will necessarily be brought about. And the three events can have very different consequences (Boudon 1986: 178, italics in original).

Note that in this formulation, chance is not "statistical noise," the inevitable consequence of errors in measurement that accompany statistical analyses; it is not "unmeasured variables," phenomena for which there are no adequate indicators, that may be categorized in the "error term" of statistical analyses; and it is not a benchmark against which explanatory claims are assessed. Chance, in this view, is an inherent part of the political world. As a result, there is need to include chance in scientific understandings in comparative politics.

COMPLEX PATTERNS AND THE RESEARCH SCHOOLS IN COMPARATIVE POLITICS

Consider some of the implications of this ontology for the research schools in comparative politics. A political world, in which political preferences are necessarily stochastic, at any one point in time and over time, and in which there are probabilistic relationships between the preferences of any one person and the members of peoples' social networks, raises questions about the ontology implicitly used by rational choice theory: How do rational calculations proceed when preferences and options are fluid and goals unclear? A political world in which structures are inherently probabilistic and in which their effects vary at one point in time and over time raises questions about the ontology that underpins structural analysis. No matter the sensitivity to initial forms, how do probabilistic institutions constrain decisions and outcomes?

Core assumptions of rationalist and structuralist analyses limit the analytic utility of each research school.

> Microeconomic theory depends on the claim that free trading at the margin by rational traders will yield a well-behaved "Paretian" bargaining locus. This in turn presupposes that the bargaining surface has some *very* stringent mathematical properties. The moment nonlinearities, in the simplest case interaction effects, are introduced, the required mathematical properties of the bargaining surface can no longer plausibly be assumed. Indeed, the surfaces very quickly develop strange attractors and catastrophes. The claim that microeconomic laws hold *ceteris paribus* is then an extremely weak one, depending on radical measures to establish linearity by force (Dyke 1990: 380-1, italics in original; see also Nelson 1990 for additional criticisms of the microeconomic bases of rational choice theory).

Game theory cannot be easily used to develop theories of social phenomena:

> [T]he basic, formal game-theoretical models are not large enough for reality, and to the extent that the theory of games becomes large (extended in

the direction of supergames, differential games, and so on) it produces undecidable results. In the real world, of course, the situations where three, four, or many more players interact in systems of "direct or indirect interdependence" are not only common but predominant; and one must get away from all sorts of lulling but unduly restrictive binarisms to be able to map actual conditions (Kontopolous 1993: 142).

Structural analyses too are limited by the world's inherent fluidity:

> It is known that all thermodynamically open systems stabilized far from equilibrium are subject to change. They cannot remain static on pain of falling apart. This is as true of you or me as it is of hurricanes. The strong presumption is that it is also true of social systems, *which cannot avoid being thermodynamic systems* (Dyke 1990: 385, italics in original).

The ontologies of the research schools in comparative politics limit their ability to explain political phenomena.

Rationalists need to reduce the domain of what they study or expand their theoretical principles. The classic mode of thought applies to limited types of political phenomena: The simpler the game, the more defined the rules and the meanings of winning and losing, the more likely are persons to use the cognitive processes of instrumental rationality, and the more likely are rationalist principles to be useful. The more complex the circumstances, the more likely are people to draw on other sorts of knowledge and reasoning, in which instrumental calculation plays a limited role (see, for example, Douglas 1986; Gellner 1985; Meehl 1977). Indeed, in response to Meehl's critique, Riker (1982) concedes the inapplicability of rational choice theory to the analysis of vote choice, a radical contraction of the theory's domain.[15] It would seem that rationalists must choose between focusing their analytic lenses on a sharply delimited set of political phenomena – cases in which the rules of the contest and the definition of winning are clear – or altering the principles of rational choice theory in order to analyze complex political phenomena.

In turn, structural analysis needs to jettison its realist assumptions. State, ethnicity, social class, political cleavage, and other concepts are not natural types. They do not signify cohesive sets of persons; aggregate patterns are not easily predicted, and they are certainly not determined. This mode of analysis needs to combine several distinct principles:

1. the persistent effect of formative patterns and decisions;
2. the expectation of unpredictable events that have major consequences;
3. the divergence of like systems over time;
4. aggregate characteristics may not be reduced to the decisions of individuals;
5. the effect of structured relationships on individuals as inherently probabilistic.

---

[15]Ironically for rationalists, Boudon (1986: 138) cites Pareto for the claim that vote choice for members of parliament can never be a logical act.

Substantial changes in the principles of structural analyses follow from changing the understanding of the underlying political reality.

EXPLANATION AND THEORY IN COMPARATIVE POLITICS

Descriptions of the field of comparative politics underscore the need to move beyond the standards of nomological and causal explanations. No matter the formal adherence to these principles and no matter that the search has extended over decades, general laws of politics that apply to large sets of cases and generally accepted causal accounts do not characterize the field. Boudon points to three fundamental problems for nomological explanations in the social sciences: the limited domains to which they apply; the vague boundaries for the domains; and difficulties in specifying the characteristics of particular circumstances (Boudon 1986: 65-6). Indeed the chapters in this volume by Barnes, McAdam, Tarrow, and Tilly, Hall, and Migdal survey well-mined research areas that demonstrate the persistent difficulties in finding widely accepted universal principles of political phenomena. Consider the general point:

> [N]o laws concerning a specified set of objects or set of phenomena (together with initial conditions) can entail any real world encounter that has not yet taken place. In each instance of the action of the law, its fulfillment must depend on a new variety of chance occurrences (Mohr 1996: 132)
>
> Many and perhaps most of the conditional [if–then form] laws put forward by the social sciences seem to be of dubious validity, and others much more restricted in their scope than had been thought (Boudon 1986: 23).

Using the analysis of social change as the exemplar, Boudon underlines several general points: Scientific analyses of social processes are possible, even though it is dangerous to posit conditional relationships, risky to draw dynamic consequences from structural data, and without logical or sociological justification to seek causal accounts (1986: 28).

Proper explanations in comparative politics adhere to standards, even as the criteria of causal and covering law explanations do not necessarily apply. All explanations require theoretical propositions. Indeed, the greater the theoretical implications of any one explanation, the more reason there is to accept it. At the same time, theories may apply to limited sets of cases; they need not be universal in scope. Cook and Campbell (1979) established the need for causal analysis to rule out rival claims and "nuisance factors." Explanatory arguments must assess the relative ability of limited sets of variables to account for events, patterns, and processes. Where appropriate quantitative data are available, causal explanations rely on the results of various forms of regression analysis. Establishing the strength of the causal link, regression coefficients assess the impact of the explanatory variable on the dependent variable. Other techniques detail the relative ability of each and all of the set of explanatory variables to account for variance in the phenomenon that is being explained, and tests of statistical significance check for the presence of chance effects. As will be developed below, more complex arguments and process models require other statistical techniques. Where only qualitative data apply, counterfactual analysis – thought experiments that examine the implications of the absence or presence of hypothesized causal variables in different cases – helps to produce scientific understanding (see, for example, King, Keohane, and Verba 1994). In all efforts to explain, however, absolute certainty is a chimera. It cannot serve as a useful standard. Rather, the more that an explanatory hypothesis passes demanding empirical tests and the more that it is logically linked to other hypotheses, the more reason there is to accept the explanatory claim. In practice and in principle, relative certainty of explanatory claims replaces the mirage of absolute certainty.

Theories may also answer questions about the probability of an outcome, not only the absence or presence of events, and they may respond to How questions as well as Why questions. Released from the ontological assumptions of covering law and causal explanations, scientific understanding in comparative politics may include some of the following: chance and random factors; distinctions between individual and structural levels of analysis; quantitative analyses that examine probabilistic and nonlinear phenomena; formal theories that bridge the gap between the abstract models and the particular cases; and process models whose general principles display the patterns observed, not narrative descriptions alone.

Reformulating the standards for explanations in comparative politics has implications for theories derived from the research schools. Designed to offer nomological and causal explanations, each approach by itself is likely to produce theories that are inadequate to the task of explaining complex political phenomena. It is not surprising that some scholars have begun to join elements of the rationalist, culturalist, and structuralist research schools. Diverse theories have appeared: Some contain sets of generally applicable factors that are applied to specific sets of cases; some examine interactions among individual and structural levels of analysis; and some join the details of particular cases with formal models. Expanding the standards for scientific understanding in comparative politics allows for fresh combinations and new theories.

MODIFYING STATISTICAL MODELS: TAKING PROBABILITY AND NONLINEARITY SERIOUSLY

As comparativists move beyond the search for covering laws and causal explanations, those who examine quantitative data are not limited by simple regression analyses. Complex statistical models become the standard. Even as Lieberson stays within a causal logic for social analysis, he separates reversible and irreversible causal relationships.

Multivariate data analyses are especially hurt when researchers or theorists are unaware of this distinction. If a model employs a variety of independent variables to account for a dependent variable, some of the linkages may be quite easily reversed and others irreversible. Attempts, under these circumstances, to talk about the relative importance of one as opposed to another are ... foolhardy (Lieberson 1985: 70-1).

Moreover, he adds, in the presence of both kinds of causal variables, efforts to control for the effect of the different factors are inappropriate. The results are misunderstood and inaccurately explained social phenomena. There is a growing recognition of the need to include forms of regression analyses and other models that do not include the assumption of linearity. The presence of nonlinearities confounds explanations that assume linearities. There is reason to seek to account for the probability of a particular outcome, and to include interactive terms in explanatory models.

Simple forms of nonlinearity can be incorporated into the linearized statistical models used today.... But the nonlinear limits of these models are quickly reached, and more complicated structures cannot be written as linear combinations of inputs (C. Brown 1995: 6; also see Dyke 1990: 391).

Brown emphasizes the extent to which the use of regression models is a matter of convenience, required neither by theory nor method (C. Brown 1995: 52-3). Chaos theory moves beyond the logic of both causal and covering law explanations that posit explanatory and dependent variables. "Indeed, the absence of exogenous variables is actually the norm in nonlinear modeling. What takes the place of exogeneity is system interdependence" (C. Brown 1995: 7; see also Dyke 1990: 382; Kontopolous 1993: 168-9). Simple linear equations apply to a small set of the phenomena studied in comparative politics.

FORMAL THEORY IN COMPARATIVE POLITICS: BRIDGING THE GAP BETWEEN MATHEMATICAL TRUTHS AND PARTICULAR CASES

Rationalists and structuralists frequently apply formal models to political phenomena. Here, mathematical principles develop the core explanatory propositions, and the resulting abstract models explain the particular by attaching it to more general propositions. This form of scientific understanding accounts for the explanandum in a cluster of interrelated propositions that together provide a general picture. The larger is the set, the more reason is there to accept the explanation of any single element (Kitcher 1989: 430).[16] In principle, the success of an explanatory account of any one event does not depend on its ability to es-

---

[16]Kitcher does not specify the size of the set and the level of certainty required of each of the claims. This raises important qualifications. There is little reason to believe that most sciences are characterized by seamless webs of interrelated propositions; patchwork quilts provide a better image (Hull 1988: 493-4).

tablish a causal process or to show that the explanandum was expected by its association with a covering law, but on the demonstration that the explanatory statement is logically linked to a set of other hypotheses that provide a coherent account of related events.

The effort to apply formal models to explanatory accounts bedevils political scientists. Fiorina and Boudon note the necessary gap between the model's idealizations and the case under analysis. Consider Fiorina's presentation:

> These models are not "tested" against historical data; rather they are "applied." The models are logical constructions, their propositions are logically true. The question is whether they are useful, which is to say, whether they enable the scholar to better understand the empirical world. A model is compared to the historical record, and if it "fits," if its propositions are reflected in the empirical record, then it is a candidate for being an element of the explanation of that record (1996: 161).

Boudon examines the explanatory utility of Hotelling's model that prefigured rational choice analyses of voting and party systems:

> Hotelling's schema provides no *empirical* proposition and can at most be seen as a plausible interpretation of certain real elections of a very specific nature (1986: 200-1, italics in original)....
>
> Hotelling's theory is formal in the sense that it does not apply to any real situation, but is rather a kind of framework that needs to be filled out once we propose to use it to account for observations about the real world. It is *general* not in the sense that it could explain every observable situation, but in the sense that it can be used for very varied situations, provided the appropriate details are fed into it in every specific case (1986: 202, italics in original).

Indeed, Fiorina underlines the gap between theory development and empirical analysis in the spatial theory of elections, the research theme that grows out of Hotelling's seminal work:

> Even though a number of empirical researchers have challenged whether these "facts" are facts at all, these disputes have had little influence on the development of the main body of the theory. Instead, for the most part, the history of spatial theory was largely driven by an internal logic (Fiorina 1995: 254).

Formal models provide a framework for analysis, core assumptions about the nature of political reality and the factors that drive political processes. They offer interpretations, but they do not explain particular events, decisions, or processes.

Some rationalists seek to bridge the gap between their models' logical truths and particular events, making the analysis directly relevant to comparative politics. Levi's chapter in this volume introduces the method of "analytic narrative," which offers explanatory accounts of actual processes. As Levi and her colleagues apply propositions taken from rational choice theory to explain historical patterns and flows, they face the challenge of relating formal models to complex political phenomena. The more they move away from the model's idealizations and the more they examine the details of a particular case, the more they need to demonstrate the adequacy of their claims against rival plausible hypotheses. The ability to tell a story with the conceptual language of rational choice theory does not suffice. As rationalists offer causal arguments, they may rely less and less on the theoretical power of their claims. They need to examine their models in relation to other accounts.

EXPLANATIONS AS ANSWERS TO QUESTIONS ABOUT PROCESSES

Some scholars compare cases across time, in place of cross-national analyses. Comparative politics displays several efforts to analyze historical flows. The chapters by Levi, Katznelson, and McAdam, Tarrow, and Tilly in this volume depict analytical narratives, configurative studies, and cycles of political protest as related and alternative modes of analyzing changing political phenomena in single countries. These exemplars present broad-scale patterns but eschew mathematization. Chaos modelers offer geometric patterns. Comparativists who study political processes vary in the extent to which they provide narratives and general principles.

Dyke presents the research of the *Annales* school of social history as a primary example, a mode of research in which modified assumptions of Marxist theory rest at the intellectual core and aggregate processes receive analytical attention:

> [T]he *Annales* historians scan the horizons of the *longue durée*. They believe that isolated data, even quantitative data, is [sic] relatively meaningless. Brief local fluctuations may belie long-range trends, and the discernment of long-term patterns is often the key to understanding....
>
> Long-term patterns show up most often and most clearly in series of numbers: population statistics, currency figures.... Each of these series is patterned: each pattern is potentially meaningful. One of the most common patterns to have emerged so far is the cycle (Dyke 1990: 386-7).

Two fundamental points underline these claims: Scientific understanding may proceed without specifying microprocesses. Put differently, individual interests and values need not be included in an analysis. Structures are not reducible to the individuals who compose them. Second, analysis seeks patterns.

> The *Annales* confederation challenges us, as we have seen, to examine the presuppositions under which the concatenations of events as strings of independent and dependent variables can provide explanations (Dyke 1990: 389).

In this view, scientific understanding defines and describes processes, even when and perhaps especially because it does not offer covering laws or causal accounts.

Tarrow's analysis of cycles of collective action specifies the patterns that accompanied the process of political protest in Italy:

> This essay proposes ... the concept of systemic cycles of protest. I will argue that moments of madness do not transform the repertoire of contention all at once and out of whole cloth, but contribute to its evolution through the dynamic evolution of larger cycles of mobilization.... It is within these larger cycles that new forms of contention combine with old ones ... and newly invented forms of collective action become what I call "modular" (Tarrow 1995, 92; see also Tarrow 1989).

Here, research describes the process of contentious action – the balance of new and old forms and the mix of violent and nonviolent events.

Stimson aggregates public opinion in the United States into a process analysis:

> Used more rigorously, trend is a powerful idea. And unless it is used rigorously its power is sapped by subjectivity.... A trend is a process that increments or decrements a series by a fixed amount at every interval. A trending series goes off in one direction, therefore, not for a while, but indefinitely.... Nothing "just trends" by some mysterious inner driving force. Trend requires process. Process requires explanation (1991: 8).

In practice, Stimson explains by demonstrating order in the patterns of public opinion and by locating the importance of opinion leaders and social networks on the views of individuals: "Part of the answer is simply aggregation. In aggregates, order arises that is difficult to find among the individuals who compose them.... Orderly and disciplined aggregates reflect orderly individuals – opinion leaders – giving social cues" (1991: 125). Stimson's analysis of public opinion shifts attention to the "public," as he details movements in political preferences.

Baumgartner and Jones detail "punctuated equilibria," not immobilism, stability, or steady change, in the development of public policy in the United States.

> So there are certainly periods of rapid change.... However, we would make a mistake to conclude from this that politics is cyclical. A punctuated equilibrium model of the political system differs dramatically from the type of dynamic equilibrium model implicit in any discussion of cycles (Baumgartner and Jones 1993: 245).

What accounts for the pattern of movement? The authors posit the interaction of three sets of factors: cultural ones that relate to issue definitions; the organizational characteristics of policy subsystems, institutional characteristics; and the equilibria that are best analyzed from the perspective of rational choice theory.

Some scholars of political development in the United States use the concept of intercurrence, a position that reaffirms Katznelson's call for configurative studies in his chapter in this volume.

The concept of intercurrence presumes neither order nor disarray, though it can accommodate degrees of either in particular historical settings. It does so by replacing the expectation of an ordered space bounded in synchronized time with the expectation of a politicized push and pull arrayed around multiple institutional arrangements with diverse historical origins. With this image of the political universe in view, attention is directed to ways in which different ordering principles converge, collide, and fold into one another. Theories of politics formulated on the presumption of intercurrence will, like all theories, stand or fall on their capacity to tell an empirically refutable story, which is, on the known evidence, more convincing than others (Orren and Skowronek 1996: 137-8).

These scholars examine processes interacting with historically formed rules and patterns. Note that they have not provided precise definitions of the concepts that assess the flows and they have not established standards for an explanation. Here, the study of processes confronts the adequacy of historical narratives that do not provide precise measures and do not offer explanatory standards.

In contrast, direct applications of chaos theory to political phenomena offer difference equations and present their analyses around the results of figures and graphs (see for example C. Brown 1995; T. Brown 1996; and the other essays in Kiel and Elliot 1996). Consider some elements of Brown's analysis of the collapse of Weimar Germany and the rise to power of the Nazis. Like many others, Brown examines aggregate voting results across the districts of the country. Unlike all others, he presents graphs, scatter-plots, and figures displaying points of attraction and movement.

As with most nonlinear systems, and due entirely to the complexity of the potential behavior of such systems, a detailed discussion of the estimated parameter values is the least productive way to proceed. Graphical analyses ... are more helpful in analyzing such systems from a heuristic point of view (C. Brown 1995: 98).

The importance of this finding is to note that for much of the Weimar Republic, the country did not vote in a state of aggregate equilibrium in July of 1932 with regard to partisan fragmentation. This has theoretical implications with regard to the study of elections in general.... (C. Brown 1995: 105).

Here, patterned displays replace tests of particular hypotheses drawn from standing theories on revolutions and electoral behavior in Weimar Germany.

These process models move comparative analysis away from cross-national generalizations as they seek to uncover the principles that explain the evolution of political institutions and behavior in a single country. The exemplars noted underline the variation in the extent to which these analyses rely on mathematical formulations and verbal descriptions, broad-gauged and fine-grained depictions of data, and arguments about theoretical principles.

EXPLANATIONS THAT JOIN RATIONALITY, CULTURE, AND STRUCTURE

Recent work displays porous boundaries among the research schools. McAdam, Tilly, and Tarrow in this volume offer a framework for the analysis of social movements and revolution that combines structuralist and culturalist factors. In addition, their essay joins with those by Ross, Hall, and Migdal to view rationality as but one type of system of meaning, a category of the general concept of culture, not its alternative. Even some rationalists blur the distinction between the rational and the nonrational. Consider North's effort to emend the view of decision making, such that rationality becomes one element in a system of perception and meaning:

> The key to the choices that individuals make is their perceptions, which are a function of the way the mind interprets the information that it receives. The mental constructs individuals form to explain the world around them are partly a result of their cultural heritage, partly a result of the local everyday problems they confront and must solve, and partly a result of nonlocal learning (North 1995: 17).

Defining institutions as sets of rules (see also North [1995: 15] and Shepsle [1995: 286]), Levi blends rationality with structuralist elements. This position echoes Shepsle's analysis that links institutions and choice:

> Like the rational choice theories that preceded them, and in contrast to the older institutional theories in economics and political science, these efforts are equilibrium theories. They seek to explain social outcomes on the basis not only of agent preferences and optimizing behavior, but also of institutional features (Shepsle 1995: 282).

Combining the elements of the different research schools, this effort joins elements of rational and extrarational elements and the choices take place within the limits allowed by social and political institutions. When scholars erase the boundaries between the research schools, they risk entering a "messy center" (see Lichbach's chapter in this volume), devoid of precise hypotheses.

Mary Douglas offers an exemplar of combinations that enhance theory in comparative politics. *How Institutions Think* (1986) blends elements from the rationalist, structuralist, and culturalist schools, combining the data gathered by cultural anthropologists, the assumptions of calculating actors that define rational choice theory, and the effects of institutions that characterize structuralists. Douglas's slim volume challenges and extends core principles of all three research schools.

Consider Douglas's analysis of ancestor worship, a subject typically addressed only by culturalists. Dismissing the dichotomy between the rational and the irrational, she offers an explanation of this complex phenomenon. An argument that follows her principles, would start with points of equilibrium at which everyone wants to see some sort of classification of kinsmen. One could start by supposing a minimal common need for each member of the society to have some area of autonomy respected by other descendants of a great grandfather. Let us say each wishes to be protected from the interference of uncles and aunts, cousins and brothers. By an emerging cognitive convention each will be granted credibility when he invokes his dead father to protect his personal space, so long as he respects the same claim from his brothers (1986: 51-2).

More generally put, the process by which some beliefs become accepted and others rejected is a problem worthy of study. It is a form of the general problem of collective action: how people come to think alike (= together) parallels how they come to act together (= alike).

Douglas extends and limits rational choice theory. The research school's tenets may be applied across diverse cultures and to varied realms of behavior but the school's typical solutions to the collective action problem, however, do not hold. "In practice, small-scale societies do not exemplify the idealized vision of community. Some do, some do not foster trust. Has no one writing on this subject ever lived in a village" (1986: 25)? Douglas adds, "The current, more sophisticated anthropological record shows these small-scale societies as never static, never self-stabilizing, but being built continuously by a process of rational bargaining and negotiating." Contrary to a fundamental rationalist principle, smallness of scale does not solve the problem of collective action. "The individual cost-benefit applies inexorably and enlighteningly to the smallest microexchanges...." Evidence produced by anthropologists "... destroys the case for extra-rational principles producing a community at some unspecified point of diminishing scale" (1986: 29). No community coheres simply because people wish to be together, trust each other, or simply value their connections. "A community works because the transactions balance out. The risk of free-riding is controlled by the accounting system" (1986: 74). Even in small-scale societies in which people display values very different from those of the scholar of comparative politics, there is reason to suppose that individuals calculate to maximize their personal benefits and minimize their own costs.

Note too that this approach extends and limits culturalist analyses. Evidence produced by the fieldwork of anthropologists denies the principled claims of rational choice theory. Neither a shared belief in the same values nor smallness of scale exempts people from solving the problem of collective action. Furthermore, individuals think in a language that is heavily encoded by existing institutions (Douglas 1986: 63; see also Gellner 1985). Also, there is no reason to suppose that any realm of life is governed by nonrational principles. "The case for ritual stimulating the emotions is weak. Hasn't anyone ever been bored in church" (1986: 36)? Note as well: "Religions do not always make believers more loyal to their rulers.... Sometimes it [sic!] does, sometimes not. The charge of irrationality against primitive religion was in the minds of th[e] anthropologists" (1986: 36-7). Analysis begins with assumptions that erase the distinction between the rational and the irrational.

At the same time, Douglas rejects two cardinal principles of classic structuralist analysis. Functional explanations, she maintains, are flawed, not because of their logic but because they rest "on a form of sociological determinism that credits individuals with neither initiative nor sense" (1986: 32). Consider too the criticism of structural analyses of institutions:

> Equilibrium cannot be assumed; it must be demonstrated and with a different demonstration for each type of society. Before it can perform its entropy-reducing work, the incipient institution needs some stabilizing principle to stop its premature demise. The stabilizing principle is the naturalization of social classifications (1986: 48).

The formation of institutions needs to be explained, and the proposed theory must account for the decisions of individuals who choose to form and join the institution.

Douglas's presentation joins together three defining themes of the research schools in comparative politics. "The entrenching of an idea is a social process.... Conversely, the entrenching of an institution is essentially an intellectual process as much as an economic and political process" (1986: 45). Douglas denies the claims of rationalists who maintain that institutions are sets of just rules, shared conventions.[17] Citing Schelling (1978), she maintains, "We want conventions about pedestrian crossings to exist, but we will violate them ourselves if we can do so with impunity.... The conditions for stable conventions to arise are much more stringent than it might seem.... For a convention to turn into a legitimate social institution it needs a parallel cognitive convention to sustain it" (1986: 46). Conventions, Douglas maintains, need to be legitimated by something other than other conventions. Institutions are not conventions. At the heart of her answer lie understandings of the world that people take to be "natural" and that are sustained and reflected in social interactions. "It is natural for us to do it this way" underpins all institutions. These principles apply to all societies. "Forgotten ancestors [in societies in which dead forebears are worshipped] and forgotten scientific discoveries [in modern societies] are in the same case" (1986: 77). Each requires an explanation; both are examples of the problem of how to account for shared beliefs. In Douglas's analysis, evidence taken from the fieldwork of anthropologists, typically supplied by culturalists, joins with the rationalists' claim that collective action needs to be shown to be in the interests of the participants and the structuralists' insistence that social interactions sustain individual perceptions and behavior. Distinctions among the research schools dissolve.

What stands for explanation in this analysis? Douglas seeks to reformulate functional explanations. The effort to explain Y – for example, the formation of an institution, a shared belief, a political organization – needs to show all of the following:

---

[17]The reference in the text is to Lewis (1968), and see Levi's chapter in this volume and the sources cited there as well. Consider also: "[T]his view of institution selection regards an institution as an ex ante bargain the objective of which is to enhance various forms of 'cooperation' and to facilitate the enforcement of agreement" (Shepsle 1995: 286). D. Brown (1995) parallels and develops Douglas's argument.

1. Y is an effect of X;
2. Y is beneficial for Z;
3. Y is unintended by actions producing X;
4. Y or the causal relation between X and Y is unrecognized by actors in Z; and
5. Y maintains X by a causal feedback loop passing through Z (Douglas 1986: 33).

In Douglas's view, beliefs that sustain collective action are indirect consequences of individual preferences that do not relate to the shared beliefs and action. Assuming that individuals seek to minimize the ability of their relatives to influence their personal lives helps to explain ancestor worship (and presumably a host of other beliefs), because the beliefs and practices of this collective value can be traced in a causal loop through social institutions to the individual's goals. The next step is to develop and illustrate the form of functional explanation.

EXPLANATIONS THAT JOIN RESEARCH SCHOOLS AND LEVELS OF ANALYSIS AND THAT TAKE CHANCE SERIOUSLY

Some theories in comparative politics take seriously the claim that propositions that apply to individuals and to structures may be treated as distinct and interactive. This is evident in the chapters by McAdam, Tarrow, and Tilly in this volume as well as in Douglas's volume, and the research by Huckfeldt and Sprague as well as my own work cited earlier. It appears as well in studies that employ propositions about queuing and tipping processes (see, for example, Schelling (1978)). The sociologist Raymond Boudon has offered a compelling model of this type of analysis.

Rejecting the adequacy of covering laws, Boudon presents an alternative standard for explanation in the social sciences that applies directly to comparative politics. In an argument that draws on the epistemology of German sociology, especially Weber and Simmel; Italian political science, particularly Mosca and Pareto; English and Scottish utilitarianism, beginning with Adam Smith; and American sociology, namely Parsons and Merton, Boudon insists that all explanations of social phenomena must relate individual choices, agency, and surrounding structures:

> The paradigm can be summarized as follows. Let us assume the existence of any social or economic phenomenon M, for which an explanation is sought. M is interpreted as a function $M(m_i)$ of a range of individual actions m_i, which themselves are, in conditions and a way to be made explicit, functions $m_i(S_i)$ of structure S_i of the situation including the social agents or actors. The function (in the mathematical sense) $m_i(S_i)$ must be able to be seen as having an *adaptational* function for the actor $_i$ in situation S_i. Weber would say that action must be *comprehensible.* As for structure S_i, it is a function $S_i(M')$ of a range M' of defined data at a macrosocial level or at least at the level of the system in which phenomenon M occurs.

Explaining M_i means, in brief and in terms of the general paradigm, saying exactly what the terms of M = M {m[S(M′)]}are (we can express it more simply as M = MmSM′). Verbally, we can say that phenomenon M is a function of actions m, which are dependent on situation S of the actor, which situation is itself affected by macrosocial actions M′ (1986: 29-30, italics in original; see also Boudon [1980: 149-94]).

Furthermore, explanations solve Why questions. Why did some example of social change occur? Boudon proposes that a proper explanation shows that changes in certain features between the first and second instances affect the situation of one or more categories of actors in such a way as to induce them to bring about the newly observed aggregated results (1986: 124-5).

Several themes are central: Explanations need to include efforts to understand the actor's decisions; social contexts sharply constrain agency, and more general macro phenomena limit the social contexts. Following the basic postulates of methodological individualism, explanations must include propositions that make sense of individual actors, a phenomenological component. In and of themselves, however, these propositions do not suffice. Explanations must relate particular decisions to more general social patterns. Multiple levels of analysis find their place in the scientific understanding of political phenomena.

Because rationality is always specific to a particular context, Boudon maintains, it is not possible to distinguish among rationality, culture, and structure. Furthermore, the relationship between individual behavior and the surrounding context and structures varies across cases. No general laws apply.

> [C]ertain sets of K conditions give rise to structure situations that are both unambiguous and *decisive,* in which there is scarcely any doubt about what the actor will do. An a priori analysis enables us to state with virtual certainty that in circumstances K, if A, then B. There are, however, other sets of K conditions in which an a priori conclusion of this type is impossible (1986: 65, italics in original).

In different circumstances, the same factor has different consequences. Boudon notes a fundamental contradiction between the presence of Cournot Effects and the requirements of methodological individualism and covering law explanations. Variations in the meaning of rationality across cases combine with differences in the specific conditions present to deny the utility of general explanatory propositions.

What determines a successful Boudon type of explanation? How do we know whether to accept an explanatory claim? Explanations need to be tested with empirical data that apply both to the actors and to the aggregations of the actions.

> {V}*erifying* the analysis can – and can usefully – take place at two levels. One is that of m, the level of comprehension, where the object is to find out whether the psychological mechanisms postulated by the observer appraised [sic!] of the main data of situation S correspond to reality. The second, that of M, is where the object is to check whether the consequences

at the aggregated level of the microsociological hypotheses *m* are indeed in conformity with aggregated data as observed empirically (1986: 39, italics in original).

Boudon insists on the need to test the claimed understanding of the individual's goals, strategies, and tactics with data that describe the set of persons and with data that apply to structures, general patterns, and institutions. Interpretations of individuals do not suffice; they are explanations when they pass demanding tests of empirical verification and when they can plausibly account for the aggregate patterns observed. Analyses of aggregate patterns require empirical tests with regard to data that describe structures and actors. Theory demands plausible accounts and verification at multiple levels of analysis.

EXPLANATIONS THAT ASSUME THE PRINCIPLES OF METHODOLOGICAL COLLECTIVISM

Must the analysis of political phenomena explain the behavior of the persons who take part in the process? Although most comparativists share the core assumptions of methodological individualism, recent work across the sciences sustains the utility of examining collectivities as such, offering analyses that explain without reducing holistic phenomena to smaller parts. Following in a tradition that extends back to Durkheim and encompasses the French *Annales* school as well as new research in chaos and complexity theory, this mode of analysis denies the need for explanations to make sense of the behavior of individual actors. Kontopolous states the general claim:

> [I]t is not the inherent capacity of free, individual micro-parts but self-organization processes and ensuing properties related to relational-structural and ecological-selectionist constraints that account for both the emergence of the mechanisms themselves and the emergence of higher (structured structuring) structures populating our multilayered universe (Kontopolous 1993: 38).

Breaking with the tenets of methodological individualism, efforts to apply these views to social and political phenomena see individuals as necessary but not sufficient components in social explanations. "The institutions are at once enabling, constraining, and availing to the individuals" (Kontopolous 1993: 83). Here, analysis focuses on the patterns of relations – from party systems to families and from government organizations to neighborhoods – that exist apart from the intentions and behavior of individuals.

EXPLANATION AND THE RESEARCH SCHOOLS IN COMPARATIVE POLITICS

There is reason to alter the standards of scientific understanding used in comparative politics. General theoretical propositions may include law-like propositions that apply to specific sets of cases; they need not be universal principles. The effort to establish open-ended covering principles stands in the way of other kinds of explanations. It directs research to examine the accuracy, the reliability, and the domain of general laws. It directs attention away from the analysis of more tractable problems. It is impossible to establish general laws and causal mechanisms with absolute certainty. All explanations require assessments of their relative certainty. All benefit from tests that eliminate nuisance factors and assess the power of rival plausible hypotheses. Note as well that all explanations require theories; in their absence, the selection of explanatory variables is arbitrary.

When comparativists apply theories to limited sets of cases, they combine general claims and particular details. Formal models in comparative politics require bridges that link the abstract mathematical claims to the explanation of particular cases and sets of cases. Statistical models should not be bound by the assumptions inherent in linear models. Why questions need to include the probability of the emergence of particular events, not only their absence or presence. Process models respond to How questions, moving the analytic focus away from questions about emergence and cross-national variation. Chance finds a central place in political analysis. The complexities of the political world need to be incorporated into the theories of comparative politics.

Fresh theoretical combinations emerge. Rationalists, culturalists, and structuralists examine rationality as one element in a system of meaning. Scholars from all three schools examine the relationship between individual decisions, social contexts, and institutions. Blending theoretical positions risks obliterating distinctions without necessarily leading to theoretical gains. Rigorous adherence to the standards of explanation in comparative politics enables theory to advance, distinguishing the path of scholarship from the swamp of the "messy center."

REFERENCES

Almond, Gabriel A., and Stephen J. Genco. 1977. "Clouds, Clocks, and the Study of Politics." *World Politics* 29:489–522.

Alvarez, R. Michael, and Charles E. Franklin. 1994. "Uncertainty and Political Perception." *Journal of Politics* 56:671–88.

Archer, Margaret. 1995. *Realist Social Theory: The Morphogenetic Approach.* Cambridge: Cambridge University Press.

Bartolini, Stefano, and Peter Mair. 1990. *Identity, Competition, and Electoral Availability: The Stabilization of European Electorates 1885–1985.* New York: Cambridge University Press.

Baumgartner, Frank R., and Bryan D. Jones. 1993. *Agendas and Instability in American Politics.* Chicago: University of Chicago Press.

Boudon, Raymond. 1980. *The Crisis in Sociology.* New York: Columbia University Press.

———. 1986. *Theories of Social Change: A Critical Appraisal.* Berkeley: University of California Press.

Brass, Paul. 1985. "Ethnic Groups and the State." In *Ethnic Groups and the State,* ed. Paul Brass. Totowa, NJ: Barnes and Noble Books.

Brown, Courtney. 1995. *Serpents in the Sand: Essays on the Nonlinear Nature of Politics and Human Destiny.* Ann Arbor: University of Michigan Press.

Brown, David W. 1995. *When Strangers Cooperate: Using Social Conventions to Govern Ourselves.* New York: The Free Press.

Brown, Thad A. 1996. "Nonlinear Politics." In L. Douglas Kiel and Euel Elliot, eds., *Chaos Theory in the Social Sciences: Foundations and Applications.* Ann Arbor: University of Michigan Press

Browne, Eric C., John P. Frendreis, and Dennis W. Gleiber. 1984. "An 'Events' Approach to the Problem of Cabinet Stability." *Comparative Political Studies* 17:167-97.

———. 1986a. "The Process of Cabinet Dissolution: An Exponential Model of Duration and Stability in Western Democracies." *American Journal of Political Science* 30:628-50.

———. 1986b. "Dissolution of Governments in Scandinavia: A Critical Events Perspective." *Scandinavian Political Studies* 9:93-110.

Cook, Thomas D., and Donald T. Campbell. 1979. *Quasi-Experimentation: Design and Analysis Issues for Field Settings.* Boston: Houghton Mifflin.

Dalton, Russell J., Scott C. Flanagan, and Paul Allen Beck. 1984. *Electoral Change in Advanced Industrial Democracies: Realignment or Dealignment.* Princeton: Princeton University Press.

Douglas, Mary. 1986. *How Institutions Think.* Syracuse: Syracuse University Press.

Dyke, C. 1990. "Strange Attraction, Curious Liaison: Clio Meets Chaos." *Philosophical Forum* 21:369-92.

Esterhazy, Peter. 1994. *The Glance of Countess Hahn-Hahn (Down the Danube).* Richard Aczel, trans. London: Weidenfeld and Nicolson.

Fiorina, Morris. 1995. "The Development of the Spatial Theory of Elections." In James Farr, John Dryzek, and Stephen T. Leonard, eds., *Political Science in History: Research Programs and Political Traditions.* New York: Cambridge University Press.

———. 1996. "Looking for Disagreement in All the Wrong Places." In Ian Shapiro and Russell Hardin, eds., *Political Order.* New York: New York University Press.

Gadda, Carlo Emilio. [1957] 1984. *That Awful Mess on Via Merulana.* Trans. William Weaver. New York: George Brazziler.

Geertz, Clifford. 1973. *The Interpretation of Cultures.* New York: Basic Books.

Gerth, Hans, and C. Wright Mills, eds. 1958. *From Max Weber.* New York: Oxford University Press.

Gellner, Ernest. 1985. *Relativism in the Social Sciences.* Cambridge: Cambridge University Press.

Glass, Leon, and Michael C. Mackey. 1988. *From Clocks to Chaos: The Rhythms of Life.* Princeton: Princeton University Press.

Goldstone, Jack. 1991. *Revolution and Rebellion in the Early Modern World.* Berkeley: University of California Press.

Hempel, Carl. 1965. *Aspects of Scientific Explanation and Other Essays.* New York: The Free Press.

Holt, Robert T. 1967. "A Proposed Structural-Functional Framework." In James C. Charlesworth, ed., *Contemporary Political Analysis.* New York: The Free Press.

Holt, Robert T., and John M. Richardson. 1970. "Competing Paradigms in Comparative Politics." In Robert T. Holt and John E. Turner, eds., *The Methodology of Comparative Research*. New York: The Free Press.

Huckfeldt, Robert. 1990. "Structure, Indeterminacy and Chaos: A Case for Sociological Law." *Journal of Theoretical Politics* 2:413-33.

Huckfeldt, Robert, and John Sprague. 1987. "Networks in Context: The Social Flow of Information." *American Political Science Review* 81:1197-1216.

———. 1988. "Choice, Social Structure, and Political Information: The Informational Coercion of Minorities." *American Journal of Political Science* 32: 467-82.

———. 1991. "Discussant Effects on Vote Choice: Intimacy, Structure, and Interdependence." *Journal of Politics* 53:122-57.

———. 1992. "Political Parties and Electoral Mobilization: Political Structure, Social Structure, and the Party Canvas." *American Political Science Review* 86:70-86.

———. 1993. "Citizens, Contexts, and Politics." In Ada W. Finifter, ed., *Political Science: The State of the Discipline II*. Washington, D.C.: American Political Science Association.

———. 1995. *Citizens, Politics, and Social Communication: Information and Influence in an Election Campaign*. New York: Cambridge University Press.

Hull, David. 1988. *Science As a Process: An Evolutionary Account of the Social and Conceptual Development of Science*. Chicago: University of Chicago Press.

Katznelson, Ira. 1986. "Working-Class Formation: Constructing Cases and Comparisons." In Ira Katznelson and Aristide R. Zolberg, eds., *Working-Class Formation: Nineteenth Century Patterns in Europe and the United States*. Princeton: Princeton University Press.

Kellert, Stephen, H. 1993. *In the Wake of Chaos*. Chicago: University of Chicago Press.

Kiel, L. Douglas, and Euel Elliot, eds. 1996. *Chaos Theory in the Social Sciences: Foundations and Applications*. Ann Arbor: University of Michigan Press.

Kinder, Donald R. 1983. "Diversity and Complexity in American Public Opinion." In Ada W. Finifter, ed., *Political Science: The State of the Discipline*. Washington, D.C.: American Political Science Association.

King, Gary, Robert Keohane, and Sidney Verba. 1994. *Designing Social Inquiry: Scientific Inference in Qualitative Research*. Princeton: Princeton University Press.

Kitcher, Philip. 1989. "Explanatory Unification and the Causal Structure of the World." In Philip Kitcher and Wesley Salmon, eds., *Scientific Explanation*. XIII. Minnesota Studies in the Philosophy of Science. Minneapolis: University of Minnesota Press.

Kocka, Jurgen. 1986. "Problems in Working-Class Formation: The Early Years 1800–1875." In Ira Katznelson and Aristide R. Zolberg, eds., *Working-Class Formation: Nineteenth Century Patterns in Europe and the United States*. Princeton: Princeton University Press.

Kontopolous, Kyriakos M. 1993. *The Logics of Social Structure*. New York: Cambridge University Press.

Kuran, Timur. 1991. "Now Out of Never: The Element of Surprise in the East European Revolution of 1989." *World Politics* 44:7-48.

Lewis, David. 1968. *Conventions: A Philosophical Study*. Cambridge: Harvard University Press.

Lichbach, Mark Irving. 1995. *The Rebel's Dilemma.* Ann Arbor: University of Michigan Press.

Lieberson, Stanley. 1985. *Making It Count: The Improvement of Social Research and Theory.* Berkeley: University of California Press.

Lipset, Seymour M., and Stein Rokkan. 1967. "Cleavage Structures, Party Systems, and Voter Alignments: An Introduction." In Seymour M. Lipset and Stein Rokkan, eds., *Party Systems and Voter Alignments: Cross-National Perspectives.* New York: The Free Press.

Mandelbaum, Maurice. 1987. *Purpose and Necessity in Social Theory.* Baltimore: Johns Hopkins University Press.

McCloskey, Donald. 1991. "History, Differential Equations, and the Problem of Narrative." *History and Theory* 30:21-35.

Meehl, Paul E. 1977. "The Selfish Voter Paradox and the Thrown-Away Vote Argument." *American Political Science Review* 71:11-30.

Meehl, Paul E. 1986. "What Social Scientists Don't Understand." In Donald W. Fiske and Richard A. Shweder, eds., *Metatheory in Social Science: Pluralisms and Subjectivities.* Chicago: University of Chicago Press.

Mohr, Lawrence B. 1996. *The Causes of Human Behavior: Implications for Theory and Method in the Social Sciences.* Ann Arbor: University of Michigan Press.

Nelson, Alan. 1990. "Are Economic Kinds Natural?" In C. Wade Savage, ed., *Scientific Theories,* XIV. Minnesota Studies in the Philosophy of Science. Minneapolis: University of Minnesota Press.

North, Douglas. 1995. "Five Propositions about Institutional Change." In Jack Knight and Itai Sened, eds., *Explaining Social Institutions.* Ann Arbor: University of Michigan Press.

Orren, Karen, and Stephen Skowronek. 1996. "Institutions and Intercurrence: Theory Building in the Fullness of Time." In Ian Shapiro and Russell Hardin, eds., *Political Order.* New York: New York University Press.

Overman, E. Samuel. 1988. *Methodology and Epistemology for Social Science. Selected Papers. Donald T. Campbell.* Chicago: University of Chicago Press.

Panebianco, Angelo. 1988. *Political Parties: Organization and Power.* Trans. Marc Silver. New York: Cambridge University Press.

Przeworksi, Adam, and Henry Teune. 1970. *The Logic of Comparative Social Inquiry.* New York: Wiley-Interscience.

Reddy, William. 1987. *Money and Liberty in Modern Europe: A Critique of Historical Understanding.* Cambridge: Cambridge University Press.

Reisch, George. 1991. "Chaos, History, and Narrative." *History and Theory* 30:1-20.

———. 1995. "Scientism Without Tears: A Reply to Roth and Ryckman." *History and Theory* 34:45-58.

Richter, Frank. 1986. "Non-Linear Behavior." In Donald W. Fiske and Richard A. Shweder, eds., *Metatheory in Social Science: Pluralisms and Subjectivities.* Chicago: University of Chicago Press.

Riker, William H. 1982. "The Two-Party System and Duverger's Law: An Essay on the History of Political Science." *American Political Science Review* 76:753-66.

———. 1990. "Political Science and Rational Choice." In James E. Alt and Kenneth A. Shepsle, eds., *Perspectives on Positive Political Economy.* New York: Cambridge University Press.

Rokkan, Stein. 1970. *Citizens, Elections, Parties.* New York: David McKay Co.

Rose, Richard, and Derek Urwin. 1970. "Persistence and Change in Western Party Systems Since 1945." *Political Studies* 18:287-319.

Roth, Paul A., and Thomas A. Ryckman. 1995. "Chaos, Clio, and Scientistic Illusions of Understanding." *History and Theory* 34:30-44.

Roth, Randolph. 1992. "Is History a Process? Nonlinearity, Revitalization Theory, and the Central Metaphor of Social Science History" *Social Science History* 16:197-243.

Ruelle, David. 1991. *Chance and Chaos.* Princeton: Princeton University Press.

Salmon, Wesley. 1984. *Scientific Explanation and the Causal Structure of the World.* Princeton: Princeton University Press.

Salmon, Wesley. 1989. "Four Decades of Scientific Explanation." In Philip Kitcher and Wesley Salmon, eds., *Scientific Explanation.* XIII. Minnesota Studies in the Philosophy of Science. Minneapolis: University of Minnesota Press.

Sartori, Giovanni. 1970. "Concept Misformation in Comparative Politics." *American Political Science Review* 64:1033-53.

———. 1994. "Compare Why and How: Comparing, Miscomparing, and the Comparative Method." In Mattei Dogan and Ali Kazancigil, eds., *Comparing Nations: Concepts, Strategies, Substance..* Oxford: Blackwell.

Scharpf, Fritz W. 1987. "A Game-Theoretical Interpretation of Inflation and Unemployment in Western Europe." *Journal of Public Policy* 7:227-57.

Schelling, Thomas C. 1978. *Micromotives and Macrobehavior.* New York: Norton.

Schofield, Norman. 1995. "Modeling Order in Representative Democracies." In Ian Shapiro and Russell Hardin, eds., *Political Order.* New York: New York University Press.

Shamir, Michal. 1984. "Are Western Party Systems 'Frozen'? A Comparative Dynamic Analysis." *Comparative Political Studies* 17:35-79.

Shepsle, Kenneth A. 1995. "Studying Institutions: Some Lessons from the Rational Choice Approach." In James Farr, John Dryzek, and Stephen T. Leonard, eds., *Political Science in History: Research Programs and Political Traditions.* New York: Cambridge University Press.

Shermer, Michael. 1995. "Exorcising LaPlace's Demon: Chaos and Antichaos, History and Metahistory." *History and Theory* 34:59-83.

Sklar, Lawrence. 1993. *Physics and Chance: Philosophical Issues in the Foundations of Statistical Mechanics.* New York: Cambridge University Press.

Skocpol, Theda. 1979. *States and Social Revolutions: A Comparative Analysis of France, Russia, and China.* New York: Cambridge University Press.

Sniderman, Paul M. 1993. "The New Look in Public Opinion Research." In Ada W. Finifter, ed., *Political Science: The State of the Discipline II.* Washington, D.C.: American Political Science Association.

Stimson, James A. 1991. *Public Opinion in America: Moods, Cycles, and Swings.* Boulder, CO: Westview.

———. 1995. "Opinion and Representation." *American Political Science Review* 89:179-83.

Tarrow, Sidney. 1989. *Democracy and Disorder: Protest and Politics in Italy: 1965–75.* Oxford: Clarendon Press.

———. 1995. "Cycles of Collective Action: Between Moments of Madness and the Repertoire of Collective Action." In Mark Traugott, ed., *Repertoires and Cycles of Collective Action.* Durham: Duke University Press.

Waldrop, M. Mitchell. 1992. *Complexity: The Emerging Science at the Edge of Order and Chaos.* New York: Viking.

Woodward, James. 1989. "The Causal Mechanical Model of Explanation." In Philip Kitcher and Wesley Salmon, eds., *Scientific Explanation.* XIII. Minnesota Studies in the Philosophy of Science. Minneapolis: University of Minnesota Press.

Yancey, William, Eugene Eriksen, and Richard N. Juliani. 1977. "Emergent Ethnicity: A Review and a Reformulation." *American Sociological Review* 82:533-48.

Zaller, John. 1992. *The Nature and Origins of Mass Opinion.* New York: Cambridge University Press.

Zaller, John, and Stanley Feldman. 1992. "A Simple Theory of the Survey Response: Answering Questions versus Revealing Preferences." *American Journal of Political Science* 36:579-616.

Zolberg, Aristide R. 1986. "How Many Exceptionalisms? In Ira Katznelson and Aristide R. Zolberg, eds., *Working-Class Formation: Nineteenth Century Patterns in Europe and the United States.* Princeton: Princeton University Press.

Zuckerman, Alan S. 1975. "Political Cleavage: A Conceptual and Theoretical Analysis." *British Journal of Political Science* 5:231-48.

———. 1982. "New Approaches to Political Cleavage: A Theoretical Introduction." *Comparative Political Studies* 15:131-44.

———. 1989. "The Bases of Political Cohesion: Applying and Reconstructing Crumbling Theories." *Comparative Politics* 21:473-95.

———. 1991. *Doing Political Science: An Introduction to Political Analysis.* Boulder, CO: Westview.

———. 1995. "On the Structure of Ethnic Groups: Crisscrossing Ties of Ethnicity, Social Class, and Politics in Europe." In Calvin Goldscheider, ed., *Population, Ethnicity, and Nation-Building.* Boulder, CO: Westview.

Zuckerman, Alan S., Laurence A. Kotler-Berkowitz, and Lucas A. Swaine. In Process. "Anchoring Political Preferences: The Structural Bases of Stable Electoral Decisions and Political Attitudes in Britain."

Zuckerman, Alan S., Nicholas Valentino, and Ezra W. Zuckerman. 1994. "A Structural Theory of Vote Choice: Social and Political Networks and Electoral Flows in Britain and the United States." *Journal of Politics* 56:1008-33.

SUBJECT INDEX

Analytic narratives, 29-31

Business (*see* Political economy)

Causal explanation, 278-83
Central banks (*see* Financial systems)
Chaos theory, 283-4
Civic culture, 55-6
Civil rights movement, 160-2
Class, 177
Collective action, 21, 23-4, 52-4
Collective identity, 47-8
Comparative politics
  Common heritage, 3-5
  Competing traditions, 5-8
  Origins, ix, 3-5
Comparative statics, 27-8
Comparison, 253-6
Complexity theory (*see* Chaos theory)
Communist states, 227
Configuration (*see* Structure)
Conflict (*see* Contentious politics)
Contentious politics, 12, 47, 59-60, 142-73,
  288-9, 297
Counterfactuals, 31
Covering laws, 278-83
Culture, 6, 10-11, 42-80, 118-20, 129-30,
  148-51, 183-6, 212-15, 242, 246-7,
  250-1, 254-5, 257, 259-60, 269,
  271, 276
Cultural change, 119

Economic policy (*see* Political economy)
Economics of organization, 191-2
Elections, 11, 178-80, 286-7, 297
  Electoral behavior, 115-41
  Turnout, 121-3
Endogeneous growth theory, 192-3
Equality, 195-6
Explanation, 13

Falsification, 33-4
Financial systems, 181-2
Framing processes, 157-9

Galton's problem, 62
Globalization, 187-9, 195, 209-10
Group boundaries, 48-9

Historical institutionalism, 218-21
Holism/individualism (*see* Structure-Action)

Ideal types, 265-7
Ideas (*see* Culture)
Industrial relations, 181-2
Institutions (*see* Structure)
International, 181-4
Interests (*see* Rationality)
Interpretation, 44, 49-52, 67-72, 197

Keynsianism, 186-7, 189

Left-Right identification, 130-1

Macroanalysis (*see* Structure)
Markets (*see* Political economy)
Mass politics (*see* Elections)
Methodology, 249-53
Mobilizing structures, 155-7
Modernity, 267-72

Nationalism, 227-9
Neocorporatism, 180-1
Neoinstitutionalism, 181
New Institutionalism, 193-4
Nominalism (*see* Ideal types)

Ontology, 245-9

Paradigms (*see* Research communities)
Path dependence, 28-9
Partisan
    Choice, 123-5
    Identification, 125-9
Personality, 54-5
Political
    Business cycle, 178-9
    Coalitions, 186, 192, 196-7
    Economy, 12, 174-207
    Opportunity structures, 145, 153-5
Producer group coalitions, 176
Protest (*see* Contentious politics)
Protest cycles, 152-3
Public opinion (*see* Elections)
Public policy, 297

Rationality, 6, 10, 19-41, 31-3, 120-1, 147-8,
        176-80, 190-2, 216-18, 224-5, 242,
        245-6, 249-50, 253-4, 256-7, 259, 268-71

Realism (*see* Ideal type)
Representation, 196
Research communities/traditions/schools, ix,
        5-9
Richard-Vine model, 177
Ritual, 58-9

Samuelson-Stolper theorem, 177
Social
    Capital, 193
    Constructivism, 149
    Theory, 12-13, 239-76
Socially embedded unit act, 160-7
Social movements and revolutions (*see*
        Contentious politics)
Spatial models, 132
State, 12, 208-35
State-society, 221-30
Structuralists, 6, 11, 22, 25, 26, 82-112, 120,
        122, 145-6, 180-3, 215-16, 243, 247-9,
        251-3, 255-8, 269-72
Structure-Action, 261-5
Subtraditions, 7-8, 258-60
Surveys, 115-17

Theory, 133-6

Unit-of-analysis, 61-3

Voting (*see* Elections)

Weberian theory (*see* Modernity)
Welfare state, 196

AUTHOR INDEX

Abell, Peter, 30
Abrams, Philip, 96, 264
Abramson, Paul R., 123, 126
Alberoni, Francesco, 145
Albert, Michel, 196
Aldrich, John A., 121, 122
Alesina, Alberto, 179, 182, 184
Alker, Hayward R., 210
Allerbeck, Klause R., 87
Almond, Gabriel A., 5, 8, 46, 55, 62, 82, 120, 126, 208, 214, 281, 285
Alt, James, 179, 190
Alvarez, R. Michael, 181, 286
American Political Science Review, 240
Ames, Barry, 19
Aminzade, Ronald, 156
Anderson, Benedict, 47, 48, 71, 150, 158, 228
Anderson, Perry, 83, 94
Andeweg, Rudy B., 128
Anker, Hans, 126
Ansell, Christopher K.,107
Aoiki, Masahiko, 191
Apter, David E., 5,8
Archer, Margaret S., 212, 214, 230, 285
Arendt, Hannah, 47
Aron, Raymond, 98
· Arrow, Kenneth, 20, 22
Athur, Brian, 28
Avruch, Kevin, 74
Axelrod, Robert, 26

Baker, K.L., 119
Baldwin, David A., 242
Banfield, Edward C., 46, 54
Barker, Rodney, 211
Barkun, Michael, 57
Barnes, Samuel Henry, 87, 118, 127, 128, 131
Barry, Brian M., 36, 83
Bartels, Larry, 7
Barth, Fredrik, 61
Bartolini, Stefano, 87, 125, 288
Barzel, Yoram, 121
Bates, Robert H., 19, 20, 22, 32, 57, 184, 216, 219, 241, 242, 246, 249, 250, 253, 256, 271
Baumgartner, Frank R., 217
Beck, Paul Allen, 87, 127, 128, 288
Becker, Gary S., 259
Becker, Howard S., 7, 87
Beer, Samuel H., 5, 196
Belkin, Aaron, 31
Bendix, Reinhard, 83, 90
Benedict, Ruth, 54
Benford, Robert D., 149, 157
Bensel, Richard Franklin, 84, 107
Berelson, Bernard R., 125
Berger, Bennett M., 45
Berger, Suzanne D., 85, 189, 190, 195-7
Berijikian, Jeffrey, 154
Berlant, Lauren, 225, 230
Bill, James A., 8

Billiet, Jaak, 131
Billingsley, Keith R., 127
Blaug, Mark, 174
Bloom, Allan, 271
Bonnell, Victoria, 95
Boone, Catherine, 221, 224
Borg, Sami, 122
Botz, Gerhard, 164
Boudon, Raymond, 289-92, 295, 303, 304
Boulding, Kenneth E., 143
Boyer, Robert, 182, 185, 189, 193, 195
Boyte, Harry C., 148
Brady, Henry E., 7
Brass, Paul, 286
Brenner, Robert, 255
Breuilly, John, 226, 227
Brockett, Charles D., 152
Brown, Bernard E., 81, 82
Brown, Courtney, 284, 285, 287, 294 298
Brown, David W., 301
Brown, Thad A., 284, 285, 287, 288 298
Browne, Eric C., 289
Brubaker, Rogers, 71
Brunk, Gregory G., 121
Brysk, Alison, 46, 52, 58, 65, 73, 144, 149
Buchanan, James M., 22
Budge, Ian, 124
Bueno de Mesquita, Bruce, 31

Caldwell, Bruce, 174
Calhoun, Craig, 250
Calmfors, Lars, 181
Cameron, David, 180, 181
Camic, Charles, 261
Camillari, Joseph A., 210
Campbell, Angus, 126, 127
Campbell, Donald T., 7, 53, 72, 279, 280, 292
Campbell, John L., 183, 185
Cantori, Louis J., 8
Caporaso, James, 7
Cattacin, Sandro, 164
Cawson, Alan, 180
Cecil, Roseanne, 70
Chagnon, Napoleon, 46
Chartier, Roger, 149
Chilcote, Ronald H., 8
Chong, Dennis, 153, 160, 161
Chrystal, K. Alec, 179
Clarke, Harold D., 128
Cloward, Richard A., 145, 161
Cohen, Abner, 52, 57, 67
Cohen, G., 179

Cohen, Raymond, 60
Cohn, Bernard S., 95
Cohn, Samuel R., 164
Colburn, Forrest, 144, 151
Cole, Robert A., 188
Coleman, James S., 5, 193
Collier, David, 87, 221, 224
Collier, Ruth B., 7, 221, 224
Comaroff, John, 96
Converse, Philip E., 126, 127, 131
Cook, Karen Schweers, 134
Cook, Thomas D., 7, 279, 280, 292
Costain, Anne N., 152
Cox, Andrew, 181
Crepaz, Markus M.L., 122
Crewe, Ivor, 128
Crist, John, 156
Crombie, A.C., 95
Crotty, William, 8
Crozier, Michel, 74
Cruz, Rafael, 164
Cukierman, Alex, 182
Culpepper, Pepper D., 193

D'Andrade, Roy G., 45, 49, 64, 66, 68
Dahl, Robert A., 5
Dahrendorf, Ralf, 101
Dalton, Russell J., 87, 119, 123, 125, 128, 288
Darnton, Robert, 67
Daston, Lorraine, 83
David, Paul, 28
Dayan, Daniel, 59, 70
deCecco, Marcello, 187
Denver, David, 128
Denzau, Arthur T., 34
deSwaan, Abram, 84
Dewey, John, 225
DeWitte, Hans, 131
Diermeier, Daniel, 20
DiMaggio, Paul, 193, 194
DiNardo, James, 153
Dirks, Nicholas B., 229
Dobbin, Frank, 194
Dogan, Mattei, 8
Dore, Ronald, 189, 195
Douglas, Mary, 104, 291, 299-303
Downing, Brian M., 84
Downs, Anthony, 6, 20, 132
Drache, Daniel, 189, 195
Driffill, John, 181
Duchacek, Ivo D., 210
Durkheim, Emile, 229

Duyvendak, Jan Willem, 146, 152
Dyke, C., 284, 285, 290, 291, 294, 296

Easton, David, 57
Eckstein, Harry F., 3, 5, 7, 8, 65
Edelman, Murray J., 47, 52, 58, 59
Edgerton, Robert B., 67
Eisinger, Peter K., 145, 152
Ekman, Paul Wallace, 49
Elkins, David J., 210
Elliot, Euel, 284, 298
Ellis, Richard, 62
Ellsworth, P., 49
Elster, Jon, 20, 24, 31, 261, 267
Elton, G.R., 96
Emirbayer, Mustafa, 158
Emsinger, Jean, 19
Enelow, James M., 132
Epstein, A.L., 57
Erfani, Julie A., 210
Ericksen, Eugene, 286
Erickson, Kenneth Paul, 8
Ersson, Svante, 122
Ertman, Thomas, 84
Esherick, Joseph W., 214
Esping-Andersen, Gosta, 196
Esterhazy, Peter, 277
Eulau, Heinz, 133
Evans, C. Lawrence, 126
Evans, Peter B., 68, 84, 86, 103, 215, 221, 224
Evans, Sara M., 148
Evans-Pritchard, E.E., 57
Eyerman, Ron, 150

Falk, Jim, 210
Fantasia, Rick, 148
Farah, Barbara, 128
Farlie, Dennis J., 124
Fearon, James D., 31
Feldman, Stanley, 286
Ferejohn, John, 34
Ferguson, Thomas, 177, 186
Ferree, Myra Marx, 156, 158
Filllieule, Olivier, 164
Finegold, Kenneth, 93, 181, 191
Fioretos, Karl-Orfeo, 188
Fiorina, Morris P., 20, 133, 179, 295
Firmin-Sellers, Kathryn, 21
Fiske, D.W., 72
Flanagan, Scott C., 87, 128, 288
Fleron, Frederc L. Jr., 65
Fligstein, Neil, 184, 194

Foran, John, 150
Fortes, M., 57
Frank, Robert H., 35
Franklin, Charles E., 286
Franklin, Mark, 123, 125, 128, 129
Franzese, Robert, Jr., 181, 182, 191
Franzosi, Roberto, 164
Frendreis, John P., 289
Frey, Bruno. 179
Frieden, Jeffry A., 177, 187, 192
Friedman, Debra, 155
Friedman, Milton, 120
Friedrich, Carl J., 51
Friesen, V., 49
Frohlich, Norman, 36
Fuchs, Dieter, 129
Fulcher, James, 178
Furet, François, 151
Furner, Mary, 187

Gadda, Carlo Emilio, 277
Gambetta, Diego, 21
Gamson, William, 149
Ganguillet, Gilbert, 164
Garner, Roberta Ash, 155
Garrett, Geoffrey, 181, 182, 184, 243
Gaudet, Hazel, 125
Geddes, Barbara, 19, 32, 219
Geertz, Clifford, 6, 45, 47, 49, 63, 150, 157, 213-15, 281
Gellner, Ernest, 71, 291, 300
Genco, Stephen J., 281, 285
Gern, Christiane, 144
Gerschenkron, Alexander, 177, 219
Gerstein, Dean, 261
Gerth, Hans, 286
Gibson, Gloria D., 149
Gill, Anthony, 19
Giugni, Marco G., 146, 152
Glass, Leon, 285
Gleiber, Dennis W., 289
Gluckman, Max, 57
Glyn, Andrew, 195
Goffman, Erving, 149
Golden, Miriam, 19, 144
Goldstein, Judith, 184
Goldstone, Jack A., 146, 184, 216, 281
Goldthorpe, John A., 180
Goode, Judith, 65
Goodman, John, 182
Goodwin, Jeff, 158, 164
Goody, Jack, 57

Gorer, Geoffrey, 54
Gottlieb, Gidon, 210
Gourevitch, Peter A., 177, 178, 186, 197
Graber, Doris, 124
Gramsci, Antonio, 208, 214
Granovetter, Mark, 193
Green, Donald P., 21, 128, 134
Greif, Avner, 19, 26, 29, 33, 48, 51
Grilli, Vittorio, 182
Grofman, Bernard, 121, 122, 132
Grossman, Gene M., 192
Guibernau, Berdun, 228
Gurin, Gerald, 126
Gusfield, Joseph R., 58, 144

Haas, Peter M., 184
Habermas, Jurgen, 145, 157, 227
Hacking, Ian, 83
Hager, Carol J., 69
Haggard, Stephan, 215
Hagopian, Francis, 221, 224
Hall, Peter A., 85, 175, 181, 182, 184, 186, 188,
    189, 191,193, 195, 198
Hammel, E.A., 86
Hancke, Bob, 191
Hansen, John Mark, 124
Hardgrave, Robert L., 8
Hardin, Russell, 20, 26, 27, 29, 35, 153
Hargreaves Heap, Shaun P., 26
Hartz, Louis, 82, 99
Hawthorn, Geoffrey, 267
Hayward, Jack, 185
Hechter, Michael, 20, 29, 33, 155
Heclo, Hugh, 243
Helpman, Elhanan, 192
Hempel, Carl, 278, 279
Hennis, Wilhelm, 267
Herrigel, Gary, 185, 193
Herz, John H., 81, 82
Hibbs, Douglas, 179
Hicks, Alexander, 180
Hildebrandt, K., 119
Hinich, Melvin J., 132
Hipsher, Patricia, 152, 156
Hirschman, Albert O., 101, 147, 269
Hobsbawm, Eric J., 71, 96
Hoeber Rudolph, Susanne, 68, 84, 86, 87
Hoerder, Dirk, 164
Hollingsworth, J. Rogers, 82, 183, 185, 193
Holt, Robert T., 5, 280
Homer, Elizabeth L., 62

Horowitz, Morton, 57
Horowitz, Donald L., 60, 61, 71
Huckfeldt, Robert, 285, 287
Hull, David, 294
Hunt, Lynn, 146, 150
Huntington, Samuel P., 5, 8, 61, 82, 220

Ikenberry, John, 93
Immergut, Ellen M., 85, 104
Ingelhart, Ronald, 56, 72, 123, 127, 128, 130, 258
Inkeles, Alex, 54
Iversen, Torben, 132, 182, 188, 191, 196

Jackman, Robert W., 122, 126, 221, 223
Jackson, Robert H., 209
Jacobson, Gary C., 133
James, Alan, 209
Jamison, Andrew, 150
Jenkins, J. Craig, 152
Jennings, Kent, 128
Jenson, Jane, 184, 186
Johnson, James, 185
Johnston, Hank, 144
Johnston, R.J., 127
Jones, Bryan D., 297
Joppke, Christian, 164
Jordan, W., 185
Joseph, Gilbert M., 214
Jowitt, Kenneth, 228
Juliani, Richard N., 286

Kaase, Max, 87, 125, 128, 129
Kahn, Robert L., 126
Kalecki, M., 175
Kalyvas, Stathis N., 19, 20, 29
Katz, Elihu, 59, 70
Katzenstein, Mary Fainsod, 152
Katzenstein, Peter J., 68, 84, 86, 87, 180, 181, 255
Katznelson, Ira, 286
Kazancigil, Ali, 8
Kegley, Charles W., Jr., 242
Keller, Edmond J., 210
Kellert, Stephen H., 277-9, 283-5
Kelman, Herbert C., 71
Keohane, Robert O., 7, 20, 184, 189, 242,
    280, 293
Kernell, Samuel, 133
Kertzer, David I., 47, 52, 59, 66, 149, 156, 229
Kiel, L. Douglas, 284, 298
Kiewiet, D. Roderick, 133, 179
Kim, Jue-on, 56

Kimmerling, Baruch, 226
Kinder, Donald R., 133, 286
Kindleberger, Charles, 197
King, Desmond, 181, 188
King, Gary, 7, 20, 280, 293
Kiser, Edgar, 19, 20, 30-2
Kitcher, Philip, 279, 282, 283, 294
Kitschelt, Herbert, 19, 29, 145, 146, 152
Klandermans, Bert, 145, 146, 149, 154
Klingemann, Hans-Dieter, 129
Kluckholm, Clyde, 45
Knapp, Peter, 96
Knetter, M., 182
Knight, Jack, 25, 36
Knutsen, Oddbjorn, 129, 131
Kocka, Jurgen, 286
Koelble, Thomas A., 85, 223
Kohli, Atul, 68, 84, 86, 87, 221, 222
Kontopolous, Kyriakos M., 284, 285, 289, 291,
    294, 304
Koopmans, Ruud, 153, 164
Kornberg, Allan, 128
Koselleck, Reinhart, 96
Kotler-Berkowitz, Laurence A, 286, 287
Krasner, Stephen D., 211, 215
Kriesi, Hanspeter, 146, 152, 164
Kroeber, A.L., 45
Krueger, Anne O., 19
Krugman, Paul, 192
Kuehls, Thom, 210
Kuper, Adam, 57
Kuran, Timur, 289
Kurth, James, 177
Kurtz, Donald V., 58
Kurzman, Charles, 154

Laitin, David D., 7, 20, 31, 45, 46, 52, 56, 57,
    59, 67, 71-3, 94, 154, 159, 212, 213, 230
Lakotos, Imre, 249
Lane, Jan-Erik, 122
Lane, Ruth, 225
Lange, Peter, 181
LaPalombara, Joseph, 58
Laraña, Enrique, 144
Lasswell, Harold, 89
Latouche, Daniel, 210
Layton, Azza Salama, 160
Lazarsfeld, Paul F., 125
Lee, Bradford A., 184, 187
Lehmbruch, Gerhard, 85, 180
Lester, Richard, 181

Levi, Margaret, 19, 23, 27-34, 95, 134, 219, 225
LeVine, Robert A., 45, 63
Levinson, David J., 48, 54
Levy, Jonah, 193
Levy, René, 164
Lewis, David, 301
Lewis-Beck, Michael S., 133
Lichbach, Mark Irving, 26, 143, 144, 153, 154,
    157, 250, 255, 259, 263, 265, 288
Lieberson, Stanley, 283, 285, 294
Lien, Da-Hsaing Donald, 32
Lijphart, Arend, 6, 87
Lindberg, Leon N., 183, 185
Lipset, Seymour M., 5, 87, 128, 288
Listhaug, Ola, 132
Little, Daniel, 150, 251
Lloyd, Christopher, 252
Locke, Richard, 185, 193
Lohmann, Susanne, 121
Longstreth, Frank, 85
Luebbert, Gregory M., 84
Lustick, Ian S., 99
Lyons, Gene M., 210

MacDonald, Stuart Elaine, 132
Mack, John, 68
Mackey, Michael C., 285
Mackie, Tom, 123, 125, 128, 129
Maddens, Bart, 132
Mahon, James, 7
Mair, Peter, 87, 125, 128, 288
Malone, Martha J., 48
Mandelbaum, Maurice, 289
Mann, Michael, 87, 215
March, James G., 194, 218, 219, 225
Mares, Isabela, 196
Marglin, Stephen, 195
Marshall, William, 191
Martin, Andrew, 186
Martin, Cathie Jo, 178
Marx, Karl, 222
Masciandaro, Donato182
Mastanduno, Michael210
Masters, Roger D., 49, 57
Mattei, Franco, 127
Matthews, Donald R., 74
Mayer, Lawrence, 8
McAdam, Doug, 145, 147, 152-5, 160, 162, 166
McCarthy, John D., 147, 156
McClelland, David C., 50
McCloskey, Donald, 285

McDonough, Peter, 127, 131
McPhail, Clark, 156
McPhee, William N., 125
Mead, Margaret, 54
Meehl, Paul E., 284, 291
Melucci, Alberto, 124, 144, 145, 149
Merelman, Richard M., 44, 46, 55, 56, 63, 65, 71, 72
Merkl, Peter H., 8
Merritt, Richard L., 8
Merton, Robert K., 101
Meyer, David S., 152, 164
Meyer, John W., 194
Middendorp, C.P., 133
Migdal, Joel S., 146, 222, 223
Milgrom, Paul R., 19, 30, 191
Mill, John Stuart, 86, 87, 99
Miller, Frederick D., 156, 158
Miller, Ross A., 122
Miller, Warren E., 126, 127
Mills, C. Wright, 273, 286
Milner, Helen, 178, 189
Minow, Martha, 222, 229
Mitchell, J.C., 57
Mitchell, Timothy, 95, 222, 226
Moaddel, Mansoor, 150, 151
Moe, Terry, 191
Mohr, Lawrence B., 7, 283, 289, 292
Montserrat, Maria, 228
Moon, David, 121
Moore, Barrington, Jr., 5, 83, 88, 89, 146, 177, 215, 226, 255
Moore, Dahlia, 226
Morton, Rebecca B., 121
Mosca, Gaetano, 213
Most, Benjamin A., 164
Mueller, Carol McClurg, 152
Muir, William K., Jr., 74
Mulvihill, Robert F., 60
Murdock, George Peter, 57
Murray, Henry C., 50

Nannestad, Peter, 133
Naroll, Raoul, 48
Narveson, Jan, 210
Nelson, Alan, 290
Nelson, Benjamin, 267
Nelson, Richard R., 182
Nettl, J.P., 82, 92, 103
Newton, Kenneth, 125, 129
Nie, Norman, 56
Niemi, Richard G., 126, 127

Nisbet, Robert A., 267
Nordhaus, William D., 179
Nordlinger, Eric A., 215
North, Douglass C., 19, 22, 25, 29, 30, 34, 216, 219, 299
Notermans, Ton, 188
Nugent, Daniel, 214, 230

Offe, Claus, 145, 181, 196
Oi, Jean, 19
Olsen, Johan P., 194, 218, 219, 225
Olson, Mancur, Jr., 6, 20-2, 33, 121, 147
Olzak, Susan, 163
Opp, Karl-Dieter, 144
Oppenheimer, Joe A., 36
Ordeshook, Peter C., 121
Orloff, Ann Shola, 93
Orren, Karen, 81, 298
Ostrom, Elinor, 19, 23, 25, 28, 193
Ott, J.S., 119
Overbye, Einar, 121
Overman, E. Samuel, 284

Padgett, John F., 107
Page, Benjamin I., 94
Paige, Jeffrey M., 60, 146
Paige, Karen Ericksen, 60
Paldam, Martin, 133
Palmquist, Bradley, 128
Panebianco, Angelo, 288
Parsa, Misagh, 151
Parsons, Talcott, 194, 241, 261
Passy, Florence, 164
Pattie, C.J., 127
Pelassy, Dominique, 8
Perotti, Roberto, 182
Perrow, Charles, 152
Perry, Elizabeth, 149
Pierce, Roy, 127, 131
Pierson, Paul, 85, 175
Piña, Antonio Lopez, 127, 131
Piore, Michael, 190
Piven, Frances Fox, 145, 161
Plott, Charles R., 24
Polanyi, Karl, 104, 175, 219, 220
Pontusson, Jonas, 178, 187, 188
Popkin, Samuel, 21, 124, 146, 150, 157
Popper, Karl J., 25, 239
Porter, Bruce, 164
Porter, Michael, 192
Pospisil, Leonard, 57
Powell, G. Bingham, Jr., 62, 122, 127

Powell, Walter, 194
Przeworksi, Adam, 5, 6, 19, 20, 33, 66, 68, 84, 86, 87, 133, 181, 280
Putnam, Robert, 29, 56, 193
Putterman, Louis, 191
Pye, Lucien W., 5, 54, 64, 90

Rabinowitz, George, 132
Ragin, Charles C., 87
Ramseyer, J. Mark, 21
Ranger, Terrence, 71
Rattinger, Hans, 133
Reddy, William, 286
Regan, Patrick M., 56
Reisch, George, 285
Richards, Audrey I., 57, 213
Richardson, Bradley M., 128
Richardson, Jeremy, 185
Richardson, John M., 280
Richter, Frank, 285
Rickman, John, 54
Riker, William H., 5, 6, 20, 121, 281, 291
Roberts, John, 191
Robertson, David Brian, 85, 223
Rochford, E. Burke, Jr., 149, 157
Rochon, Thomas R., 152
Rogow, Arnold A., 81, 82
Rogowski, Ronald, 7, 8, 19, 20, 177, 186, 187, 192, 240
Rohrlich, Paul Egon, 197
Rokkan, Stein, 5, 83, 87, 128, 288
Roll, Eric, 174
Romer, Paul, 192
Rosanvallon, Pierre, 184, 187
Rose, Richard, 288
Roseberry, William, 230
Rosenbluth, Frances, 21
Rosenstone, Steven J., 116, 122, 124
Rosenthal, Jean-Laurent, 32
Rosenthal, Naomi, 148
Ross, Jennie-Keith, 71
Ross, Marc Howard, 46, 47, 51, 57, 60, 62, 68, 69, 71, 74
Roth, Paul A., 285
Roth, Randolph, 285
Rothchild, Donald, 210
Rothstein, Bo, 36, 188
Roubini, Nouriel, 179, 182
Rucht, Dieter, 145, 166
Ruelle, David, 289
Rueschemeyer, Dietrich, 103, 215
Rupp, Leila J., 158

Russell, A.P., 127
Rustow, Dankwart, 8
Ryan, Michael, 222, 229
Ryckman, Thomas A., 285

Sabel, Charles F., 185, 188, 190, 193, 197
Sabetti, Filippo, 29
Sachs, Jeffrey, 182
Salais, Robert, 185
Salant, Walter S., 184, 187
Salmon, Wesley, 279, 282
Samuels, Richard J., 85
Sanders, John T., 210
Sarat, Austin, 222, 229
Sartori, Giovanni, 5-7, 280, 281
Scarbrough, Elinor, 125, 129
Schaltschneider, Elmer E., 177
Scharpf, Fritz W., 29, 30, 181, 289
Schein, E., 119
Schelling, Thomas C., 30, 184, 249, 301, 302
Scheper-Hughes, Nancy, 73
Schermer, Victor L., 60
Schmidt, Manfred, 179
Schmitter, Philippe C., 85, 180, 183, 193
Schneider, Joanne A., 65
Schofield, Norman, 285
Schor, Juliet, 195
Schroeder, Ralph, 267
Schudson, Michael, 214, 229, 230
Schumpeter, Joseph, 175
Schwartz, Michael, 148
Schweder, Richard A., 45
Scott, James C., 45, 48, 58, 66, 68, 69, 70, 72, 84, 86, 87, 144, 150, 151, 241, 242, 246, 250, 254, 257, 258, 271
Scott, W. Richard, 194
Sculli, David, 261
Selbin, Eric, 150
Seligman, Adam B., 263, 270
Selznick, Philip, 243
Sewell, William, Jr., 94, 144, 146, 156, 163, 166
Shamir, Michal, 288
Shapiro, Ian, 21, 134
Shapiro, Michael J., 210
Shapiro, Robert Y., 94
Shephard, Walter James, 102
Shepsle, Kenneth A., 190, 299, 301
Shermer, Michael, 285
Shils, Edward, 47, 194, 214, 225
Shirk, S.L., 19
Shonfield, Andrew, 175, 185
Shorter, Edward, 164

Shue, Vivienne, 221, 222
Sikkink, Kathryn, 184
Silberberg, Eugene, 121
Silberman, Bernard S., 84
Simon, Herbert A., 104
Siu, Helen F., 214, 229, 230
Sklar, Lawrence, 279, 282, 283
Skocpol, Theda, 7, 68, 83, 84, 86, 87, 90-4, 103,
      105, 106, 146, 154, 158, 187, 208, 215,
      241, 242, 248, 249, 251, 252, 255, 257,
      272, 281
Skowronek, Stephen, 81, 84, 107, 298
Smith, Anthony D., 71, 228
Smith, Christian, 152
Smith, Jackie, 156
Smyrl, Marc, 193
Sniderman, Paul M., 124, 287
Snow, David A., 149, 157
Solow, Robert, 181
Somers, Margaret R., 7, 20, 86, 92, 96, 149
Soskice, David, 181, 188, 191, 193, 196
Spiro, Melford E., 45, 64, 68
Sprague, John, 19, 20, 33, 287
Spruyt, Hendrik, 87, 209
Staniland, Martin, 174, 175
Stanley, Harold W., 126
Starr, Harvey, 164
Steinmo, Sven, 85, 219, 224
Stern, Paul C., 228
Stevenson, Garth, 210
Stevenson, John, 164
Stimson, James A., 286, 297
Stokes, Donald E., 126, 127, 132
Storper, Michael, 185
Strauss, Claudia, 49, 50, 63, 66
Streeck, Wolfgang, 183, 193
Stretton, Hugh, 100
Sullivan, Denis G., 49
Summers, Lawrence, 182
Supple, Barry, 187
Sutcliffe, Bob, 195
Swaine, Lucas A., 286, 287
Swedberg, Richard, 193
Swenson, Peter, 178, 187, 188
Swidler, Ann, 194, 269

Tabellini, Guido, 182
Tambiah, Stanley Jeyaraja, 71
Tanke, P.R. Kolkhuis, 133
Tarrow, Sidney, 7, 56, 84, 144-6, 152, 153, 162,
      163, 166, 289, 297
Taylor, Charles, 44, 47, 63, 67-9, 146

Taylor, Michael, 26, 32, 144, 154
Taylor, Rosemary C.R., 193
Taylor, Verta A., 158
Teixeira, Ruy, 122
Tembruck, Friedrich H., 267
Tetlock, Philip E., 31
Teune, Henry, 56, 66, 133, 280
Thelen, Kathleen, 85, 181, 191, 219, 224
Thompson, E.P., 148, 214
Thompson, Michael, 62
Tilly, Charles, 52, 82, 83, 87, 92, 143, 145, 152,
      156, 163, 164, 166, 222
Tilly, Louise A, 83, 145
Tilly, Richard, 83, 145
Tocqueville, Alexis de, 87
Tolbert, Pamela S., 194
Touraine, Alain, 145
Traugott, Mark, 52, 156, 164
Trevor Roper, H.R., 94
Tsebelis, George, 21
Tucker, Clyde, 127
Tufte, Edward R., 179
Tullock, Gordon, 22
Turner, John, 5, 48
Turner, Victor, 47, 57, 157

Uhlaner, Carole J., 121
Ulam, Adam B., 5
Urwin, Derek, 288

Valen, Henry, 123, 125, 128, 129
Valentino, Nicholas, 286, 287
van der Eijk, Cees, 125
van Deth, Jan W., 129, 134
Varoufakis, Yanis, 26
Verba, Sidney, 5, 7, 20, 46, 56, 82, 120, 126,
      208, 214, 280, 293
Verdier, Daniel, 21
Vitalis, Robert, 221, 224
Volkan, Vamik D., 70
Voss, Peter, 144

Waldrop, M. Mitchell, 285
Wallace, Anthony F.C., 45, 54
Wallerstein, Immanuel M., 83, 215
Wallerstein, Michael, 19, 181
Walt, Steven, 146
Waltz, Kenneth N., 247
Warner, Carolyn M., 94
Wasserstrom, Jeffrey, 144, 156, 214
Waterbury, John, 221
Watkins, Frederick Mundell, 102

Wattenberg, Martin P., 123, 125
Way, Christopher, 182
Weber, Eugen, 49
Weber, Max, 31, 87, 98, 208, 222, 226, 243,
    244, 261, 265, 268-70
Weiner, Myron, 5, 8
Weingast, Barbara R., 19, 30
Weingast, Barry R., 19, 30, 31, 184, 191, 243
Weir, Margaret, 184, 187, 189
Wendt, Alex, 242, 252
Whiting, Beatrice Blythe, 66
Wiarda, Howard J., 8
Wickham-Crowley, Timothy, 146, 154
Wildavsky, Aaron, 46, 50, 62, 105
Wilentz, Sean, 213, 215, 229
Williamson, Oliver, 191
Wolf, Eric R., 144, 146, 150
Wolfinger, Raymond E., 122
Woo-Cumings, Meredith, 215
Wood, Stewart, 181, 188
Woodward, James, 279, 283, 285

Worden, Steven K., 149, 157
World Politics, 14, 240
Wren, Anne, 196

Yancey, William, 286
Young, Michael, 47

Zald, Mayer N., 147, 155
Zaller, John R., 124, 286
Zeitlin, Jonathon, 185
Zelle, Carsten, 128
Ziegler, Andrew H., Jr., 8
Ziegler, Nicholas, 185
Zolberg, Aristide R., 89, 286
Zucker, Lynne G., 194
Zuckerman, Alan S., 8, 284, 286, 287
Zuckerman, Ezra W., 286, 287
Zukin, Sharon, 193
Zwicky, Heinz, 164
Zysman, John, 181, 190, 192

Continued from the front of the book

Paul Pierson, *Dismantling the Welfare State?: Reagan, Thatcher and the Politics of Retrenchment*

Marino Regini, *Uncertain Boundaries: The Social and Political Construction of European Economies*

Yossi Shain and Juan Linz, *Interim Governments and Democratic Transitions*

Theda Skocpol, *Social Revolutions in the Modern World*

Sven Steinmo, Kathleen Thelan, and Frank Longstreth, eds., *Structuring Politics: Historical Institutionalism in Comparative Analysis*

Sidney Tarrow, *Power in Movement: Social Protest, Reform, and Revolution*

Ashutosh Varshney, *Democracy, Development, and the Countryside*